1877: *Year of Violence*

Robert V. Bruce is Professor of History at Boston University. He is also the author of *Lincoln and the Tools of War*, *Bell: Alexander Graham Bell and the Conquest of Solitude*, and *The Launching of Modern American Science, 1846–1876*, for which he won the Pulitzer Prize in history in 1988.

1877: *Year of Violence*

BY

Robert V. Bruce

Elephant Paperbacks
Ivan R. Dee, Inc., Publisher, Chicago

First ELEPHANT PAPERBACK edition published 1989 by Ivan R. Dee, Inc., 1169 South Plymouth Court, Chicago 60605. Manufactured in the United States of America.

ISBN 0-929587-05-7

CONTENTS

PART I. *Powder Keg*

PART II. *Explosion*

PART III. *Reverberation*

To my mother,

BERNICE IRENE BRUCE

1877: *Year of Violence*

I

Powder Keg

CHAPTER 1

The Charge

TO CELEBRATE the hundredth anniversary of the nation's independence, Philadelphia put on a gaudy, vulgar, high-spirited Centennial Exhibition. The Exhibition's sponsors meant it to sum up the age. And it did. The Exhibition displayed everything from gothic soda fountains to Professor Bell's telephone, from the majestic Corliss engine to "an alto-relievo in butter" of "Iolanthe Dreaming"—a thousand works of groping art and sure-handed technology. Capping it all, the great cultural barbecue demonstrated that the finer things of life could turn a profit right in the middle of the worst depression the nation had ever suffered.

While everyone within the grounds behaved himself admirably, crime, vice and violence ran rampant just outside. Nobody bragged about that; and yet, like the show within, it caught the spirit of the times. So did the summer's big news story. At the height of Centennial jubilation word came suddenly from the Little Big Horn that General Custer's command had been wiped out by the Sioux. The event shocked the nation, not so much because several hundred Americans had been slaughtered in the Indian country, as because this time some two hundred fifty of them were white, and United States troops at that.

Without some such twist violence was not news in the America of 1876. Violence flickered incessantly on every man's horizon that year, and thunderheads of fury had been massing for some time. In Pennsylvania, host to the Centennial crowds, Governor John F. Hartranft complained to the legislature about "the growth of lawlessness in our national life." The South's Ku Klux Klan, he charged, had provided an example of systematic murder, arson and other crimes, committed with impunity. During the past decade the violent elements latent in every civilized society had been getting "a dangerous education," and commencement exercises seemed in progress. Hartranft aimed his message at terrorism in the mining regions, but his remarks could have applied as well to festive Philadelphia. In 1875 Philadelphia's homicide rate shot up by more than 50 per cent, and the City of Brotherly Love maintained its killing pace right through the Centennial Year.

In Texas lynch law had almost supplanted the courts. In Ohio the *Cleveland Leader* noted that no murder had been committed in the Cleveland area between 1815 and 1867. "How," it asked, "can we account for this almost sudden eruption of murders during the last eight years?" In the wild mining camps and cowtowns of the West sudden death was commonplace. In the South, where life had always been taken lightly, bloody race riots became instruments of political strategy. In New York City every anniversary of the long-past Battle of the Boyne led to strife, often bloody, between Protestant and Catholic Irish.

Vicarious gore was a breakfast staple in those days. It came with the morning newspaper. When a man was caught in a machine or showered with molten iron or brutally beaten, every moan was rendered, every contusion, fracture, laceration and disfigurement described with a painter's feeling and a surgeon's vocabulary. The press had lots of chances, for in the mid-seventies employers did not pamper their men with safety devices. Mine explosions were routine, factory mishaps normal and railroad accidents a matter of course. Even without the assistance of the internal combustion engine the Machine Age had begun to munch on its victims.

Along with violence went contempt for law. Ex-Governor Seymour of New York saw "an ebbtide in American morals." Corruption had spread from top to bottom. The foremost preacher of the day, Henry Ward Beecher, had just been dragged through the courts on a convincing charge of having committed adultery with the wife of a close friend. A stolid military hero savored the perquisites of the Presidency—cigars, horses and carriages, fine houses, thick-spread flattery —while his administration sank into a bubbling bog of corruption. The Secretary of War fled impeachment and prison, the President's private secretary connived with the Whisky Ring to defraud the Treasury of millions, the President's brother-in-law traded on his influence for a bone tossed by Wall Street speculators, the Vice-President quit politics under a cloud of bribery.

A falling out among thieves disclosed the surrender of Congress to bribery in the Credit Mobilier scheme. In June 1876 another exposure cost ex-Speaker Blaine the Republican nomination for the Presidency. The Senate was the tool of big business, its allegiance not hidden by all its pompous hypocrisy. A Grant-appointed nonentity presided over a timid and vacillating Supreme Court, recently humbled by Congressional threats in the legal tender cases.

State legislators were bought and sold in lots by corporations and political rings. The rankness of carpetbag corruption in Southern states was nearly matched by that at Albany, under the rule variously of Tammany boodlers and of the financial pirates who had boarded and captured the Erie Railroad. State laws were heavily weighted in favor of corporations. And the judges of state courts, most of them past and future corporation lawyers, planted greasy thumbs on the scales of justice whenever the statutes fell short of their purpose.

The fall of the notorious Tweed Ring in New York City left other municipal leeches sucking away undisturbed throughout the nation. In New York itself corruption scarcely paused for breath. There was more truth than poetry in the doggerel comment of a cheap periodical for boys:

> Of course we all knew it was not a square game,
> But show me the man who would not do the same.

Boss Tweed was but one head of the hydra. Graft as usual continued for the police, the courts and other functionaries in a position to swap favors for cash.

Among the nobility of wealth were men of honor. But their honor was a tender thing. They nurtured it in quiet and let Jubilee Jim Fisk hog the headlines with his amours, his floutings of law, his flamboyant caperings, until he came near being the public's beau ideal of success. Furtive and deadly as a spider, his sometime partner Jay Gould fed on the betrayal of friends, fattened on the ruin of stockholders, lied and bribed his way to a power that raised him above the law. Cornelius Vanderbilt, profane, ignorant and ruthless, stood on legality to overturn justice and multiplied his millions by watering railroad stock on an unprecedented scale. Railroad officials gave generous contracts to construction and freight companies controlled by themselves, and so used their trusts to line their pockets. Men like these overshadowed the decent majority. What lesson, then, did Wall Street seem to hold for the seventies? "Steal largely or not at all; for it is preached in Gotham that he who steals largely and gives donations to the Church shall enter the kingdom of heaven, while to him who confines his stealings to modest peculations shall be opened the doors of Sing Sing."

Not all modest peculators went to jail, though the population of New York's Eastern State Penitentiary hit a new high in 1876. In the Southwest the James boys and the Youngers and their confreres defied the depression. Vigilantes had to deal out what passed for justice in Montana. At Deadwood in the Dakota Black Hills (themselves the prize of a broken Indian treaty) the local paper remarked: "We have again to repeat the hackneyed phrase, 'the stage has been robbed!' "

In the cities, growing with cancerous vigor, poorly policed, sickeningly overcrowded, there flourished crime of all kinds. Prostitutes —facetiously called "soiled doves" in the press—strutted by the score along Houston and Amity and Wooster and a dozen other New York streets, in the French Quarter of New Orleans, through the gaslit night of every American city. In the mill towns of Massachusetts, where employers were partial to the cheaper labor of women, some unemployed men found crime preferable to dependence on their wives for support. The gangs of thieves and ruffians that infested New York City's "Arch Block" or Eighth Ward or the Bowery or Water Street had their counterparts in a dozen other cities. The Canal Street section of Buffalo was as lawless and depraved as any in the country. Cleveland complained of being overrun by organized gangs of thieves and vagabonds, and the local press set up a cry for more police.

The nation's children seemed to be aping their elders. The New York Society for the Reformation of Juvenile Delinquents found its business "largely on the increase." Commitments of children to the New York House of Refuge on criminal charges reached a peak in 1875 and the next highest number in 1877.

In the early seventies, teen-age gangs in San Francisco gave rise to the new word "hoodlum," and by 1876 they were notorious. An English traveler described the San Francisco hoodlums as "young embryo criminals—regularly organized gangs of boys and girls, whose ages vary from fifteen to twenty-five," who waylaid, robbed and sometimes killed at night, using knives or revolvers. They also held up or levied tribute from storekeepers and saloonkeepers. Each gang had a name, usually by district, as the Bernal Heights gang, the Hayes Valley gang, the Beach Combers and so forth.

New York also had its teen-age criminal gangs, like the Baxter Street Dudes. Some adult gangs even had their apprentices or cub scouts: the Dead Rabbits had a junior auxiliary in the Little Dead Rabbits; the Forty Little Thieves tagged after the Forty unqualified Thieves. There was no doubt about the youthfulness of the Nineteenth Street Gang, spawned in a Tenth Avenue block known as "Misery Row." These "street rats," as the police called them, were children who knew little beyond the indescribable squalor of nineteenth-century tenement life, some of them orphans shifting for themselves, others sent into the streets by drunken parents to beg or steal. Most of them "had never been in school or church, and knew of God and Christ only in street-oaths." Nor was there doubt about the Daybreak Boys, a gang of harbor thieves, so called partly because they operated at dawn and partly because none of them was over twelve years old.

And of course there was that gregarious species, obnoxious enough yet not so deep-dyed in criminality, which might be called the banded whooping adolescent. An offended patron of the arts in Cleveland complained in 1876 about "a lot of hoodlums that infest the Heights, who had broken up an amateur concert on the South Side." "There is a bad element passes up Jackson Street every evening that requires looking after," thundered the *Scranton Republi-*

can. "We mean certain young fellows, in age ranging from 15 to 18 and 20 years, who think it very smart and cunning to insult ladies, knock people down, and yell with all their might as they pass along that thoroughfare."

No need to speculate on the whys and wherefores of the homeless or nearly homeless juvenile delinquents of the city streets. Cruel environment made them what they were. As for boys born to better circumstances, lax discipline at home, quarrelsome parents, bad company, drunkenness and lack of religious training were all blamed. So was what the chaplain of the New York House of Refuge called "a morbid and demoralizing literature."

Since the dime novel in its original form bit the dust some fifty years ago, it has come to seem as innocent as the old oaken bucket. And yet it may have been even more deadly. Cynics may dismiss the New York chaplain as a Victorian prig, but they cannot so easily laugh off William Graham Sumner, one of the greatest sociologists of his day and as hardheaded and unsentimental a man as ever lived. In the summer of 1877 Professor Sumner examined certain cheap periodicals which he had found to be immensely popular "not only among the idle and vicious boys in great cities, but also among schoolboys" from twelve to sixteen. He was shocked and angered.

The literary material [he wrote in part] is either intensely stupid, or spiced to the highest degree with sensation. The stories are about hunting, Indian warfare, California desperado life, pirates, wild sea adventure, highwaymen, crimes and horrible accidents, horrors (tortures and snake stories), gamblers, practical jokes, the life of vagabond boys, and the wild behavior of dissipated boys in great cities. This catalogue is exhaustive. There are no other stories. There is a good deal of the traditional English brutality in exaggerated forms. These stories represent boys as engaging all the time in the rowdy type of drinking. The boy reader obtains a theoretical and literary acquaintance with methods of fraud and crime. [The stories teach the following lessons:] The first thing which a boy ought to acquire is physical strength for fighting purposes. Every youth who aspires to manliness ought to get and carry a revolver. No fine young fellow, who knows life, need mind the law, still less the police. The latter are all stupid louts. If a boy's father is rich, he can easily find smart lawyers who can get the boy out of prison, and will dine with him at Delmonico's afterward.

All this did not move children to run out and slaughter their neighbors in lieu of Indians. Its real danger lay in its tendency to make violence seem normal, to lower the ignition point of its readers. A crowd of such boys could flare up like tinder should a spark of excitement be fanned by winds of social unrest. And in 1876 the winds were rising.

Within the lifetime of the average teen-ager, the nation had broken violently out of one era and rushed into another—the age of mechanized industry, great corporations and nationwide competition.

The old citywide trade unions were outmoded when the postwar spread of railroads turned the whole continent into one big economic arena. Skilled workers met the new situation by organizing national craft unions, some thirty of them by 1870 with a membership of about 300,000. But these unions included only a very small fraction of non-farm workers, about one in twenty. Even this happy few presently ran head-on into advancing technology. Barrel machines struck the coopers, pegging machines the shoemakers, molds the cigar makers, and so on. Even in less easily mechanized trades like iron puddling, the new large scale of production opened the way to subdivision of skills, each worker being allotted a simple step in a complex operation. So the industrial worker became an unskilled cipher, an interchangeable unit of labor, competing with hundreds of thousands of equally usable men throughout the nation.

The rise of great corporations hastened the degradation of labor. In these the worker's wages and conditions of labor were set not by the man that hired and bossed him, but by a distant board of unapproachable directors in the name of a thousand unseen stockholders, none of whom knew he existed, or much cared. Panting along behind events, social theorists talked about the worker's "freedom to bargain." For the individual worker bargaining was no longer possible. His only freedom was to work at the lowest wages and under the worst conditions acceptable to his hungriest rival anywhere, or not to work at all. And the strange new power that threatened to rob him of both bread and self-respect seemed none the less sinister to him for being invisible.

In the old days community opinion and his own conscience had usually kept the employer from pushing his inherent advantage too ruthlessly. In the new era local opinion was too puny and national opinion too slow-moving and unchanneled; besides, blame had to be spread over a multitude of anonymous stockholders. Conscience, too, lost its voice, as intellectuals deserted the humanitarian philosophy of Jeremy Bentham for the "Social Darwinism" of Herbert Spencer. Most business tycoons did not know or care whether Herbert Spencer was a philosopher or a penman, but they sensed the climate of opinion. "Laissez faire!" cried the Spencerians. Let the laws of nature take their course. Let wages be set in the open market by God's own law of supply and demand. The struggle for existence will then eliminate the unfit and perfect the human race. On Herbert Spencer's map the road to paradise lay through the jungle.

And what a jungle the worker now struggled in! Much more beset him than mere wage cuts. The "truck system" prevailed in mining and extended into other fields, such as iron, steel, stone and glass. Under this system the employer forced his workers to buy their necessities at stores which he himself owned and operated. Having a captive clientele, the employer cut service to the bone, setting up shop in sheds or barns if he chose, carrying a limited variety of poor quality goods, and charging 10 or 20 per cent more than independent stores. He kept his trade by paying off his men in scrip or orders for goods redeemable only at the company store, or by firing those who traded elsewhere.

Many cigar-making establishments paid their workers in cigars at more than the retail price. In Cincinnati, a city where the machine had triumphed early, a cigar maker would often get two boxes of cigars, usually the poorest specimens available, in lieu of his weekly wage of six dollars. Then he had to go from saloon to saloon peddling them, perhaps spending a dollar, selling the cigars for five, and bringing home four dollars to support his family for a week. If unlucky, he might come home with two dollars and a box of cigars. Or he might even give in to what must have been very strong temptation and drink up what little cash he got.

Working conditions shortened or cut off the industrial worker's life. Cooped up in dim light and foul air during his daily ten-hour stint (in some cases still as much as twelve or fourteen hours), he grew listless. Unguarded machinery lay in wait for the moment of carelessness that might kill, cripple or disfigure him. Dust of various kinds—metallic for brass workers, file cutters, iron molders and machinists, tobacco for cigar makers, sawdust for woodworkers, stone dust for quarrymen and stone cutters, lint for textile workers—attacked his lungs. Fire trapped him without adequate escapes. The miner went down to work as to an open grave, not knowing when it might close on him. The victim of an industrial accident seldom went to law about it. Even if he had the funds to do so (and he seldom had) the courts held that the worker accepted the risks with the job.

The courts seemed to be against the workingman on general principles. After much agitation labor had got Congress and several states to pass laws declaring eight hours, instead of the prevailing ten, to be a legal working day. As the courts saw it, these laws merely granted an individual worker the right to give up two hours of work a day—and the pay that went with it. Furthermore, employers were left free to hire men who would work the normal sixty-hour week; and so the sixty-hour week remained normal.

The times themselves were against the industrial worker. The year 1873 had brought a depression like none before, a vale of tears that grew wider and deeper until by 1876 it seemed like the valley of death itself.

Hard times smashed the national craft unions. With thousands of desperate job hunters on tap, employers no longer worried about strikes. As wage cutting began in earnest, some unions fought back. There were bitter strikes in textiles, coal mining and cigar making. In 1874 the iron puddlers and boilers—the "Sons of Vulcan"—were told at their annual convention that no parallel existed for their strike activity that last year. When the next convention came around, their leaders could only say "this year takes the rag off the bush. . . . Every Forge in the organization, excepting a few in the Ohio Valley, has been smitten with the aggrandizing power of monopoly." In fighting back, a trade union seemed merely to trade a slow death for a quick one. By 1876 only 50,000 union men remained in the whole nation—one worker out of a hundred. In New York City alone, union membership plummeted from 45,000 to 5,000. The nine surviving national unions had all the fight knocked out of them. Their only hope seemed to be in lying low. The Cigar Makers' Union, which had lost more than 80 per cent of its enrollment and was down to a cozy 1,000, begged its less docile members to "remember the adage that prudence is the better part of valor."

Legal harassment, the firing of unionists and industrywide blacklisting, all more thorough and merciless than ever before, combined to drive organized labor underground. A delegation of French un-ionists at the Centennial Exhibition reported that in the hundredth year of American independence many workers were afraid to serve on welcoming committees; a union man, the Frenchmen were told, was "hunted down like a mad dog." Labor organizations therefore turned to secret rituals, handgrips and passwords, met in secret, concealed their membership, their purposes, even their names. Yet secrecy made unionism seem sinister and lawless. Centennial or no Centennial, the public smelled subversion in the very name of the "Junior Sons of '76"—though, in fact, that semisecret organiza-tion proposed to elevate labor primarily by inflating the currency.

Northern intellectuals had long been uneasy about the temper of labor. "Fear haunts the building railroad," wrote Ralph Waldo Emerson back in 1843, "but it will be American power and beauty, when it is done. And these peaceful shovels are better, dull as they are, than pikes in the hands of these Kernes; and this stern day's work of fifteen or sixteen hours, though deplored by all the human-ity of the neighborhood . . . is a better police than the sheriff and his deputies to let off the peccant humors."

In Pennsylvania, Irish "Kernes," along with their Welsh cousins and British ex-foemen, now dug most of the nation's coal. With the hours of labor down to ten or twelve, and with layoffs frequent, their "peccant humors" had fuller play. Even the "sheriff and his deputies" could not always handle them. "In these days," complained Governor John F. Hartranft, the *posse comitatus* "is painfully in-efficient." He had reason to know; time after time he had sent state militia to restore peace in the mining regions. Though an ex-soldier Hartranft had little stomach for that sort of job. He conceded that rioters had often been "grievously wronged, and goaded to mad-ness by what they conceive to be the injustice of the law, which seems to protect their employer and leaves them exposed to his ca-price or avarice." And he had a bagful of remedies to offer—even including a state court of arbitration for labor disputes.

But in the end, the only action taken was to sharpen the state's main instrument of force, the militia, under the Hartranft-inspired law of 1874. By 1876 increased state funds and rigid inspections had made "a wonderful improvement," said Hartranft, an improve-ment demonstrated in the course of the latest disturbances. He did not mention the recent rise of an ominously powerful private constabulary, commissioned by the governor under a Civil War statute but paid and commanded by the corporations. In years to come it would be notorious as the "Coal and Iron Police."

The collapse of trade unionism exposed American workers to the full shock of hard times. While the cost of food (which took three fifths of a workingman's pay) dropped only 5 per cent between 1873 and 1876, his daily wage fell at least 25 per cent in the same time—50 or 60 per cent by some estimates. As layoffs became longer and more frequent, total yearly earnings fell off even more. By 1878 some classes of shoe-factory workers in Massachusetts, for example, earned about $300 a year. In a family with four children, after rent and fuel were taken care of, each member thus had about sixty-five cents a week for food, clothing, schoolbooks, medical care and other needs. This cruel reduction of living standards probably caused a greater sum of misery than did out-and-out unemployment.

The usual contemporary estimate of unemployment was 3,000,000. This seems a bit wild, since most unemployment occurred among the nation's 4,500,000 non-farm workers. Sixty per cent unemployment, or even 40 per cent, is too big a figure to swallow. In 1878, on the other hand, Massachusetts made the first and only systematic survey of unemployment in that period and came up with a figure too low to believe: 5 per cent of all wage earners, farm and non-farm —equivalent to about 600,000 nationally.*

Perhaps an estimate of 1,000,000 totally unemployed would be nearer the mark. Considering the desperately low earnings of the rest, one still finds misery enough to go around. But it did not go around evenly, for agriculture got off lightly in that depression. It was the great cities that bore the brunt of hard times.

During the winter of 1874-1875 relief applicants besieged Boston's Overseers of the Poor in numbers that suggested "some great fire or more serious calamity." Twenty-five per cent of New York's workingmen were said to be jobless, and the figure is not entirely

---

*This figure was based on estimates by local authorities of those nineteen or over in their communities who "really want employment"—three chances for error right there. Besides, the state swarmed with vagrants whom some Massachusetts authorities may have considered in but not of their towns, and hence not really to be counted. "Temporary" layoffs could not have been counted either, inasmuch as most workers in the state were laid off at least 10 per cent of the time.

implausible. In every city soup kitchens ladled out watery stew by the tankful. Police-station basements filled up with huddled masses, doubtless yearning to breathe free but settling for a plank to lie on and a refuge from the cold or wet of the night. They were called "revolvers" in New York, because they could only stay a night or two in any one station house; and there were said to be 30,000 in circulation there early in 1874. Private charitable organizations abounded, but their handouts were meager, haphazard and uncoordinated. All aspects were summed up by the case of a man who worked nine of them for what he could get—a total of $8.00 a month.

In New York, therefore, hundreds of jobless, homeless, hungry men begged the police to send them to Blackwell's Island as vagrants. At San Francisco, "dumpies" built huts of scrap wood and picked over garbage heaps for food. Everywhere men drifted aimlessly, hopelessly. Nowadays such men are referred to as "transient unemployed." In the seventies they were called "tramps." Records of the Massachusetts Board of State Charities from 1865 on showed a close correlation between business slumps and "the tramp evil." With the worst depression yet known, there came tramps in numbers beyond all previous experience. Some put the figure at more than 1,000,000.

Tramping as a way of life had not always been without honor among Americans. The itinerant preacher and the Yankee peddler had been welcome everywhere in the old America. Even in the industrial age, the wandering craftsman remained a matter of course. Among printers, especially, only a scorned few had not "tramped it," "carried the banner," followed the road and lived by their wits and an occasional job in passage.

The depression forced other workmen to join the printers on the road. The *Iron Molders' Journal* denounced wandering nonunion molders as "the real bane of the working class. . . . No wonder the workingmen call them 'scabs' in lieu of anything more contemptible." Yet a month later it acknowledged that "the opening of spring will start many of our members on tramp." The iron puddlers' convention in 1875 noted that as the hard times forced shutdowns, union puddlers "apply for their cards and migrate to other sections in search of employment." In 1876 the *Cigar Makers' Journal* carried a regular column of advice to readers "on tramp," usually discouraging. "Tramps had better keep away unless they want to swim out," warned Local Sixty at Keokuk. "Eleven men on strike, tramps keep away for the present," wrote Local Seventy-three at Fort Wayne. From New Haven came the sardonic advice: "Those on the road would confer a favor by bringing a little change with them when this way to assist some that are here, instead of expecting assistance."

Wandering job seekers of the mid-seventies shared the conveniences of boxcar, park bench, hayrick, bridge abutment, barn and hen roost with men, women and children of all ages and origins. At Altoona, for example, three tramps were locked up, one of them "a bit of a boy"; after sending the older pair up for a considerable stretch, the magistrate gave the youngster "fifteen minutes to leave the city." A Pinkerton agent came across a tramp gathering near Wilkes-Barre and noted among the congregation "old men, abandoned women, the wretchedest of wretched hags, young persons in the heyday of health and strength, and little children, prematurely old and shrewish." Many a story was told of solid citizens caught by the depression, stripped of money and hope and set adrift. Yet perhaps there was a basic type: the register at Cleveland's "Poverty Barn," a sort of municipal hostelry for vagabonds, showed nearly all lodgers there in January, 1876, to be white, literate and "quite young." Young America, it seems, was on the march.

By 1876 the ecology of depression tramps had been well studied. In the winters they holed up in the big cities, subsisting on soup and sheltered by municipal authorities (to whom they sometimes rendered a *quid pro quo* on election days). In Connecticut, it was reported, tramps made a point of conspicuous petty larceny in the fall so as to get winter accommodations in jail. With the coming of spring they swarmed out over the countryside. From New York City they seemed to head upstate and then west to Ohio and Illinois. The Boston contingent moved west to Poughkeepsie, then down the west bank of the Hudson to New Jersey and Pennsylvania. Ohio, with its good roads and prosperous farms, was said to be "the paradise of tramps." New England, on the other hand (at least according to the *Cigar Makers' Journal*) was "the worst place in the country" for a wanderer seeking work. For some reason the South was little troubled by tramps; perhaps because tramps were the offspring of an industrial society, consequently Northern, consequently unwelcome in postwar Dixie. Or again, it may have been the region's poverty, bad roads and miserable jails.

People grew less tolerant and more fearful of the tramp as his tribe increased. In proportion, the tramp grew more desperate and less peaceable. Justly or not, he was blamed in large part for the recent rise in rural crime. Newspapers carried more and more stories of tramp misdeeds in the countryside. Some town authorities began paying tramps' railroad fares to the next station to get rid of them, figuring it was cheaper than keeping them in the jail or poorhouse. Any riddance was good. Five tramps sleeping in an abandoned lime kiln in Pennsylvania were crushed to death when the walls caved in, and the story was cheerfully headlined "A Few Tramps Less."

By 1876 the tramp seemed to have become "a permanent institution in the United States," and demands were made for new laws to deal with him. Committees reported on the problem, conventions met to consider remedies, legislatures enacted harsher penalties for vagrancy and stiffer requirements for public charity. Still the "tramp evil" increased. As the year drew to a close, northern Ohio was said to be overrun by tramps. New Hampshire granaries, clotheslines and poultry yards suffered as never before, while in the cities and towns of that state theft and burglary became common. When would it all end? And where?

Sick and exhausted though a tramp might be, bankrupt of purpose and dignity, blown like dust on a rising wind, nevertheless he had blessings of sun and air that were denied to thousands with legal residences. For the age of industry was also the age of gigantic slums.

American cities of the 1870s bulged with newcomers from the farm and the immigrant ship. Even yet, a retreating edge of green lingered tantalizingly close to the heart of many a city. Farmers tilled their fields as near as nine blocks to Public Square in Cleveland; forty blocks away, children picked huckleberries and cows grazed. New York's Broadway ran into the country beyond Fifty-seventh Street; and Central Park charmed foreign visitors with its hills and valleys, its tiny lakes, its groves and tree-lined walks. But wage earners had to live very close to the machines they served or to the bosses who put out the homework they sweated over.

After a day's work of ten or twelve hours, they had neither the time nor the strength to walk far. Urban transit remained horse-drawn —New York City had only just begun its elevated railway—and fares were high, thanks to corrupt monopolies. Carfare would have taken from 10 to 15 per cent of the average worker's total earnings. And Sundays were for resting—or "sleeping it off." So the workers and their children spent their short lives almost entirely immured in the barren tenement districts, seeing no living green from year to year but the scum on fetid puddles or the mold of pushcart fruit. Out of a public school class of fifty New York boys who were questioned on the subject, only three had ever seen Central Park.

While Indians and buffalo roamed the Great Plains, spacious America brought forth slums more crowded than any others on earth. By 1880 some 1,000,000 people lived on Manhattan Island. The Tenth Ward had a population density of 276,000 per square mile, and there were several close runners-up. On Crosby Street, 192 people, including ninety-one children, were found living in one tenement house; on Mulberry Street, seventy-five "lodgers" slept on the filthy floors of a single building, this being in addition to the regular tenants. Cleveland had its Flats, St. Louis its Cross Keys and Clabber Alley, Boston its North End, Philadelphia its Bedford and St. Mary's Streets. Even a comparatively small industrial city like Fall River had tenements where twelve people lived in three rooms, or fifteen people in four. Everywhere the depression led to "doubling up," two or more families using the same room or rooms, the same fire, the same table.

The squalor of these warrens was beyond any description, though many a writer attempted one. The people themselves made a stab at it when they coined neighborhood names: Kerosene Row, Poverty Gap, Hell's Kitchen, Bandits' Roost, Bone Alley. Tenements four, five, six stories high, were jammed back-to-back along narrow streets. In a specimen tenement the bedrooms measured seventy-eight by eighty-four inches, and only six out of the twenty-one bedrooms had windows. Sunlight rarely touched most windows anyway. Many a child knew June as the month when the sun at last reached down to his family's window, and he knew the very spot on the scabrous wall that marked the high point of light and the beginning of summer. This was apt to be the extent of his education in the exact sciences. Out of 600 children living at the infamous

Five Points in 1870, only nine attended any kind of school. Nevertheless, in the swarming tenements with their pasteboard partitions, curtained-off subtenants and rooftop orgies, children learned other things not known to their more sheltered contemporaries.

Death—by fire, assault, suicide, falls, alcoholism, malnutrition and above all, disease—provided daily diversion in a tenement block. Life was as cheap as it was plentiful. At Gotham Court, a blot upon blots —condemned in 1871 but not torn down for another twenty years— the cholera epidemic of 1866 boosted the death rate to 195 per thousand. For tenement districts generally, in New York and elsewhere, normal mortality rates ran to more than twice present levels. Children, especially infants, died in large numbers.

The state of sanitation, both in the tenements and in the cities as a whole, explains the death rate fully. Most of the tenements were filthy, some of them alive with vermin and rats. Pitch-dark hallways, piled with trash, contained the only wash basins. Many cellars ran inches deep with polluted seepage. Old brick sewers, their very existence forgotten by the authorities, had been plugged for years and drained only into adjacent soil. Hand pumps drew water from wells sunk next to backyard privies. Much of New York's waste emptied into sluggish rivers and channels, leaving the city in a sea of sewage. Cincinnati drew its water from a point in the Ohio only a few hundred yards above a municipal discharge sewer, and the same was true of many other river towns. Three thousand died of cholera in the Mississippi Valley epidemic of 1873. The great cities were periodically terrorized by outbreaks of typhus, yellow fever, scarlet fever and smallpox.

During the cholera epidemic of 1866, a well-to-do New York diarist set down a bitter condemnation of his own class. "It is shameful," he wrote, "that men, women, and children should be permitted to live in such holes. . . . We are letting them perish of cholera and then (as Carlyle suggests somewhere) they will prove their brotherhood and common humanity by killing us with the same disease—that capacity of infection being the only tie between us that we could not protest against and decline to recognize."

There was another tie, however, which many of the city's elite recognized by proxy on rent day. The tenements yielded fantastic profits to their owners, profits ranging up to 50 or 75 per cent a year on the original investment. Some tenement owners had graduated from the very deathtraps they were now exploiting. Others, of gentle birth, had never known the life out of which they drained their profits. There were tenements which had fallen by purchase or bequest into the hands of churches; and yet these, or their agents, seemed to squeeze their tenants as hard as did the most grasping of publicans.

With all this came the heyday of conspicuous consumption. In Tiffany's, New York City had "perhaps the most extensive and elegant jewellery establishment in the world." The trains of costly dresses swept through the dirt of Fifth Avenue. New York millionaires seemed not to mind if their gold-faced palaces stood within sight and smell of shantytowns. Matthew Smith's best-selling *Sunshine and Shadow in New York* (1868) illustrated its title by a frontispiece pairing A. T. Stewart's $2,000,000 white marble mansion with a notorious old ruin of a tenement. Many other books of the period dwelt on the same theme.

Workingmen did not miss the point. The *Iron Molders' Journal* took note of Cornelius Vanderbilt's reputed $85,000,000 fortune (actually he had $105,000,000). "What an amount of robbery those figures represent!" it roared, pointing out that if every iron molder in the United States saved $100 a year (an unlikely event), the molders would be eighty-five years in matching the fortune.

Of course, American mythology instructed the young that wealth was the sure and just reward of merit and hard work. A long parade of Horatio Alger heroes carried the banner marked "Excelsior" to every Main Street and Mulberry Bend. But the gospel was an obvious fiction. Many years later one of its preachers called upon United States Senator Robert F. Wagner to bear witness to it, for the senator himself had been an immigrant slum child of the seventies. "That is the most God-awful bunk," said Wagner. "I came through it, yes. That was luck, luck, luck. Think of the others." A survey of nearly all American industrial leaders of the 1870's— more than 300 of them—shows that the typical leader came not from a log cabin or a tenement, but from an upper or middle class family of English stock, Congregational, Presbyterian or Episcopalian in religion, and already established in business. The young hero usually graduated from an academy or college and almost never went to work before the age of eighteen.

If you have merit, you will become rich. Ergo, if you remain poor, you have no merit! Few workingmen of 1876 let the implied insult distract them from the injury. Their resentment of the latter grew more and more threatening. In the Michigan Legislature that winter a member denounced "the oppressive magnates of these corporations, who wallow in all the luxury the imagination can think, torn from and drawn from the blood and hard labor of their employes." Boston's Overseers of the Poor were pleased "that in this period of general depression, . . . public order has been so well preserved," but their tone of mild surprise betrayed a growing worry. Goldwin Smith, an Englishman who knew many wealthy Americans, found them "pervaded by an uneasy feeling that they were living over a mine of social and industrial discontent, with which the power of Government, under American institutions, was wholly inadequate to deal: and that some day this mine would explode and blow society into the air."

At the end of 1876, however, it began to look as if the two major political parties would do the job first. They began on the night of the Presidential election (the night on which a party of grave robbers broke into Abraham Lincoln's tomb and tried to steal his body). Amid fraud and intimidation on both sides, the Democrats had apparently won. But a shift in the electoral votes of three Southern states, currently occupied by Federal troops under a Republican administration, could change the result. As soon as they realized this, the Republicans made the necessary claims and set about with all their well-developed resources of fraud and force to make the claims good. The Democrats, denied the spoils of office for sixteen years past, talked bitterly of taking up arms in defense of right and patronage. A leading Kentucky editor called for 100,000 Democratic volunteers to ensure the inauguration of their man. Joseph Pulitzer of the *New York World* offered to "bare his breast to the bullets of the [Republican] tyrant and rush headlong upon his glittering steel." "Millions of men will be found ready to offer their lives," shouted an Indiana politician to a huge and enthusiastic mob; "resistance to tyranny is obedience to law," an Ohio orator informed another. "I am a revolutionist," wrote the Democratic Speaker of the House to a friend. "When I vote next for a President, I expect to enforce it with a bayonet. You may think I say this in anger. I do not." At the year's end, with no solution in sight, it looked as though the United States might "decompose into anarchy" without any assistance from the "lower classes."

Looking back over the first century of American independence, platform orators of 1876 hugged the theme of material progress with pathetic gratitude. The nation heard at great length that it was much bigger, more populous, stronger and richer under General Grant than it had been in the days of General Washington. And the pointers with pride spoke some of the truth, even if not all of it. The spirit of 1876 was not all bad, any more than the spirit of 1776 was all good. George Washington's America had its quota of grafters, time servers, turncoats, profiteers, counterfeiters, even bread rioters. The Grant era had its peaceable, law-abiding, patriotic, honest majority. A portrait of Centennial America which ignored that majority would be like a graph in which the bottom line equals 90 per cent—accurate in detail but misleading in effect.

Still, averages can mislead as well as truncated graphs. The elements of social upheaval were not evenly spread over the land, but instead were bunched together in the great cities. There one found what might be called "the mob-in-being": thousands of people massed together as never before, not by sympathy or excitement, but simply by the terms of their life. Whenever quitting time poured thousands into the streets, whenever warm weather emptied the tenements onto sidewalks and front stoops, there stood the mob, ready-made. Working on the minds of these people were the dishonesty and cynicism of politics, the injustice of law and courts, the weakness of law enforcement. They knew death as a daily acquaintance and violence as the normal response to frustration. They brooded on the oppression of labor, the arrogance of capital, the wild inequality of fortune, the misery of tenement life, the fear and hunger and degradation of hard times. The makings of a grand social bonfire were heaped high. Beneath them, like shavings, were scattered the tramps, bitter, desperate, standing to lose nothing but life and counting that small loss. And everywhere ran the volatile children and teen-agers, eager for excitement, full of dime-novel yarns, acting on pure impulse, ready like so much kerosene to take fire at the drop of a spark.

Amid these well-laid combustibles, railroad managements now began to crack down on their employees—like flint on steel.

CHAPTER 2

The Fuse

NO YEAR in the history of American railroading has ever ended more terribly than 1876 or begun more bleakly than 1877.

Darkness and blinding snow filled the night of December 29. Shortly before eight o'clock, the Lake Shore Road's Pacific Express, drawn by two locomotives and carrying 159 human beings, started over an iron truss bridge at Ashtabula, Ohio. As the lead locomotive reached the far abutment, its engineer heard a cracking sound beneath him, felt the bridge sink and instinctively opened the throttle. The locomotive sprang forward, tearing loose from its coupling. He looked back from the cab window in time to see the second locomotive turn turtle and fall into the ravine sixty-nine feet below. The bridge crumpled slowly from one end to the other and crashed down, carrying with it four baggage cars and seven stove-heated passenger cars. After the long drawn-out tumult of the fall came a hush in which only the wind was heard. Then, here and there along the wreck, orange tongues of flame sprang out of darkness and began licking at the broken cars. Perhaps as many as twenty people already lay broken and dead within. At least sixty more were trapped and burned alive in the wreckage.

Since at least half of the dead were consumed utterly, no exact accounting was possible. Nevertheless, the Ashtabula horror stood unchallenged as the worst rail disaster America had ever suffered. The Lake Shore's chief civil engineer shot himself a few days later; the strong-willed financier who had insisted on an unsound bridge design endured five years of reproach before following suit. The impact on the public mind was tremendous. Just as the public had come to believe railroads perfectly safe, observed the *Railway World*, "a new horror occurs to weaken confidence."

On the same stormy night of December 29, 1876, every train in motion west of Montreal on the Grand Trunk Railway of Canada was being stopped and the locomotive fires drawn. Thus the Brotherhood of Locomotive Engineers replied to the Grand Trunk's violation of agreements and dismissal of Brotherhood leaders. Aided by the storm, the strikers completely blocked the single-track road. Next day they turned back strikebreakers, while sympathizers held the roundhouses. On January 3, 1877, the Grand Trunk capitulated, even to reimbursing the Brotherhood's Grand Chief Engineer, Peter M. Arthur, for travel expenses he had incurred during the strike.

Only a similar victory over the Central of New Jersey in the previous October matched this latest triumph of the Brotherhood. A new force confronted railroad management. Before 1876 railroad strikes had almost all been wildcat affairs. The Brotherhood of Locomotive Engineers had concentrated on temperance work and mutual insurance. Now, with its membership passing 10,000 and its treasury well filled, it was brandishing a club which had proved formidable even in the hands of a leaderless, planless few. And management did not like it.

The day after the Grand Trunk's surrender, ragged newsboys yelled, "Extry, extry, death of Commodore Vanderbilt!" The indomitable old man who had hammered together the great New York Central system, whose death had been awaited since May by relays of card-playing reporters across the street, who had outlived two of the doctors attending his last illness, was mastered at last. In his final hours he quavered a favorite hymn, which ran "I am poor, I am needy." This was only a little premature. Of the $105,000,000 which he proved unable in the end to take with him, more than $90,000,000, including absolute control of the New York Central, went to his eldest son, the prudent, plodding William H. Vanderbilt. The Commodore's death had been discounted for months, the son had been managing the Central for years, and yet the final stilling of the formidable old man seemed to mark the end of an era. The railroad world wondered.

Three blows in one week—and in those days, when the railroads shivered, the nation shook.

Mark Twain had already pinned a label on the times with his novel *The Gilded Age*. He could as well have called it *The Rail-*

road Age. Wherever you looked in the America of 1877—in politics, industry, agriculture, morals, technology, even in the arts—you saw somewhere, plain or subtle, the mark of the rails.

A locomotive in passage, the new prime mover of the nation, roused Walt Whitman as it did his fellow Americans in those years:

> Thy black cylindric body, golden brass and silvery steel . . .
> Thy great protruding head-light fix'd in front,
> Thy long, pale, floating vapor-pennants, tinged with delicate
>   purple,
> The dense and murky clouds out-belching from thy smoke-
>   stack,
> Thy knitted frame, thy springs and valves, the tremulous
>   twinkle of thy wheels . . .
> Type of the modern—emblem of motion and power—pulse
>   of the continent . . .
> Fierce-throated beauty!

Whitman voiced the wonder that kept boys of the seventies hanging around depots at traintime, stopped them in fields to watch passing freights, stirred them from sleep at the far-off hallooing of night trains in pursuit of the horizon. They hardly needed Oliver Optic's "Lake Shore" stories about heroic young engineers and firemen. (" 'She is safe!' cried Tom, at the top of his voice, as he leaped from the engine upon the ground, and placed the little girl in the arms of her mother.") They read the stories nevertheless, and others too, and dreamed of more. And now and then, when a fast express thundered through the town, even the grownups felt their pulses beating to its rhythm.

The railroad! On it depended almost all that made the new America different from the old. Where would the new West of the farmer be without it? The railroad took the farmer there in the first place—lured him there sometimes with its high-spirited handbills and easy rates for settlers. The railroad sold him his land, brought in his supplies and, above all, provided his only outlet to the markets of the world. If the railroad were cut off, the buffalo would be saved; but the Great Plains farmer would be a vanishing species.

Industry? Railroads were big customers, as the people of Pittsburgh well knew. But that was only part of it. What made the new industry different from the old was the scope of its markets and the scale of its operations. Whole cities took up specialties. Chicago turned hog butcher for the nation, Minneapolis became the nation's miller, Lynn its cobbler, Paterson spun its silk, St. Louis brewed its beer. Railroads made possible that triumph of mass production and marketing.

Railroads drew the map of the new urban age. They turned fields into cities and cities into backwaters. Altoona was a child of the Pennsylvania. The Lackawanna made Scranton out of Slocum's Hollow. Without the Baltimore & Ohio, Baltimore would have been much quieter, greener and smaller than it was. Having helped create the new towns and cities, railroads hauled in the herds of cattle, rivers of milk and mountains of flour that kept their millions fed.

There were highways still, of some use for local horse-drawn traffic. The rivers still ran, and people read about the race of the *Robert E. Lee* with the *Natchez*. Even at Pittsburgh towboats were thick along the forks of the Ohio. Some canals kept up a rearguard fight against weeds and silt; and now and then in the warm season, the larger ones, like the Erie Canal or the Chesapeake and Ohio, roused themselves to a flurry of serious competition with the rails. Nevertheless, those arteries flowed too sluggishly to sustain by themselves the vigor of the world's newest industrial giant. It was the railroads that carried the lifeblood of America in 1877.

All this had come about within the memory of living men. Peter Cooper, whose Tom Thumb of 1830 had been the first locomotive built in America, was alive and busy in 1877, a year after running for President on the Greenback ticket. Men still putting in a long day's work on the railroad could remember when Cooper's contraption had eaten the dust of a horse-drawn rail car. Starting from nothing, railroads had grown faster and farther than had the United States itself in those expansive years. Now they spanned the nation and accounted for a tenth of all its property.

Much of that growth was the work of a half-dozen years. In 1865, after marking time through nearly a decade of turmoil and civil war, American railroads had leaped forward, sped by huge Federal and state grants of land and credit. The Great Plains lay open for development, the newly industrialized East needed connecting and feeder lines, great systems awaited only the shaping hands of organizers like Vanderbilt, railroad builders moved at last to link the oceans. The railroads themselves pumped in streams of immigrants, who swelled the pent-up demand for housing, spread out over the plains and spilled into the labor market. Railroad consolidations and technical advances lowered freight rates, and industry quickened in turn. Business was good, money was easy and confidence was boundless. The railroads had no trouble selling their stocks and bonds. Indians and buffalo might be the only commuters present along some of the projected Western lines, but investors considered high interest rates, government benevolence and, above all, the glowing future; and they bought. Over 1,000 miles of new road were laid down in 1865. By 1867 the annual new mileage was topping 2,000. It hit 3,000 in 1868, 6,000 in 1870, and more than 7,000 in 1871.

With that year the country's current needs were nearly satisfied. In 1872 new mileage dropped under 6,000 and in 1873 barely reached 4,000. After the Credit Mobilier scandal broke, subsidy bills were political poison; and so in 1872 every party included an anti-land grant plank in its platform. Meanwhile, crop production went up 50 per cent, farm prices fell accordingly and the hard-pressed Western farmer began kicking at the floor of railroad rates. Members of a farmers' social organization known as the Grange moved into state politics and put through rate-regulating "Granger laws" to curb the railroad "robber barons."

Back east, on September 18, 1873, came a sudden crash that froze bankers and businessmen in their tracks: Jay Cooke and Company had closed its doors, bankrupt! Cooke, the leading banker of his day, had tried to finance the building of the Northern Pacific Railroad by selling $100,000,000 worth of its bonds. But railroad investors were growing wary. With a 1,000-mile gap still unclosed, Northern Pacific bond sales fell off. To keep the road going Cooke borrowed heavily at short-term, counting on a revival of confidence among long-term investors before the loans came due. He soared out over the tanbark with a nonchalance surprising in a man of such solid repute, only to find no one on the other trapeze. And when he looked down, lo! there was no net.

The fall of Cooke caused a brief banking panic, which in turn forced a short but deadly slackening of trade. No more was needed.

The nation slid down a spiral of depression which was to last longer than any other in its history. And the railroads suffered like the rest.

To be sure, total net earnings were a shade higher in 1876 than in 1873. But they had to be spread over 6,540 more miles of road. And they had been shored up only by ruthless economizing in the face of sagging revenues. Between 1873 and 1876, operating expenses per mile, including wages, were cut 18 per cent. Furthermore, the burden of capital stock and bonded debt had grown by 16 per cent. Perhaps as telling as any statistic was the fact that road after road went crashing down into foreclosure or receivership—seventy-six in the Centennial Year alone.

With it all, 1876 brought rate wars of unprecedented ferocity among the five main lines linking the Northeast to the West—the Grand Trunk, the New York Central, the Erie, the Pennsylvania and the Baltimore & Ohio. Railroad competition in hard times was a deadly game. Bankrupt roads were run by their receivers not so much for profit as for business—at any price. Their competitors had to match their rate cutting in order to pay interest on bonds, maintain equipment and keep a minimum corps of employees. The Grand Trunk happened to be bankrupt. So in 1876 rates fell like Lucifer from Heaven. Along the Baltimore & Ohio they were cut in two. One could ride the New York Central from Chicago to New York City for thirteen dollars. A hundred pounds of farm products could be shipped from Chicago to New York for eighteen cents instead of the usual fifty, and to Boston via the Grand Trunk for twenty cents instead of seventy-five. Among its other effects, the trunk-line war of 1876 finished off the Atlantic & Great Western Railroad.

This, as 1877 began, was the climax now capped by the Ashtabula horror, the Grand Trunk strike and the death of Commodore Vanderbilt. No wonder the *Railway World* omitted allusions to a "Happy New Year." "Railway management has been more than one-half failure," it noted. "The stockholder is alarmed, and not without cause; the bond-holder sees his security weakened . . . Anarchy prevails in the conflict of roads."

Talk as one might about "long lanes" and "darkness before dawn," the sunrise could warm only those who lived through the night. And as the first weeks of 1877 wore by, no rosy glow lighted the horizon. On the contrary, darkness deepened on March 1 when the Supreme Court upheld the Granger laws. The *Railway World* threw up its hands at what it called "the most important, and, in some respects, the most unfortunate decision ever made by an American court of last resort."

Reported receipts of seventeen western lines during January and February fell a half million dollars short of the same period in 1876. Bad spring floods cut down business and raised expenses on the Atchison, Topeka & Santa Fe. The breaking up of a hard winter made tributary wagon roads almost impassable in the Kansas Pacific's territory, and railroad business fell off in consequence. Later in the year the Chicago & Alton lost through failure of the corn crop in its area, the Central Pacific through a drought in California, Rocky Mountain locusts, which had lately devastated vast areas of the Great Plains, sowed the ground thickly with eggs in the fall of 1876. Fearing fresh onslaughts in 1877, farmers husbanded their money and merchants kept their stocks low. Railroads felt the effects.

"The distress in railways is greater than ever before," wrote the board chairman of the Illinois Central in April. "It is important," he warned the road's president, "that we should have every dollar that we can possibly command before August 1st for the quarterly dividend of 2 per cent." The receiver of the Kansas Pacific ordered all expenses cut "to the very lowest points"; and his general superintendent began filling every vacancy at lower wages, taking off trains, laying off construction gangs and reducing the number of section men.

On the stock exchange, rails sank lower and lower. Baltimore & Ohio stock dropped from 191 at the start of 1876 to 79 in the early summer of 1877. Lake Shore fell from 96 to 50, Pennsylvania from 56 to 32. Even the rock-solid New York Central slipped from 117 to 90. In London, a vital source of railroad capital, American railroad bonds, good and bad, inspired an "intense feeling of anxiety and distrust." That winter and spring, 7,225 more miles of railroad went into receivership or under foreclosure.

And then, in one sector after another, the tide of battle seemed to turn.

The first break came on the labor front. Early in 1876 the Boston & Maine had cut wages 10 per cent for all employees. After its usual 6 per cent dividend, the road ended 1876 with a surplus. In January 1877 it raised the salaries of its president and superintendent. Self-confident after drubbing the Jersey Central and the Grand Trunk, the Brotherhood of Locomotive Engineers demanded a raise of ten cents per day for the road's sixty-seven engineers. President White contemptuously refused to spend an additional $6.70 a day. On the afternoon of February 12, after a four-hour ultimatum, the Brotherhood engineers stopped trains wherever they happened to be. "The result," commented the *Railway World*, "is awaited with much interest, because the failure of the strike will probably lead to the avoidance of future conspiracies against railway companies and the traveling public."

The company having put non-union standbys aboard every train, a sketchy and haphazard service was resumed within hours. And the hard times brought in crowds of job seekers. Most were unqualified, but some usable men turned up. The Brotherhood tried to buy off the strikebreakers. Other roads serving Boston offered aid and men to the Boston & Maine, a development which goaded Grand Chief Arthur into a vague threat of a general rail stoppage at Boston.

Despite Arthur's ill-judged threat, the public cheered for the Brotherhood. Commuters said they would rather walk than see the men beaten down. One prominent stockholder asserted publicly "that he didn't care if he missed his dividends for years to come, but he wanted the engineers to gain their point, for he believed they ought to be paid well." Another element showed its temper in a preview of things to come: Boston police were called in to clear the Boston & Maine station "of the crowd of loafers which has infested it since the beginning of the strike."

But public sympathy counted for nothing in a contest of treasuries. The road's officers ignored sentimental stockholders and stood on principle. Gradually the Brotherhood ran out of money. Train service improved steadily, though the road was not back to normal until midsummer. The striking engineers were replaced and, in most cases, were still looking for work a year later.

During the strike, Boston heard from a son of the Adams family, a family long noted (with an exception named Samuel) for its impatience with both crowds and loafers. In 1866 Charles Francis Adams II, a firm-jawed ex-colonel of thirty-one, had deliberately mapped out the campaign of his life. "I fixed on the railroad system," he recalled later, "as the most developing force and largest field of the day, and determined to attach myself to it." First he wrote a stream of magazine articles on railroad problems. Then he proposed a State Board of Railroad Commissioners and in 1869, after three years of lobbying, saw it created—the first effective body of its kind in the nation. At once Adams became one of the three members and, as he frankly admitted, "by common consent the controlling mind."

The Boston & Maine strike was, in the opinion of himself and his friends, Commissioner Adams' finest hour. On the evening after his board's hearings on the strike, he wrote a report which was adopted and published without the change of a word. "A good, square blow well got in," he labeled it in his private diary. Condemning the strikers, it suggested impartial public investigation as the cure-all for labor disputes. As a supplement Adams offered the draft of a law imposing a heavy fine or a year or more in jail on any railroader who refused to handle the rolling stock of his own or another struck road, or abandoned a train between stations or intimidated strikebreakers. Even peaceful dissuasion of strikebreakers on company property would incur a $300 fine or three months in prison.

Adams' proposed strike law encountered some angry dissents. The *Railroad Gazette* warned against abridging the liberties of one class "in order to secure to another complete immunity from loss." "Mutterings of discontent are heard all over the land," said the *Engineers' Journal*, "and unless this policy is abandoned, we shall hear the dread cry in our own land of 'bread or blood.'" And Adams' own state refused to enact his strike bill. But somewhat milder measures, punishing the obstruction or abandonment of trains but not the mere quitting of work, were passed that spring by Pennsylvania, Delaware, Michigan, New Jersey and Illinois.

Adams was not yet done. Early in March 1877, needing the money to buy himself a new bookcase, he dashed off a two-part article on "The Brotherhood of Locomotive Engineers" for the *Nation*, the country's most influential weekly. In light-hearted anonymity, he spoke his mind: "the Brotherhood of Locomotive Engineers has got to be broken up. . . . it has become a mere common nuisance . . . a standing public menace. The only question is how to proceed so as to break it up most quietly and most effectually." He offered an answer: the corporations must create a regular graded service, with its promotions, its life insurance and its pensions. "The men would [not] . . . sacrifice, by joining in strikes, what represented the accumulation of years of service." In short, railroaders would serve under a sort of peace bond.

A week before Adams' *Nation* article appeared, a committee of engineers and firemen on the Philadelphia & Reading Railroad had petitioned the Reading management for a 20 per cent raise. Their petition set no time limit, it threatened no strike and it had nothing to do with the Engineers' Brotherhood. Five days after the *Nation* article, with the wildcat petition as a pretext, Reading engineers suddenly were told by the management to quit either the Brotherhood or the Reading. Those who stayed with the road might, if they chose, enjoy the benefits of a proposed company-run substitute for Brotherhood insurance. All the money an employee paid in, however, would be forfeited, if he quit his job or went on strike. "The Reading Railroad seems to agree with the Nation," commented the *Railroad Gazette*.

Denouncing the "scurrilous sheet" which he considered to have been the Reading's inspiration, Grand Chief Arthur hurried off to Philadelphia. Arthur must have grasped the meaning of the struggle. As the *Railroad Gazette* put it, "in this case, really, it is the company and not the Brotherhood which strikes." Evidently the forces of management were on the move not just to tame the Brotherhood but to "break it up." And in this crucial fight, the Brotherhood was up against a man who had already proved himself to be organized labor's most brilliant and remorseless enemy: the Reading's president, Franklin B. Gowen.

In 1877 Franklin Gowen was forty-one and at the height of his fame. In an age of business giants few matched his command over the public's emotions. Finance was his field; but his soul, like his magnificent voice and his solidly handsome face, belonged to an actor. In his heyday he could deliver a stockholders' report from the stage of the Philadelphia Academy of Music and hold a large audience spellbound. His wit, eloquence and stage presence seemed to administer a local anesthetic to the seat of logic. Even in cold print, and in this age of understatement, his speeches tend to unsettle the judgment.

Gowen's talent for melodrama had served him well as a young

Pottsville lawyer. In his adventurous career as president of the Philadelphia & Reading Railroad—a height he scaled in his early thirties—that talent was indispensable. His life was a cavalcade of thrillers, written, produced and directed by their star. Most grandiose of all, perhaps, was his move to make the coal-carrying Reading its own principal customer by purchasing a lion's share of the Schuylkill County coal fields it served. This massive gulp gave the Reading a case of financial indigestion which in 1877 was already acute. But Gowen's gift of corporate faith healing staved off the collapse for years.

Gowen never set up company stores through which to gouge his employees. He insisted on investigation of every injustice charged against bosses. In 1870 he arranged for the first written contract between American miners and operators, and in 1875 set up the first company-supported benefit system in the anthracite industry. The public knew Franklin Gowen best, however, by his crusade for (as he put it) "the right of the individual laboring man against the tyranny of trades unions."

Gowen's reputation as a union buster was solidly established in 1875 with the destruction of the Workingmen's Benevolent Association, an organization of anthracite miners which had been the first notable industrial union in the United States. It seems to have been the individual mine operators, rather than Gowen, who polished off the W. B. A. But Gowen helped rally and inspirit the operators. And he himself later bragged to the Reading stockholders that he had done the deed, though it cost the company $4,000,000.

In 1877 Gowen was fresh from his greatest dramatic success: the overthrow of the "Molly Maguires." Under the spell of his romantic oratory, the entire country came to believe that a secret band of labor terrorists who called themselves "Molly Maguires" had held the Schuylkill mining region in their grip for twenty years past, murdering mine foremen, superintendents and strikebreakers in vague but enormous numbers. After diligent research some historians remain unconvinced that any such secret organization ever existed. Two brief spells of violence had indeed troubled the Schuylkill region like many another community in those brawling times, one outbreak in the mid-sixties, the other in the summer of 1875. Six murders were committed by members of the Ancient Order of Hibernians in the latter period; but the murderers seem to have acted in a purely private capacity, and only three of the victims could have been involved in labor troubles.

Nevertheless, Gowen's forensic fireworks cast such quibbles into the shade. As one of the counsel for the prosecution, Gowen dominated the trial of six alleged "Mollies" in the spring of 1876. The climax came when a Pinkerton detective took the stand with a thrilling story of counterespionage in behalf of Gowen and the Reading. Perhaps the world believed it all because it was just too good to be false. Certainly the story, scarcely altered or embellished, did well as a play, *Secret Service*, and provided Conan Doyle with a full-length Sherlock Holmes novel, *The Valley of Fear*.

By March 1877, when Gowen struck at the Engineers' Brotherhood, ten "Mollies" lay under sentence of death; and before the long hysteria ended, the gallows would claim ten more. The Reading's "Coal and Iron Police" was meanwhile being transformed from a group of mine guards into an efficient police force. Violence and crime were to continue in Schuylkill County, but no one thereafter would dare lift a hand against the Reading.

Peter Arthur and his Brotherhood met the Reading's attack squarely. The grand chief, himself a fluent and persuasive orator, spoke to large and sympathetic audiences throughout the region. When the Reading's superintendent turned down a request for arbitration, the Brotherhood called a strike for midnight on Saturday, April 14, 1877. Half of the Reading's engineers quit, carefully taking all trains to their destinations first, so as to keep clear of the new Pennsylvania law.

Surprised in his turn, Gowen recovered quickly. Loyal men were given raises. Dispatchers and superintendents were called out of Sunday services and put to work, some still wearing silk hats. On Monday Gowen began hiring new men. Unlike the Boston & Maine, he took on many greenhorns, to the heavy cost of the road in burned-out engines and wrecked cars. The Brotherhood made the most of these mishaps, ringing changes on the Ashtabula theme; Gowen counterattacked with charges of Brotherhood sabotage. But trains were running regularly even if hazardously within a week. And Gowen was able to announce "with pardonable pride" that not one of the Reading's 22,000 men "will hereafter be obliged to submit to the degradation of asking his fellowman for leave to earn his daily bread."

With head high, but treasury low and prestige trailing, the Brotherhood of Locomotive Engineers was now in full retreat.

Meanwhile, peace impended on another front. The trunk-line rate wars had scarcely started in 1874 when the combatants began seeking a durable settlement. Time after time agreements were negotiated only to collapse. Sometimes the fault lay with ambitious underlings, anxious only to make a good showing for their own divisions. Sometimes the top men turned marplots. The death of Commodore Vanderbilt changed the picture. The father had loved a good fight for its own sake. The son, William H. Vanderbilt, preferred a compromise, so long as there was profit in it.

On March 9, 1877, therefore, President John W. Garrett of the Baltimore & Ohio wrote jubilantly to his London banker: "I have recently spent a week in New York, engaged in what will prove, I hope, the most important conference ever held between the Trunk Lines." The other conferees were Vanderbilt, Hugh J. Jewett of the Erie and Thomas A. Scott of the Pennsylvania. Conversations, reported Garrett, were "full and free." For the first time in trunk-line history, all troubles and difficulties were reviewed minutely, "in a spirit of candor and justice, without the slightest interference or influence on the part of subordinates." Garrett used all his "personal influence" to bring Vanderbilt and Jewett into harmony, and Scott of the Pennsylvania "joined cordially and heartily in this work . . . Mr. Vanderbilt, for the first time in my knowledge at such a meeting fully representing his entire lines, showed . . . a sincere . . . cooperative spirit." Rates on westbound freight were hiked 50 per cent immediately as a sort of aperitif. "The great principle upon which we all joined to act was," wrote Garrett, "to earn more and to spend less."

After this heartwarming agreement in principle came a series of conferences, lasting through the spring, for the working out of details. In mid-May the four leaders developed a traffic pooling scheme like one already successful among southern roads. It applied only to freight westbound from New York, the Erie and the New York Central each to get 33 per cent of the tonnage, the Pennsylvania 25 per cent and the Baltimore & Ohio 9 per cent. Eastbound freight could not be pooled so well, because many independent feeder lines were involved. Later, however, similar pools might be made for

freight westbound from other cities. Though the Grand Trunk
still held aloof, circumstances had toned down its former intransi-
gence. On June 8, after "a very harmonious meeting," the heads of
the four major American lines formally signed the pooling treaty.
The war was over.

It seemed that railroad luck was finally turning. The grasshopper
scare in the West proved to be a false alarm; by late spring, a
bumper crop seemed in prospect, with consequent fat freight earnings at harvesttime. The disputed Presidency of the United States
was awarded to Rutherford B. Hayes just in time to avert anarchy
and possible bloodshed. Under pressure from public opinion and
his Southern Democrat allies, the new President pulled Federal
troops out of the last three occupied states of the South. Reconstruction was over. The new tranquillity of both North and South encouraged business planning. Even the outbreak of the Russo-Turkish War in late April brought a certain ghoulish satisfaction. Grain
prices rose immediately.

Yet this was not enough. The trunk lines were determined not
only to "earn more," but also to "spend less." How to do this? They
could drop unprofitable services formerly maintained for competition's sake. Higher rates for grain tended to reduce volume and
hence operating expenses. Above all, the recent routing of the Engineers' Brotherhood invited a cut in wages.

The Boston & Maine strike in February had led to numerous
proposals that employers combine against organized labor. In April
it was noted that a recent traffic pool among the anthracite carriers
had helped the Reading to weather its shutdown. Guaranteed its
share of the season's coal business anyway, that road could hold out
all summer without actually losing a ton of coal freight, the major
source of its income. Naturally enough, in view of all this, people
now suspected a similar strike insurance plan among the four trunk
lines. One of the four would reduce wages. The other three would
hold off, and the pooling arrangement would make up to the fourth
for any strike losses. Then the remaining roads would take their
turns.

The Pennsylvania made its cut a month before the pool took
effect, but a secret agreement could have taken care of this. The
trunk-line pool as published did not include eastbound traffic to
New York or any at all to Philadelphia. But later testimony by Scott

implied the existence of an unpublicized eastbound pool, beginning a month before the wage cut and lasting into the summer. Scott denied under oath that the trunk lines had agreed among themselves to cut wages. But in weighing this, we might remember that a prominent Baptist layman named John D. Rockefeller stated not long afterward—also under oath—that he had no interest in the Standard Oil Trust. And Scott was less noted for piety than was Rockefeller. The best that history can do is to bring in a Scottish verdict of "not proven."

In any case, financial desperation, plus the notion that labor had been tamed, made the pay cuts logical enough. "The Brotherhood is destroyed as a dictatorial body," said the *New York Times* in April; "neither railroad nor engineer will fear it henceforth or regard its ukases. . . . Both steps in the action of the Reading Company—the stand against the union and the plan of substitution as to its benefits—are an example which should be imitated by employers generally." A few days later, the president of the Illinois Central wrote the board chairman: "If Mr. Gowen is successful . . . all the companies in the west could combine and offer the engineers the same or even better advantages than they now obtain in their own association." And he sent to Gowen for a half-dozen copies of the Reading's insurance plan. Other roads did likewise, and included in their letters best wishes for Gowen's success. On May 15 the Missouri Pacific cut engineers' pay by 12 per cent. The men took it quietly.

But the real test would come only when the eastern trunk lines made the experiment. And the railroad world therefore braced itself expectantly on May 24 when the Pennsylvania announced a 10 per cent reduction, to take effect June 1 for all employees earning more than a dollar a day. On the Pennsylvania, this would be the second such cut since the Panic.

Would the men submit? Or would the "mutterings of discontent" heard by the *Engineers' Journal* indeed harden into "the dread cry of 'bread or blood' "?

CHAPTER 3

The Match

NO PRIVATE enterprise in the nation's experience had ever equaled the Pennsylvania's wealth and power. Even Nicholas Biddle's Bank of the United States, though it gave Andrew Jackson the fight of his life, had been a puny thing compared to Tom Scott's barony. In 1873 the railroads and canals controlled by the Pennsylvania were capitalized at $398,000,000 (eleven times as heavily as "Emperor Biddle's monster") and netted $25,000,000 a year (about equal to the annual revenue of the Federal government under Jackson).

Originally the Pennsylvania's name had been apt; the parent stem ran from Philadelphia to Pittsburgh. But in the fat postwar years, it had proliferated like a banyan tree. Now the parent company alone accounted for nearly 1,000 miles of road through the richest industrial area on earth, Great Britain possibly excepted. Other lines owned or operated by the company brought the total to 1,600 miles. And the lines controlled but not owned outright by the system added up to nearly 5,000 miles more. From the Hudson to the Mississippi, from the Great Lakes to the Ohio and the Potomac, from the prairies of Illinois to the marshes of the Jersey coast, the rails of the Pennsylvania system stretched shining and unbroken. Speaking of "ukases," Tom Scott's pay-cut decree had imperial scope.

News of the cut leaked out a couple of days before the official announcement on May 24. Superintendents, auditors, business agents and master mechanics were in on it early, with cashiers, bookkeepers and other clerks not far behind. Word spread through the shops, among boilermakers, blacksmiths, machinists, carpenters, painters. Out along the line, in the close valleys of the Appalachians, amid the rolling hills of Ohio and Indiana and the broad fields of the Midwest, in sooty towns and green villages, the news fell upon

43

switchmen, helpers, dispatchers, baggagemen, station agents, pumpers, signalmen. Even longshoremen at the company's New York freight docks felt the blow. To perhaps 20,000 men the news came as a personal misfortune, the latest of a series. It was the trainmen, however—the engineers, firemen, brakemen and conductors—whom the company watched most narrowly.

Among trainmen the brakemen had the lowest pay, a shade more than hod carriers but considerably less than carpenters. In the spring of 1877 American railroad brakemen got anywhere from $1.00 to $2.15 per twelve-hour day, averaging $1.75 (which happened to be the rate on the Pennsylvania). Monthly earnings averaged $55 on the Northern Pacific, $37 on the Lackawanna and probably somewhere between on most other roads. Yearly earnings on Illinois roads ran to about $500 or $550. But in 1878 brakemen on the Indianapolis & St. Louis averaged a pitiful $330.

Yet no railroader had a harder or more dangerous job than the brakeman. As he walked along freight-car roofs, a low bridge might snap the thread of his life in the middle of a careless thought. Handholds, the brackets used for climbing cars, were seldom if ever inspected. Brakemen on the Pennsylvania now had the new Westinghouse air brake and Janney automatic coupler, but on many roads they still had to race along swaying roofs to spin the brake wheels car by car. And almost every road except the Pennsylvania still used link-and-pin couplings. On such roads the brakeman had to jig with death every day, darting between cars or leaning from the beam that contained the coupling slot, while he guided a link into place and dropped the pin through. A brakeman with both hands and all his fingers was either remarkably skillful, incredibly lucky or new on the job. In running between the cars to uncouple them, the brakeman stood a fair chance of catching his foot in a switch frog (not blocked as now) or the open rail end of a switch. Then would come a brief, futile struggle to free himself before the rolling wheels sliced through his flesh and bone. Most railroads waited years before installing well-known safety devices, because, the men bitterly assumed, condolences came cheaper.

In snow or freezing rain the brakeman who did not slip on a glaze of ice might be so numbed by cold that he misjudged a leap and fell between cars. In Massachusetts an average of forty-two railroad men were killed on the job and fifty-four injured during every year of the mid-seventies, and half of these accidents occurred to brakemen coupling cars or riding freights in cold weather. Some deaths may have been voluntary. In Baltimore a reporter talked with several brakemen: "In two instances, it is said, brakemen after loss of rest and under the depression of reduced wages, etc., have purposely thrown themselves under the wheels. Nearly all the men talked with said [that] at one time and another when melancholy, they had meditated about stepping over the bumpers and meeting instant death."

This did not concern railroad management, however, for reasons stated in the official regulations of the Pennsylvania system:

6. The regular compensation of employes covers all risk or liability to accident.
7. If an employe is disabled by sickness or any other cause, the right to claim compensation is not recognized. Allowances when made in such cases, will be as a gratuity, justified by the circumstances of the case and previous good conduct.

In theory an injured employee might have had some legal redress. In practice he was stymied by lack of money, the railroad's abundance of skilled lawyers and the prejudice of judges. Systematic company insurance plans did not begin among railroads until 1880. Private insurance companies either charged all trainmen prohibitive rates or cheated them out of benefits. Engineers, firemen and conductors had their brotherhoods to look to for help in emergencies. The brakemen had none.

Brakemen took orders from the conductor, who had charge of the train as a whole. Besides collecting fares and answering questions, the conductor bore final responsibility for his train's regularity, safety and general upkeep. He had to know the duties of engineers, baggagemasters, brakemen, mail agents, express messengers, porter and news agents, and see to it that each did his job. He made sure that brakemen maintained and used their signals, lamps and tools properly. On passenger trains he directed the brakemen in keeping the cars properly heated and ventilated. At every terminal he had air brakes and couplings inspected. He was expected to keep passengers in order, not always an easy task in those rowdy times. On a freight train he collected manifests, noted damages, delivered way freight, kept track of and reported on cars used. In

short, though the engineer tended to regard him with disdain and
a touch of jealousy, the conductor earned his pay. This averaged
only $545 a year on the Pittsburgh, Fort Wayne & Chicago. On some
roads in Pennsylvania conductors got as little as $1.30 a day, on
others as high as $3.66, the average being $2.78. Most roads outside Pennsylvania and the South paid conductors between $3.00
and $3.50, which put them roughly on a par with bricklayers.

Between the pay of brakemen and conductors stood that of firemen, about $1.90 a day on most roads. But the Lehigh Valley paid
$2.50, the Lake Shore $1.19, and Virginia roads only 99 cents.
Monthly, firemen averaged $50 on the Lackawanna, $61 on the Jersey Central, $48 for freight and $55 for passenger service on the
Pennsylvania. On the B. & O. they averaged $421 a year, even though
the average B. &. O. brakeman made $493.

In return for this, railroad firemen shoveled coal into furnaces
"hot enough to melt glass," worked the tender brake at the engineer's direction, kept a lookout along the road, helped the engineer
clean and polish his engine after every trip, and on occasion clambered out over the speeding engine to oil it. One duty they prized
was taking charge of the engine in the engineer's absence. This
privilege kept them proudly mindful that engineers began as firemen.

To become an engineer was no mean ambition. Engineers considered themselves the aristocrats of the train crews. Yet they too
endured hardship, drudgery and danger. It was the engineer who
watched the track and everything near it, unrelaxing hour after
hour, knowing every spur, every siding, every blind curve, every
bridge, every grade crossing so well that not even fog and night
could dull his awareness. It was the engineer who might be called
upon at a split second's notice to save or forfeit scores of lives, including his own, by right or wrong use of throttle, brake and whistle.
For twelve hours of this wearing duty, most roads paid about $3.25.
Some, like the Reading or the Boston & Albany, paid only $2.75. The
Pennsylvania's Jersey division and the Lackawanna gave out to the
public that their engineers earned $100 a month; but on the Bur-
lington in the spring of 1877, monthly earnings averaged $84.85.
Annual earnings averaged about $900 on the Burlington and $1065
on the Rock Island, as against only $540 on one small Illinois road.

Later, after the unthinkable had happened, a cry went up from the well-to-do that railroad labor had been pampered, especially engineers. Yet in the summer of 1877 President Harris of the Burlington admitted privately that railroad pay was "fully as low as with other industries." In spite of the risk and responsibility of their work, brakemen earned little more than common laborers, engineers about the same as plumbers.

Railroaders had a grievance peculiar to themselves: the layover. At the end of a run the train crew had to lay over at their own expense until they were needed for a return trip, or else ride back on their own time, paying regular fares. Sometimes a man laid over for days, meanwhile maintaining two homes with no money coming in.

Even at their home terminals, trainmen were expected to be ready for work at any time, though unpaid when idle. By 1877 idle days came more and more often. Most railroad officials hated to trim the force, knowing the misery that sprang instantly upon a jobless man and his family. So they divided up the work, doling it out in smaller and smaller portions as times grew worse. And the men hung on, afraid to gamble on finding a full-time job elsewhere. One brakeman on the Pennsylvania bitterly displayed a month's pay of $18 on which he had to support a family. A fireman complained: "A man never makes much money unless freights are very good, and he is running all the time, and is half dead . . . of course engineers, with their big wages, they can make money."

Even before the June 1 cut, the Pennsylvania's men felt that they were "down to hard pan." But railroad officials failed to sense their mood. "The men were always complaining about something," grumbled Superintendent Pitcairn of the Pittsburgh Division. Lesser officials snarled back at them. At least one conductor regarded the abuse he took from dispatchers as his chief grievance.

On the evening of May 22 the Newark division of the Engineers' Brotherhood held an angry protest meeting, though Chief Arthur had made not a peep. Next day the Jersey City lodge met also, found a majority in favor of striking, and put out feelers to other railroad organizations. Like Arthur, the national leaders of both the Conductors' and Firemen's Brotherhoods held aloof. Nevertheless, by June 1, the day the cut took effect, engineers' and firemen's locals throughout the Pennsylvania system had chosen delegates to a joint grievance committee. All that week newspapers and the public speculated on the outcome, with wise money on a strike.

When the grievance committee, some thirty or forty strong, filed nervously into the Philadelphia office of President Thomas A. Scott, they faced a formidable bargainer. Before them stood a handsome, mild-mannered gentleman of fifty-three, erect and dapper, his blandly amiable face framed by a silky set of muttonchop whiskers. He looked for all the world like a self-assured clergyman with a rich and placid congregation, the sort of minister whom female parishoners in particular would find enchanting. His disarming suavity constituted a major weapon in Tom Scott's well-stocked arsenal. With it went tremendous energy and industry, an aptitude for intrigue, a dauntless spirit, and insatiable ambition. His middle name was Alexander, and it was not unfitting.

Bull-necked Franklin Gowen charged his obstacles head-on. Tom Scott seemed to flow through and around them, like a rising tide. The seventh of eleven children, fatherless at the age of twelve, not blessed with family fortune, young Tom Scott had nevertheless risen fast. Starting with the Pennsylvania in his twenties as a station agent, he soon won promotion to the superintendency of the Western Division, with headquarters at Pittsburgh. His three Pittsburgh years turned out to be among the most trying of his career. The Pennsylvania had managed to block entry of the B. & O. into that city and thereby had deeply angered the Pittsburghers. Scott's tact and charm softened their hostility, though nothing could have removed it. Promoted to the vice-presidency in 1860, Scott further proved himself in putting through favorable legislation at Harrisburg. In 1864, after a legislative battle which once more turned back the B. & O. from Pittsburgh, a state senator drily asked: "Mr. Speaker, may we now go Scott-free?"

Early in the Civil War, Scott became Assistant Secretary of War in charge of all government railroads. After resigning in 1862, he reappeared briefly in military annals as an organizer of the most brilliant large-scale troop movement of the war, the rushing of Hooker's corps by rail from Virginia to Tennessee in time to help win the battle of Chattanooga. After the war his imagination and ambition soared. Under the grimly single-minded J. Edgar Thomson, Scott played a conspicuous part in expanding the Pennsylvania

Railroad to a size and power unprecedented in American business history. He had been weighing an offer of the Erie's presidency in 1874 when the Pennsylvania's directors unanimously chose him to succeed the deceased Thomson as president.

The fateful year 1877 brought Tom Scott to a new height of power and prestige. "We have thirty-eight one-horse legislatures in this country," said Wendell Phillips, an old abolitionist whose anti-slavery impulse had not been put to sleep by the Emancipation Proclamation, "and we have a man like Tom Scott with three hundred and fifty millions in his hands, and if he walks through the States they have no power. Why, he need not move at all; if he smokes, as Grant does, a puff of the waste smoke out of his mouth upsets the legislatures." Phillips exaggerated, of course. Most observers put the score for Scott at only twenty legislatures.

Yet Scott wanted something more. For years he had schemed and maneuvered to stretch the Pennsylvania system clear across the continent. Now, as president of the unfinished Texas & Pacific Railway, he needed only a Congressional subsidy to achieve his ambition. But since the Credit Mobilier scandal, Congress had grown skittish of railroad subsidies. Hired publicists in the South beguiled Southern voters with the prospective delights of a Southern transcontinental route. In Washington, Scott money flowed like brooks in spring, and Scott lobbyists talked as incessantly. Presently Scott had a substantial bloc of supporters in Congress—but still not a majority.

Then came the disputed election of 1876. A fantastic balance of technicalities left the two contenders, Republican Rutherford B. Hayes and Democrat Samuel J. Tilden, each within a hairsbreadth of the White House. Historians concede Tilden the better title, but the Hayes men had more nerve and bargaining prowess. They won the necessary support of Southern Democrats by promising the South a Cabinet post, withdrawal of Federal troops, patronage—and "internal improvements of a national character." Hayes was exceedingly vague in his endorsement of the last point; but the Tilden men offered no hope at all, and so Tom Scott threw his bloc of Southern Congressmen to Hayes. This, in the opinion of the Hayes managers, was indispensable to the Republican victory. Even so, it was not until the dawn of March 2, 1877, that Hayes got a telegram confirming his election. He received it while en route to Washington in Tom Scott's own luxurious private railroad car.

Despite all this, the Texas & Pacific subsidy remained unsettled on June 4, 1877, when the trainmen's grievance committee confronted Tom Scott. The new Congress would not meet until December; and Hayes's inaugural address had shunned even the words "internal improvement," merely recommending attention to the South's "material development . . . within the just limits prescribed by the Constitution and wise public economy." This last phrase must have chilled Tom Scott, inasmuch as the Southern Pacific was now offering to build a southern road without any subsidy at all.

At the same time, Scott, through his Empire Transportation Company, was now engaged in mortal combat with John D. Rockefeller's Standard Oil Company. The Empire Transportation Company had sunk a huge sum in petroleum transportation—520 miles of pipeline, a telegraph system, a fleet of tank cars and other expensive equipment. Standard Oil countered by acquiring its own pipelines and tank cars. Empire then challenged Standard's near-monopoly of refining. Rockefeller struck back by taking Standard Oil's business away from Scott's Pennsylvania Railroad until such time as Scott's Empire Company sold him its refineries. The war was on. The Pennsylvania immediately sacrificed 65 per cent of its oil traffic, meanwhile carrying Empire oil at cost. By June the road had lost $1,000,000.

June 4, 1877, was therefore a day to try Scott's temper. Though he had good reason to shy from a strike, one must still admire his self-control. He listened patiently, politely, even sympathetically, while the grievance committee spun out its story. Besides the pay cut, the engineers complained about the system of assigning trains: the first crew in was the first out, without a chance to rest or see their families. They wanted regular runs, to stabilize pay and working days. They wanted passes home in case of long layovers. The system of "classification"—setting up grades of pay based on efficiency and length of service—was often used (the men believed) to keep wages low; and they wanted the system abolished.

For an hour Scott parried the men's complaints and bewailed the Pennsylvania's desperate situation. Since the panic, the annual dividend had been reduced from 10 to 6 per cent. A 40 per cent cut! And until now, wages had been cut only 20 per cent! Was it unjust to ask one small sacrifice more in this time of the company's need? From president to section hand they were all in the same boat, all victims of the depression. Come better times and pay would surely rise again.

Actually the Pennsylvania had netted enough in 1876 to pay an 8 per cent dividend and still set aside a million and a half—just what the new pay cut would save in a year. The latest cut in dividends would save another million. And so far in 1877 net earnings were higher by $165,000 than in the same months of 1876. Even with no Centennial business that summer, even with the Empire-Standard battle to sustain, the pay cut seemed needless, at least to the *Engineers' Journal.* "Facts are stubborn things," said the *Journal*, "and figures will not lie. . . . It is time some decided steps be taken to stop these unjust and uncalled for reductions."

Under the Scott spell, however, the committee finally decided to accept the cut. Back home some hot heads repudiated the surrender. Most brakemen, many conductors and even a few engineers were for striking. The newspapers predicted, however, that no strike could succeed without a majority of the engineers, who were better organized and harder to replace, and the men seemed to agree. At least, after meeting behind closed doors, the locals of the brotherhoods issued no strike call.

Just the same, it had been a near thing. One small, stout-hearted group of Pennsylvania Railroad employees actually did take up the challenge. Since 1873 the longshoremen at the company's New York docks had seen their hourly pay drop from twenty cents to fifteen. Working sometimes late into the night, with long unpaid delays in the middle of the day, they earned from six to eight dollars a week. Rents of ten or twelve dollars a month left them little enough to feed and clothe their families. When the June 1 cut brought their pay down to thirteen and a half cents an hour, they struck, more than 100 of them. All day on June 1 they lolled in the shade about Battery Place, drank beer in Hugh McHugh's saloon, and looked on critically as the red-faced, hard-breathing agent and foreman strained at barrels and crates. Fifty city policemen patrolled the the area, just in case, but found nothing to do. Nervously Tom Scott wired a compromise offer of fourteen cents an hour, and a few men took it. The company brought over shipping clerks to fill in. The clerks were not happy about it, having themselves been cut from eighty dollars a month to forty-five since the panic, but the immediate discharge of a grumbler recalled the others to a sense of duty. For their trouble the clerks got ten cents an hour—probably more than they were worth.

The longshoremen's defiance was gallant but foredoomed. A strike by trainmen, even a small group, would have sent a thrill of sympathy through the whole system. But the longshoremen had neither kinship nor contact with the trainmen. And so a note appeared in the sympathetic *Irish World* toward the end of June: "The longshoremen's strike has ended. They have concluded to accept fourteen cents an hour."

Without awaiting the result of Tom Scott's experiment, the Lehigh Valley Railroad had boldly announced a general 10 per cent cut for June 1. The Lehigh engineers held portentous secret meetings all through the last week in May. Reporters from the big city papers descended on Bethlehem, Easton and other towns along the Lehigh; and the *New York Times* said flatly that a strike had been voted. But as June 1 rolled by, so did the trains.

The day after the Pennsylvania's grievance committee bowed to Scott, the Lackawanna announced a reduction—the standard 10 per cent—to take effect on June 15. But the conductors' and firemen's brotherhoods clung tighter than ever to their no-strike policy. And by now the Engineers' Brotherhood seemed thoroughly discredited, stripped of power to do more than grumble, reduced to its old role of a benevolent society so far as it was suffered to exist at all. Thus prostrated, on July 1 it underwent that old Chinese torture known as "the death of a thousand cuts." Michigan Central, Lake Shore, Bee Line, Vandalia, Union Pacific—the roll of reductions would read like the index to *Poor's Manual*. When the Indianapolis & St. Louis, a low-paid line, announced its 10 per cent cut on June 30, the yardmen and switchmen at St. Louis quit, as did those of the Vandalia; but their gesture was futile.

The unkindest cut of all those on July 1 was that of the New York Central. To be sure, 85 per cent of the Central's stock had for years been the chief support of orphans: namely, Cornelius and William H. Vanderbilt, in that order. Still, of all railroads, the Central least needed retrenchment. In 1877 it netted more than 10 per cent of the total cost of the road and all its equipment. Its 8 per cent dividend amounted to more than a tenth of all dividends paid that year by all the railroads in the United States. Besides, the Central's wage rates were comparatively low to start with. Why the cut then? Did it come from a mere passion for conformity? Or was there really something to the popular suspicion of a wage-cutting pact among the trunk-line conferees at the Brevoort House that spring? We are never likely to know.

The Erie had a better case. For years its blood had been sucked by the greediest vampires of Wall Street: Daniel Drew, Jim Fisk and Jay Gould. Since the panic its stock had dropped from 75 to 5. In receivership since 1875, its net earnings in 1876 fell $1,000,000 short of the interest on its bonds—not that the bondholders were much surprised. With every year of railroad progress, necessity pressed harder on the pallid Erie to shift its broad gauge to standard, replace iron rails with steel, double-track its lines, rebuild its bridges, modernize its facilities generally. Thanks perhaps to a militant labor force, the Erie at the same time paid considerably better wages than its wealthy competitor, the New York Central.

On June 28, after rumors of a July 1 10 per cent cut had been officially confirmed, a delegation of fifty trainmen waited on Receiver Jewett in his New York office (fortunately moved from the palatial headquarters of the late Jim Fisk). The guiding spirit in the group was Barney J. Donahue, a sharp-eyed little brakeman with sandy hair and mustache. His twenty-five years of Erie service had left Donahue with a crippling case of inflammatory rheumatism, a crushed hand and a shortened left leg, the result of a fracture. Despite his handicaps, Donahue managed to keep on the "extra brakeman list" and earned about enough each month to pay his board bill.

In contrast, Donahue's adversary was getting the highest salary that had ever been paid a railroad executive. After Tom Scott turned down the Erie's presidency in 1874, the directors had cast about widely before landing Congressman Hugh J. Jewett of Zanesville, Ohio. Jewett's price for the luckless job was a ten-year guarantee of $40,000 a year, of which $150,000 was paid in advance and the rest in equal instalments. As a Democratic politician, Jewett had given no evidence of brilliance. He tailored his pompous speeches to fit the prejudices of his constituents. In the roles of lawyer, banker and railroad manager, however, he wore a different aspect—direct, shrewd and systematic as his political oratory was rambling and rootless. In time, the Erie's deal with Jewett proved to be a bargain. But at the moment, as the court-appointed receiver of the bankrupt road, Jewett's greatest triumph seemed to have been in negotiating his salary.

To the complaints of Donahue and the others, Jewett replied curtly that the cut had to be made and would be made. His only gesture toward conciliation was to point out that their pay would still be higher than on other lines. The men in their turn remained unmoved, unless by anger. They had, in fact, already decided to strike if Jewett did not rescind the wage cut. Probably Jewett knew this: a couple of informers had tipped off the company that very day. He certainly know about the time in 1874, just before he came to the Erie, when 1,000 mechanics at the Susquehanna shops struck for back pay. On that occasion, the strikers had played rough, blocking the tracks, seizing trains, dismantling locomotives, defying the sheriff and yielding at last only to state troops dispatched by Governor Hartranft of Pennsylvania. The Erie's victory cost it a million dollars.

Jewett profited from his predecessor's experience. After the grievance committee had "dispersed to neighboring hotels and saloons," the receiver applied to Governor Lucius D. Robinson of New York for state troops to prevent expected rioting. Only a month before, New York militia had been called to break up a riot between strikers and scabs at a Haverstraw brickyard. This time the call came before the riot. Despite that peculiar fact, the governor, who happened to be a stockholder and director of Erie, showed what the *New York World* called "an extravagant readiness to credit the rumor." For several days the militia in their gaudy uniforms paraded the streets of Buffalo and Rochester at public expense. An Erie official said "any demonstration would be speedily put down, even if it should be found necessary to sacrifice life" (presumably not his own). The *World* deprecated this hasty and uncalled-for state intervention in a private quarrel. "The military arm," it warned, "is not to be lightly stretched forth either by the Government of a State or by the Government of the nation."

Justifiable or not, the governor's action served its purpose. Despite all of Barney Donahue's haranguing, the strike threat fizzled; and Jewett fired the leading troublemakers in successive batches, ending with Donahue himself. (The Erie had stopped using outside detectives, but now had an efficient secret service of its own.) To railroad leaders the Erie's triumph may have carried a moral: when in doubt, call the militia.

Three large roads waited until after July 1 to cut wages. One was the Baltimore & Ohio—already notorious for low pay—of which more will be said later. Another was the Northern Pacific on which wages had already been cut "as low as the lowest of neighboring roads." As July began, Northern Pacific officials took note of eastern successes. "Although the experiment has not yet been attempted in the Northwest," reported Vice-President Stark, "it is possible that we now might make some reduction in this department without serious inconvenience." On July 18 the directors authorized a pay cut on the Minnesota and Dakota divisions, if the president "shall deem it expedient." (What happened then is not certain, but events of that week must have made the move seem decidedly inexpedient.)

The Chicago, Burlington & Quincy, like the New York Central, could not cry poverty as convincingly as some other roads. Nevertheless, when lower earnings forced a retreat that spring from a 10 per cent to an 8 per cent dividend, the directors clamored for economy. "The shortest and best way to accomplish this," suggested one, "is to adopt the same plan that the Penn. Central has done, namely a reduction of 10% on all salaries that average over $1.00 a day. . . . There certainly can be no cause of complaint . . . while stockholders are to have their income reduced 20%."

President Robert Harris, a civil engineer turned administrator, had an unusual sympathy for the men. He could not wholly resist the pressure, but he tried to confine the cut to certain classes, mainly engineers and firemen. It was to be kept secret until July 10, so as not to endanger holiday business. Harris and his colleagues feared the men might take Independence Day too literally—as one official put it: "too much whiskey around and too many idle men."

General Manager William B. Strong was already writing hopefully that "by January 1st we will be able to make another cut." Harris tried to forestall this. "Early in July [wages will be] very nearly down to bed rock," he wrote a leading director, significantly enclosing a *Chicago Journal* editorial. "Had there been no soulless and inexorable monopoly," wrote the *Journal*, "there would have been no remorseless and undaunted Mollie Maguires." "I have read the newspaper slip you sent me," came a sniffy reply, "but think it applies more to the great coal combination, who I fancy have unduly pressed on their employees, than to us. The experiment of reducing the salaries has been successfully carried out by all the Roads that have tried it of late, and I have no fear of any trouble with our employees if it is done with a proper show of firmness on our part and they see they must accept it cheerfully or leave."

Most railroad leaders did not share Robert Harris' qualms about the wage-cutting experiment. Yet those leaders were not really callous or brutal. Their labor policy sprang not from innate cussedness, but from the system and the times. The enormous growth of railroads had meant an enormous hunger for capital. Railroads therefore, from necessity, became financial pioneers: the first great American business corporations. Legal ownership, and hence responsibility, resided in a vast impalpable cloud of stockholders. Actual management was delegated to a few executives and directors. "Your first duty and mine also," wrote one railroad president to another, "is to the property with which we are respectively connected and we have no duty or right, even, to sacrifice that for anything or anybody." These men, in short, felt morally bound to put maintenance of dividends ahead of their own humanity or sense of social justice. By 1877 the phrase "soulless corporation" had become a cliché, and it almost always referred to a railroad.

Railroad leaders, like most businessmen of the seventies, held fiercely to the doctrines of Social Darwinism. They were themselves the products of natural selection, the survival of the "fittest"—or at any rate, the most heavily endowed with energy, shrewdness and ruthless will. Applied to themselves, the doctrine was flattering. Applied to their employees, it was useful.

No leader expounded the dogma more fluently than the Burlington's vice-president, Charles Elliott Perkins, an expatriate Boston Brahmin who carried with him to Iowa an Emersonian urge to philosophize. Wrote Perkins: "the sooner employers as well as employees make up their minds that the labor question is primarily one of supply and demand and discuss it on that basis, the better for the country and everybody in it. . . . Some of the newspapers talk about corporations paying the wages they feel able to pay. . . . [But] the spirit of the age . . . has not required and ought not to require a man to buy what he does not want . . . If work is plenty and labor scarce, [railroads] must pay what laborers, from the president down, can get elsewhere, or shut up shop. . . . When work is scarce and labor plenty, and thousands of men and women idle, laborers, from railroad presidents down, must take what they can get or remain idle. . . . Railroads can only reduce wages because they can find plenty of new men at the new rates if the old men can do better and desire to leave. . . . The number of idle men about is a standing argument that is stronger than anything on paper."

Railroad managers suspended their reverence for the law of supply and demand when it came to freight and passenger rates. Where, for example, was their devotion to natural economic law in the trunkline conferences of that spring? Sometimes, also, they allowed better pay to men living in certain Western areas where prices were high, even though men could have been hired for less.

Yet whatever inconsistencies the railroad leaders themselves may have fallen into, they resisted with holy zeal any challenge to the doctrine by labor unions. "Capital," protested the *Scranton Republican*, "cannot consistently advocate combination among the employers, and at the same time denounce it among the employed." Railroad leaders cared nothing for what was thought in Scranton. To them a strike was a wicked violation of natural law and a union was an outrageous conspiracy to that end. After some labor trouble on the Michigan Central in 1864, the president wrote his superintendent: "I hope you will find out who the leaders are or were and be sure to let them go one at a time . . . But be sure to do it unforgettingly." In the summer of 1876 President Garrett of the B. & O. not only refused to see a grievance committee of firemen, but also ordered them all discharged the next day. In the case of known or suspected labor agitators outside the three established railroad brotherhoods, vengeance pursued its prey still further by means of the black list, which circulated widely among railroad officials. A man whose name appeared on such a list would not find work on a railroad again.

Job seekers often had to take an ironclad oath later known as a "yellow dog contract," like one used by some officials on the Burlington in June 1877:

In consideration of the C. B. & Q. R.R. Co. giving me work, I do agree to keep out of all combinations of men encouraging strikes, and in case of strikes or combinations, will work faithfully for the company's interest, and will run my engine to the best of my ability if other men do strike, or combine to quit, to force the R.R. Co. to terms made by any combination of men.

Some railroads hired private detectives to keep tabs on labor. First among such agencies stood that of Allan Pinkerton, already world-famous for supplying the detective who brought down the "Molly Maguires." "All the officials of the [Pennsylvania Railroad] Company are my friends," boasted Pinkerton that very spring.

Such was the spirit in which railroad managers trooped along the way blazed by the Boston & Maine, the Reading and the Pennsylvania. They saw it as the path of righteousness. When the great storm burst at last, the strength of the typical railroad leader was as the strength of ten, because his heart felt pure.

CHAPTER 4

Hangfire

TOM SCOTT'S masterly handling of the June 4 grievance committee seemed to be the climax of the drama. Pay cuts on the other roads provided an apparent denouement. As soon as the Baltimore & Ohio made its midsummer cut, the final curtain would presumably be rung down on a scene of general jollification about the green baize. But the audience misjudged both the structure and length of the play. A curious episode in June turned out to be not a bungling anticlimax, but the prologue to Act Two.

On Saturday evening, June 2, 1877, a group of Pittsburgh, Fort Wayne & Chicago Railroad trainmen met at Dietrich's Hall in Allegheny City, across the river from Pittsburgh. They felt, as a brakeman put it, that the engineers "generally patched things up for themselves" and "didn't look after anything else." So they formed the Trainmen's Union, a secret, oathbound organization to include not only engineers but also conductors, firemen, brakemen, switchmen and all other workers in the transportation departments. As they saw it, the trunk-line managements had ganged up to subjugate their employees in detail. To counter this, the new union would organize at least three fourths of the trainmen on each of the trunk lines. Then it would move against the cuts, the "classification system" and other long-standing grievances. If it came to a strike, firemen would not take engineers' jobs, men on nonstriking roads would not handle struck equipment—in short, unity of capital would be met at last by unity of labor.

The master spirit in that first meeting was oddly cast as a labor leader. Far from being an intellectual or a crusader, he represented nothing so much as the Gilded Age itself, with all its restless energy and easy morals. In the hurly-burly of a springtime Saturday night at Dietrich's Hall it was no halo that picked him out from the crowd

59

but a worldly self-assurance, six feet of height and a pair of leather lungs. His stubborn chin, down-curving mustache, slightly aquiline nose, clear brown eyes and dark hair parted neatly in the middle all hinted at his upper-class Prussian ancestry. What might have been military harshness in his ancestors, however, was tempered and mellowed in him by American blood and birth, as well as by a fine singing voice and a taste for bonded Pennsylvania rye. Both the voice and the taste, it is pleasant to note, were to remain strong and true right through the era of "Sweet Adeline." For on June 2, 1877, Robert Adams Ammon was still a week short of his twenty-fifth birthday.

Despite his youth he already had marvelous stories to tell, most of them true. Born in New Jersey, he grew up in Pittsburgh. His father, August Ammon, a prosperous insurance company executive known about town as "Squire" Ammon, sent the fourteen-year-old Robert to Western University (now the University of Pittsburgh) for courses in arithmetic, geography, reading and German. Young Ammon then attended the Capital University at Columbus, Ohio, but was expelled at the age of sixteen for his escapades in concert with the son of a prominent railroad official.

If any part of his formal education influenced Robert Ammon's career, it must have been the geography. After his expulsion, he went west, joined the United States Cavalry as a bugler, suffered a calf wound in a fight with the Blackfeet Indians and was discharged. The seventeen-year-old veteran clerked it for a while in San Francisco and visited China as a purser on the Pacific mail steamer. Back in the United States at nineteen, Ammon, in behalf of a Californian financier, led a party of men through the mountains of Arizona in search of a fabulous diamond mine (later shown to be one of the most notable swindles of that fraud-filled era). After a pleasure trip to South America, he became an insurance agent for various companies, doubtless helped by his father's connections and probably also by his own love of talk and travel. Married in September 1873, he settled down for a couple of years as a hotelkeeper near Cleveland, until the hotel burned down.

Late in the summer of 1876, August Ammon's prodigal son turned up in Pittsburgh again with his wife, his first child and a letter of introduction to J. D. Layng, general manager of the Pittsburgh, Fort Wayne & Chicago Railroad (a subsidiary of the Pennsylvania).

Young Ammon assured Layng that he was willing now to settle down for good, and Layng gave him a job as a brakeman. Until the fateful pay cut, Ammon kept his word. Having an income of $40 a month in addition to his brakeman's pay, he lived better than his co-workers. By the spring of 1877 he and his family were established near the upper end of Adams Street in a little white cottage surrounded by a green lawn, trellised grapevines and beds of flowers—the picture of contented domesticity.

The fateful meeting at Dietrich's Hall changed all that. Ammon became "grand organizer" as well as head of the new Trainmen's Union, and off he went on June 4 to propagate the faith. The union paid his expenses, which were small, since his fellow workers let him ride free. Railroad men everywhere had been waiting for someone, anyone, to lead them; and they rushed to join the new union. For three weeks Ammon traveled over the Fort Wayne road, the Baltimore & Ohio, the Cleveland & Pittsburgh, the Lake Shore and others, organizing lodges and swearing in members until the Trainmen's Union included thousands of trunk-line railroad workers all the way from Baltimore to Chicago. The precise total enrollment of the union will never be known, but in Pittsburgh alone it reached 400 or 500. Nothing quite like this had ever happened to American labor before. With all due allowance for the "grand organizer's" energy and gift of gab, such phenomenal growth foreshadowed a new era in American history.

On June 16 Grand Chief Arthur of the Engineers' Brotherhood paid a visit to Pittsburgh "by special request" and conferred with Brotherhood men from both Pittsburgh and Allegheny. After his return the *Engineers' Journal* announced significantly that no existing rule or law of the Brotherhood prevented its members from also joining the Trainmen's Union.

Unfortunately for the Trainmen's Union Robert Ammon's wholesale inductions let in detectives and informers who kept the various managements well posted on the union's plans and membership. The ax began falling at once. On the Pan Handle punitive discharges began only four days after the birth of the union. "Determined to stamp it out," as one official stated to the press, the Baltimore & Ohio issued a general order for the discharge of all men belonging to "the [new] Brotherhood or Union." The Pennsylvania had apparently resolved to cut down its working force anyway, and the advent of the

Trainmen's Union presented it with a fine list of candidates for the sack. Ammon himself, whose railroad job was being done by an "extra" brakeman, escaped until June 24 only because he jumped around so. At last, however, an official of the Fort Wayne road managed to intercept him and hand him his walking papers.

In spite of this Ammon and his Trainmen's Union went ahead. On Sunday, June 24, forty men fanned out over the several lines to notify all lodges of a general railroad strike at noon on the following Wednesday, unless the roads yielded to union demands. On Monday a committee presented formal demands to the Pittsburgh railroad officials, who refused to receive them. The committee could not get passes to Philadelphia to see Tom Scott; it would not or could not pay its own way; and so the negotiations, such as they were, ended there.

Though no official notice was granted the committee, it got immediate unofficial notice: its five members were fired in a body. So were several score Trainmen's Union members who had thus far dodged the ax. These blows, with their implication that all was discovered, shook the nerve of the union. On the evening before the strike, at a council of war in Dietrich's Hall, a number of men (including some who had been among the first to champion a strike call) "kicked up a rumpus" which "came near ending in a row." A sizeable faction refused to go along with the strike. Some of these, unknown to the union, went out on night trains after the meeting and spread false word east and west that the strike had been called off. Next morning, with the strike only hours away, telegrams poured in on Ammon and his colleagues asking if the news were true. And Ammon found the telegraph lines closed to him by railroad officials when he tried to reply.

The inevitable fiasco had its moments of excitement. At the zero hour of noon, about 200 men gathered around the grain elevator and the Rush House in Pittsburgh. They were in a bitter mood, most of them having been discharged for union activity. After an hour of milling about, a half dozen or so detached themselves from the crowd and went into the Pennsylvania yards to stop an incoming freight. The police, who had been keeping the crowd in check, ran after the little group and ejected them. Here was the point at which real trouble might have flared up. But the trespassers left quietly; and after railroad authorities had announced that any loiterers would be jailed as vagrants, the crowd thinned out and drifted sadly away.

After it was all over, a prominent railroad official bragged to reporters that the roads had never been worried by the strike threat. He admitted, however, "that if the employes could be thoroughly organized, a great deal of trouble could be given." Robert Ammon had the same idea. He and his fellow unionists knew "that the bubble would have to burst, that there would be a strike sooner or later," perhaps in the early fall. The Trainmen's Union was not dead. It was not even sleeping. By mid-July it was larger than ever.

Even if the Trainmen's Union had been as dead as the public mistakenly supposed, its influence would have lived on. Every railroad town that Ammon visited was like a saturated solution into which he dropped a seed crystal of unionism. For a while at least, whatever might happen to the Trainmen's Union as a national movement, the railroad men of those towns could turn in time of need to ready-made organizations with recognized leaders. The idea of unity among all trainmen remained, and likewise the fact that it had been put into practice, however fleetingly. A psychological channel had been opened. Perhaps it was shallow. But the shallowest of channels can change the course of a mighty river when the water is running right. And the current was strong that summer.

People had hoped, for no very good reason, that the Centennial Year would be the turning point of the depression. It was not. In July 1877 Secretary of the Treasury John Sherman took some comfort from the sound position of the Treasury. But "in regard to wages, rents, transportation, prices, and all questions of political economy which enter into the commonweal of the people," he wrote a friend, "you can judge as well as I."

Depending on whom you listened to, and when you listened, the Baltimore & Ohio Railroad Company was either prospering hugely or about to collapse. It paid 10 per cent on its stock, but its stock capitalization was extraordinarily low in comparison to its bonded debt. This annoyed some people, who pointed out that you could omit a stock dividend and stay solvent, whereas bond interest had to be paid willy-nilly. They also charged that in his annual reports, President John W. Garrett laid on the rose paint with much too heavy a brush. Under these attacks, Baltimore & Ohio stock prices fell by 50 per cent in the first half of 1877.

Garrett did display a certain shiftiness in writing to his London banker, Junius Morgan. Frantically anxious to borrow more money in London, he sent Morgan cheery news of the road's finances. But he begged Morgan to use his statements without publication lest they get back to the United States, where he was singing a different tune "upon the subject of taxation." As to Garrett's borrowing plans, Morgan complained in mid-June about the bad effect of the collapse in B. & O. stock prices. Morgan's brilliant son, J. Pierpont, added to his father's pessimism with a cable from America reporting B. & O. floating debt at more than $8,000,000. "Your position will soon become one of great danger," the elder Morgan warned Garrett, "if you continue to pile up these large amounts of floating obligations." He insisted that Garrett must reduce stock dividends, regardless of the effect on the market. It was "either that or something far more disastrous. . . . The storm is upon you."

Garrett thought he saw another alternative. Portly, rubicund, ponderous in word and motion, he had a keen, cold mind; and his bluish gray eyes missed little. Garrett's middle name was "Work." He forced his way more like a glacier than a torrent. Yet this ex-provision dealer without railroad experience had taken over the B. & O. just before the Civil War, brought it through that great conflict and built it up into one of the nation's four great eastern trunk lines in less than twenty years. He hated unionism and, indeed, any display of employee independence. Reluctantly he sent a man in 1863 to look into the grievances of demonstrating laborers at Locust Point. "If there be any weak, old, or inferior workmen," he directed vindictively, "they should certainly be dismissed if an advance is made." Advance or not, the instigators of the protest were to be ferreted out and fired, and no labor organization was to be recognized or dealt with. When a trackmen's strike broke out four months after the end of the war, Garrett called on Major General William H. Emory to break the blockade with United States troops; and Emory promptly obliged.

So now Garrett characteristically decided to cut wages instead of dividends, even though wages had been reduced 10 per cent only eight months before. At the regular directors' meeting of July 11 another 10 per cent reduction was decreed to take effect on Monday, July 16, for all employees earning more than a dollar a day. That done, the directors adjourned until mid-September, omitting the August meeting because so many would be away on vacation.

In an official statement Garrett tried clumsily to placate the men. He said that all officers were subject to the same cut (which was a lie in his own case, for his salary was not trimmed by so much as a nickel). He pleaded financial necessity. Unfortunately the men could and did read Garrett's latest glowing report to the stockholders, and they took note also of the fat 10 per cent dividend still being paid. Garrett expressed confidence that everyone would "cheerfully recognize the necessity of the reduction." This was perhaps the most thoroughly misplaced confidence since the opening of the Ashtabula bridge.

Morale on Garrett's road could hardly have been lower. The men felt that they were "treated just as the rolling stock or locomotives." Since the last cut had come a series of measures to get more work for less pay: extra cars, reduced crews, no overtime pay for Sunday work, a new "second class" rating at $1.50 for most firemen ($1.35 after the new cut). What with temporary layoffs, brakemen and firemen now averaged about $30 a month. After meeting board bills, half the firemen were left with $10 a month to support their families. On July 16 the B. & O. still owed the men for their June work; but if their pay were attached for debt, they were fired.

At Wheeling four or five men tried to talk up a strike, but in vain. Some freight firemen at Baltimore resolved to quit on Monday morning, but Garrett got wind of this and arranged to have strikebreakers on hand. That done, he took the Saturday evening train for New York. He knew well enough that his men did not "cheerfully recognize the necessity of the reduction." But he assumed that they did recognize the futility of resistance with so many jobless thousands at his command.

Passing over the vexed question of just how many thousands were jobless, we can say at least that in the summer of 1877 there were as many as ever. In Buffalo unemployment and suffering were acute. The oldest citizens of Rochester could not recall a worse year. At Albany public relief spending reached a depression peak.

Those who had work were not much happier. "The laborer is the author of all greatness and wealth," ex-President Grant told a delegation of unionists in London on July 3. "Without labor there would be no Government or no leading class, or nothing to preserve." On that very day in Washington Secretary Sherman, a leading figure in the aforesaid government, announced that his Treasury Department would take advantage of a recent court interpretation of the Federal eight-hour law and would hereafter demand ten hours' work for a day's pay. Workers electing to work only eight hours would be docked 20 per cent. Secretary of the Interior Carl Schurz had done the same thing two months earlier.

A Cincinnati cigar maker with a wife and three children was asked how he lived on his earnings of $5 a week. "I don't live," he said. "I am literally starving. We get meat once a week, the rest of the week we have dry bread and black coffee." He remarked that all three of his children were sick.

The *Labor Standard,* official organ of the Communists, reported without comment that the pay of Brooklyn policemen had been reduced by the customary 10 per cent. Similar cuts were being made in police departments all over the country and numerous layoffs too. Even the Pinkerton Detective Agency, already acquiring a national reputation for its work inside unions, felt the same pinch. "Now, when the Molly Maguires operations are finished," wrote Allan Pinkerton, "where is the work to come from? and echo answers 'Where?' I can assure you [Superintendent George Bangs] that it will be hard work to get work, should we have another dull season, such as we have had." Pinkerton felt aggrieved when the head of his Philadelphia office asked for a raise. "Mr. Franklin must certainly have got another attack of his old Complaint," he wrote. "It is impossible, that, had he been in his sane mind, and thought all the matter over, that he ever would have made such a proposition. . . . There is no demand for labor. . . . Philadelphia has got through safely and a little ahead, solely on account of the Business given to us by Mr. Gowen."

Everywhere wages kept falling. Many workers took new cuts of 10, 20, and even 40 per cent. Labor troubles consisted almost entirely of lockouts by employers or strikes against wage reductions. Usually the employers won. The Iron Molders nearly went down before an employer offensive aimed at stamping out unionism entirely, and they scarcely pretended to resist cuts ranging from 20 to 40 per cent. With the bravado of desperation, the June issue of their *Journal* predicted a revival of American unionism, because "the feeling that it is organization or extermination is growing." And it jauntily promised that "supply and demand economists will soon hear the cry of supply and be d——d." By early July it had given up the pretense. "The fates seem to be against us. Our employers are persecuting us with all the means in their power, and the press is rendering them valuable aid; even the law is called in to their assistance, all having but one object in view—the total destruction of Trade Unions. It can truly be said the war of capital and labor is now raging as it never did before."

More than ever the wealthy wondered and feared. In Pennsylvania ten condemned "Molly Maguires" awaited execution on June 21. Writing to the *Workingman's Advocate,* an Indianapolis man demanded their rescue by force. "The laboring men of Indiana 100,000 strong—will stand by you," he promised (without visible warrant). All the night before, militia patrolled the streets of Mauch Chunk with loaded rifles. When the morning of death dawned heavy and dull, thousands of miners and their families gathered there and at Pottsville and Wilkes-Barre to witness and mourn the multiple hangings. The traps were sprung in a drizzling rain, and there was no violence except on the gallows.

Yet the rope did not end it all. Within a few days rumors filled the press that the "Mollies" were still active, that three of their enemies had been murdered and three others had disappeared. The *Irish World,* a pro-labor voice of the Ancient Order of Hibernians, had been doubly stung by the hangings, which it considered a shocking miscarriage of justice. "Drive a rat into a corner and he will fight," it warned on June 30. "Drive your serfs to desperation, you grinding monopolists, chain them in enforced idleness half the year and lash them with the whip of hunger to work at semi-starvation wages— semi-starvation for themselves and their little ones—the other half, and in their desperation they will some day pounce upon you and destroy you!"

Violence hung like the smell of gunpowder in the summer air. In Montreal on July 12, the anniversary of the Battle of the Boyne, two men were killed and several wounded in a wild riot between Catholic and Protestant Irish. In Philadelphia crime was "so common that even an atrocious murder causes but momentary comment." Just published was Major John Edwards' book *Noted Guerrillas,* which made heroes of wartime bandits and bushwhackers and commenced the apotheosis of Jesse James. At the end of June the Deadwood stage was robbed again; and lawlessness was said to be growing even worse thereabouts, what with hundreds of desperate men earning nothing. The Molly Maguire hangings had raised the number of legal executions since the beginning of the year to forty-eight. There were others besides. On July 13 a body of masked men took a prisoner from a jail near San Francisco and hanged him to a tree; no arrests were made. Vigilance committees became a matter of course, not only in the West but also in the East. In Kentucky nine deaths were reported in a battle between horse thieves and a vigilance committee, seventy men being engaged on each side.

It was in dealing with the tramp problem that the forms of law seemed in greatest danger of being put aside. Tramps had never been so numerous and so bold as they were that summer. The cities saw plenty of them. Through the summer nights hundreds sprawled and snored along New York's Battery or Chicago's Lake Park. They overran the countryside, especially along the railroad lines, infesting every road and byway in some regions, "slouching in the shade of fences, under trees, skulking near barns, watching favorable opportunities to invade farm houses." Late in June a tramp hacked to death three members of a farm family near the town of Gore, Ohio. Johnstown, Pennsylvania, was reputedly the base of operations for "several thousand" tramps known as the "German Band," from which numerous small gangs sallied out in forays upon the countryside. In once peaceful country districts, doors and windows that till recently had been thrown open to the coolness of the summer night were now locked, bolted and barred, and farmers organized night patrols.

As in 1876 most tramps were on the road more out of desperation than innate depravity. "The country is full of molders travelling," noted the *Iron Molders' Journal*. But a rising hysteria seized the tramp-infested regions, and it began to seem that the only good tramp was a dead one. "The simplest plan," remarked the *Chicago Tribune* in a heavy attempt at humor, "where one is not a member of the Humane Society, is to put a little strychnine or arsenic in the meat and other supplies furnished the tramp." A greenback newspaper reprinted this under the heading: "The Bullionists' Cure for Tramps." Considering the times, there is a disturbing possibility that someone, somewhere, took the item seriously.

Much more seriously meant were widespread editorial recommendations of "a good shot gun" or "a vigilance committee and a stout rope thrown over the limb of a tree." Reports came from all over the

Eastern states of vigilance committees threatening to lynch tramps. The climax came when "96 wealthy gentlemen," including Vice-President Alexander Cassatt of the Pennsylvania Railroad, called upon the citizens of three eastern Pennsylvania counties to meet at Bryn Mawr early in July. At this "antitramp convention," it was proposed to form a corps of mounted police and to provide every resident with a horn, a watchman's rattle, a billy and colored fires for night signaling. After much publicity and several meetings, the conferees cut out the fireworks and limited their antitramp exertions to assisting the authorities in the enforcement of existing laws. Meanwhile, the press carried the running story under the heading "War on the Tramps"—not considering, perhaps, that if society had declared war on the tramps, then the tramps must ipso facto be at war with society.

Tramps aside, the farmer felt better that summer than he had for some years past. That meant a great deal. Farming was still the biggest business in the country, well behind railroads in value of improvements, but neck and neck in terms of equipment and far ahead in value of land. In numbers of gainful workers, agriculture outstripped by a whisker all other classifications put together. And country folks outnumbered city people better than two to one.

During the early seventies, farm prices had held steady while non-farm prices rose—whence the wave of farm discontent that had carried the Granger movement forward. In 1874 the balance was regained, and thereafter non-farm prices fell faster than farm prices —whence the ebbing of the Granger tide. By 1877 Granger lodges had turned from agitation to sociability, from political rallies to pie socials, oyster suppers, picnics and fairs. To the surprise of the railroads the Granger decision of March 1877 did not lead to anything like the legislative tyrannizing they had feared. "The great excitement [among farmers] against the railroad companies seems to have wholly subsided," reported the *Railroad Gazette* gratefully.

Farm excitement that summer centered instead on crop prospects. For the farmer 1877 promised to be a year of bounty. Hoping for high prices, he had put all his cash and credit into seeding. He won his gamble. Weather favored him almost everywhere. By midsummer his corn towered "gloriously," and its color was "superb." The wheat crop especially was turning out beautifully, with a rich yield per acre and a greater acreage than ever before. An avalanche of wheat rumbled toward the nation's grain-shipping centers. With the Russo-Turkish War still on and European harvests poor, prices held up. There was a smell of money on the prairie breeze, and even the languishing retailer and manufacturer picked up the scent and panted for their share.

But this whiff of distantly approaching prosperity failed to enliven most workers and businessmen as the Fourth of July came around again. People seemed to have worked the flag waving out of their systems during the whoop-te-do of '76. This did not apply to the young, of course. Schools were out, and the newly educated brought in the usual crop of cane. The traditional squibs and crackers, pin-wheels and rockets, blood and fire commemorated independence of one sort or another. Beadle and Adams started five new series of dime novels that year, and their rivals brought out six, including "The New Sensation Ten Cent Novels." The class of 1880 at Princeton managed to get itself suspended in a body and ordered out of town for serenading the faculty in boisterous and disrespectful fashion after exams. Even so, the Fourth of July passed with unusual quiet in the cities. The weather being warm and fair, most who had the wherewithal either went on picnics and excursions or took in a baseball game. It looked as though the editor of the *Wheeling Intelligencer* might have been right that spring when he wrote hopefully: "With the postponement of Congress till the middle of October, there doesn't appear to be any reason why we shouldn't have a quiet summer."

The Wheeling papers took no notice of Independence Day observances in the pleasant little West Virginia railroad town of Martinsburg. It was not the sort of place one looked to for sensational news. The shops and roundhouse of the Baltimore & Ohio Railroad had not spoiled the freshness of Martinsburg's white-painted houses, glistening church spires and red-brick buildings with bright green shutters. Round about, soft in the summer day, lay the neat fields and farmhouses, the groves and sloping hillsides of the fruitful Shenandoah Valley. A visitor in June had found Martinsburg's 8,000 citizens "a staid, quiet, peaceable, unexcitable population, social and neighborly," many of them recently come from the thrifty and hard-working farm regions of Pennsylvania. Another visitor, Robert Ammon, had come in June to organize a lodge of the Trainmen's Union. He encountered a few Martinsburg people who were not so peaceable, men who talked loudly of striking just as soon as John Garrett tried another cut on them. "I thought it was all wind," said Ammon later. "I didn't think they would strike at all."

On the Glorious Fourth, the only attraction in Martinsburg proper was a parade of Colonel Faulkner's Berkeley Light Infantry, a local militia organization. The High Street band and Captain Shaffer's company of the West Virginia Guards marched out of town in the morning to Berry's Woods on the Maryland side, where (the *Martinsburg Independent* reported tactfully) "a large crowd was gathered and the day passed in various amusements."

A Baltimore & Ohio brakeman named Richard M. Zepp composed a more detailed and less tolerant report on the doings of Captain Shaffer's company. "Their conduct on that occasion was outrageously bad, so much so, that as a member of the company I was ashamed of it," he wrote Governor Henry M. Mathews of West Virginia. "It was nothing more nor less than a drunken spree. They threw their arms and accoutrements around as if they were of no account. Capt. Shaffer has no more control over the company than some little boy would have. Myself and others of the company wish to turn our arms in to the state in good order and withdraw from the com. with your consent." Strangely enough, Zepp waited a full week before getting mad. More strangely still—or else not strangely at all—he wrote on July 11, the day on which John Garrett announced his 10 per cent pay cut.

No one, even in Martinsburg, paid much attention to the squabblings of a militia company. Threshing machines were clattering on Berkeley County farms by mid-July, and a fair yield of wheat was reported. In the woods round about, and indeed all over the East, the seventeen-year locusts were breaking up from the soil in hordes, ravaging trees and laying eggs for the first time since the troubled summer of 1860. The West, however, was enjoying a breather from the Rocky Mountain species. On the plains a grain bonanza ripened. Near Fargo on the Red River, a traveler from the East gaped at the sight of unfenced wheat fields 4,000 acres in extent. The valley would yield 4,000,000 bushels that year, he was told. Everywhere stood "wheat, barley & oats as fine as I ever saw, 40 bushels of wheat to the acre in some places." Stages loaded with settlers and their goods went out every day from Bismarck to the Black Hills; and the ferry ran steadily from dawn to dusk passing emigrant wagons over the river, as many as 100 a day.

Back east it was a rich season in the country, a time of green apples and green corn, huckleberry pie and watermelon, camp meetings and picnics, the scent of new-mown clover in the fields and the bright bow of a sickle moon in the sky. After a spring and early summer that had been "wondrously cool and rainy," the sun began to blaze, the earth cracked, roads turned dusty and the cicadas fiddled a livelier song.

In the cities it was death that called the tune. From the tenement houses of New York City, said the *Times*, "already the cry of the dying children begins to be heard. . . . Soon, to judge from the past, there will be a thousand deaths of infants per week in the city." During the first week of July in Baltimore 139 babies died. Baltimore had no system of underground drainage; all its liquid sewage ran in dirty streams through open gutters, while solid waste was carried through the streets in carts. In cities big, small and middle-sized, the story was the same. From choked gutters everywhere rose the stench of sun-cooked offal. Cleveland streets reeked with "poisonous and miasmatic vegetable and animal matter"; while in a small Ohio town hopefully named Bellaire, a press correspondent sniffed the wind coming from an alley west of Guernsey Street and called for the impeachment of the street commissioner.

Everyone got out of town who could, though not everyone could. "In the poorer parts of the city," reported the *New York Times*, "knots of languid men and women lounge in the shade. Slatternly and dirty children, ragged and half naked, swarm on the sidewalks. The sunlight rains hotly down into a street noisome with the refuge of poor kitchens. Indescribable smells arise on every hand. Everybody is sweltering in suffering silence, and the only sign of activity is the appearance of the huckster." In contrast, "the streets of the better portions of the town, where rich people live, are a silent and stony desert. The house fronts are closed, and as grim as the tombs of the Pharaohs." So it was in every city by mid-July. Everybody who was anybody had left for the Adirondacks or the White Mountains, Atlantic City or Sea Girt, Long Branch or White Sulphur Springs. Francis Murphy of temperance fame passed through Pittsburgh on his way to Ocean Grove, "looking and feeling well." Andrew Carnegie, the living vindication of Horatio Alger, left the same city on the same day for Cape May. The white tents of militia encampments blossomed forth in choice country; the Eighteenth National Guard Regiment of Pennsylvania, for example, looked forward to an eight-day encampment on Lake Chautauqua, beginning July 21. Even the Brotherhood of Locomotive Engineers made arrangements for a steamboat excursion up the Hudson on July 25.

Tom Scott put his luxurious private car "Pennsylvania" at the disposal of Governor Hartranft and family for a six weeks' pleasure junket across the continent that summer. They were to switch to Jay Gould's private car at Chicago (but did not, as it turned out). Before leaving Philadelphia on July 16, the prudent governor conferred with his adjutant general, James W. Latta. They agreed that the state was enjoying a calm such as it had not known for several years. Nevertheless, Hartranft told Latta to exercise the governor's authority to send militia against any outbreak which local authorities could not or would not handle. Then, with conscience clear, Hartranft joined his party and off they rolled to the West, far from sun-baked Philadelphia. "It is convenient to have Scott and Gould for friends," commented the *Pittsburgh Post* enviously.

On that hot Monday morning businessmen were still brooding over R. G. Dun and Company's long-awaited quarterly circular, considered the most authoritative assessment of the state of business. Appropriately issued on Friday the thirteenth, it recorded a new high in business failures during the past six months and saw few signs of recovery aside from the prospects of good crops.

In Martinsburg, West Virginia, subscribers to the *Wheeling Register* opened their papers to the normal budget of news. All was quiet on the Danube, but not on the Clearwater, whence came news of a bitter two-day fight between Chief Joseph's Nez Percés and the troops of General Howard. Outnumbered six to one, the Indians had fought brilliantly; but even as breakfasting Americans sloshed down coffee after their fried potatoes, the hapless Nez Percés were setting out on their famous retreat from Idaho across Montana. Meanwhile, back at the Indian Bureau a clerk had just been fired for taking bribes. At Montreal an inquest had been held on an Orangeman riot victim; the mortality rate in New York City's tenement districts was attracting notice; a banking panic gripped St. Louis; and the wages of Louisville printers had been cut 10 per cent.

In a column of local trivia headed "Small Talk" was an item which read in full: "The ten per cent reduction of wages of employees of the Baltimore and Ohio road goes into effect today."

II

Explosion

CHAPTER 5

First Blood

JOHN GARRETT had gravely underestimated the Trainmen's Union. It still lived all along his line, it still had leaders and those leaders now laid desperate plans. They knew as well as Garrett that a conventional strike would last only until strikebreakers could be summoned. So they yielded to the spirit of 1877. Does the law stand in your way? Then evade it if you can and break it if you must. Beat off strikebreakers by force, seize trains, yards, round-houses, do whatever is necessary.

Bob Ammon was up in the Pennsylvania oil regions looking for another job. The B. & O. sections of Ammon's union seem to have acted entirely on their own. If any one man led them, it was probably the same Richard M. Zepp who had self-righteously quit Captain Shaffer's militia company on July 11.

Dick Zepp lacked Bob Ammon's height, his taste for hard liquor, his wanderlust and his stretchable ethics. Otherwise, the two railroad brakemen had much in common. Both were in their twenties,

74

born leaders, enterprising, intelligent, ready in speech and "decidedly prepossessing" in appearance, though Zepp had a wine-colored
birthmark on one side of his face. The son of an engineer, Dick Zepp
grew up in railroad-centered Martinsburg. As a small boy during the
Civil War, he hung around the soldiers' camps. He and his brother
George, some fifteen years his senior, were two of a kind, the runts
of the Zepp family, a scrappy pair always at loggerheads. George, a
B. & O. fireman, was now bitterly opposed to the strike movement
his brother led.

At Baltimore that hot and humid Monday, events fell out pretty
much as John Garrett had foreseen. In midmorning firemen began
deserting freight trains, first at Camden Junction two or three miles
out of town, then at a couple of stations in the city. Vice-President
John King, Jr., Garrett's son-in-law and second in command, promptly sent out the waiting strikebreakers. The strikers, now joined by
some brakemen and an engineer or two, confined themselves to un-
availing words and looks. Only one strikebreaker backed down.
Around noontime railroad officials led forty Baltimore policemen
against the strikers point by point, dispersing them without violence.
By midafternoon freight trains were again running regularly along
the line. Passenger trains had never been interrupted. As the soaking
heat of the afternoon drained slowly away, John King assured reporters that there would be no more trouble. The strikers had all
been fired, and their jobs were already filled.

Meanwhile, train hands from all along the line had begun to concentrate at Martinsburg. That town was Dick Zepp's home. It was a
key railroad junction. It lay in West Virginia, which was not quite
so well regulated a B. & O. satrapy as Maryland. The town's police
force was small. And the citizens passionately supported the railroad workers. Martinsburg drew most of its livelihood from the B.
& O., and this dependency galled the town. Martinsburg people appreciated the plight of the men and resented the road's callous labor
policy. Besides, they felt that there was "too much pay and speculation among the head men—big salaries, wine suppers, free passes and
presents to Congressmen for their votes." Then there were the gro-
cers and other retailers who lived on the trade of railroad men.
These privates in the ranks of capital now turned their coats and
actively urged the railroad men to resist. If the law were to be
broken, Martinsburg was its weakest point.

The crews of waiting trains were usually to be seen hanging around the dispatcher's office. On this day knots of men formed also at the depot, the machine shops, the switch stands and along the tracks. Something unusual was up. Toward evening, after the failure of law-abiding methods at Baltimore had become clear, a fireman notified the dispatcher that a cattle train had just been abandoned by its entire crew and that no replacements could be had.

Word spread, and people hurried through summer dusk to see the unaccustomed excitement. Women and children were among them, and also a few police. The strikers coolly uncoupled the engines, ran them into the roundhouse and announced to road officials that no more trains would leave Martinsburg in either direction until the 10 per cent cut was rescinded. After conferring with B. & O. officials, Mayor A. P. Shutt tried to soothe the crowd and was hooted for his pains. Finally he ordered the arrest of the ringleaders. But darkness was falling, and rain clouds had piled up in the western sky. A cool wind swept the yard. People felt much livelier than they had in sultry Baltimore. Facing the angry crowd, Mayor Shutt's police were helpless. Zepp and the others laughed at them. No one could be found who wanted to or dared to take out a train, and so the yard was abandoned to the strikers. By midnight the machine shops, depot and roundhouse were all deserted except for a guard of union men left to enforce the blockade. Clouds hid the crescent moon. Quiet as the scene was, not many slept in Martinsburg that night. Some of the strangers from Baltimore and elsewhere were put up at the hotels or at the homes of fellow strikers. But all night long small groups of men stayed up to talk nervously on street corners and await the uncertainties of the day.

By coincidence a telegram at nine that night to the Brevoort House in New York brought John Garrett hurrying home by special train. Garrett's eighty-five-year-old mother, already bedridden, had suddenly begun to let slip her feeble hold on life.

Other telegrams that night also turned out to be heralds of death. While Dick Zepp rode the shoulders of a cheering crowd, B. & O. officials grimly and somewhat imperiously applied to Governor Henry M. Mathews of West Virginia for military protection. Mathews, who had just returned that day from a couple of pleasant weeks at White Sulphur Springs, must have wished he had stretched out his vacation a little longer. Still, the B. & O. was a power in West Virginia politics.

So the governor obediently followed the B. & O.'s Wheeling agent to the road's telegraph office. There he wired Colonel Charles J. Faulkner, Jr., at Martinsburg to have his Berkeley Light Guards preserve the peace "if necessary, . . . prevent any interference by rioters with the men at work, and also prevent the obstruction of the trains." After waiting at the telegraph office until past three o'clock without further news, Mathews went back to his rooms at the McLure House and turned in.

Old Mrs. Elizabeth Garrett died at daybreak before her only son could reach the house on Mount Vernon Place. As the edge of that same gray morning—Tuesday, July 17, 1877—crept westward to the Shenandoah Valley, the people of Martinsburg heard the shrill whistle of a locomotive with steam up.

On orders from Master of Transportation Thomas B. Sharp, a loyal engineer and fireman started out with the cattle train. Immediately the strikers' guard swooped down on it and yelled at the engineer to stop or be killed. He stopped. Notified of this, the Baltimore officials ordered Sharp to keep trying until the train got through. By now hundreds of strikers and citizens, including "a number of half-grown boys," had flocked to the yard; and at the next try the engine did not move a rail's length before it was boarded, uncoupled and run into the roundhouse. Sharp, a stern taskmaster and the austere veteran of more than one daring Civil War exploit (including the seizure of B. & O. rolling stock for the Confederacy), moved now in a swirl of mob hatred. It was later said that he had opposed the pay cut. But the crowd did not know this, if it were true, and anyway the old soldier had his orders.

At about nine o'clock the sound of fife and drum carried over the hubbub, and presently Colonel Faulkner appeared with his Berkeley Light Guards at the small hillside building that served as a depot. The crowd cheered them as they filed down the steep wooden steps to the tracks and marched to the roundhouse. Most of the militiamen were railroaders—if not strikers—and their young commander was a well-liked son of the town's leading family.

From the porch of a house on an embankment overlooking the yard Faulkner gravely explained his position to the crowd. He sympathized with the strikers, and if no one volunteered to take out a train, that did not concern him. But the militia would have to protect anyone who did choose to work. The Berkeley Light Guards were there "not for exhibition, but for effective service." And the colonel thereupon ordered the militia to load with ball cartridges.

Thus encouraged, the strikebreaking engineer and fireman tried once more to run the cattle train out. In addition to the cattle, the train now carried a number of militiamen with loaded rifles, riding the tender, the buffers, the pilot and the caboose. The train inched through the yelling crowd toward a switch that joined the siding to the main road. A soldier named John Poisal, himself a railroader, noticed from his seat on the cowcatcher that the switch had been turned so as to derail the train. Jumping down with rifle in hand, Poisal ran to the switch. Twenty-eight-year-old William P. Vandegriff, the striker who had turned the switch, stood there guarding it with a pistol. As Poisal reached for the switch, Vandegriff fired at him and missed, fired again and hit him under the temple. The ball struck glancingly and lodged under the skin of Poisal's forehead. Poisal brought up his rifle and fired point-blank at Vandegriff, and from other militia rifles came at least two more shots. One ball tore off the striker's right thumb, another lodged in his thigh, a third broke his left arm.

Later that day Vandegriff's arm was amputated. After nine days of agony he died. He had been "esteemed by his companions," the local paper asserted afterwards, "as an orderly as well as a determined man." He certainly had shown determination. A rumor circulated that he had been drunk on the fateful morning of July 17, but a member of the family denounced this as "a falsehood, the malignant invention of some enemy." "That he sent for John Poisal [while on his deathbed] is equally untrue," added the spokesman. "He did not send for him, nor did he ever express any desire to see him, nor did the family then—nor do they now—or ever desire to see him." Thus the bitter seed took root. As for Poisal, he lost the support of sentimentalists by turning up in Martinsburg hale and hearty a few days later. But it would be hard to blame him for returning Vandegriff's fire.

All this came later. As the two injured men were being taken away, the crowd, the soldiers, the strikers and officials, the mayor and the colonel saw only the blood shining wetly from the rails and spreading in a bright red splotch over the cinders. Before that violent summer ended, a red blot would spread across the nation. This first installment was enough for Martinsburg.

It was enough for the strikebreaking engineer and fireman, who climbed down from the engine and called it a day. It was enough for anyone else who had thought of sticking by the company. And it was enough for Colonel Faulkner. He had given no order to fire, and no one ever blamed him for the tragedy. After calling in vain for volunteers to run the train, he announced that the orders of the governor had been fulfilled, marched his company into town and dismissed the men until further orders.

Faulkner's telegraphed confession of helplessness drew a tart reply from Governor Mathews, who promised to send a company "in which there are no men unwilling to suppress the riots and execute the law." (Later Mathews made a point of commending Faulkner's conduct, perhaps because of the Faulkner family's political standing.) The brave tone of the governor's wire had little to back it up. The state militia was in sad shape. After the war compulsory muster and drill had been abolished. Then enrollment was prohibited. The four companies remaining on the books had just been placed (possibly as a joke) under the command of the state librarian. And of the four, two were from Martinsburg: Faulkner's and Shaffer's companies, neither deemed reliable. One of the two remaining, a forty-man company, was scattered over the countryside; and its headquarters at Moorefield were thirty-eight miles from the nearest railroad and telegraph station. The single company at Mathews' immediate disposal was a sixty-man Wheeling company, the Mathews Light Guards.

The Guards had been looking forward to action, though not of the sort now confronting them. They had planned to make a summer encampment at White Sulphur Springs, where the real object of attack (according to a local paper) would be "the hearts of the belles." In preparation, fine new twenty-dollar uniforms of Confederate gray with blue and gold trimmings had been ordered for delivery on July 16. Thirty-two of the suits arrived just before the strike, including the uniform of the commanding officer, Captain W. W. Miller. The lucky possessors of uniforms were mustered along with twenty volunteers in mufti at the state capitol building on Tuesday noon. In spite of the brand-new uniforms, the Guards did not look, to a Wheeling reporter, "as if they thirsted for martial glory."

If the Guards reflected Wheeling opinion, their diffidence did not necessarily arise from cowardice. Wheeling was "emphatically a city of laboring men," including Mayor Sweeney and his council. All morning long, wild rumors had circulated; and when the impending departure of the Mathews Light Guards became known, "the excitement knew no bounds." By two in the afternoon, when the Light Guards marched out of Capital Square to their special train with rations and twenty rounds apiece, a crowd of men, women and children filled the whole square and all of Sixteenth Street down to the depot. "As a general thing," noted one reporter, "all expressed sympathy with the strikers." Even so, it was a stirring sight, reminiscent of Civil War days, and no one blamed the Guards for their predicament. Cheers went up, handkerchiefs waved and tears were shed "sufficient to run a saw mill."

John Garrett wasted no tears on the Light Guard. Nor did the death of his mother that morning distract him from urgent business. Even before the Light Guards had entrained, he and his lieutenants began pressing Mathews to call for Federal troops. The strike was spreading over all the divisions on the line. Conductors, brakemen and engineers were joining the firemen. "The loss of an hour," warned Garrett, "would most seriously affect us and imperil vast interests." With Federal troops, he suggested, "the rioters could be dispersed and there would be no difficulty in the movement of trains." Evidently Garrett had not forgotten the effectiveness of Federal troops against B. & O. strikers in August 1865.

To have defied John Garrett openly in the West Virginia of 1877 would have required either superhuman spunk or a perfect readiness to retire from politics. Mathews assured Garrett that the riot would be stopped somehow. But he believed that the Light Guards would stop it; and in any case, he would not ask for Federal help until all the state's power had been proved insufficient.

Having shown this much backbone, Mathews consented to an interview down the line at Grafton with Vice-President William Keyser of the B. & O. When the Guards' train moved out in midafternoon, Governor Mathews rode with it in a special car. Also aboard were four newspaper correspondents; the intensity of public interest in this affair had not escaped the notice of the press.

En route to Grafton Lieutenant Lukens of the Guards drilled the volunteers in an emigrant car and "put them through the manual right lively." Crowds turned out along the way to see the train pass; and when it reached Grafton at seven that evening, hundreds of people waited at the depot. Mathews told those gathered about the hotel that he knew nothing about the merits of the quarrel between men and management, and that it was none of his official concern anyway. His duty was only to make sure that no man was forcibly prevented from working for whom he pleased and at such pay as he was willing to accept. Vice-President Keyser then explained the necessity of the cut, promised protection for those who stayed on the job and vowed to fire the others the next day. The strikers met and decided to continue the strike. Keyser asked the conductors and engineers to serve in the firemen's places. They refused and he fired them. Darkness had set in by now. At ten o'clock, as the Light Guards' train started for Martinsburg with Keyser aboard, a volley of shots made the troops jump. It turned out to have been a few harmless torpedoes placed on the track by some prankster. During the commotion strikers took off the fireman. Keyser had three strike leaders arrested and confined under guard at the hotel, and at last the train got away. "A spark would have ignited the strikers to riot," thought a reporter.

The departure of the train brought comparative peace to Grafton, and Governor Mathews prepared to make up some of the sleep he had lost in the last day or two. Opening the window of his hotel room to the warm night air, he disrobed in the full light of the gas, unaware that he had a sizable audience on the hillside by the Grafton House. He turned down the gas, climbed into bed, and had begun to drowse when a small boulder crashed into the room. Luckily for the governor, the rock struck the window sash and was deflected away from the bed. Mathews professed to be mystified by the cowardly attack. The fact that Vice-President Keyser customarily occupied that room may have had something to do with it, however. The governor changed his room and struck out again for dreamland, only to be drawn back by news that a party of strikers had come to the hotel to free their three arrested comrades. Mathews persuaded the would-be rescuers to go home. In the morning he took his own advice and returned to Wheeling.

Clouds had hung over Baltimore all that evening, and shortly before midnight a sudden warm shower drenched the city. As rain slid down the windows of Camden Street Station, Vice-President King telegraphed the B. & O.'s Washington agent that Governor Mathews might soon call for Federal troops. "It will be well," he suggested, "to see the Secretary of War and inform him of the serious situation of affairs, that he may be ready to send the necessary force to the scene of action at once." Why was King suddenly so confident that a call was at hand? After all, Mathews had told reporters that afternoon that no such call would be made unless the state militia tried and failed to restore order. The stone-throwing incident at Grafton occurred after King's wire was sent. All that had happened, so far as King knew, was that Mathews and Keyser had ridden to Grafton together and had failed to talk the strikers back to work. Perhaps Keyser had got some sort of conditional promise from the governor on the way to Grafton.

The "action" referred to by King could apparently be seen best from the middle distance. At Wheeling people talked excitedly on street corners about the strike, which by now had stopped freight traffic all along the line. Almost everyone rooted for the men. A rumor passed from group to group that strikers had burned the B. & O. shops at Martinsburg. Similar rumors circulated in Baltimore at the other end of the line; and there was talk of a general strike of all labor in that city, for the boxmakers and the canmakers happened to be on strike just then.

But at Martinsburg, aside from some wild talk about teaching John Poisal a lesson or maybe smashing some windows in Mayor Shutt's hotel, all was quiet. Nothing much had happened since noon, when the strikers had stopped a cattle train by boarding the engine with drawn revolvers. Passenger and mail cars continued to run without interference. As for freight, it was rumored that the strikers would throw the switch in front of any departing train and would shoot anyone who touched that switch. Thomas Sharp could find no one willing to test the truth of the rumor, whether protection was furnished or not; and so seventy engines and 600 freight cars now jammed the Martinsburg yards. The strikers saw this, noted the spread of the strike throughout the line and grew confident—even smug. They felt that they had mastered the situation and could now get along without violence or even open threats. A newspaperman reported "perfect order" at midnight. How then, they asked themselves, could Governor Mathews justify a call for Federal troops?

To the rest of the country the strike remained a local affair. Most newspapers of the seventeenth had found room on their front pages for a paragraph or two about the orderly beginning of the strike.

Gunplay at Martinsburg and the spread of the strike led morning papers of the eighteenth to expand their coverage somewhat. Eastern papers now gave the story a full column or more; Western papers still held it to a half or a third of a column, but displayed it more prominently than before. Editorial reaction developed slowly and variously. The *Philadelphia Record*, in an editorial headed "Criminal Strikers," said that Colonel Faulkner should have used "more powder" against "these outlaws"; and it hoped that the ringleaders, at least, would get the severest punishment allowed by the law, as an example to others. The *New York Times* condemned the strike as "a rash and spiteful demonstration of resentment by men too ignorant or too reckless to understand their own interests." It called for action to assure the "complete and absolute supremacy of law." On the other hand, the *Times* thoughtfully acknowledged the surprising strength of community support for the strikers. Most papers suspended editorial judgment, except as it entered into news treatment.

On Wednesday, July 18, while morning editorials were being made up, the Light Guards' cars, hitched to the rear of a mail train, moved cautiously toward Martinsburg. On the way, "some of the bloodthirsty volunteers lost their Murphys [temperance badges] in order to keep up their courage," and by the time the train pulled into Martinsburg at eight in the morning, Surgeon Harvey had several bad cases of bottle fatigue on his hands. Similar preparations were reported on the other side. A reporter at Martinsburg found that "some of the strikers had started on a carouse; that others said they were reckless as to what they did in the future, and that some were affected to tears in the recital of what they called their oppression." At the request of mayor and council Martinsburg saloons closed down that morning. When the Guards' train arrived, a large but orderly crowd waited on the platform. Now, presumably, would come the test of state authority which Governor Mathews had so recently insisted must precede a call for Federal aid.

Yet nothing happened. Colonel Robert M. Delaplain, Mathews' aide and deputy in command of the state militia, went into a huddle with railroad and town officials, and decided to leave the militia in the cars so as not to "further exasperate the strikers." The three militia cars stood in the broiling sun all day with shutters drawn and a single guard on each car platform. Reporters worked hard to make a story out of the situation. "There is a great deal of excitement," wrote one heroic correspondent, "but it is of that silent ominous kind. There can be no doubt but that the strikers are contemplating some deep laid scheme. Ominous silence and whispered words among the strikers portend mischief." Martinsburg, it seems, was rampant on tiptoe and rioting in whispers.

The strikers tried to win over Captain Miller of the Light Guards with an account of their sufferings from low pay and high food prices. Miller snapped back that he had nothing to do with the price of flour, and that he would carry out orders "if his entire company was used up in the attempt." The railroad shopmen kept on the job despite the strikers' pleadings and were not molested. At two o'clock the Light Guards, their new gray uniforms stained with sweat, were marched from the cars to their quarters in the courthouse. They appeared to be pretty well used up already.

All of these events must have seemed disappointingly tame to the press corps, now being swelled by recruits from the great metropolitan dailies. Colonel Delaplain came to their rescue with an extraordinary telegram, sent soon after his arrival in Martinsburg:

> The feeling here is most intense, and the rioters are largely cooperated with by civilians ... The disaffection has become so general that no employee could now be found to run an engine even under certain protection. I am satisfied that Faulkner's experiment of yesterday was thorough and that any repetition of it to-day would precipitate a bloody conflict, with the odds largely against our small force. Capt. Faulkner thinks that two hundred U. S. Marines would not be in excess of the requirement. . . .

When the weekly *Martinsburg Independent* came out a couple of days later, it called this wire "much ado about nothing" and charged Delaplain with acting "very indiscreetly." Nowhere did the wire state that any law was then being broken or would be broken in the time it might take the governor to muster more volunteers or summon the legislature. Yet on the strength of this, and this alone, Governor Mathews fired off the following telegram:

Wheeling, July 18, 1877

To His Excellency, R. B. Hayes,
President of the U. S.
Washington, D. C.:
  Owing to unlawful combinations and domestic violence now existing at Martinsburg and at other points along the line of the Balti-

more and Ohio railroad, it is impossible with any force at my command to execute the laws of the State. I therefore call upon your Excellency for the assistance of the United States military to protect the law abiding people of the State against domestic violence, and to maintain supremacy of the law.

The Legislature is not now in session and could not assemble in time to take any action in the emergency. A force of from two to three hundred troops should be sent without delay to Martinsburg, where my aid, Col. Delaplain, will meet and confer with the officer in command.

H. M. MATHEWS
Governor of West Va.

Mathews notified John Garrett of this and thereby excited that potentate to the sending of two magnificently pompous telegrams. One of these, to Mathews, lengthily congratulated the governor on his decision. The other, to President Hayes, urged immediate compliance with Mathews' request and advised Hayes to send the troops stationed at Washington and Baltimore as being the nearest. President Garrett assured President Hayes that West Virginia had done all it could "to suppress this insurrection," and that "this great national highway" (meaning the B. & O.) "can only be restored for public use by the interposition of the U. S. forces." And he warned: "Unless this difficulty is immediately stopped, I apprehend the gravest consequences, not only upon our line, but upon all the lines in the country which, like ourselves, have been obliged to introduce measures of economy in these trying times."

For all its grandiloquence Garrett's wire to the President showed keenness of vision. Nothing could scatter the seeds of labor unrest so far and so fast as a railroad strike, and never before had the waiting ground been so thoroughly plowed and harrowed. Labor was about to rise up in a form too gigantic for any one state to contain. So perhaps Governor Mathews' hastiness did not divert, but merely quickened the course of history. If not at that moment, then certainly within a week Rutherford B. Hayes, *de facto* President of the United States, would have had "this difficulty" thrust into his hands.

In his honesty and high sense of duty Rutherford Birchard Hayes belonged more to the period of his Connecticut and Vermont forebears than to the generation over which he now presided. But in other respects he suited his own times, especially in the mixture of vigor and inner tensions which had driven him forward. Born small and frail two months after his father's death, morbidly overprotected as a boy in a family of women dogged by death, anxious to live up to the ideal of his dead father and brother, he drew on his inward strength and the occasional companionship of a beloved uncle to achieve sane and self-reliant manhood. As late as his twenties he had suffered wracking fears of madness, a fate spared him but not his sister Fanny, who had been his boyhood alter ego. In the end he won through, coming out of Kenyon College and Harvard Law School a likable, energetic and able young lawyer. The Civil War lifted him out of his law practice and minor office holding in Cincinnati. Colonel Hayes of the Twenty-third Ohio Volunteers was well esteemed by a sergeant on his staff, a future President himself. "His whole nature seemed to change when in battle," wrote ex-Sergeant William Mc-Kinley. "From the sunny, agreeable, the kind, the generous, the gentle gentleman . . . he was, when the battle was once on . . . intense and ferocious."

With a fine war record and a major general's commission behind him, Hayes's number came up regularly on the political roulette wheel. Two closemouthed terms in the stormy Congresses of recon-struction days, three well-conducted if unspectacular terms as gov-ernor of Ohio, the fortunate chances of a national convention and the help of Tom Scott and Southern Democrats had brought him at last to the White House. The storms through which he passed on the way had (except the last) been largely within him, and in any case had left no mark on his countenance. At fifty-four he was stockier than in his youth, but he walked with a quick, springy step and a soldierly bearing. His blue eyes remained keen, his complexion fresh, his face unlined, his auburn hair but little grayed. A heavy mustache, blending into a grizzled beard, now hid the firm chin and gently humorous mouth that had lent attraction to the clean-shaven young man. But the high forehead and bold, well-shaped nose still pro-claimed a man of force and intelligence.

Somewhere in Hayes, as in his America, a strain of radicalism lived obscurely. Camouflaged on his family tree hung his grandfather's cousin Nathaniel Austin, who might have been hanged in real life save that he broke jail and disappeared forever while under sentence of death for his part in Shays's Rebellion. Closer and decidedly be-yond concealment was Hayes's own first cousin, John Humphrey

Noyes, utopian communist, advocate of "free love," vegetarianism and spiritualism, "probably" (says Vernon Louis Parrington) "the most radical American of the times." Hayes himself had favored state regulation of railroads, and in 1871 he had referred in a speech to "the colossal fortunes . . . already consolidating into the hands of a few men—not always the best men—powers which threaten alike good government and our liberties." Despite those stirrings, Hayes in 1877 remained a disciple of laissez-faire. One should not read too much into the fact that in the 1875 directory of Fremont, Ohio, Hayes listed his occupation as "capitalist." Still, it seemed likely that if anything gave him pause in the present crisis, it was a matter of law, not humanitarianism or concern for social justice. A labor dispute that could constitutionally qualify as an "insurrection" was something rather new under the American sun.

Governor Mathews' call for troops caught Hayes in a bad moment for presidential trail blazing. Scarcely a month before, Samuel Tilden had been guest of honor at a Democratic dinner, where the speakers all assumed that Tilden was the lawful President, and that Hayes "holds his office as a usurper by fraud and disloyalty to the Constitution." One responsible and highly esteemed Democrat noted in his diary that "the result of such a set of speeches in any other country would be immediate revolution." Tilden, to be sure, scarcely fitted the role of revolutionary leader, especially at that moment, with his health failing and his left hand crippled by arthritis. His doctors soon afterward talked him into a European tour, for which he sailed on July 18, less than four hours before Mathews' telegram to Hayes. But Tilden's departure left plenty of Democratic politicians and newspapers hacking away at Hayes's title. Members of the Republican returning board in New Orleans were under indictment for falsifying the Presidential election returns—and those returns had been essential to Hayes's electoral majority. The *New York Sun* led the cry in the Louisiana matter, running a daily cut of Hayes with the word *FRAUD* stamped across his forehead. Other Democrats took steps to test Hayes's title in the courts.

If Hayes's situation was ticklish generally, it was still more so in any controversy involving railroads. The *New York Sun* bluntly ascribed "Mr. Hayes's residence in the White House" to "the Texas Pacific enterprise" and "Col. Scott's influence." Perhaps, however, there was a grisly counterweight to this in the memorial services being held in Vermont that same July 18 for Mary Birchard, the President's cousin, who had been killed in the Ashtabula wreck.

More likely to have troubled Hayes was the condition of the United States Army. Because it had served as the main prop of carpetbaggery in the South, most Democrats cried it down. They ridiculed the possibility of foreign war and condemned the use of the Army as an internal police force. Some called for a reduction of the armed forces to a mere nucleus around which volunteers and state militia might group themselves in time of need. The *Pittsburgh Post* suggested 10,000 men as an adequate number. In May it was even widely rumored that Hayes was about to disband the entire force. Within the limits allowed them Army leaders carried on a desperate holding action; and the commanding general, William T. Sherman, made a speech, later counted prophetic, which warned of possible widespread mob violence if the Army were weakened. These efforts helped to keep the Army's authorized strength up to 25,000. But in July 1877, with Mexican border troubles holding down some troops and Chief Joseph's Nez Percés making a hot handful for others, even that figure seemed much too low. Consider the bitter words of Lieutenant General Philip Sheridan, reporting that year on his Military Division of the Missouri:

> The troubles on the Rio Grande border, the Indian outbreak on the western frontier of New Mexico, and the Indian war in the Departments of the Platte and Dakota, have kept the small and inadequate force in this Division in a constant state of activity, and almost without rest, night and day. This condition of affairs is not only true for the past year, but it has been nearly the same thing for the last ten years. During the last two years, the ratio of loss in proportion to the number engaged in this Division in the Indian wars has been equal to or greater than the ratio of loss on either side in the late civil war.

At the moment the Army labored under an absurd new handicap. Because of a wrangle between the Democratic House and the Republican Senate over the use of troops in the South, Congress had failed to pass the Army Appropriation Bill for the fiscal year beginning July 1, 1877. So the Army was now serving without pay. A group of bankers led by Drexel, Morgan and Company, and including that good and very rich Democrat August Belmont, offered to advance the officers up to 95 per cent of their pay in anticipation of an eventual appropriation. The enlisted men could look for no such favor. But they were used to the situation, since most of them had not been paid for months anyway.

In Idaho and Montana these men, unpaid and unsung, were even now offering up their lives for their country, steeped though it currently was in greed and cynicism. Could they also be expected to kill their fellow Americans in defense of property rights? The depression had driven many jobless workers into military service. One of these, John Woodside of Company K, Ninth United States Infantry, wrote the *Iron Molders' Journal* from Omaha Barracks that March to let his old friends know where he was. He had met other union men in his company. "It does not follow," he remarked, "that a change of dress involves a change of principle." If Governor Mathews could not trust Captain Shaffer's West Virginia Guards to fight the strikers —and he said as much publicly—could President Hayes trust Company K and others like it?

Another man than Rutherford Hayes might have worried also about the voters' reaction to harsh measures against labor. For some reason Democrats posed more successfully than Republicans as friends of the workingman. Perhaps a faint bouquet of the Jacksonian era still clung to the Democratic Party. Perhaps Republican reliance on industrial and railroad magnates struck the common man more forcibly than Democratic dalliance with bankers and Southern Bourbons. Perhaps the Democrats profited from being out of the White House in time of depression. Or maybe the Democratic leaning toward greenbackism appealed to workingmen, who had acquired an unaccountable taste for that doctrine. Anyway, if Hayes should send troops against workingmen, the Democrats might easily make a campaign issue of it.

The possibility must have crossed Hayes's mind. As governor of Ohio in the spring of 1876, he had sent state militia to suppress disorders growing out of a coal miners' strike. "I am glad you agree with me as to the treatment of the mining riots," he wrote Ohio Congressman James A. Garfield. "We shall crush out the lawbreakers if the courts and juries do not fail." Hayes crushed the disorders, but Ohio Democrats brought up the affair in a bid for labor votes during the Presidential campaign of the following November. The Republicans were worried enough to reply: they charged that "demagogues" like Samuel Tilden would have refused to call out troops in defense of law and order for fear of losing votes.

But now the next election was far off, and anyway Hayes had already announced his "inflexible purpose . . . not to be a candidate for election to a second term." Besides, Hayes was proud of a slogan he had coined in his Inaugural Address: "He serves his party best who serves his country best." And he tried hard to live up to it.

Federal military intervention in a labor dispute was not really unprecedented. By request of the Maryland legislature, President Andrew Jackson, no less, had sent Federal troops to quell a labor disturbance among construction workers on the Chesapeake and Ohio Canal forty-three years before. Probably Hayes knew nothing of that remote precedent, although John Garrett or his legal advisers may well have remembered it. More to the point, the Reconstruction Era had thoroughly familiarized Americans with the maintenance of the peace by Federal troops on the application of a state governor. From 1865 to 1877 Federal troops were so used on twenty-five occasions—more than in all the years before. Southern states under carpetbag rule had been unwilling beneficiaries on all but one occasion (the Fenian invasion of Canada in 1866). Consequently, there was a piquant irony about the present call of a Southern Democratic governor. Much was said later about that odd twist of fate. But the basic situation was thoroughly familiar.

Van Buren in 1838 and Pierce in 1856 had demurred on the grounds that the states involved had not done their best to restore order. A similar doubt arose in Hayes's mind now. He called Secretary of War George W. McCrary to the White House and talked the problem over with him. Presently the Secretary wired Governor Mathews: "The President is averse to intervention unless it is clearly shown that the State is unable to suppress the insurrection. Please furnish a full statement of facts. What force can the State raise? How strong are the insurgents?" The healthy skepticism, the refusal to jump at the first command, doubtless came from Hayes himself; it was characteristic of him. One is left to wonder, however, which of the two men ballooned the strike into an "insurrection" and raised the strikers to "insurgents." Similarly baffling is the ease with which Mathews' reply laid Hayes's doubts to rest. After briefly pointing out the scarcity of immediately available state troops, the governor asserted: "I have no doubt that within ten days I could organize within the State a force sufficient to suppress any riot, but in the meantime much property may be destroyed, and what is more im-

portant, valuable lives lost." The "insurrection," it will be noted, had
been deflated again to a "riot." But Mathews did not explain why or
how death and destruction might result if the state spent a week or
two raising more men.

Despite the brevity and vagueness of the governor's argument,
Hayes accepted it. At 3:50 p.m., July 18, the Adjutant General wired
the commanding officers at the Washington Arsenal and at Fort Mc-
Henry in Baltimore to send every available man to Martinsburg as
soon as possible. Transportation would be provided by the B. & O.
(but not gratis, as it later turned out).

Samuel Tilden heard the news on July 27 when he debarked in
Ireland with his friend John Bigelow (who would have been his
Secretary of State, save for Tom Scott). "Tilden thinks," wrote
Bigelow in his diary, "we are both to be congratulated for being
spared the necessity of meddling with a question so beset with difficulties & bad feeling. He criticizes the action of the Federal govt
in sending troops to do a duty which should have been discharged
by State authorities until proved to be incapable of it & doubts
whether any one can do his duty and not make more enemies than
friends." Here is a pleasant little exercise for historical "if" baiters.

But however narrow the margin had been, Hayes, not Tilden, was
President; and Hayes had chosen to send the troops.

Andrew Jackson may have been the first President to use Federal
troops in a labor dispute. Rutherford Hayes was the first to be remembered for doing it. The reasons for this are worth exploring.
Jackson's unprecedented intervention can be explained by his mili-
tant temper and possibly by the fact that one of his closest friends
happened to be president of the affected corporation. His readiness
to act is significant mainly as evidence that Jackson's tenderness
toward the workingman was not what it was later cracked up to be.
Hayes's action, on the other hand, far from being his normal response,
ran counter to his resolution not to intervene in state affairs. Only four
months before, he had written in his diary: "My policy is trust, peace,
and to put aside the bayonet." Plainly something more than one man's
predisposition lay behind his decision. Jackson's intervention, furthermore, stood alone for more than forty years; whereas, since Hayes,
Federal troops have been used in labor disputes more than twice as
often as in all other kinds of civil disorders put together.

Rutherford Hayes's decision on that humid July afternoon made history, not by its constitutional novelty nor by its illumination of Hayes's character, but rather by what it betokened for the nation. A great transition was in painful progress, and the President's action threw a spotlight on it. Hayes already saw himself as a "national" President, meaning a healer of the division between North and South; and the characterization went deeper than Hayes himself realized. In the time of Rutherford Hayes, not just politics but all of American life was becoming "national." Especially were industry and labor growing too big for states to handle alone. That fact was soon to be burned into the American mind beyond effacement. John Garrett had been right in his guess. The United States was about to encounter its first—and bloodiest—nationwide strike.

CHAPTER 6

The Bell Tolls in Baltimore

THAT afternoon, rain swept over West Virginia from the Ohio Valley. To Wheeling it came as a blessing. It clinched the Wheeling Standards' four-run lead over the Bridgeport Browns by ending the game after five innings. West Virginia's state capital was soon to be shifted from Wheeling and relocated according to a popular vote; and by an embarrassing coincidence, an open air rally in behalf of Martinsburg had been scheduled for that very evening. Its sponsors now gratefully postponed it to some more suitable date than July 18, 1877. Best of all, the rain reached Martinsburg itself in the early evening and dispersed the crowds, leaving only motionless freight trains, backed up now for two miles east and west, to stand as evidence of an "insurrection."

All along the line, the strikers were quiet, though determined. At Keyser they met and resolved to stand by the other divisions. At Grafton no freights moved. The mayor warned against intimidation of strikebreakers and, amid derisive laughter, proclaimed his determination to enforce the law at all hazards. No one else had much to say.

The Federal government's chosen defenders of railroad income happened to be men of the Second United States Artillery, whose regimental fund had just taken a severe beating from unlucky investment in railroad bonds. The men themselves had not been paid for seven months. At dusk, under heavy skies, eight officers and 112 men of that hard-bitten regiment left Baltimore's Fort McHenry for Washington, where they joined twelve officers and 200 men of the same regiment from the Washington Arsenal. All were under command of the Arsenal's peppery commandant, Colonel William H. French, forty years out of West Point and a veteran of the Seminole, Mexican and Civil Wars, in the last of which he had commanded

93

a corps. Even when things went well, French's puffy cheeks and narrowed eyes gave him the look of a man about to explode; and, in time of trouble, he often did.

French's command left Washington by train at ten that night. In Martinsburg all was quiet except Colonel Delaplain, who still emitted telegraphic twitters. The governor's excitable aide had French's train stopped at Harper's Ferry to wait for daylight, "as they would probably be wrecked coming through to-night." He forgot to explain this to French, who finished his journey in a mood of bitterness at "having been detained by the officials of the road without consultation with me for reasons belonging to themselves." Deeming a force of 300 rifles insufficient, Delaplain also wired Secretary Mc-Crary for another 100 riflemen and two pieces of artillery. McCrary had two field pieces made ready and tried to round up a couple of Gatling guns for good measure, but without success. At Martinsburg a Wheeling reporter did his best to match Delaplain, but could work up nothing more sensational for a midnight dispatch than a tale of "scattered groups in different portions of the city" whose "actions are of the most secret and suspicious order."

French's troops arrived at Martinsburg early the next morning, July 19, in a gloomy drizzle, to find a small peaceable crowd awaiting them. The "insurrection" remained a fairly well-kept secret. The regulars bivouacked in the roundhouse, while most of the strikers prudently hung about just beyond the town line. Late that morning the rain stopped, and the sheriff's deputies and the town police passed out copies of a Presidential proclamation commanding the "insurgents" to disperse and retire to their homes by noon. Nothing much happened. Even Colonel Delaplain calmed down at last, wiring Mc-Crary that additional troops would not be needed after all.

That afternoon, as the Light Guards and several squads of regulars patrolled the yards, a coal train started out for Baltimore, the first freight to leave since the strike began. The engineer's wife and stepdaughter talked him into quitting, but a replacement was found. Ten regulars rode with the train as far as Harper's Ferry; and all the way to Baltimore it moved with excruciating caution—taking nearly ten hours for the trip. It met no opposition.

Westbound freight Number 423 left soon after, also with a squad of regulars aboard. When 100 armed strikers menaced it on the west side of town, the fireman jumped off and refused to continue. The sheriff, augmented by the entire Mathews Light Guard, marched to the scene, seized the ringleader, Dick Zepp, and escorted him to jail (he was released on bail that evening). Dick Zepp's pugnacious brother George came walking down the track, dramatically flourishing a Navy revolver and followed by his remonstrating mother. Fireman George Zepp had stood about all he could of his younger brother's nonsense and now proposed to take out Number 423 and be done with it. Short, stocky and blackhaired, he measured up to his brother in fighting spirit; at eighteen, he whipped the town bully of Cumberland in a saloon, threw him out into the street and then in his pride walked down the street and had his photograph taken. He was in such a mood now. Ignoring his mother and keeping back the strikers with his revolver, George Zepp joined the engineer in the cab of Number 423, and the train moved out.

Despite the departure of a freight each way without bloodshed, B. & O. officials could find no one to take any more out that day. Nevertheless, they looked for an early triumph. The arrival of the regulars and the arrest of Dick Zepp had cut the heart out of the Martinsburg strike. The men told a reporter that evening that "they would not molest the United States troops." In the morning, strikebreakers from Baltimore took out freight trains freely, and by evening the yards had been largely cleared. The sheriff and a detachment of the Light Guards arrested two more strike leaders, one of whom was immediately discharged and the other let out on low bail. "The riot here," wired Delaplain to Mathews, "may be regarded as suppressed." Martinsburg's brief spell of notoriety had ended.

But the strike had not. On the contrary, some disturbing new elements now began to appear. One of these was the rallying of other trades to the side of the railroad workers.

Boatmen of the Chesapeake and Ohio Canal took the lead in this. Something more than class feeling brought them in, to be sure, for they laid their own troubles to the B. & O.'s doing. A naïve New Yorker wrote a Baltimore banker that month about interest payments on bonds of the Chesapeake and Ohio Canal Company. Brown and Sons replied that interest had now been paid up to July 1, 1864. "When a further payment may be expected, we cannot say," they added somberly, "the revenue of the Company, through competition with low railroad freights, having been heavily reduced." Boatmen as well as bondholders were caught in the squeeze. The boatmen

collected freight charges, paid tolls to the company and lived—or
tried to live—on what was left. When the B. & O. cut its competing
rates early that spring and again in mid-June, the boatmen had to
cut charges. Yet the canal refused to reduce tolls. So after the second
B. & O. cut, the boatmen, out of money, credit and luck, simply tied
up their boats near their homes or where there was good pasture. By
July canal traffic had nearly ceased.

On Thursday evening, July 19, westbound freight Number 423,
the one George Zepp was riding, reached Sir John's Run, a favorite
gathering place for the canal strikers. Hundreds had assembled there
that fine summer evening. Hatless and barefoot, some wearing only
shirt and pants, they waited like savages in the dark laurel thickets
along the railroad. As Number 423 passed, a volley of rocks bounded
off the boiler and rattled into the engine cab. One stone gave George
Zepp a good thump. The train eased to a stop, the regulars jumped
off and the boatmen vanished howling into the underbrush, all with
no great harm done. At Cumberland, Maryland, a canal port as well
as a railroad town, a jeering, hooting crowd of boatmen, railroaders
and citizens swarmed around the train, shook fists at Zepp and the
rest of the crew and uncoupled cars. Two hours later, at midnight,
railroad officials managed to get the cars coupled again and the train
moved on. At Keyser, West Virginia, a still more determined mob
ran it on to a side track and took the crew off by force. Lieutenant
Curtis and his detachment of United States troops could only look
on helplessly. Even George Zepp gave up at last and rode a passenger
train back home to Martinsburg.

Thus the pacification of Martinsburg proved a hollow triumph.
The embolus had not dissolved, but had merely shifted to another
point in the artery.

At Grafton the strikers had shown their temper early that afternoon. When B. & O. officials found a man to take the way freight to
Parkersburg, a score of strikers with Colt revolvers stepped out of
the crowd and threatened to kill him. A discharged conductor shouted
that he had fourteen shots in his two Colts and would "die in his
tracks before that train should move." The Parkersburg man stepped
down, presumably saving a number of lives. No more freight de-
partures were attempted. Grafton stayed quiet the rest of the day.
At a meeting of the local strike committee with a deputation of
strikers from Keyser, it was resolved to negotiate with railroad of-

ficials for a wage of two dollars a day for firemen and brakemen.

Main Street in Wheeling languished dull and lonesome all day, and the freight depot slumbered like a graveyard. No local fireman would work, and threats from a strike committee scared off some jobless men who came to town looking for work as strikebreakers. Crowds clustered around the newspaper offices to watch the bulletins. Everyone sympathized with the strikers' plight, and all workingmen hoped the B. & O. would get thoroughly trounced. Most people thought the troops should have been kept out of the fuss. "Let them [strikers and management] fight it out," they said.

The Light Guards, and especially the volunteer contingent, had fallen from public favor since their brave departure two days earlier. The *Wheeling Register* remarked sarcastically: "The friends, parents and sweethearts of the Light Guards will be happy to learn that they arrived safe, and do not propose running into danger." Local wits did not overlook the Guards' bibulous night ride to Martinsburg, and the factory men of Wheeling proposed to "get up a big dinner" for the Guards on "their return from their brilliant campaign." Some of the volunteers had already straggled back for various reasons: they were "heartily sick of sleeping on the benches in the [Martinsburg] Court House," or "hell would be to pay out there, and they thought best to return," or Captain Miller had slighted those without uniforms. On their way back some of the voluntary veterans attended a fund-raising dance given by the strikers at Grafton.

At noon, Friday, a train left Martinsburg carrying a number of railroad officials, a telegraph operator and linesman, eleven reporters (including one or two from Chicago) and about fifty United States troops, all jammed into a baggage car, two coaches and Colonel Sharp's private car. Two armed soldiers sat on the front of the engine, legs dangling over the cowcatcher; four guarded the engineer and fireman in the cab; and the two troop-laden coaches literally bristled with rifles, one or more of which stuck out of every window. As the train passed Sir John's Run, a motley crowd, white and black, yelled at it from the woods. Ominously some coal miners had now joined the boatmen and railroad strikers. They had already detained one train for some time that morning, pulling out coupling pins so as to split it and dragging off the engineer and fireman. Now a squad of regulars dropped off to prevent similar interruptions.

At five that afternoon, the train stopped in front of the B. & O.'s

Queen City Hotel at Cumberland, Maryland. A dense crowd gathered about the train, shouting and threatening. The reporters heard a new note, more strident and capricious than before, and noticed that the crowd was mostly made up of boys. The police could not keep the youngsters off. They ran agilely between cars, tugged at brakes, taunted the troops, even boarded the train. School was out; and the boys sensed that here was an opportunity for mischief of a rare sort, mischief which the grownups not only tolerated but even egged on. Soldiers in blue with real guns, the steam and shine of massive locomotives, the hoarse crowd, all this on a cool, clear summer afternoon—what a combination! "Much of the excitement, indeed the greater portion of it, is caused by boys," scolded one reporter, "and their parents would do much towards restoring peace if they would keep their children at home." Soldiers aboard the train raised and aimed their rifles at anyone making as though to grab the weapons, and if militia rather than disciplined regulars had been aboard, there might have been weeping in Cumberland homes that night. But no one got shot; and after supper in the Queen City Hotel, the train's passengers boarded again and departed without further molestation.

Running cautiously, now and then serenaded with curses and cat-calls from along the road, the grim excursion soon afterward reached Keyser, West Virginia. Things looked bad there. One striker, arguing with an old watchman, was heard to yell: "What in hell do I care if I do get killed; it might as well be so as to starve to death!" Some strikers were drunk though not quarrelsome; all were bitterly determined. They talked of resisting the regulars, and said that 1200 local miners had promised to help. Just before midnight the miners met at Piedmont four miles away, and resolved to go to Keyser in the morning and help stop trains. Rumor reported parties of miners stationed in the mountains to wreck any freights that passed. Someone at Piedmont printed up a long and rather eloquent manifesto, warning the B. & O. that 15,000 miners, the united citizenry of local communities and "the working classes of every State in the Union" would support the strikers. "Therefore let the clashing of arms be heard; . . . in view of the rights and in the defence of our families we shall conquer, or we shall die." Sharp wired Delaplain that no crews could be found at Keyser to take out trains, and that strikebreakers refused to leave the soldiers' quarters because of violent threats "by all classes here."

It was Cumberland, however, that now held the center of the

stage. Of sixteen freights sent west from Martinsburg on July 20, only one arrived at Keyser that day, and that had a strong military escort. The rest were stopped at Cumberland. Even on the train that got through, a shot from someone in the Cumberland mob had cut through the pants of a trainman, "making a slight hip wound." An editorial in the *Wheeling Intelligencer* suggested that Cumberland had been chosen for a stand by the strikers because it happened to lie in Maryland, the governor of which had not yet called for United States troops. But the fury at Cumberland could be explained in other ways. Depression suffering had reached a climax in that town. A few days before, a check on eleven families of jobless men in the Sixth Ward showed all of them "in sore need—some of them starving." On the Friday before the strike began, a crowd of unemployed men had met in the shade of the trees near the Baltimore Street crossing. Speakers addressed them from the top of a hogshead. "The laboring men of the city have little to eat and little to wear," said one. "The rolling mill is idle, and no prospect of starting. Merchants in this city have trusted men until they have ruined themselves by so doing." Another urged that the city make work by building a reservoir, with borrowed funds if necessary. Similar meeting were held that week end and during the B. & O. strike. Local politicians, especially greenbackers, managed somehow to push to the front of the agitation and, in so doing, to shove aside the proposals for public works. But though the politicos blunted the point of the movement, the force of desperation still worked in and on the city.

Many jobless rolling-mill men joined the crowd in the broad open space before the Queen City Hotel that bright, cool Friday. Very likely a contingent of tramps roved through the crowd also, for tramps had been thick in West Virginia and Maryland all that month. Thirty-five vagabonds had been seen in Cumberland on Wednesday, washing their clothes in the canal near the steelworks; and on the morning of that very Friday a gang boarded a passenger train near Cumberland and rode to Baltimore on the authority of a loaded revolver. Boatmen were in the thick of the excitement, too. At midnight about 400 of them marched up to, though not into the city, beating a drum as they came. All accounts agree, however, that "boys from 14 to 18 years of age" formed the most active and perhaps the most numerous element in the mob.

The railroad strikers themselves were now only a small fraction of the mob. The few railroaders who took part in the Cumberland disorders followed the lead of a burly stranger named Rench. Late that night Rench and another man were arrested and locked up. A great crowd of sympathizers demonstrated before the mayor's house and got the prisoners released, on their promise to appear before the magistrate next day. The two men rode off into the night on the shoulders of the jubilant crowd. B. & O. officials had given up trying to move freights through. Those that came in were left in the yards, and by morning thousands of freight cars stretched in long lines from Harrison Street to the Oldtown Road.

A day or two earlier the railroad strikers might have rejoiced at the temper of the town. Matters, they might have bragged, were now well in hand. But some of them were already a little frightened by what was stirring in the social jungle. All they had in hand (they began to suspect) was a tiger's tail. And from Baltimore, as Friday ended, came a blood-chilling roar.

In the seventies, little more than a third of Baltimore's wage earners worked in factories, the rest being in trade, transportation and services. Still, 40,000 factory workers constituted a formidable bloc, and, anyway, all workers felt the pinch of the great depression. That spring the British consul reported great "distress and suffering among the laboring classes," and the Democratic Club of Ward Seventeen complained to Mayor Latrobe about the "degradation of the workingman and his family" inflicted by hard times. After Baltimore's jobless petitioned for a program of public works, the city got a few projects going. In July 1877 several large piles of loose bricks and cobbles near Front and Fayette streets signalized one of these, the laying of some gas pipe. The city projects eased distress as far as they went, but they went not nearly far enough.

The depression had hit trade unionism at least as hard in Baltimore as elsewhere. Of the fifteen trade unions mentioned in local newspapers during the early seventies, only four or five now survived. But the mounting pressure of hard times, which at first had made organized labor flinch and cower, nerved it now to fight back. During the second week of July, 700 canmakers struck for more pay, tying up an industry which in Baltimore ranked second only to ready-made clothing. And on the very morning that the railroad strike began, some 160 boxmakers struck for a 10 per cent raise.

Both the canmakers and the boxmakers had thus far behaved themselves. The striking railroaders kept quiet, too. Many of them had gone to Martinsburg, Cumberland and other points of interest along the line; and anyway, the B. & O. made no attempt to move freights, though shippers (especially the oil companies) complained bitterly. Those who knew Baltimore wondered at the quiet and doubted that it could last. Early in the nineteenth century Baltimore had taken Boston's place as the most mobbish town in the land; and as if to set a seal on the change, Baltimorean plug-uglies and rebel sympathizers had mobbed the Sixth Massachusetts Regiment in the streets of the city at the start of the Civil War. Everyone in Baltimore knew about that occasion and others like it. The historically minded could recall four vicious riots on the B. & O. alone. And an especially ugly mood now gripped Baltimore workers. "The working people everywhere are with us," said a leader of the Baltimore railroad strikers to an out-of-town reporter. "They know what it is to bring up a family on ninety cents a day, to live on beans and corn meal week in and week out, to run in debt at the stores until you cannot get trusted any longer, to see the wife breaking down under privation and distress, and the children growing sharp and fierce like wolves day after day because they don't get enough to eat." On July 17 the *Evening Bulletin* sounded a nervous warning. It urged "those contemplating violence" to remember that "they are not in Martinsburg, nor yet in Montreal." Baltimore, it insisted, "cannot afford to have any rioting, and all acts leading to it must be promptly repressed."

Such was the nature and the mood of the city to which John Garrett, on news of the blockade at Cumberland, recalled Governor John Lee Carroll from Carroll's country place on the fine summer morning of Friday, July 20.

Garrett and King met Governor Carroll at the Camden Street Station, told him what was what along the road and led him to a sheaf of dispatches, which Carroll read over. Then they drove him to Barnum's Hotel, where he set up his headquarters. After lunch Carroll officially called upon all citizens of Maryland to "abstain from acts of lawlessness" and to aid the legal authorities "in the maintenance of peace and order." These were preliminaries. The main event began in midafternoon when Carroll ordered Brigadier General James R. Herbert of the Maryland National Guard to restore order at Cumberland with whatever portions of the Fifth and Sixth regiments he deemed necessary. Evening papers reached the streets with this news shortly after five o'clock.

If the order surprised anyone, it was probably because it had not come sooner. The militia officers themselves had met Wednesday afternoon to lay plans for the expected summons. Among other things, they had decided on the alarm signal 151 as a call to arms. This alarm, unlisted on the regular alarm cards and never yet used in Baltimore, signified riot or other extraordinary civic danger; and the proposal to use it suggests a somewhat boyish yearning for excitement, as if the officers simply hated to miss the chance. Now, having ordered Captain Zollinger of the Fifth and Colonel Peters of the Sixth to assemble their regiments under arms at their respective armories, General Herbert urged the sounding of 151 to hasten the assembly. Carroll demurred, fearing the effect on Baltimore's excitable citizens.

By five o'clock impatient B. & O. officials had their troop train waiting with steam up at Camden Station. An hour passed. Just after six Captain Edward Johnson of the Fifth Regiment reported 150 of his men ready at the armory and 100 more expected. He suggested eagerly that if the fire bells and the City Hall bell—"Big Sam"—sounded 151, "the general would have more men than he wanted." A few minutes later Colonel Peters of the Sixth reported less than thirty of his men on hand. General Herbert put more pressure on Carroll, and the governor weakly yielded. After arranging for the sounding of 151, Herbert ordered 250 men of the Fifth and 150 of the Sixth marched to Camden Station by eight o'clock, and directed Colonel Peters of the Sixth to wait with another 100 at his armory for further orders. At seven-thirty Herbert and six of his staff officers drove to the station in a hack.

The bells rang at 6:35 p.m. Stores were open—in those days they did business every evening until nine—but factories had closed and sent their workers out into the city. As at Cumberland the day was a rare one for July, cool and fair. People were in no great hurry to get home. Crowds flowed thickly along the sidewalks and spilled over into the streets. Then, dropping from the bright sky, came the clamor of the riot call.

People started walking faster and more purposefully. Boys ran to where they thought excitement might develop. A small crowd already loitered at Camden Station, and within fifteen minutes thousands more were gathered there, many of them in work clothes with sleeves rolled up. At seven-thirty distant cheering and the throb of drums drew the mob up Eutaw Street. The Fifth Regiment had just come out of its armory on Garden Street. Before it stood a close-packed crowd of several thousand, which, to the troops' happy surprise, broke into applause. Captain Zollinger had tightened discipline in his regiment a month before, and the boys made a smart appearance. Cheers continued as they marched behind their drum corps to Eutaw Street by way of Madison. Then came a change. From the crest of a downward slope the whole of Eutaw Street lay open to view below them. People jammed it, looking from a distance like pebbles on a stony beach. But, as in a nightmare, it was the stones, not the wind and surf, that roared. Toward Camden Street the roaring grew harsher. At the corner of Eutaw and Lombard a hail of bricks and stones beat upon the militia. Some missiles were thrown from windows by shrieking women. An advancing party of the hostile mob appeared at this point, shouting threats. The main body of the mob waited nearer the station. A dozen soldiers had been hurt by the rock barrage, and their comrades helped them along. Captain Zollinger ordered the troops to fix bayonets. At Camden Street a solid mass of "rough-looking men" barred the way. Zollinger halted his column, commanded the crowd to make way, and when they would not, ordered his men forward on the double. The crowd broke, and the men of the Fifth reached the shelter of the depot through a fusillade of brickbats and a scattering of shots. Zollinger himself knocked a brawny man out of the way with the blunt edge of his sword. Some twenty-five of the militia had been injured in the course of the evening's march. No one on either side had been killed.

If the Fifth Regiment had a guardian angel, he was watching that night. But it was the angel of death who spread his wings over the Sixth Regiment. The Sixth's armory occupied the entire second story of a large building at the corner of Fayette and Front streets. A flight of steps led from the street to a pair of glass-paned doors, behind which were a small landing and a narrow flight of stairs to the armory. The building stood in the factory district and a furni-

ture factory took up the first floor. The crowd that greeted the Fifth
Regiment on Garden Street had been interspersed with women and
small children, and it had shown a holiday mood, as though looking
forward to an unscheduled parade. Outside the Sixth's armory a
different mood prevailed. Dominant in the Front Street crowd were
"a rough element eager for disturbance; a proportion of mechanics
either out of work or upon inadequate pay, whose sullen hearts
rankled; and muttering and murmuring gangs of boys, almost outlaws, and ripe for any sort of disturbance." According to the policemen on duty there, the teen-age element, as at Cumberland, bulked
largest. Here on Front Street the violence and misery of the era bore
its full and perfect fruit.

By seven-thirty several thousand people filled Front Street almost
to Baltimore Street, and packed Fayette Street on both sides of
Front. Yells and taunts came fitfully at first. Then began the spell
that transmutes a collection of rational individuals into a single
beast with power multiplied and mind contracted, driven by emotion and by one emotion at a time. When a mob feels rage, it
knows no fear. When it tastes fear, it seeks only escape. Neither
reason nor consistency has any part in its make-up. With immense
and irresistible enthusiasm it can run directly counter to its own
plain interests and the interests of its individual components. Argu-
ments by themselves can never turn it aside. Yet it can be reversed
in a flash by a word or a phrase, a gesture, a trick of weather, a
laugh or scream or tone of voice—whatever happens to touch some
hidden nerve.

The emotion that filled the crowd on Front Street was fury, en-
gendered by the life sentence of toil and misery which the age had
pronounced upon them, turned against the great-bodied and soulless corporations, narrowed in this place to hatred of Maryland's
dominant corporation and its master, John Garrett, and bearing
now upon the troops who defended John Garrett's interests. By the
pseudo logic of the mob such enemies must be attacked immediately and physically. So when straggling militiamen in forage caps,
blouses and gray pants were spied hurrying toward the armory, the
mob manhandled them. "Is your life insured?" someone asked a
fat, panting sergeant, and another chimed in, "I guess you'd take a
five by seven box." The mob bore one struggling man to the railing
of the Fayette Street Bridge and heaved him over into Jones Falls;

he managed to catch a beam and save himself. Others saw what was up and made for home as unobtrusively as possible, though not without cuts and bruises.

In the armory 180 militia listened nervously. "Hurrah for the strikers!" shouted the mob in the streets below. Loose bricks and stones left by the gas-pipe project gave the crowd ammunition, and they made the most of it. Boys began to pelt the armory door with stones. Four soldiers, standing guard outside the doors, were called inside for safety's sake. As they turned to enter, the mob yelled in triumph and flung bricks at the doorway, instantly smashing the glass panes. Most of the city's police had been sent to guard railroad property, and the small squad at Front Street could do nothing to restrain the mob. By eight o'clock every pane of glass on the Front Street side of the armory had been shattered. A few panes were gone on the third floor, perhaps from pistol shots.

At quarter past eight, pursuant to General Herbert's orders, Colonel Peters chose three companies to march to Camden Station. Company I led the way down the narrow stairs, two men abreast. The first two men to reach the doorway ducked back inside under a shower of missiles. "Keep your heads down, boys," one yelled. Panic seized the others, and they turned back up the stairs. One fired his breech-loading rifle, perhaps by accident, certainly without orders. The pungency of gunsmoke filled the stairway. On the second try, urged forward by Colonel Peters, some managed to get out to Front Street only to be met by flying stones, brickbats and pieces of iron. Almost reflexively they raised their rifles and fired in the air. The sound pierced through the general uproar. For a moment the crowd wavered. Then someone shouted, "Give 'em hell, boys, they're only using blanks!" And the assault began again. The troops leveled their breechloaders and began firing directly into the crowd. "For God's sake, men, quit firing!" yelled Captain Tapper. They did not quit. Dusk had settled over Baltimore, and the flashing of rifles stood out vividly. Pistol shots came from the mob, musketry rattled, men, women and children screamed with rage, pain or fear.

After seeing his brother James off to join the Fifth Regiment, Thomas V. Byrne of North Gay Street had tried to calm his three excited sisters by strolling over to the Sixth's armory to see what was happening. In his late thirties, a salesman in Strassburger's clothing store, Tom Byrne was well liked in that part of Baltimore.

He had begun to try his hand at politics and was now the Fifth
Ward's register of voters. The last sight Tom Byrne ever saw was
the emergence of Company I. A rifle bullet smashed through his
right temple and buried itself in his brain. Some bystanders carried his body away, leaving a pool of blood on the sidewalk near
the corner.

Satisfied now that the troops were not using blanks, the crowd
scattered down side streets. The rest of Company I came out, formed
in company front and began a march unparalleled in Baltimore
history since the ordeal of the Sixth Massachusetts more than sixteen years before. After Company I had set out on the double along
Front Street toward Baltimore Street, a pause emboldened the mob
to reassemble. Company F, next out, got the same welcome as Company I and replied to it as fiercely. Some of its men became separated from the rest and sought shelter in the armory. Company F
followed Company I down Front Street, the rear ranks firing back
on the crowd now and then.

In Company B was a large proportion of teen-age recruits. The
greeting they got from their civilian contemporaries in the street
sent them scrambling back up the stairs in a panic, some of them
nearly impaling their comrades on fixed bayonets. On the next attempt they found that the crowd had either gone after the first two
companies or else had got its fill of lead. Captain Duffy took them
by a different route along Gay Street, where (until they reached
Baltimore Street) they were only sporadically stoned.

Behind them in the twilight wounded men and boys limped away
or were helped off by their friends. Blood stained the pavement. A
single ball had pierced both thighs and the groin of a teen-ager
named James Barner, who lay screaming on the sidewalk. Though
maimed for life, he survived to ponder at leisure the meaning of
what had happened to him on that strange summer evening. Around
him, those who walked past bullet-scarred houses, crunching shards
of glass underfoot, now spoke softly and gravely. From the distance, therefore, one could hear the mob raging after the troops and
the crackle of rifles replying.

At the corner of Front and Baltimore, Patrick Gill, aged forty,
stood bewildered as the mob eddied past him. A tinner by trade,
not long from Ireland, he had no friends in town and no clear notion of what was happening. Nor did light now come but only

darkness; for, as he stood perplexed, a bullet drove through his right side into his stomach. He died two hours later in a law office near by, a sacrifice (if he had asked the authorities) to the maintenance of peace and order, or (the mob might have assured him) to the cause of social justice. His corpse was taken to a police station, where the police chipped in eighteen dollars toward his funeral.

At the same corner, John Norton, aged eighteen, had been vending poultry to help support his mother and sisters. When he realized his danger, he turned and tried to push through the crowd toward his near-by home. Then he dropped with a bullet hole through both thighs.

Rounding the corner into Baltimore Street, the militia marched at quickstep in company front formation. The scene took on a nightmare quality, deepened by hovering night. Level and narrower than Eutaw Street, Baltimore Street had a closed-in feeling about it. Passing cross streets in daylight, one could catch a glimpse of the waterfront and open sky, but dusk had shut off this view. On both sides, the ugly brick buildings of the seventies stood stiffly in close ranks; and the arches over their high, narrow windows looked like eyebrows raised in horror. The stores and saloons were still open, and people crowded the sidewalks. But the street itself was almost deserted, as if cordoned off for some macabre parade. Three streetcars had stopped along it, and frightened passengers still huddled in one of them. The mob had stopped yelling; and now there was a businesslike hush, a deadly serious quiet, frayed only a little by the tramp and shuffle of feet and the spattering of rifle fire. Two men were carried into a drugstore, one shot in the stomach, the other in the bowels; just outside the store, still another teen-age boy fell wounded. The flash of rifles lit up frightened faces in brief tableaux. Brickbats knocked two militiamen unconscious. The men of the Sixth Regiment marched along in good order; and on reaching the first stalled streetcar, they deflected with eerie precision, passed around it and resumed their line of march.

At the corner of Baltimore and Holliday a big man led the mob in a rush at the troops. Bricks were thrown and someone fired a pistol. A number of the troops turned and fired a volley into the crowd, riddling the Dime Restaurant on the corner. A gang of fleeing rioters burst pell-mell into Chenoweth's Saloon. Chenoweth later said there were five men among them and about thirty boys,

most of them carrying stones. Two men and a boy lay prostrate on
the sidewalk in front of the Dime Restaurant. Dragged inside, none
of them lived more than a few minutes. A half-pound stone was
found in the pocket of one, forty-year-old Otto Manecke, a fresco
painter with a wife and five children. Cornelius Murphy, aged
twenty-three, an unemployed oyster dredger, left a widow. The
third corpse had been Willie Hourand, a fifteen-year-old newsboy.
His father, a jeweler, had died some time before, and Willie, whom
the *Baltimore News* described as "one of the brightest" of its newsboys, had been bringing in a dollar or two a day to help support his
mother. Earlier that day the mother and son had begun moving
their belongings to new rooms on Stricker Street. The four o'clock
edition of the *News* on this day of excitement offered the boy too
good a chance to miss. "Good-bye," he said; "leave the heaviest
work till I get back." There was heavy work indeed for Mrs. Hour-
and that night. At the police station she found the body of her son
lying on a bench, his skull crushed by a bullet which had entered
the right eye and passed out on the left side.

From Holliday to Light Street firing was brisk. A cobbler, a
grocery clerk and a carpenter, all in their twenties, fell dead from
bullet wounds in the head or heart. A bullet opened the skull of an
eighteen-year-old messenger boy, who nevertheless clung to life
with astonishing tenacity for nearly two days afterward. As the
troops approached another of the stalled streetcars, a hysterical
woman started to jump off. Sixteen-year-old John Reinhardt, a
serious young man who wanted to become a photographer, pushed
her back in, saying, "For God's sake, ma'am, stay where you are!"
Before he could take cover himself, a rifle bullet killed him. Altogether, ten men and boys died as a result of that evening's deadly
parade, and more than a score were badly wounded. According to
rumor other casualties were concealed. None of the known dead or
wounded were railroad strikers.

Among the troops, the only serious casualty was William Young,
a prompter at Ford's Theater, who suffered a flesh wound in the
back of the head from a pistol ball, and whose nose was broken and
face disfigured by a large stone. Nevertheless, the ranks thinned
rapidly as men dropped out and fled to the Central Police Station,
where they changed to civilian clothing. Of the 120 men who had
set out from the armory, only fifty-nine remained in line when the

harassed companies at last came in sight of Camden Station. Set against the harshly angular structures of later years, the red-brick depot building, its ornate white trimmings made lacy by distance, had an ample, comforting, almost motherly look, like a placid matron among desiccated spinsters. So, at least, it must have seemed to those of Colonel Peters' men who won through to its haven.

Inside the depot, besides the men and officers of the Fifth Regiment, the newcomers found General Herbert, Governor Carroll, Mayor Latrobe, the Board of Police Commissioners and various railroad officials (including Vice-President King but not President Garrett). Also present were some frightened citizens who had been waiting for trains when the uproar began. Their wait was vain. No trains left that night, passenger or freight. About 200 rioters drove away the engineer and firemen of the waiting troop train and beat back a squad of police who tried to restore order. Rioters also attacked the engine of the Chicago express which had been scheduled to leave at eight o'clock. Shortly after nine o'clock, three half-drunk boys or young men boarded that same engine, ran it into the yards and jumped off. Going full tilt, it smashed grandly into some freights, tore up part of the platform at the Lee Street end of the station, demolished the dispatcher's office and came to rest upside down.

At nine o'clock police cleared all civilians, excepting officials, from the depot building proper. Under orders from General Herbert, Company C fixed its bayonets and charged a mob which had forced its way northward halfway along the platform to a point above Barre Street. Flying stones knocked out two militia men, who were taken to King's private car at the rear of the troop train. The mob fell back from the platform and made a stand in the yards. Reinforced by Company K, the militia charged again. They were ordered back after meeting pistol fire as well as brickbats from a mob of several thousand. The defiant mob tore up tracks and demonstrated before the depot on Camden Street. Anxious to stretch the civil power to its limit before invoking further military force, Governor Carroll asked Mayor Latrobe to summon all available city police. By ten, Baltimore police were present in force guarding the depot and the yards. Vice-President King made a telegraphic report to John Garrett, adding: "It is said to be the fiercest mob ever known in Baltimore."

By now 15,000 people were massed around the depot. Again a strange silence had fallen, broken by the tramp of feet and occasional yells from boys in the crowd. Suddenly the sound of a fire alarm stirred the crowd, and people pointed to three flaming passenger cars. Woodwork on a locomotive took fire, and the south end of the passenger platform blazed up. Firemen arrived, laid hoses and started up their pumps. Some rioters attacked one of the fire engines, cutting its hose and quenching its fire. Police exchanged pistol shots with the attackers and drove them back, wounding several. Rumors swept the mob: first, that all railroad property was to be burned; then, that rioters meant to burn out the whole city. (People well remembered the fate of Chicago six years before.)

When he saw the flames and heard the rumors, Carroll immediately wired President Hayes that the rioters had got beyond the state's power to control, that they had "taken possession of the Baltimore and Ohio Railroad depot, set fire to same, and driven off all firemen who attempted to extinguish the flames," and that in Maryland's name, he must now call upon the United States government for military aid. Without troubling this time to ask questions, Hayes promptly authorized Federal intervention. That night Secretary McCrary ordered General William Barry, commanding Fort McHenry, to report to Governor Carroll with all available men and to act under Carroll's orders in quelling the riot. Three companies were also ordered to Baltimore from stations in New York Harbor.

Even before these orders had been received, Carroll had discovered that the rumors were false, that the fires were out and the crowd was drifting away. By one o'clock in the morning of the twenty-first, most police had been withdrawn from the depot and the militia had bedded down within. Carroll notified McCrary that order had returned and United States troops would not be needed right away. "There is," he added, however, "increasing lawlessness at Cumberland and as I will not be able to send a force from here I may be obliged to ask the Government for aid." In all these transactions, Carroll behaved rather less like the rider than like the balky steed, equally galled by thorns to the front and spurs to the rear.

Carroll let his original request stand; and on Saturday afternoon, in a proclamation replete with whereases, Hayes officially brought Maryland alongside West Virginia within the fold of Federal protection. Giving General Barry command of Baltimore operations,

Hayes sent that knightly major general, Winfield Scott Hancock, commander of the Military Division of the Atlantic, to confer with Governor Carroll on the situation—unofficially, in fact, to take chief command of what was rapidly assuming the form of a major campaign.

The sunlight of Saturday morning seemed to have driven off the fears of Friday night. Baltimore had apparently, in Emerson's phrase, let off its peccant humors. The crowds that filled Baltimore Street that morning came as sight-seers. They stood in pleasurable awe before Chenoweth's Saloon, the Dime Restaurant, the Sixth Regiment Armory, pointing out smashed panes, bullet scars and spots that could be blood. Merchants boarded up windows and locked doors, not in fear of tumult, but in disgust with such unprofitable notoriety; for those who gawked did not buy. Calm surrounded the B. & O. depot, more calm, indeed, than ever before in its history. In what its foes considered a mere petty spite of all the world, the B. & O. had stopped passenger trains, which the strikers (if not the Friday rioters) had never molested. Along the whole line east of the Ohio River not a wheel turned that day.

Around noontime, nevertheless, fears revived. City authorities closed all saloons (the Murphy temperance movement had not taken hold in Baltimore). "There is a horrible feeling with the populace, which will result in a fearful riot tonight," King warned Garrett. Carroll, suddenly glad that Federal troops were now at his command, asked General Barry to call and confer "on the subject of keeping the peace in this city tonight." "It may," he said nervously, "be extremely important for the safety of the city that a show of force should be made." At ten-thirty Friday night, independently of Carroll's application to Hayes, the War Department had sent a guard of Federal troops from Fort McHenry to the B. & O.'s great harbor terminal at Locust Point, on the collector of customs' insistence that the riot endangered the United States (and B. & O.) bonded warehouses there; and the Treasury Department had sent a revenue cutter, guns shotted with grape, to fend off possible rioters at the same place. This, and the earlier dispatch of troops to Martinsburg, left Barry with no infantry at all and only enough artillerymen to serve three guns. Ever since late Friday night the sending of troops from New York Harbor stations had been dizzily on and off, off and on, to the confusion of their commanders. Now it was finally on. At Barry's call the War Department ordered the New York detachments to entrain. The Navy sent 100 marines from the Washington Navy Yard.

Around Camden Station all remained quiet until dusk. Men of the Fifth Regiment walked guard about the depot building. Had those of the now-hated Sixth shown themselves, they would have baited trouble; and, anyway, two-thirds of them had sneaked out, changed to civilian clothes in a near-by saloon and gone home. Knots of angry men began to appear in the circles of dim gaslight under the street lamps. Fifty police in blue uniforms and shiny badges formed a cordon around the station. "Herbert reports turbulent crowd at station," wired Carroll to Barry; "bring your men and guns . . . the Marines are expected every moment." Before Barry's men got there, the crowd broke through the police cordon. Pistol fire erupted, mostly from the police, who aimed low to avoid fatalities, but some also from a gang of thirty boys equipped with old-fashioned pepperbox revolvers. More than a score of rioters limped away wounded, two of them dangerously and one of these a boy of fifteen. Suddenly, by a well-ordered plan, the police moved into the crowd, each officer selecting and collaring a man. The riot collapsed limply. Guardsmen with fixed bayonets herded the prisoners—with accidental irony—into the gentlemen's waiting room. Locked in, and increased by succeeding batches to about 100, they raved with comic impotence, sang and swore in chorus, pounded on the door and broke off bench legs for bludgeons, all to no purpose. Arraigned next day, most were held over for hearings on Wednesday. Thus the expected "fearful riot" turned into anticlimax.

At York and Light streets that night, "South Baltimore roughs," canalmen and some miners engaged a police squad in a brief scuffle until police reinforcements came. After yells, pistol shots and the sound of running feet, the skirmish ended with the police in possession not only of the field but also of fifty more candidates for the magistrates' attention.

Except for an apparently incendiary fire which destroyed a lumberyard, the only other excitement of the night occurred at Mount Clare Station elsewhere in the city. At ten o'clock about 100 rioters attacked the foundry, but were routed by a volley from twenty-five police armed with Springfield rifles. Near by, four hours later, flame and smoke burst from a train of petroleum cars. "Quiet as death" till then, the night suddenly rang with the shouts of a mob on an embankment overlooking the track. In the face of threats and missiles, police and a B. & O. passenger brakeman uncoupled the burning cars and pushed the others out of danger, saving all but seven. The mob gave up and dispersed.

To be self-sustaining, a popular frenzy must develop progressively greater sensations. Momentum must be more than maintained, it must be increased. This had not happened in Baltimore. After the lethal march of Friday night Saturday's mere scuffles forecast peace on Sunday; and so it turned out.

So it would probably have turned out even if Federal troops had stayed away. The arrival of those troops only reinforced an ordinance of human nature. Coming from Washington, the Marines reached Camden Station just before Saturday midnight, arriving first, as in popular tradition (even though a little after the crisis had passed). Some of them were sent to patrol the yards at Mount Clare after the police had dispersed the crowd. Just after midnight Barry's artillery, three three-inch rifles, were planted at Howard and Camden streets. Sunday morning brought regulars from New York and from Fortress Monroe, Virginia. To avoid "an unnecessary march through the city," most were taken directly from Canton Street Station by tug to Fort McHenry. One detachment of 100 men went on to President Street Station and marched thence to the Sixth Regiment Armory. Along the way stones were thrown experimentally and then, when the troops stoically ignored them, more boldly and accurately. At last, one stone dropped a soldier. "Halt!" shouted Brigadier General Henry Abbott. "Fix bayonets! Forward march!" Almost before the commands were out of Abbott's mouth, the crowd had fled; and the rest of the march was peaceful. Taking the hint, however, General Abbott borrowed a suit of civilian clothes from Colonel Peters before calling on General Hancock at Barnum's Hotel. And when late that night, Governor Carroll ordered all troops and arms transferred from the Sixth's armory to the Fifth's, General Abbott contrived to carry off the movement before daylight "and thus avoid bloodshed."

So peace had come to Baltimore. By Sunday night, some 500 Federal troops, including the Marines, were stationed in the city. The B. & O. was running passenger trains again and without incident—though the strike against freight service remained unbroken.

That day a Baltimorean wrote his wife that the killing of citizens had been "universally condemned," and that Colonel Peters of the Sixth Regiment "would be mobbed if he should venture upon the streets." Also writing privately, the United States District Attorney blamed "the folly and incompetency of the authorities in sounding the fire alarm to call out the militia," compounded by a demoralization of the Sixth Regiment, "consisting largely of overgrown boys."

"I want you to state," said the chairman of a strikers' committee to a *Philadelphia Inquirer* reporter, "that we had nothing to do with this outbreak. Not one of our men was in it. . . . When we found there was going to be trouble we passed the word among our men to keep out of it, and nearly every one of them went home and stayed there." The *Inquirer* printed the statement; and most other newspapers did the strikers similar justice, though many charged them with indirect responsibility.

On the score of indirect guilt, the public had other ideas. That Sunday a friend wrote John Garrett that "believing your life and property to be in danger," he would if desired "endeavor to raise a sufficient force" to protect them. A full week after the riot, a visiting New York politician wrote home that "the poor misguided laborers will, as must always be the case, be the greatest sufferers—but I hope that the lesson will not be lost on the managers of our great trunk roads who are indirectly (at least) responsible for a great deal of the mischief done." John W. Garrett, added the letter writer, "keeps himself entirely out of sight. No one has seen or heard from him for days. He is most bitterly denounced by all classes of society, and will I think be forced to retire from the Presidency of the Company."

Thus ran Baltimore opinion. But in the rest of the nation by that time (for whatever consolation it may have afforded John Garrett) the Sixth Regiment's bloody march had sunk out of mind beneath the terrible, almost incredible tidings from Pittsburgh.

CHAPTER 7

The Great Strike

ROBERT PITCAIRN, a bullet-headed, square-faced Scotsman, advanced in life side by side with his countryman, Andrew Carnegie—up to a certain point. After that, Pitcairn's path leveled off and Carnegie's kept rising. Like his friend Andy, Bob Pitcairn began as a telegraph messenger boy in Pittsburgh at two and a half dollars a week. He and Andy entered the service of the Pennsylvania Railroad together, and in 1865 Pitcairn succeeded his fast-climbing friend as superintendent of the Pennsylvania's Pittsburgh division. There he remained in 1877.

Why, with their backgrounds and chances so much alike, did Pitcairn stop and Carnegie go on? Both were alert and hard-working. They shared many tastes, including a boyhood love of the shows at the old Pittsburgh Theater. Pitcairn, to be sure, was a bit more self-indulgent than Carnegie. In later years he grew fleshy. He had a ravenous sweet tooth. "He explained to me confidentially one day," recalled Carnegie, "that he had live things in his stomach that gnawed his insides until fed upon sweets." But Pitcairn's basic deficiency seems to have been in a quality for which Carnegie was noted: the ability to see things through another man's eyes. That failure of empathy, that fatal gap in Pitcairn's understanding, was to be lit up by flashing guns and burning buildings.

On Monday, July 16, 1877, Pitcairn ordered all through freights to be run as double-headers eastward from Pittsburgh to Conemaugh, beginning on July 19. A double-header was a train with two locomotives. On the uphill run westward, all freights had long been double-headers of about thirty-six cars, more or less, depending on their lading. On the uphill run eastward, some trains had been double-headers, others single engines with seventeen or eighteen cars (as against fifty or sixty on the Philadelphia end of the line). Pitcairn's order simply made double-headers of *all* eastbound through freights as far as Conemaugh, where one engine would cut the train and the other would take it on to Philadelphia. This would save the delay and trouble of having one single-engine train wait for another to join it at Conemaugh. It would also cut labor costs. As many engineers and firemen would be needed as before, but only half as many conductors and brakemen.

There came the rub. The men considered double-headers dangerous, especially in winter. Each brakeman had to handle twice as many cars as before. The trains were more apt to break; and in rain or fog a break might not be noticed until one section came crashing into the other. Besides, the men calculated that some fifty or sixty of them would be thrown out of work by the order, and no one felt safe. Crowding around the bulletin boards that Monday, they read the order, grumbled and speculated on who would be fired. Some talked of not going out on the double-headers. The grumblers made no formal complaint, perhaps because they remembered what had happened to the last ones who did. If Pitcairn had been aware of the grumbling, it would not have bothered him anyway. "The men were always complaining about something," he said later.

Pitcairn's folly lay in the timing of his order. He could not possibly have picked a worse day, a worse week or a worse year. The Trainmen's Union was not dead. It had a considerable membership of Pinkerton agents alone, or so Allan Pinkerton later implied (observing with unconscious humor that anyone could get in, "no matter how low and vile"). Pitcairn must have known of the union's vague but earnest plans for a strike in the fall. He knew the B. & O. cut was to take effect that very Monday. He knew that the men of his division were to be paid that day for their June work and would thus be in the best possible situation for a strike. How can we explain Pitcairn's failure to wait just a week or two? Only by assuming that he underestimated the combined strength of his men and sadly misjudged both their temper and the temper of the times.

In Pitcairn's place, Tom Scott might have shown more sense. Standard Oil was pressing Scott hard in its fight with his Empire Transportation Company over the oil traffic. The Texas Pacific scheme still hung in the balance; and Scott could not afford to alienate the public by provoking a bitter labor struggle, especially when he needed a Congressional subsidy so desperately. But Scott was not aware of Pitcairn's double-header order, "a matter," he said later, "of detail management of the respective divisions that scarcely ever comes to me at all."

On Tuesday and Wednesday the men who labored in Pittsburgh's steel mills, factories and glass works talked about the strike on the B. & O. "It'll be here," they said, "it'll be here in a day or two." The smell of coming trouble reached the countryside. According to the sheriff, police and citizens, an unusual number of strangers, mostly tramps, had begun coming in during the preceding week. Perhaps those recollections credited the tramps with too much foreknowledge. But certainly since the beginning of trouble on the B. & O., the shabby strangers had been entering Pittsburgh by wagon road and railroad, riding in on tenders, cowcatchers, even car steps, drifting along Pittsburgh streets by ones and twos at first, then in gangs of six or eight. In St. Paul some weeks later thirteen tramps brought in for vagrancy were found to possess loot from Pittsburgh; and they confessed to having heard or guessed in advance that Pittsburgh pickings would be good.

According to later testimony, the parties who should have been most aware of what was coming were just the ones who suspected least. Robert Ammon left town on July 18 to take a job in the oil regions. Samuel Muckle, president of the Pittsburgh division of the Trainmen's Union, had no idea that trouble was at hand. Neither did railroad officials. From Yard Dispatcher Joseph McCabe to Vice-President Alexander Cassatt, none of them saw the barometer falling. Pitcairn himself chose the very morning his order took effect, Thursday, July 19, to leave with his family for a seaside vacation at Long Branch, New Jersey.

At three o'clock that morning the first of the new double-headers pulled out of Pittsburgh in darkness and rain. Old "Bobby" Atchison, sixteen years an engineer on the Pennsylvania, took it out as far as Derry. He expected no trouble and saw none. On the way back to Pittsburgh Engineer Atchison noticed with surprise that the usual outbound freights were not passing him. "Must be a wreck on the road," he said to his fireman. When he came in, shortly after noon, a conductor got on the engine and rode down with him. "What's the matter?" said Atchison, "there's nothing out." The conductor told him: "The boys wouldn't let anything go out this morning." They passed a crowd by the track, and Atchison yelled down: "What's going on here?" "Lots of fun," someone yelled back.

The "fun" had begun at half past eight that morning. The rain had stopped a couple of hours before, leaving Pittsburgh's air temporarily laundered. Chips of blue sky gleamed from puddles along the tracks. A hundred miles or so away, at Martinsburg, West Virginia, Colonel French and his Federal troops had just arrived and were bivouacked in the B. & O. roundhouse. In the Pennsylvania's roundhouse at Pittsburgh, half a dozen engineers and firemen listened while a fireman read them a morning paper's account of "The Railroad War" and the dispatching of Federal troops. "Bloody Work Expected To-Day," said the headline. In the yard outside, freight conductor William Ryan made ready to take out the eight-forty double-header.

At the last minute Flagman Augustus Harris, generally known as "Gus," refused to go out. The decision was his own, not part of a concerted plan or a general understanding. Had he lain awake that past night, listening to the rain, asking himself if he dared quit, wondering if anyone would join him, weighing the chances? Or had he simply risen to a breakfast that did not fill him, seen his children go off shabby and half-fed, walked brooding through the damp morning and then yielded impulsively to stored-up rage? If he ever told anyone, his story was not written down. Gus Harris opened the floodgates, and the torrent of ensuing events swept him beyond the sight or hearing of history.

Conductor Ryan appealed to the rest of his crew, but they joined Harris in refusing to go out on a double-header. They could hardly make a living as it was, they said. Now some of them were bound to lose their jobs altogether. This was the moment to act, and they were determined to seize it. At nine o'clock Chief Clerk David Watt sent for replacements. Twenty-five brakemen and conductors in the trainmen's room declined to take out Ryan's double-header and were discharged on the spot. Instead of leaving the yard, they hung around to watch developments.

At last Dispatcher McCabe persuaded a trio of yard brakemen to serve as crew for Ryan's freight. With that, the strike turned ugly, for the strikers hotly resented the use of yard men on a "long road" job. As Trainmaster David Garrett walked out in front of the engine, he encountered a crowd of about twenty angry strikers, of whom the most violently demonstrative was a flagman named Andrew Hice. Hice shouted that the train would not go out, nor would any other double-header freight. When one of the volunteer brakemen tried to couple a caboose to the train, a striker who was "a little the worse for his beer," threw a link which hit the brakeman on his side, knocking the breath and courage out of him. The brakeman took refuge in the Philadelphia express, which stood near by, and the rest of the volunteer crew gave up. By now, the nine-forty trains were due to go out, but a steadily growing crowd had blocked the switch leading onto the main track west of Twenty-eighth Street. No eastbound trains could leave.

Thus casually, almost as a matter of course, the Pennsylvania strikers and their sympathizers took the way of the B. & O. strikers, which was also the way of their lawless times. Trainmaster David Garrett, standing on the tracks between an idle locomotive and a stubborn crowd, had accurately summarized the legal status of strikers, both in his day and ever since: "Hice, you have a perfect right to refuse to go out, but you have no right to interfere with others." And the reply of Flagman Andrew Hice, with equal brevity and precision, had summed up the mood and the morals of the age: "It's a question of bread or blood, and we're going to resist."

Hice was wrong on every count: law, morals, even strategy. Like Robert Pitcairn, he believed in the justice of his course. But, like Pitcairn, he did not know all the relevant facts in the case, and he did not understand all of the facts he knew.

Some of those facts now became plain. Freight crews joined the strikers as their trains came in and were stopped; yet by noontime railroad men were outnumbered by others in the crowd at the Twenty-eighth Street crossing. A city detective, who estimated the crowd at about a hundred, noted that "quite a number of the people there were boys"—the fulminate in almost every explosion of that terrible fortnight. They were as eager for a show as former teen-agers Carnegie and Pitcairn had once been. The noon hour brought more outsiders. Some may have been the advance guard of the tramp army. Others were probably men from the mills. Here was the first easy stirring in Pittsburgh of the same beast which was soon to rage through Baltimore.

Pittsburgh was a workingmen's town. Its dedication to heavy in-

dustry was best appreciated after dark. At night the city looked and
sounded like "hell with the lid off." From Mount Washington, opposite the confluence of the Allegheny and the Monongahela, visitors looked down toward a dark wedge of land spangled with the
fires of hundreds of furnaces and mills. Among these by 1877 were
73 glass factories, 33 iron mills, 8 steel rolling mills, 7 white lead
factories, 29 oil refineries and 158 coal mines. Stern-wheelers towed
coal barges along the broad Monongahela and joined their whistles
to the shore noises of exhaust steam, gears, rollers, flywheels, steam
hammers and blast furnaces. Though the panic of 1873 had hit
Pittsburgh hard, the city had recovered sooner than the rest of the
country. The pull of advancing technology helped overcome the
drag of depression. Two years after the panic Andrew Carnegie
opened his great Edgar Thomson Steel Works, named after Tom
Scott's predecessor on the Pennsylvania Railroad. The year 1877
brought a quickening of recovery. By spring Pittsburgh's mills were
running at about 75 per cent of their pre-depression rate, or 25 per
cent better than in the spring of 1876.

Pittsburgh's millmen were not a docile lot. They knew how to
strike, and they had tasted victory even in depression. In December 1874 Pittsburgh iron manufacturers had tried to cut puddlers'
wages about 25 per cent, rejecting a union offer to take a compromise 10 per cent cut. After four months of a stubborn strike, the
employers gave in. During that strike the Pittsburgh Bolt Works
imported Negro strikebreakers from Virginia, and violence threatened for a while. Major General Alfred L. Pearson, commander of
the local militia, called four companies to arms. But Governor
Hartranft put a damper on Pearson's militance, and the episode
ended peacefully. As business improved, Pittsburgh iron workers
remained touchy. They resented especially the employers' abandonment of the so-called "hot dollar"— a bonus of a dollar per ton
for work in the hot months of July and August, with which puddlers
might hire an extra helper or seek other relief from the heat, Murphy
pledge permitting. Now July was here again and hot weather with
it. Two successful defensive strikes by the boilers in May and June
had helped to build up self-confidence. And 1877's wave of pay
cuts gave millmen a fresh grievance. The local literary society reflected the prevailing mood when it scheduled a lecture on "Labor
and the Capital that Oppresses It" for the evening of July 19.

Still more ominous was the unity of all classes in Pittsburgh against the Pennsylvania Railroad. Out in the clear air of Pittsburgh's wealthy suburbs, amid the felicities of lawns and drives, croquet grounds and bright parterres, one heard grumblings more elegantly couched but just as bitter as those vented in the smoke-darkened tenements of the South Side. Like Martinsburg and Cumberland, Pittsburgh deemed itself the victim of a greedy monopoly. In the late sixties, the city had lost its pre-eminence as an oil-refining center; and it blamed the Pennsylvania Railroad for that, because the Pennsylvania's rates to Philadelphia were as high from Pittsburgh as from Oil City, more than a hundred miles further away. The Baltimore & Ohio reached Pittsburgh in 1871, but through freight had to be ferried slowly and expensively from its Monongahela terminal to that of the Pittsburgh & Western on the Allegheny. The alternative of river shipments did not console the Pittsburghers. In 1876 a Pittsburgh newspaper expressed the city's feeling in an editorial called "Railroad Vultures." "This community," it warned, "is being aroused into action, and presently the torrent of indignation will give place to condign retribution." It denounced the railroad kings as "money jugglers," led by greed into "all known ways and byways of fraud, scheming, and speculating, to accomplish the amassing of princely fortunes."

In June 1877 the Chamber of Commerce pointed out that freight rates to San Francisco were 20 per cent higher from Pittsburgh than from New York, where there was railroad and steamship competition. In a unanimous resolution the Chamber called on Congress to use its interstate commerce power against "undue or unreasonable discrimination."

July brought more direct and certain relief within sight. For two years there had been talk about building a competing line seventy miles to Youngstown, Ohio, where it would tap extensive railroad connections to the West. During the second week in July leading businessmen took the project in hand and reorganized the embryo Pittsburgh & Lake Erie Railroad. Construction was begun that year and completed in 1879; Pittsburgh then saw its dream of railroad competition come true. In July 1877 the revival of newspaper agitation served to remind Pittsburgh's elite of the Pennsylvania's injustices. It also reminded workingmen they had powerful, if unaccustomed, allies in their struggle against the great corporation.

Chief Clerk David Watt came up against that pervasive local hostility in midmorning when he went to Mayor William McCarthy's office to get police aid. "Billy" McCarthy was a man of decided opinions, upon which he would discourse fluently in a cracked but vigorous voice, emphasizing his remarks by pounding the head of his ever handy hickory cane on the nearest desk or table. In this way he had left his mark on every editorial desk in town. Pittsburgh's anger at rate discrimination and its sympathy with the men were both strong in him, for he owed his political success to the labor vote. When Watt asked Mayor McCarthy to come down in person with a squad of police, the mayor answered curtly that he had been sick and was not fit to go. He did not say what he had been sick of, but Watt gathered that it was the Pennsylvania Railroad Company.

Watt also wanted ten policemen, to which Mayor McCarthy replied that they were not to be had. This happened to be true. For years Pittsburgh's credit standing had been so low that not even 7 per cent bonds could be sold at par. City revenues from all sources were 50 per cent below those of 1873. Early in 1877 an adverse court decision had unexpectedly thrown an additional burden of debt on the city, and a provision of the state constitution now restrained the city from further borrowing. Already police pay had been cut to what the *Pittsburgh Post* called "the starvation point." By the end of June the city had run out of money to pay even those low wages. And so, only a few days before, half of Pittsburgh's policemen had been fired for lack of funds to pay them. The night force was cut to nine lieutenants and eighty-two patrolmen; a policeman might cover his new beat in twenty minutes if he walked fast and did not look for trouble. The day force available for service away from the station houses amounted to only eight men.

McCarthy did consent to send what men he could spare; and he suggested that Watt hire as many more as he needed from among the recently discharged men, who happened to be calling at City Hall for their final pay that very morning. The laid-off men were not especially eager to serve in such a cause for only one day's pay. Besides they had neither uniforms nor weapons. Nevertheless, after Watt agreed to assume the expense, Mayor McCarthy hired ten and sent them to the Twenty-eighth Street crossing under the command of a day force detective.

The crowd at the crossing had blocked an outgoing freight by refusing to let the switch be turned. "I'll turn that switch," announced Watt gallantly and stepped to the task. An interloper from the Pan Handle Road (whose men had a reputation for ruggedness —the "Pan Handle Roughs," they were called) placed himself in front of the switch. "Boys," he shouted melodramatically, "we may as well die right here!" Watt grabbed him by the coat and called for an officer. Suddenly a fist shot out from behind the Pan Handle man and blacked Watt's eye. Besides being dexterous, the owner of the fist, a striker named Thomas McCall, showed himself to be "limber as an eel" before the police finally caught up with him and hauled him off, struggling, to the lockup. (For his offense, McCall was eventually fined $1500 and sentenced to a year in the penitentiary.) After being struck, Watt sent the mayor a request for fifty more police. With some difficulty, the chief of police managed to raise six or seven. Meanwhile, Dispatcher McCabe set the switch right, and the freight went through on its way to Wilkinsburg.

It was to be the last freight out of Pittsburgh for some time. And the pursuit of McCall, with all its farcical elements, brought another twitch of the tiger's tail. Even though the small crowd of strikers and spectators made no violent response to McCall's cries for help, the police found it exasperatingly slow in making way for authority and decidedly nimble in yielding to the fugitive. Still more ominous was the small cloud of stones that flew, as if by a law of social physics, from the hands of boys assembled on the hillside by the tracks. On this Thursday noon juvenile stone throwing brought forth only some cursing from the police.

The crowd at Twenty-eighth Street grew slowly. By three o'clock perhaps 200 men, women and children stood around chatting and waiting for the next excitement. This came, however, at Torrens Station about three miles further east and just beyond the stockyards. Watt sent Trainmaster Garrett to move out forty-six cars of livestock from Torrens while there was still time. Before Garrett could do anything, Andrew Hice and his followers reached the scene. About 150 men, women and children gathered to look on and lend the strikers moral support. Garrett's train crew climbed down as soon as the hint of a threat gave them an excuse. Garrett walked to the telegraph office to wire for police. There he met Hice. "Be careful not to do anything you'll be sorry for," said Garrett,

"It's a question of bread or blood," Hice said. "If I go to the penitentiary I can get bread and water, and that's about all I can get now." After rejoining the crowd in the yard, he called out: "They're going to bring the militia! I want four good men." Four young men, two of them strikers, came forward. "I want you to go to Pittsburgh and get out two thousand millmen," he said.

No such army rose that day, and the bluff may not have disturbed Garrett. Nevertheless, the passenger train which presently arrived and let off a half dozen police also brought scores of strikers and their sympathizers. Watt, wearing his purple badge of courage, came too; and he and Garrett succeeded in sending off a train of livestock by pretending to move it to another siding. After that single stroke there were no more attempts to move freight from Torrens.

At four o'clock, an effort was made to start a double-header from Twenty-sixth Street with four policemen aboard each engine. Before starting, the engineers had privately confessed to the strikers that they were highly susceptible to intimidation. And so they proved to be. The engines wheezed twice, the train moved ten or twelve feet, the crowd gave a yell, a tall young striker named David Davis stepped onto the tracks and waved his hands and the train crews, professing mortal terror, abandoned the train. The road foreman and the civil engineer sidetracked the cars and put up the engines in the roundhouse. That ended the company's attempts to move freights that day. Passenger trains, however, continued to move in and out on schedule; the strikers, far from obstructing, took special pains to expedite them. Some pains were necessary; for in the crowd at the crossing, sympathizers far outnumbered actual strikers, and the enthusiasm of these allies required guidance.

Many people were to charge that the Trainmen's Union planned all this. In the case of the Pennsylvania Railroad, the evidence suggests otherwise. Men like Andrew Hice or Gus Harris or David Davis assumed the lead briefly at one point or another, but only because they happened to be foremost in nerve or vehemence. The president of the Pittsburgh division of the Trainmen's Union, Samuel A. Muckle, formerly a conductor on the Pan Handle Road, had been fired in June for his union activity. He happened to sleep late on July 19 and so did not even hear about the strike until nearly noontime. His first comment was: "Impossible!" Though he approved of the strike and hurried to Twenty-eighth Street, he busied himself there chiefly in trying to persuade his former Pan Handle comrades to go home and keep out of trouble.

The Trainmen's Union nevertheless gave the Pittsburgh strike movement a nucleus. Under its auspices the strikers met that evening at Phoenix Hall on Eleventh Street. Reporters badgered the doorkeepers for more than an hour before the strikers decided to admit them. Exactly what had happened meanwhile was not revealed, but the rest of the meeting impressed the newspapermen with the intelligence and zeal of the strikers. A rolling-mill man took the floor and assured the railroaders of support from Pittsburgh labor generally. "We're with you," he said. "We're in the same boat. I heard a reduction of ten per cent hinted at in our mill this morning. I won't call employers despots, I won't call them tyrants, but the term capitalists is sort of synonymous and will do as well." Another man said he had heard that the strikers would not meet serious resistance if they took guns from the armory of the local militia, the Duquesne Grays. "We don't want arms!" the men yelled at him. The next speaker renounced violence and intimidation of any sort, specifically repudiating the assault on Watt; and he promised that "moral suasion" alone would be exerted against men who chose to run trains on the company's terms. The proceedings were twice broken into by announcements of good news for the strikers— that the B. & O.'s Connellsville branch to Pittsburgh would be on strike by morning (loud cheers), and that another freight crew had joined the strike and were bringing their train in (more cheers). After some discussion the meeting adopted a statement of demands drawn up by a strikers' committee (of which Gus Harris was a member): no more double-headers, a restoration of pay to pre-June levels, all dismissed strikers to be taken back and pay grades to be abolished. Double-headers had been the immediate occasion of the strike. These further demands made it an extension of the movement begun on the B. & O. And with that extension the B. & O. strike became what historians have called the "Great Strike"—a revolt of American railroad workers against their lot generally and the 10 per cent cut in particular.

Indeed, the rising would soon spread to other classes of industrial labor. And as if to raise an anemometer in that mounting gale, the meeting at Phoenix Hall concluded with a resolution inviting "all workingmen to make common cause with their brethren on the railroad."

It seemed for a while as though the engineers might decline to embrace the "common cause." At a meeting of the Brotherhood local that same evening the older engineers opposed mixing into the strike. It was a conductors' and brakemen's affair: let them fight it out. After all, the engineers' June committee had formally accepted the 10 per cent cut, and the subsequent double-header order did not hurt engineers. The entry of some half-drunk and boisterous members broke up the meeting. Another, held the next morning, settled nothing except that the young hotheads were gaining support. A third, on Friday afternoon, made it official: the freight engineers of Pittsburgh joined both the strike and the Trainmen's Union.

Young Robert Ammon, summoned from the oil regions by a friend's wire, arrived at the Union Depot in Pittsburgh that Friday morning. There some men from the Pittsburgh, Fort Wayne & Chicago Railroad asked him to lead them in a strike of their own; but Ammon, dog-tired, brushed them off and headed home to Allegheny. "I got my breakfast," he said later, "and fooled around the house with my wife and baby for about an hour, and then went to bed." Early that afternoon, after more appeals from Trainmen's Union men, the sleepy grand organizer called down to his wife, "All right, if they're going to strike, I'll be there." As he rolled over for a final snooze, Mrs. Ammon called up excitedly, "Bob, they're going to put No. 15 engine on the siding!" Ammon jumped out of bed, confirmed the news with a glance from his window and dressed hastily. At his front door a half dozen union men met him with word that Mayor Ormsby Phillips and twenty-five police were on their way to the Fort Wayne yards.

Ordinarily the "outer depot" of the Fort Wayne road at Allegheny drew little notice from travelers. Along the tree-shaded street stood a few boardinghouses, a little wooden shack for the vending of lunch and villainous cigars to the suffering trainmen and a lonesome brick house converted into a telegraph and dispatcher's office. Not far off stood the road's extensive machine shops. Now, however, an excited crowd of several hundred swirled about the yards. Ammon took immediate command. He assured Mayor Phillips that the strikers would preserve both property and order as long as they could and then, if overborne by the mob, would call on the police for support. According to Phillips and the chief of police, Ammon also bragged that the strike was organized all over the country, that "if he sent a telegram to Martinsburg the strike would stop, and if he would turn over his hand here, the thing would be stopped." Ammon denied any prearrangement. For his part, Ammon claimed that Mayor Phillips promised him immunity from arrest so long as he committed no violence, and that Phillips agreed to "leave that portion of Allegheny in my charge." "That's stuff," said Phillips in rebuttal later, "that ain't my style!" "Stuff" or not, Phillips made no effort to dispossess Ammon and his men.

The Great Strike had reached Ohio even before it broke out in Pittsburgh. At Newark, a small city in central Ohio where four divisions of the B. & O. came together, B. & O. freight brakemen and firemen met quietly on July 18 and resolved to strike against the 10 per cent cut. Newark's last outbound freight train left at ten minutes to eight that cool, damp evening. As elsewhere, passenger trains ran without hindrance. The engineers hung back, like those at Pittsburgh, but their sympathy was plain; and anyway the blockade was effective without their open support.

The Newark strikers maintained a sober decorum. They were reported to have sworn off liquor for the duration. Not jubilation but calm dejection prevailed among them—so calm, indeed, that rumors of a strike were not confirmed by railroad officials until well into the next day. Till then, the officials chose to blame freight delays on the eastern tie-up. Reporters hurried to the scene and found it "painfully quiet," though by noon 250 cars and a dozen or more engines had accumulated in the yards.

Even before noon a B. & O official called at Governor Thomas Young's office in Columbus to ask for state troops. Finding the governor away in Cincinnati, the railroad officials wired him to come back. That afternoon a brick mason who had once been a railroad fireman volunteered to help take a freight train out at Newark. Just as it was about to move, a striking fireman held up his hand. He had lost three fingers in a railroad accident. "This," shouted another striker, "is the man whose place you're taking. This is the man who works with a hand and a half to earn a dollar and a half a day, three days in the week, for his wife and children. Are you going to take the bread out of his mouth and theirs?" The strikebreaker hesitated a moment, then jumped down amid cheers.

Governor Young came back that night and insisted on waiting for Licking County authorities to try their hand first, in line with the precedent most recently followed the year before by Governor Rutherford B. Hayes. On the morning of July 20, the calm prevailing in the Newark yards was broken by the arrival of the sheriff. The strikers readied themselves; and when the expected engine, one of the famous B. & O. "camel-backs," came puffing down and was coupled to some freight cars, the men blocked the track and swarmed over the tender. Someone recognized the strikebreaking fireman: "it's that man that was shot in the melon patch last summer!" "Well, if it ain't you can shoot me!" Amid noise and confusion, the sheriff could occasionally be heard exhorting the crowd: "I now command you, one and all, to disperse to your business and to your homes, and cease to interfere with peaceable citizens." "We don't blame you, Mr. Schofield," someone called up to him, "but we can't stand this. I've got a wife and two children now suffering for victuals. I'll stand this thing as long as I've got a drop of blood in my heart." And others cried out: "We can't bear no more; we're crowded to the wall; but we'll die right here!" When the engineer, obviously unhappy, at last put his hand to the throttle lever and started the engine forward, three men boarded the cab from an adjacent boxcar. One stopped the engine, the other two gently hauled the engineer out of the cab window onto the boxcar. The engineer bore himself with resignation. In fact, he grinned broadly. The would-be fireman slunk home, escorted by a policeman and followed up by a crowd of jeering boys.

Sheriff Schofield at once called on the governor to send state militia (an action which ruined the sheriff politically, for the people of Newark were solidly pro-strike). Governor Young ordered four companies to Newark and solemnly warned lawbreakers that he would use all his powers to protect property and the right to work. None of this shook the nerve of the strikers. They remained decorous and determined. That afternoon two drunks reeled into the yards and were promptly tossed out again by the strikers. No single individual seemed to command the Newark strikers. They followed the sense of the meeting, as Quakers might say, on such proposals as one or another of them happened to conceive and put forward. Yet they proceeded with notable coherence, as though fused by their common adversity.

Governor Young's departure from Columbus with two militia companies that night touched off no such uproar as had troubled Baltimore a few hours earlier. Two or three hundred spectators at the depot looked on glumly but peaceably. By early morning on Saturday about 170 troops had assembled at Newark, including a company which had done duty for three weeks in the previous year's labor riots. The people of Licking County resented the sending of troops, and the county commissioners pettishly refused to pay for their rations. At this, the strikers themselves volunteered to feed the soldiers. Newark businessmen subscribed liberally to the fund. As the day ended calm and cool, troops and strikers were hobnobbing in high good humor. Governor Young, however, did not join in the jollity. Giving up hope of breaking the strike that day, he called up heavy reinforcements of militia from Dayton and Cincinnati and set the zero hour at 6:00 a.m. the next day, Sunday, July 22. "Anxious to prevent the destruction of human life," he commanded the citizens of Newark to keep away from the railroad grounds at that hour.

In the spirit of their eccentric road, the men of the Erie gave the Great Strike a few new twists. For one thing, the movement on the Erie had a known leader—soon to be widely known. He was Barney J. Donahue, the sandy-haired little half-crippled brakeman who had led the protest against the July 1 cut and had been fired for his imprudent enterprise. The Erie sent its monthly pay car along the western divisions of the road just as the B. & O. strike began to make headlines. With their pittance in their pockets and an example in view, the firemen and brakemen of three western divisions met at the important junction town of Hornellsville, New York, a little before midnight on July 19. For them it proved to be a witching hour indeed. Donahue's bitter eloquence carried them into the Great Strike as of 1:00 a.m. on July 20, a deadline not revealed to the bewildered superintendent until five minutes after it had expired.

Their demands (not formally presented until the following afternoon) included other novelties. First of all, they wanted reinstatement of Donahue and a dozen or so other discharged members of the recent grievance committee. The strikers also objected to the company's late decision to charge twenty or twenty-five dollars a year as rent for the little patches of company land on which the men had for years been occupying shanties and raising vegetables. Their demand for the withdrawal of the July 1 pay cut, however, linked the Erie men firmly to the Great Strike. All these demands were rejected at once and with finality by Receiver Hugh Jewett.

The tactics of both the strikers and the company also showed Erie individualism. Donahue's men stopped passenger as well as freight trains. Wary of the Federal intervention already plaguing their B. & O. brethren, they let mail cars go through after cutting out passenger and other coaches. Otherwise, the only exception made was for a madwoman and her keeper, who were permitted to ride on to Elmira. Erie officials in their turn shrewdly halted all trains headed for Hornellsville, bringing back the passenger trains and leaving freights on sidings. This prevented the congregating of strikers and the jamming up of rolling stock at Hornellsville (though some determined strikers got through anyway on commandeered handcars).

Besides all this, the Erie strike raised a novel point of law, one which would loom monstrously in the path of organized labor for generations to come. Since the Erie was in court receivership, obstruction of its business could be (and would be) construed as contempt of court. The broadax of the court injunction hung over the neck of little Barney Donahue.

For the moment, few heeded this technicality—except for the Erie officials at New York, who quietly went about procuring warrants. More spectacular was the prospect of military high jinks. Just as he had done three weeks earlier, Governor (and Erie director) Lucius Robinson hastened to call out state militia. Six hundred of them reached Hornellsville from Elmira and Rochester early in the evening of July 21. As at Newark, Ohio, the troops seemed to find the strikers jolly good company. It may have been the militia's shaky will to fight that persuaded railroad officials to delay a showdown for another day or two, or until sterner stuff could be mustered.

As the Sabbath dawned, therefore, a truce prevailed at both Newark, Ohio, and Hornellsville, New York. Fuses burned short in both cities, nevertheless. And the fuse had already run out at Pittsburgh, the plumpest powder keg of all.

CHAPTER 8

The Crossing

AT QUARTER to five on Thursday afternoon, July 19, Mayor McCarthy of Pittsburgh left for his home, eight miles from the crowd at Twenty-eighth Street. His wife was sick, he later explained, and anyway the police at the crossing reported all quiet. Fifteen minutes later David Watt, who took a different view of affairs, hurried into City Hall and asked for fifty more police. "What will I do?" he asked, when the mayor's clerk told him there were none to spare. "If you're afraid for your property," said the clerk, "you'd better call on the sheriff, and the sheriff can call a *posse comitatus.*" "I'll do that," said Watt.

But the sheriff happened to be out of town for the day. Pending his return, Watt went back to the yard. Pitcairn had been wired the news and was now on his way back. For the present Watt could do nothing more than nurse his black eye and watch incoming freight cars accumulate in the yard. By eight o'clock more than 400 of them, many loaded with perishable meat and fruit, stood idle between the Union Depot and Twenty-eighth Street. Beyond the latter point oil cars waited in growing lines.

The sun was setting red behind the Union Depot a mile or so down the yard from the blockaded crossing. In its fiery glow, groups of people—strikers, millmen, tramps, women and children—stood talking or rambled quietly among the cars. Most of the men looked desperate enough, dressed as they were in shabby or ragged clothes, the uniform of the depression; and the slanting light of the blood-red sun left shadows like war paint on their grimy faces. Now and then a passenger train made its regular stop at the outer depot near by to take on and let off passengers. Some of the arrivals joined the crowd. Toward nine o'clock the crowd halted a livestock train; but after some palavering, the self-appointed leaders of the strike de-

131

cided to make an exception of cattle cars for the sake of the animals, and the train was waved on.

At nine-thirty that evening Adjutant General James W. Latta was summoned from a G.A.R. post meeting in Philadelphia. At the West Philadelphia depot, Pennsylvania Railroad officials showed him dispatches from Watt reporting the failure of Pittsburgh authorities to put down the disturbance. Tom Scott, visiting his daughter's family eighteen miles up the Delaware, was just now being roused from bed by a messenger with news of the strike. Not waiting for Scott's arrival, the railroad officials told Latta: "We want troops." "You'll have to take some other steps first," said Latta. "It appears the mayor has been doing something, and now you must look to the sheriff." Presently Scott joined the group and sent orders for the sheriff to be duly called upon.

At Pittsburgh Tom Scott's wish was being anticipated by the road's general counsel, John Scott (no relation). Two years before, John Scott had completed a term as United States Senator, to which he had been named in 1869 by a quiet order of Tom Scott to members of the Pennsylvania legislature. Now ex-Senator Scott made a payment on his debt by going with David Watt to Sheriff Robert H. Fife's home. They got there at about eleven. The sheriff rose from bed, hustled into his clothes and ushered his callers into the parlor. Sheriff Fife was not a peace officer of the Wild Bill Hickok or Bat Masterson stamp. On the contrary, he was a mild-mannered, soft-spoken, middle-aged gentleman who had suffered three severe heart attacks in the past year. As Fife stood there blinking through his spectacles, John Scott assured him that the railroad only wanted him to go out and make a *pro forma* call upon the crowd to disperse. If the crowd did not obey, the sheriff would then be expected to call upon the governor for state troops. Pulling on his coat, Sheriff Fife went along with his visitors.

Superintendent Pitcairn arrived at the outer depot on the train from the east a few minutes after eleven, listened to the crowd there and prudently rode on to the Union Depot. As he walked back to his office at Twenty-sixth Street, he was picked up by the sheriff's carriage. At Pitcairn's office the party found Major General Alfred L. Pearson, commander of the Sixth Division of the Pennsylvania National Guard, who had come there to investigate the situation at Adjutant General Latta's telegraphed request. Sheriff Fife, General

Pearson, David Watt, a deputy and a few loyal employees walked on up Liberty Street to Twenty-eighth. By now it was after midnight. On the way Fife noticed small groups carousing, sleeping or talking in almost every empty freight car and caboose. At Twenty-eighth, Fife thought there must be about a thousand people. Watt guessed two hundred. The sheriff knew hundreds of Pittsburghers. These people all looked strange to him. Not many seemed to be railroaders. Some might have been millmen. Others looked like tramps. The night sky was clouded over, but gaslight and railroad lanterns disclosed enough to make Fife nervous. And the sudden sound of pistol shots fired into the air made his uncertain heart jump.

Nevertheless, he mounted a pile of lumber, identified himself to the crowd, told them they were violating the law and ordered them to disperse. Someone in the crowd promptly shouted: "Go to hell, you gray-headed old son of a bitch!" Others suggested disagreeable alternatives. Fife kept talking. The company was bound to win, he told the mob. Why prolong a hopeless struggle? The law was against them; and if he could not enforce it now, he would have to find means to do it. "You and Pearson can both go to hell," yelled a leader of the mob. "Go and bring your posse, we don't care a damn for you or your posse. Mayor McCarthy and his police are with us." Others called out that the merchants were with them, that T. C. Jenkins was going to give them a thousand barrels of flour, and Alexander King was donating a thousand dollars. (Both Jenkins and King later denied this.) "You don't know these gentlemen as well as I do, or you wouldn't talk that way," protested Fife. "We know them," someone said, "and you'd better take a walk." Just then a man came running up with a piece of paper which purported to be a dispatch from the Monongahela Valley: "Hold your position until to-morrow morning, and we will send five hundred coal miners to assist you." The crowd broke into a wild cheer. Fife talked on, over increasingly foul abuse, while similar "dispatches" came from Wilkes-Barre and Mansfield. Finally Fife and his companions acted upon at least one piece of the mob's advice—they took a walk.

Back at Pitcairn's office Fife seemed for a moment to wonder if he were being railroaded into a rash action. He asked General Pearson what he ought to do, Pearson being a lawyer and the only other man present not in railroad employ. Pearson firmly advised the sheriff to call out a *posse comitatus* and to notify Adjutant General Latta of the situation. Having received the advice, Fife disregarded it. He judged (and rightly, as it turned out) that few Pittsburghers would serve on such a posse; and to bring a force of Allegheny County farmers into the city would, he felt, lead to bloodshed and everlasting bit'erness. So instead, ex-Senator Scott wrote out a dispatch calling on the governor to send state troops, and Fife signed it. Since Hartranft was known to be junketing through the West at Tom Scott's expense, copies were also sent to the principal state officers on the theory that one of them must possess delegated power to act.

Adjutant General James W. Latta was the man. Hartranft had explicitly authorized him to act in any such emergency only four days before. At midnight in the West Philadelphia depot Latta had seemed "very much disturbed." But Tom Scott's persuasive lecture on "the importance of preserving the highways of the country intact," together with an awareness of recent events on the B. & O., had by now prepared the Adjutant General's mind for Fife's call. At once he wired Pearson to call out a regiment. The telegram reached Pitcairn's office at about three-thirty, and Pearson sent word to Colonel P. N. Guthrie to assemble the Eighteenth Regiment. An hour later the little conference at Pittsburgh broke up. In the yards strikers and sympathizers still roamed around noisily; but the weary railroad officials bade good night to Pearson at the Union Depot Hotel and turned in there for some sleep. Pitcairn had scarcely stretched out on his bed when wires began coming in from President Scott and others at Philadelphia with orders for train movements—evidently on the assumption that the strike would be broken by morning. As it turned out, Pitcairn was not to get any sleep until Sunday.

No freight trains ran Friday morning after all. Pitcairn had engines fired up and crews waiting, but the crowds controlled the switches. Outsiders swarmed aboard passenger trains and rode as they pleased without paying fares, mostly back and forth between Twenty-eighth Street and Torrens Station. The conductors could do nothing about it. One conductor thought many of the intruders were millmen, because "they seemed to work somewhere where the sun did not strike them." An engineer thought most of them were there out of curiosity. Perhaps the novelty of riding free attracted many. Pitcairn claimed to recognize no more than six or eight railroad men out of all the hundreds he saw. Still, some must have had railroad experience, for they would hook locomotives onto cattle cars, run them up to the stockyards near Torrens and turn the cattle out to graze. Railroaders provided some guidance still—a brakeman seemed to have things in charge at Twenty-eighth Street—but only Hice remained in evidence of those who had been prominent on Thursday.

At Torrens 500 or 600 men, women and children, most of them "a pretty hard class," stood talking in groups on or by the tracks. Fife, Pearson and some others went up there that morning. Fife urged the crowd to disperse and read them a proclamation purporting to be from the governor (actually written by Hartranft's private secretary and issued by Latta). Jeers and the rallying cry of "Bread or blood!" went up again, and someone shouted that they would wade in blood to their knees before they would disperse. Fife warned the women and children to leave, lest they be hurt when the military arrived, but the women told him they were there to urge the men on. Pearson saw quite a few people he knew by sight. Hoping to have some influence, he climbed up on a tender and made a short speech of his own. "We don't care a damn for you and your troops!" came the reply. Afterward Fife talked to a young man who seemed to be taking the lead. "Why are you acting this way, and why is this crowd here?" asked the sheriff. "The Pennsylvania Railroad has two ends," said the young fellow, "one in Philadelphia and one in Pittsburgh. In Philadelphia they have a strong police force, and they're with the railroad. But in Pittsburgh they have a weak force, and it's a mining and manufacturing district, and we can get all the help we want from the laboring elements, and we've determined to make the strike here." "Where do you live?" asked Fife. "In the eastern part of the state," said the rioter. "Are you a railroader?" "No, I'm a laboring man."

The *Pittsburgh Leader* came out that day with an astonishing editorial headed "The Talk of the Desperate." "This may be the beginning of a great civil war in this country, between labor and capital," it began. "It only needs that the strikers . . . should boldly attack and rout the troops sent to quell them—and they could easily do it if they tried. . . . The workingmen everywhere would all join and help ... The laboring people, who mostly constitute the militia, will not take up arms to put down their brethren. Will capital, then, rely on the United States army? Pshaw! These ten or fifteen thousand available men would be swept from our path like leaves in the whirlwind. The workingmen of this country can capture and hold it, if they will only stick together . . . Even if so-called law and order should beat them down in blood . . . we would, at least, have our revenge on the men who have coined our sweat and muscles into millions for themselves, while they think dip is good enough butter for us." After several hundred words of this, the *Leader* sanctimoniously assured its readers that it was all "a faithful re-production of what a representative workingman said on the subject this morning." "It will be seen," the *Leader* commented, "that he is really a communist."

In such an atmosphere—and encouraged further by a telegram from Barney Donahue at Hornellsville, New York, reporting that the men of the Erie had struck and were with them in spirit—the strikers' committee met Superintendent Pitcairn on the platform of the Union Depot and presented the men's demands as agreed upon the night before. Vice-President Cassatt, who had arrived in Pittsburgh that morning, came out to listen. Pitcairn read the paper over and handed it to him. After Cassatt read it, he handed it back. "Have no further talk with them," he said. "They've asked for things we can't grant them at all. It isn't worth while to discuss the matter." "I can't possibly send such a paper to Mr. Scott," Pitcairn told the men. And so the committee departed.

By his own lights, Cassatt would have been a fool to yield an inch when he knew that the Commonwealth of Pennsylvania was committed to break the freight blockade by military force. The process had already begun. After ordering out Colonel Guthrie's regiment early that morning, General Pearson had come down to the city, managed to stop the presses of two morning papers and inserted notices of the call to arms. Unlike Baltimore, Pittsburgh's militia had no prearranged alarm signal; press notices and the exertions of individual officers were the only means of getting the men together. Furthermore, some men coming in by train were put off by strikers and strike sympathizers. Several excuses could thus be pleaded by those who chose not to show up for a disagreeable and unpopular duty. Guthrie's 326 men had been ordered to march to the Union Depot by seven; all considered, it spoke well for their fidelity that two thirds were on hand by noon. Pearson sent Guthrie's command to Torrens, fearing that the crowd there might try to burn the stockyards. Convinced by now that one regiment would not be enough, Pearson had already called out the rest of the division. Those other troops were to open Twenty-eighth Street.

So Guthrie waited expectantly out at Torrens for the freights to start coming. The crowd of 1,200 made no demonstration, did not even hiss. Andrew Hice assured Guthrie that the strikers would resort to no intimidation or obstruction of any kind. He confidently promised to stake the success of the strike on the company's inability to find crews. A few minutes later a train came up from Pittsburgh heavy-laden with toughs, most of them apparently from out of town and all of them belligerent. As soon as they scrambled off, trouble began. One of them, a man known as "Monkey John" Richardson, stood on top of a car and slanged Guthrie loudly and systematically. The crowd grew threatening on three occasions during Guthrie's two-day vigil, but each time they were pacified bloodlessly by the troops' determined advance with fixed bayonets. Despite his success as a peacemaker, Guthrie presently began to get impatient for word of effective action down the line at Twenty-eighth Street.

The trouble there was that only a fraction of the other units had shown up. By midafternoon of Friday not a man of the Fourteenth Regiment had yet arrived. But Captain Breck and twenty-five men of his battery were on hand with their two artillery pieces, and Colonel Howard had fifty men of the Nineteenth Regiment ready. So Pearson started them up Liberty Street on the way to Twenty-eighth. It was a cool day for July. The breeze was from the north, and a cloud shadow now and then drifted past. At this crucial moment Pearson drew back. He explained to the railroad officials that seventy-five men were not enough to overawe the crowd at first sight. The troops would have to fire. With artillery the crossing could surely be cleared, but only at great cost in lives. The implacable Cassatt thought Pearson ought to go ahead anyway. John Scott and Vice-President William Thaw of the subsidiary Fort Wayne road were Pittsburgh men, and the prospect of such slaughter appalled them. At their urging, Pearson recalled the troops.

While the troops waited on the Union Depot platform, Pearson and the railroad officials reached the conclusion that Pittsburgh militia could not be trusted to fight their fellow townsmen—in some cases, their fellow workers or relatives. Cassatt pointed out that Philadelphia militia could be brought in quickly by special train and that they would not take the strikers' part. The others fell in with the suggestion. Telegrams urging that course went out from the railroad officials to Tom Scott and from Pearson to Adjutant General Latta. That evening Latta called out the First Division of the Pennsylvania National Guard, commanded by Major General Robert M. Brinton, and, on Brinton's assurance that his men were all right for any emergency, ordered them to Pittsburgh. Some of Brinton's command were away on vacation, others could not be reached in time, but General Brinton managed to have 600 men, nearly half his total strength, on trains by two o'clock Saturday morning. Summer soldiers though they were, and most of them workingmen at that, almost half were veterans of the Civil War. Brinton himself had served through the war, rising from private to brevet lieutenant colonel. Class sympathy with the strikers would therefore have to contend with the war-instilled habit of discipline. It would also come up against an intercity rivalry of long standing.

Pittsburgh's quarrel with Philadelphia went back at least thirty years. In 1846 Philadelphia's influence in the legislature denied the B. & O. a right of way to Pittsburgh. Pittsburghers held an indignation meeting against "Philadelphia capitalists," and the *Pittsburgh Gazette* condemned "the bitter hostility of Philadelphia to our interests in this respect." A Philadelphia reporter wrote home from Pittsburgh that "not only the citizens but the merchants generally are now greatly exasperated against Philadelphia." A generation later, in 1877, Pittsburghers regarded Philadelphia as the seat of Tom Scott's empire, and they were sure to look upon Philadelphia militia, more than any others, as myrmidons of the oppressor. The failure of John Scott and William Thaw to warn Cassatt of this—or perhaps Cassatt's indifference to a warning—can only be put down as one of the vagaries of minds under stress.

By one o'clock on the morning of Saturday, July 21, when Adjutant General Latta arrived at the Union Depot on a fast train from the East, Colonel Gray had finally reported with what he could muster of his Fourteenth Regiment. Together with Breck's battery and Howard's Nineteenth Regiment, this made 350 Pittsburgh troops available to Pearson at the depot, besides 250 now under Guthrie at Torrens. While waiting for the Philadelphia militia, Pearson moved the Pittsburgh troops out to Twenty-eighth Street, choosing two-thirty in the morning as about the quietest hour possible.

Out of the east, between the converging valleys of the Allegheny and the Monongahela, a great ridge ran toward the city of Pittsburgh. The ridge loomed steeply over the Pennsylvania Railroad yards, which lay by its northern or Allegheny side. Half a mile before reaching the actual juncture of the two rivers, the ridge sank down to a camel-back elevation, on part of which stood the courthouse and other county buildings. Thence the hill descended to the flat triangular space which formed the heart of the city. At the end of the great central ridge stood the Union Depot, a square substantial brick building, part railroad station and part hotel. Once a bright red, it had long since been mellowed by Pittsburgh smoke, like an old meerschaum pipe, to a rich chocolate brown. Facing it across a cobblestone square towered a huge slate-sided grain elevator, one of Pittsburgh's landmarks. The tracks of the railroad yard fanned out behind the depot in an intricate network of rails, contained on one side by the smoke-blackened hillside and on the other by Liberty Avenue. From the Union Depot at Eleventh Street eastward to the outer depot at Twenty-eighth, the steepness of the great hill ruled out the extension of side streets beyond the tracks. At Twenty-eighth, however, the ridge sagged enough to let a road cross the tracks and run slanting up and over to the Monongahela side. On the hill stood the dingy brick West Penn Hospital, from which a private road came down to join Twenty-eighth Street near the bottom.

As expected, not many people were there. Gray posted his men halfway up the hillside, Breck's two six-pounders commanded the crossing, and Howard's men swept back the small crowd without difficulty. Amid "considerable howling," Pearson told the crowd that he and his men meant business, that the Philadelphia troops were due soon and that the crowd must stay off the tracks. To cries for bread Pearson replied: "I'll send you a carload of bread if you go away and let these tracks alone." Then he jumped on a locomotive and returned to the Union Depot, leaving the brigade commander, a hardware merchant named Joseph Brown, in charge.

Brigadier General Brown had made an excellent war record; "a braver man never breathed," said Colonel Guthrie afterward. But Brown was high-strung, garrulous and fussy. Lately he had been ill, and he was ill now. Moreover, the call had surprised him in mid-morning on the way to his store, and he still wore his civilian suit. This may have added to his uneasiness. And Pearson had been right in doubting the enthusiasm of Pittsburgh troops for such work. All of this helps explain the rapid deterioration of discipline among the troops at the crossing.

By the time Saturday morning dawned fair and cool, Brown's men had left their arms stacked under guard on the hillside and were chatting cosily with the citizens, eating hardtack with them, walking up and down the street with them, behaving in general—as a passing regular army lieutenant from the Allegheny Arsenal saw it—"as though they were going to have a party." "You won't shoot work-ingmen," people said to them. Occasionally Brown and his officers tried to clear the crossing by marching a rank of men across it and along Twenty-eighth Street a few yards. But the crowd would flow good-humoredly around and in back of the troops even as the man-euver went forward. In midafternoon a Pittsburgh lawyer talked with one of the militiamen on the hillside. "You may be called upon to clear the tracks down there," said the lawyer. "They may call on me," said the soldier, "and they may call pretty damn loud before they will clear the tracks."

The militiaman was a true Pittsburgher. Just about everyone in town, high and low, sympathized with the strikers and thought Sheriff Fife had been too hasty in calling for troops. After all, total injuries so far consisted of an official's bruised eye, a brakeman's aching ribs and a sheriff's hurt feelings. The editor of the *Dispatch* thought there was "a good deal of farce" about calling out the militia on such trivial grounds, though he feared the consequences. The editor of the *Leader* stopped quoting the "talk of the desper-ate." Perhaps the news of Baltimore's riot worked this change. At any rate, the *Leader* alluded a bit nervously to that tragedy and laid it to "the inbred lawlessness of southern blood." Pennsylvania troops, it felt sure, "will endure insult and even stone-throwing be-fore they will shed blood"—not that "either insult or violence will be offered them."

Nevertheless, a feverish excitement possessed the city. Hundreds of people at the Twenty-eighth Street crossing watched the Philadelphia troops of General Brinton come in from the east early that afternoon in two trains bearing the marks of heavy stoning by mobs at Harrisburg, Johnstown and Altoona. Stones and half-bricks littered the cowcatchers and car roofs, and rifles protruded from broken windows as the trains puffed slowly past. The hillside, a natural grandstand, was black with spectators, men, women and children, old and young, some of them sitting on the steps of their hilltop homes. The people on the hillside—including the Pittsburgh militia who stood or sat among them—were almost all mere bystanders with no intention of mixing into the action below, should any develop. None did develop at this juncture. Far from attacking the troop trains, many in the crowd sent up a cheer as they passed, hoping, no doubt, to win the good will of the Philadelphia men.

As they rode down the yard to the Union Depot, the Philadelphia soldiers saw more than 2,000 cars and locomotives lying idle around them. Water from melting ice trickled from refrigerator cars full of meat for the Eastern market. The railroad company had disposed of large quantities of fruits and other perishable commodities, but much still remained, doomed to spoilage. In other cars were all the necessities and most of the luxuries of nineteenth-century civilization: clothing, furniture, books, whisky, silverware, oil, coal, flour, machinery, carpets, ornaments—everything from cribs to coffins.

These idle cars, this lost business, weighed on the mind of Vice-President Cassatt as he watched the 600 new troops come into the depot, gulp down sandwiches and coffee, add another ten rounds of ammunition to the ten they already carried and then sit around waiting for orders. Cassatt, chafing at the delay, found an added annoyance scarcely endurable: a Pittsburgh steel manufacturer named James Park met him around four o'clock and urged him not to send the troops out at all that day, since most Pittsburgh workingmen had Saturday afternoon off. "I think I know the temper of our men pretty well," said Park, "and you would be wise not to do anything until Monday." Besides, he added, "you can't depend entirely on our Pittsburgh militia in case of a riot."

"The Philadelphia regiment won't fire over the heads of the mob, if there is a mob," retorted Cassatt.

"If there's going to be firing," said Park, "you ought to have at least ten thousand men, and I doubt if even that many could quell the mob that would be brought down on us."

"We must have our property," said Cassatt stonily. He took out his watch. "We have now lost an hour and a half's time." At that, Park gave up and went home.

Cassatt was still not left in peace. William Thaw took up the argument for a delay, even putting his views in writing. John Scott came into the office just then and took Cassatt's side, after which Thaw tore up his note. Even so, at the last minute Thaw made a strong personal appeal. But Cassatt insisted that affairs were in the hands of the state officials. "It's their problem," he said with finality.

General Brinton, who had got a good look at what was in store at the crossing, asked General Pearson if he still thought the plan was wise. Both Pearson and Latta stuck by it. But since Brinton seemed to doubt that General Brown's men had the crossing as well in hand as had been assumed, Pearson agreed to go along and "look over the ground." Cassatt promised that double-headers would move out as soon as the tracks were cleared. In a last-minute briefing, Brinton told his men: "No matter what is done to us—even if they spit in our faces—I don't want a shot fired. But if they attempt any personal violence, we have the right to defend ourselves, and we shall do it."

The troops marched out in a column of fours, a rear detachment pulling two shiny Gatling guns laboriously over the ties. After protracted efforts, Sheriff Fife had managed to press seventeen deputies into service, including members of his family; and these civilians, carrying warrants for the arrest of eleven alleged ringleaders, walked two by two ahead of the troops. Superintendent Pitcairn went along to point out the malefactors, and years later a Philadelphia soldier recalled the imposing spectacle of Alexander Cassatt in a tall white hat, stalking along the tops of a line of freight cars. A large crowd had gathered around the depot, some looking over the fences into the yards, some already inside and roaming the tracks. As the troops marched along, a growing throng followed close behind.

The crowd in front also grew steadily denser. At Twenty-fourth Street, Pearson left Colonel E. Decius Loud and the 300 men of his Second Brigade to guard the hundreds of loaded cars standing there; Loud threw out a skirmish line and drove the crowd back far enough to permit the coupling of cars and the making up of trains. For a while the crowd opened before the rest of the troops as they continued toward the Twenty-eighth Street crossing. Amid much hooting there sounded a few cheers; for the soldiers made a stirring picture in the afternoon sunlight, marching along in regular order, dressed in fine uniforms of blue or red or gray, one outfit distinguished by black-plumed hats. Their rifles, polished to a bright gleam, flashed and glittered handsomely.

At the crossing itself and well beyond, a crowd of from 5,000 to 7,000 jammed the tracks and surrounding ground. Most of those in the yards proper seemed to be millmen or tramps, many boisterous, some "half tight." As James Park and William Thaw had feared, millmen had come by the hundreds as the plants shut down. Pittsburgh millmen usually wore dark clothes, but some of the noisiest of these men wore light-colored pants, and two of them wore velveteen coats. This led one spectator to identify them as strangers, probably tramps. On the hill was a cross section of the city's population, including women and children, workers and professional men. Most were there for the reason given by a gas company solicitor: "I had nothing more to do that day, and I thought I would come up and see what the railroad men were doing." A lawyer said: "I had never seen a strike before, and I went up to see what it looked like."

When Fife and his posse reached the crowd at the crossing, Pitcairn failed to see any of the men for whom warrants were out. Fife promptly washed his hands of the affair, since he did not himself know the men. But the mere presence of the sheriff set off an uproar of jeers and curses; and one particularly belligerent man upbraided Fife so boisterously that one of the officers had to propel the ranter forcibly into the crowd, whence he raved and bellowed incontinently. General Pearson, meanwhile, had pushed through the mob and up the hillside in search of General Brown. Brown could not be found, but Colonel Howard of the Nineteenth Regiment turned up on the hospital road. To Pearson's questions he replied gloomily: "You can place little dependence on the troops of your division; some have thrown down their arms, and others have left, and I fear the situation very much." Privately Pearson felt no more hopeful. "Meeting an enemy on the field of battle," he said later, "you go there to kill. The more you kill, and the quicker you do it, the better. But here you had men with fathers and brothers and relatives mingled in the crowd of rioters. The sympathy of the people, the sympathy of the troops, my own sympathy, was with the strikers proper. We all felt that those men were not receiving enough wages." Keeping his thoughts to himself, Pearson ordered Colonel Howard to ready his command for action in case of a clash. Then the apprehensive general headed downhill to explain the impasse to Adjutant General Latta and request more troops.

Meanwhile, General Brinton's command, marching along the tracks below, had come up against the close-packed crowd at the Twenty-eighth Street crossing. In the words of sundry witnesses, the troops recoiled "like jumping up against a rock," the crowd stood "right like a wall," there was "no give." "Hold the fort," yelled the audience on the hillside to the crowd below; "stand to your post!" The advice was superfluous, since the sheer density of the crowd prevented a retreat. Among the Philadelphia troops one soldier collapsed from sunstroke or a fit and, stiffened in spasm, was carried off to the telegraph office two blocks back.

The great ridge loomed over the crowd and the soldiers like a long, dark comber, always about to break, yet never breaking, giving the scene an aspect of grotesque unbalance, as in a dream landscape where the laws of nature fail. The troops who found themselves in this nightmare spot had already been rudely roused from civilian slumber, hustled off to an unforeseen and unpredictable duty, cursed and stoned along the way, hastily and scantily fed and turned out onto a hot grid of tracks with a howling crowd on all sides. Yet, astonishingly, they still preserved the aplomb of veterans. As General Pearson came down to the yard and shouldered his way through the crowd, he saw the Philadelphians perform an evolution that would have done them credit on a parade ground. At Brinton's command, the First Regiment's column of twos faced right, parallel to the tracks. One rank stayed on the Liberty Street side of the main tracks, while the other swept across to the foot of the ridge. Then ten men of the Washington Grays and twenty of the Weccaco Legion marched along the tracks between the two parallel ranks, like a piston in a cylinder. In effect, Brinton's men had formed a hollow square, a maneuver much talked of during the late Civil War but seldom if ever achieved. The Grays dragged up their two Gatlings and aimed them up the tracks. Within the square Sheriff Fife stood nervously, while Robert Pitcairn sat on a plank in the middle, chatting with another railroad official. Brinton asked Pearson for further instructions, and after a moment's hesitation Pearson said: "The tracks must be cleared." Then he turned and walked back along the tracks toward the telegraph office, for the purpose (he told Pitcairn) of requesting more troops.

A quiet order was passed to the blue-clad east rank to advance up the tracks with fixed bayonets. The men stepped back a pace, lowered the shiny points and moved forward into the crowd. Those before them tried to get away, but could not break through the rearward mass. Several felt the steel enter their flesh; a machinist got a bayonet in the back. Others instinctively grabbed the bayonets to turn them aside, and some soldiers lost hold of their rifles. Howls, curses, yells erupted. "Now," said an officer plaintively, "why don't you men go back?"

A couple of small boys, eight or ten years old, had been playing around in a sand house to the left of the tracks. Finding some pebbles there, the boys flung them out over the heads of the shouting crowd. "Quit that, boys," said a railroad constable; "there'll be trouble here." Behind a watch box on the hillside opposite, three or four teen-age boys stooped and picked up such objects as were loose and handy. They let fly with a stone or two, then half a dozen clods, lumps of coal, sticks, finally a couple of old shoes—perhaps offered up to the cause by their excited owner. Before the watch box volley had slackened, other people along the hillside were joining in. One young man raked together a little pile of stones and commenced to pitch them systematically into the ranks of the Philadelphians. "Don't do that," said a detective nervously; "they'll fire up here." "They dasn't shoot," said the young fellow, and he pulled a revolver from his hip pocket. By now missiles were raining down on the troops from all sides. To Robert Pitcairn, sitting aghast in the hollow square, it seemed as though they "clouded the horizon." On the left-hand side of the tracks stood four loaded coal cars crowded with spectators. From these, testified a witness, "the coal just appeared to be raising off the cars and dropping on the soldiers." Two or three soldiers staggered, others got suddenly sick from the sun or fear. One "had the whole side of his face knocked off by a brick." Another dropped down for a moment, struggled to his feet, leaned on his gun and began wiping blood from his face. His black-plumed hat lay among the cinders. An officer was jarred by a chunk of wood thrown from behind the watch box by a boy of sixteen or seventeen.

"Shoot!" yelled a rioter in sudden crazy defiance. Others took up the taunt: "Shoot, you sons of bitches, why don't you shoot!" A loud crack or two sounded near the watch box. The Fourth of July was scarcely two weeks gone, and Haines and Company were still advertising "Fire Crackers, Torpedoes, Percussion Caps, and Pistols at bottom prices." Whether or not some of those playthings made the first noise, real shots almost immediately issued from the crowd. The young man on the hillside fired his revolver; a man wearing a cap drew a pistol and fired at the troops. A shot came from a man on a coal car, another from behind a small house on the hospital road. The crowd at the crossing grabbed at a soldier's musket; the soldier stepped back and fired into the crowd. Everyone was yelling, and witnesses later disagreed on whether or not any officers gave a command to fire; none of the officers admitted doing so, but almost all freely said they would have, if firing had not commenced of itself. General Brinton felt that his men had properly acted on his standing order to defend themselves. At any rate, a rattle of musketry began at the head of the formation and then spread along the sides irregularly, two or three shots a second, like a string of firecrackers. The crowd was struck dumb for a moment. Men fell silent in mid-curse, their mouths agape. Civil War veterans in the crowd dropped flat, still governed by old battle reflexes.

At first the troops fired impartially in all directions outward from their hollow square. The soldier with the battered face fired, wiped the blood from his eyes and fired again in aimless anger. Then, for some reason—perhaps because the first volley of stones had come from that direction—the Philadelphians centered their fire on the hillside. The rank facing Liberty Street turned about and fired over their comrades' heads at the ridge. Most of the people up there had thought themselves out of it, had been looking down on the spectacle with lofty detachment, participating only vocally, if at all. It took a few seconds for them to realize their danger. Some stood frozen while bullets kicked up puffs of dust around them. Eventually most of the crowd ran up over the ridge or took refuge in the little gullies and ravines that scored the hillside.

Some, however, missed the last chance that life was to offer them.

How many died in those few seconds cannot be determined. The
Pittsburgh Commercial Gazette estimated a day or two later that
about twenty were killed in the Twenty-eighth Street area. Ten
deaths are certain. Some of the wounded, carried away by friends
and not reported, may have died later on from their injuries. One
sixteen-year-old boy, last seen at that point just before the firing, was
still missing ten days later. An eighteen-year-old Pittsburgh militiaman died of bullet wounds on the hospital grounds. Fourteen-year-
old John Ruhl was listed as dead in the first reports, a bullet having
smashed into his right cheek and out through his left eye; but he
pulled through (surviving, indeed, long enough to read with his
one good eye about the Wagner Act, the unionization of steel and
other triumphs of organized labor under Franklin Roosevelt's New
Deal). Of the positively known dead whose occupations were listed,
only one or two were railroaders, but all were workingmen.

Many more were wounded, including several small children. One
bullet shattered the knee of a little girl, four years old, who lived on
the hill. A lawyer saw her from his refuge in a near-by ditch, pulled
her to cover and tied a handkerchief around her leg. Later that
night doctors cut her leg off, after which she died, or so the lawyer
heard. At least thirty, possibly as many as sixty or seventy people
were hurt seriously, but the exact number will never be known.
Since the coroner dealt only with deaths, no official count was made.
Newspaper reports contain obvious duplications. John Ruhl seems
to have turned up three or four times in the same list under various
approximations to his right name. Estimates at the scene were thrown
off by the flopping down of unhurt veterans. Certainly there was
blood and pain on the hillside; certainly the firing which cut short
some lives also twisted others and made them ugly.

Fifteen of the Philadelphia troops were hurt. None were killed.
Through the firing, the Pittsburgh militia stood fast on the hillside
at carry arms and only broke for cover when they saw "the dreaded
Gatling guns" working to the front. Consequently they suffered more
heavily. How much more is uncertain.

All this misery had been set going in a matter of four or five
minutes' gunfire shortly after five o'clock. As soon as the crowd started
running away, Brinton shouted "Cease fire!" This having no effect, he
and several of his officers moved up and down the lines, repeating
the order, striking up muskets with their swords, pulling men back-

ward into the hollow square. At last the racket sputtered out, and there was comparative silence.

Down at Twenty-sixth Street, with the moral support of Colonel Loud's detachment, David Watt had got steam up in a dozen or so locomotives with crews standing by, ready to take out double-header freights. The crackle of musketry two blocks away cut through the puffing and hissing of the engines and drew Watt's attention up the tracks. There he saw a panicky mob stampeding toward him. With commendable self-possession, Watt had the gate opened out to Liberty Street, while Colonel Loud threw a detachment across the tracks, thus shunting the human herd out of the yards. Nevertheless, the firing, the excitement, the lateness of the hour all combined to give the waiting train crews a fine excuse for refusing to go out. Watt gave up hope of breaking the freight blockade that day, though passenger trains (except for the five-twenty) continued to run through the crowds, which willingly gave way. One witness to the firing went home a few minutes afterward on the six o'clock train.

At the moment of the firing General Pearson stood at a window of the railroad telegraph office on the corner of Twenty-sixth and Liberty. Roundhouse racket and the clicking of the telegraph keys masked the sound of gunfire. Pearson's first chilling suspicion of the tragedy came from a cry in Liberty Street. People began streaming past, some carrying dead and wounded. Alexander Cassatt rushed in with confirmation of the general's fears, having seen the slaughter from the roundhouse roof. Cassatt seemed chiefly concerned with the safety of railroad property, the locomotives, the workshop machinery, the goods-laden freight cars. Robert Pitcairn followed with further details, and at Pearson's summons General Brinton presently came in to report. Pearson had known slaughter before, more fearful than anything at Twenty-eighth Street. Congress had voted him a medal of honor for bravery in the Wilderness, at Cold Harbor and in the Petersburg lines. This was different. He shrank from battle against unarmed friends and neighbors, women and children. In his agony he looked beseechingly to Cassatt for guidance: what should be the next move? Should the troops hold the crossing, occupy the hill or take over the roundhouse? Before Cassatt could answer, Pitcairn told his superior meaningfully: "I don't think you have any opinion." Cassatt took the cue. "I have nothing to do with the movements of the troops," said he, "I know nothing about that whatever." General Brinton was not so shy. The line was clear, Brinton told the officials, and they were now at liberty to send out their double-headers. Cassatt and Pitcairn had to confess that crews were no longer to be had. In that case, Brinton said vehemently, his troops could not stand around at the crossing like dummies; they should either be given free rein against the crowd or be moved to a more tenable position; and if the latter (as Pearson's face told him it must be), Brinton favored occupying the Twenty-sixth Street roundhouse for the night. Pearson gratefully adopted the idea: the roundhouse it would be then.

At the crossing the Philadelphia troops held sway. A few lay prostrate from exhaustion or sunstroke, and their comrades doused them with water, while small parties of citizens moved about on the hillside succoring the civilian wounded. The firing had jolted most onlookers from passive ill will into fighting hatred; but as the crowd reassembled, it hovered prudently about the corner of Liberty and Twenty-eighth rather than at the crossing. When some bold spirits came closer, raging at the Philadelphians, the command to bring pieces to the ready scattered them immediately. The Pittsburgh militia were no help, now or later. Most of them had thrown down their arms and gone home—or joined the mob. At Pearson's order the rest of the local troops occupied the long wooden transfer sheds that ran from Twenty-third Street to Twenty-fourth. And as darkness settled along the tracks and crept up the hillside, the Philadelphians themselves retired to the "lower roundhouse" at the corner of Twenty-sixth and Liberty.

At the news of the slaughter at Twenty-eighth Street the whole city went mad. A Philadelphia soldier in civilian clothes, carrying dispatches along Liberty Street, heard the crowd yelling that "they wanted every damned Philadelphia soldier to go home in a box, that they would tear them to pieces." A Philadelphia militia surgeon was shocked to find Pittsburgh doctors in hearty sympathy with the mob. Local politicians followed the mob or, in one or two cases, led it. Businessmen—not all but most—joined in the outcry against the great monopoly now stained (they felt) with innocent blood. Most of all, "it was evident"—at least to the *Dispatch* reporter—"that the whole labor interest of Pittsburgh was about to fight the Pennsylvania Railroad." The street crowds of young men and boys, many fifteen and under, were heavily weighted with factory workers from the South Side. A delegation of 600 workingmen marched in from Temperance-ville with full band and colors. From at least one factory that had not shut down for the afternoon, men rushed home for pistols, muskets, butcher knives and whatever other weapons might be found. By eight o'clock as the night deepened, an immense crowd yelling with rage, packed Liberty Street from Twenty-fifth to Twenty-seventh and jammed Twenty-sixth Street halfway to Penn Avenue. Those outside the superintendent's office, next door to the roundhouse, howled for Pitcairn and Watt. "Get them out of there," they yelled, "we've got coffins for them." But the railroad officials had already gone to the Union Depot Hotel.

City authorities did not strain themselves to put down the mob. According to Mayor McCarthy, the railroad officials had told him the day before that they could get along thenceforward without his police; and now he took them at their word. No police were regu-larly on duty in the city until eight o'clock at night, and McCarthy had made no effort on Friday and Saturday to recruit an emergency force. As the mob gathered near the roundhouse, loudly claiming the mayor as an ally, General Pearson wired McCarthy to come and talk sense into them. McCarthy did not show up. At the suggestion of railroad officials, however, McCarthy sent a couple of men out along Liberty Street to close all saloons from Eleventh to Thirtieth. Most saloon-keepers complied with the request, but many in the crowd managed to get half-drunk anyway.

McCarthy also sent word to the proprietors of gunshops and pawn-shops to hide or remove their weapons. A couple of hundred rioters banged on the doors of Johnston's gunshop; but Johnston, by doling out a few muskets one by one, managed to stall the mob off till sev-eral night patrolmen arrived and turned it away with a show of force. The mob, continually augmented by squads of South Siders, swept on up Liberty Street and cleaned out Shute's store. Another crowd broke into the militia armory on Market Street and made off with all but a few arms which had been hidden away. At James Bown and Son's, the city's leading cutlery, gun and sporting-goods store, were sixty feet of cases and a large store window, all full of arms and ammunition. Young Bown and a couple of employees struggled to make ready for the mob, clearing out the window display, putting up screens, blocking the doors with a couple of scantlings and moving what arms they could down to the magazine in the cellar. Before many of the arms had been put away, a gang of fifty or so "half-grown boys," some South Side workingmen, a few respectable citizens and a number of thieves and tramps marched down Wood Street with a few old muskets, a makeshift battering ram and a drum. The eight policemen outside Bown's were helpless against them. For a moment the ram thudded against the door; and then, to the dismay of young Bown, who in the illogic of excitement had given no thought to the vulnerability of glass, the mob crashed in through the big store windows and thundered through the store. It sounded to the frightened Bown as though "bedlam had broken loose." Within minutes the gun cases were cleaned out. The mob got away with more than 400 guns, many of costly make, besides pistols, powder and carving knives. They also took spoons, fishing tackle, postage stamps and other items of dubious military value. In the opinion of one police officer, the mob was mainly bent on plunder. "I don't think," said he, "that many of those guns ever went into the riot."

On the western edge of the city, along Penn Avenue, stood the warehouse of the Allegheny Arsenal, a major arms depot of the United States Army. Here were more than 36,000 stand of rifles and muskets, besides thousands of carbines and revolvers, a number of cannon and two large powder magazines filled to capacity. To get all this the mob needed only to brush aside twenty soldiers and sweep over a low retaining wall surmounted by a frail wooden picket fence. Several months earlier, some premonition of trouble had led the arsenal's commandant, Major A. R. Buffington, to break up the prepared small arms ammunition, storing the powder and consigning the balls to the lead pile; perhaps he had read General Sherman's speech about the menace of mob violence. Nevertheless, the makings of much trouble lay thus accessible, and meanwhile Buffington's twenty men retained only forty rounds between them suitable to their own Springfield muzzle-loaders—two shots apiece. One of General Pearson's first reactions to news of the outbreak at Twenty-eighth Street had been to send Buffington a warning telegram. That evening Buffington waited apprehensively. All he could do in preparation was to lock the gates and run a loaded six-pounder up to them. A little past ten o'clock a shouting mob marched up to the gate with drums beating, heedless of the ease with which it could have pushed down and walked over the picket fence not far away. Not wanting to "flourish a red handkerchief in the face of the bull," Buffington kept his force out of sight. All the crowd saw at the gate was the gun, a sentry and Buffington in civilian clothes. "Boys," said Buffington, "what's the matter?" "Philadelphia troops have fired into a crowd down here and killed a lot of women and children, and we come to get arms to fight them." "It's a sad thing," said Buffington, "but it is impossible for me to help you." The major kept up the talk as long as he could, hoping for some distraction; and miraculously it came—a cry of fire down the street, which drew the mob away. "The guns are spiked," shouted a ringleader; "we'll all go." Buffington saw no more of the mob. But the encounter left him shaken, or so we may suppose from his curious conduct on the following morning.

For a while after the Philadelphia soldiers had filed into the lower roundhouse and posted guards at its windows, quiet prevailed around it and the other railroad buildings at the corner of Twenty-sixth and Liberty—the adjacent telegraph and superintendent's office, the enginehouses, the paint, upholstery, carpenter and machine shops. As General Pearson stared gloomily down from the second-story window of Superintendent Pitcairn's office, he saw an express wagon rolling along Liberty Street with a hot supper from the Union Depot Hotel for him and his fellow officers. He was able to deduce its errand from the fragments of crockery presently pitched through the window by the swelling crowd outside. "After that," recalled Pearson reminiscing under oath, "an Irishman—I know he was an Irishman by the cut of his jib and his language—drove up on a bob-tailed, lantern-jawed horse and made a very inflammatory speech to the mob. . . . One of them pulled a piece of board off a fence and struck the horse over the back, and the last we could see of this Irish orator he was going down Liberty Avenue." The mob's reaction, it presently became clear, expressed not so much disagreement with the orator's sentiments as impatience with further talk. If words alone could kill, life in the roundhouse would already have been extinct. The crowd at the gate kept "making faces like fiends and yelling." Said Captain John Ryan of the State Fencibles:

They were blackguarding us in the most scandalous manner. Men, women and half-grown boys. It was the most outrageous language I ever heard in my life. When we would go up and attempt to drive them away, they would just stand and spit at us, and call us all sorts of names. But my men stood it, and walked up and down, and paid no attention to them.

Now pistols began flashing in the darkness. Several balls whined through the broken windows of the telegraph office and lodged in the ceiling. Two sentries were nicked by pistol fire, after which Colonel Loud ran the Gatlings into position to sweep the crowd. "I don't think we can stand it any longer," said a corporal to Captain Ryan, "unless you give us permission to kill some of those people out there." "If I get permission," said Ryan, "I will give it to you very quick." The application passed up the chain of command to Pearson. But Pearson turned it down. Liberty Avenue, where most of the active rioters were, ran along below the level of the yards. The troublemakers, Pearson believed, could easily get down out of range, leaving the less active spectators on Twenty-sixth Street, including many women and children, as the only target. "I turned away perfectly disgusted," recalled Captain Ryan. General Brinton felt the same way. "I can't stand it," he told Pearson, "we must defend ourselves."

General Pearson could not stand it either. But neither could he stand the thought of "defending" himself by killing his friends and neighbors. He found himself in an intolerable and insoluble dilemma; and like most men in such a case, he fled. Also like most men, he tried to disguise flight as duty—disguise it not so much to others as to himself. He announced his intention of going to find Mayor McCarthy, "which would do more good than our bullets would." When Brinton remarked that the men needed both bullets and rations if there were to be a siege, Pearson seized upon this as a more soldierly errand. He would go down to the Union Depot for provisions and ammunition and would be back in an hour, he told Brinton. Meanwhile Brinton was to take command. "Do you have any new instructions?" asked Brinton. "Hold on until I return," said Pearson.

Pearson never came back. He and his staff, in full uniform, walked unmolested between the long lines of freight cars which stretched to the Union Depot a mile away. At ten o'clock, just as Pearson walked into the depot, the telegrapher reported that communication with the roundhouse had been cut off. Up in Adjutant General Latta's room on the second floor of the hotel, Pearson found a nervous group of state and railroad officials. From outside came the noise of men marching about with drums and fifes. Latta and the others were astonished at Pearson's arrival unharmed. They could not get the requested supplies through to the besieged roundhouse, they told him, and it would be impossible for Pearson himself to get back. Parties of rioters, they said, had ransacked the hotel from cellar to roof with the object of finding Pearson and hanging him. Pearson scoffed at the idea. "If anyone is hanged," he said jokingly, "somebody will be hurt." "This is no time for levity," snapped Latta, "the situation is very serious, and your life isn't worth a penny. You've been blamed for the whole thing, and you're doing an injury by remaining in command of the troops." "What do you want me to do?" asked Pearson. "Is General Brinton in command out at the roundhouse?" asked Latta. "He is." "Then I think the best thing is for you to go away from here." "Do you wish me to change my headquarters?" asked Pearson. "If so, will I go to the Monongahela House?" "No," said Latta, "you'll be just as bad off there as here." One of Pearson's staff offered his house as a refuge for the general, and Latta accepted the suggestion. Latta spoke with the delegated authority of Governor Hartranft, and the other state officials supported Latta's views. So Pearson gave in. "Very well," he said wearily, "I take this as an order." Thus Alfred Pearson made his exit from the stage.

At the roundhouse Brinton and the other Philadelphia officers welcomed Pearson's supposedly temporary absence as a deliverance. At least one of them panted for a chance to "extinguish the rioters." In the cold blood of the winter after, this man testified that in General Pearson's place he would have "opened fire with every weapon we had, at just about dusk. The mob was so dense at that time they could hardly have got out of each other's way. They were composed of the criminal classes, vagrants, bummers, and tramps of every kind, and such men as we call night owls, never seen in daytime, a class that would benefit the community by fertilizing the soil." Brinton, not so thirsty for blood, would not permit Gatling or artillery fire. But with his consent the troops fired their small arms into the crowd at the gate and thus drove them off. After that, the besiegers settled down to sporadic firing with pistols and muskets from behind corners, chimneys and piles of lumber.

The men in the roundhouse were far from happy, sitting or crouching in darkness while stones and bricks hurtled through the broken windows and bullets thudded against the walls. Someone outside had got hold of explosive bullets, devilish curiosities renounced years before by most nations as beyond the limits of civilized warfare. These exploded from time to time against locomotive plates or brick walls, though fortunately not in flesh. To such harassments were added hunger, fatigue and the frustration imposed by General Brinton's scruples against the use of Gatlings or artillery. Yet all these together did not spell doom. The real danger lay in the fact that the stronghold of the Philadelphia troops stood at the bottom of a gentle incline, scores of loaded oil and coal cars stood at the top, and railroad tracks ran between. As one of the rioters presently summed it up at the top of his lungs: "We'll have them out if we have to roast them out."

The great barbecue began at about quarter to eleven with the firing of a freight car two or three blocks beyond the Twenty-eighth Street crossing. Some said that small boys began it; but whoever struck the match, strong backs must have given the burning car the impetus with which it careered down the grade, trailing smoke and sparks through the darkness. Perhaps deliberately, a misplaced switch sent the car tumbling off the track near the "upper roundhouse" at Twenty-eighth Street. Then a half dozen coke cars rumbled down and fetched up against the derailed car with a crash heard plainly by the thousands of spectators on the hillside opposite. Oil cars were touched off and shoved along. Great clouds of smoke boiled up from the flaming mass. Whenever cars slowed up on their descent into the inferno, a gang of twenty or so would give them a fresh start. According to one spectator, these expediters were "nearly all boys, fourteen to sixteen or seventeen years of age." The prime movers in all this, however, were grown men who went at it systematically, passing orders back and forth like a gang of efficient workmen. One of these, a machinist from the city of Allegheny across the river, was recognized as he crouched in a coke car setting fire to a pile of shavings; as a result, he later drew a six-year term in the penitentiary.

The sand house caught fire first. Then, very slowly, the flames worked to the upper roundhouse. Long before the buildings got going, however, the light from strings of burning cars had reddened the night sky. Before the huge crowd on the hillside a spectacle unfolded to be remembered for a lifetime. Reflected fire glittered from the eyes of thousands. General Brinton, at bay in the lower roundhouse, first saw the glare in the sky about eleven. Latta and his frightened colleagues watched the spreading colors from their hotel window a mile away. Before the night was out, farmers a dozen or so miles out in the country began to wonder about the strange glow on the horizon over Pittsburgh way.

The same financial pinch that cut off half the Pittsburgh police force in July had also nipped twenty-two men from the fire department, leaving a working force of ninety-four. These did their best. At about eleven o'clock the crowd on the hillside clearly heard Number Seven's steam engine start up at Twenty-third and Penn, heard the clatter of hoofs, the noise of the gong and the rumble of wheels, and then a significant lull, peppered by the sound of distant oaths: at pistol point in a Penn Avenue gutter Number Seven's crew were drawing their engine's fire. Other engines rocked along the streets, horses at a gallop, until the cursing crowd grabbed the halters. Number Three ran a gauntlet of musket and pistol fire for several blocks, but all in vain. When hose was laid, the crowd cut it. A fireman knocked down one elegant gentleman whom he found strolling alongside the hose, punching holes in it with a sword cane. One gang of rioters hauled a cannon along Penn Avenue, paused at Twenty-third, aimed the gun at some hose carriages and yelled: "If you don't get out of that, we'll blow you to hell!" Four men with pistols menaced a hose-laying crew until the firemen explained that the hose would only be used to safeguard nonrailroad property. At last the firemen reeled in their hose to save it from the knives of the crowd. All that night the flames fed without stint.

A large part of Pittsburgh's population stayed up to see the show. Thousands made the hillside their grandstand, notwithstanding its recent unhealthiness for onlookers. Thousands more filled Liberty Street down to the Union Depot and beyond. The spectator element watched quietly, almost raptly. The shouts of individual actors in the drama therefore could be heard for a considerable distance. These active participants were comparatively few. Before the lower roundhouse several hundred took the part of besiegers, stupidly collecting on the Liberty Street side, though the yard side was far more vulnerable. A much smaller group, perhaps less than a score, cast themselves as incendiaries and went to work with quiet absorption. Much burning was done at the top of the grade, near Thirty-first and Thirty-second streets. All along the car-packed yards, however, new fires broke forth from time to time at one isolated point after another. In the Pan Handle's yard near Eleventh Street, a city fireman begged: "Don't do it, or you'll set the city on fire!" "We don't care a damn if we do," shouted the arsonists and lit their fires. Still other participants confined themselves to pillaging—or "salvaging," they might have called it. Looting began as a by-product of the burning, then became an end in itself. At midnight, most of the pilferers were teen-age boys and girls, perhaps obeying parental directions, perhaps working on their own hook (for this was, after all, the age of enterprise, and a good Alger hero seized his every chance to acquire goods). Adults soon joined in. By one in the morning, the streets teemed like ant runs with files of citizens bearing burdens. The pillagers, like the firebrands, proceeded almost sedately. At the stationhouse near Penn and Twenty-sixth, the police arrested evident looters as they passed, and the culprits submitted with remarkable passivity. Elsewhere vagrant rumors occasionally scattered the looters in brief panic, but always they returned to the job.

The derailment of the first few cars near Twenty-eighth Street had frustrated the besieging mob's initial attempt to burn out the Philadelphia troops at Twenty-sixth; accessions to the blaze merely piled up at the higher point. At about two o'clock Sunday morning General Brinton's attention was called to a dark object at Liberty and Twenty-seventh. Presently a cloud passed away, and moonlight glinted from a brass fieldpiece—captured, it later transpired, from the Pittsburgh militia. The gun was aimed at the machine shop, where a number of troops were ensconced. Brinton had fifty men cover the gun with their rifles. As a rioter took the lanyard in his hand, Brinton gave the command to fire. When the smoke cleared away, eleven men lay dead or wounded in the street. Dogged volunteers took their places. Brinton's men shouted a warning, then drove them off with renewed rifle fire. For several hours the shout was heard at intervals, "Go back, go back, one, two, three," followed by the cracking of rifles. Not once did the besiegers manage to fire their little cannon.

As the pale light of Sunday morning dawned, the besiegers gave up the effort and resorted once again to the torch. A track of the Allegheny Valley Railroad ran unobstructed along the Liberty Street wall and passed near the lower roundhouse. Defying the Philadelphians' bullets, a gang of rioters leaped up on the wall and began shoving burning freight cars toward the roundhouse and its adjacent buildings. The troops threw car wheels on the tracks and blocked the fire cars, but not at a very comfortable distance. Fire extinguishers and a hose were discovered inside the roundhouse and put to work. For a couple of hours the fire was held at bay. At last the rioters found some cars loaded with whisky and "high wines," pushed them as close as possible and set them ablaze. Somehow the burning liquor found its way into the cellar of the machine shop, which was presently bathed in flame. Thence the fire spread to other buildings. The roundhouse held out longest, though burning cinders big as a man's hand filled the air around it. Coughing in dense smoke, General Brinton and his staff decided that the time had come to march. At ten minutes past eight Sunday morning the troops made their exit in perfect order. The roundhouse roof was burning. Across Liberty Street lumberyards and shanties were aflame for an entire block, ignited not by the crowd but by heat and sparks from burning railroad property.

CHAPTER 9

The Smoky City

IN NEW YORK CITY on the night of July 21, while the mob howled and pillaged at Pittsburgh, City Hall Park lay quiet. Gaslight flickered through swaying leaves; a few tramps slept on the benches; the high dark buildings on the Broadway side rose massive and imperturbable. Signs of activity appeared, however, on the other side of the park, where blocks of yellow light glowing from upper stories marked the offices of the great morning newspapers. Within the low-ceilinged rooms a blue fog of tobacco smoke muffled the glare of Argand burners, and scribbling men tossed page after page of manuscript to copy boys. Night editors struggled to channel the flood of news from maddened Pittsburgh. Already the presses pounded in their subterranean rooms and shook the pavements where ragged newsboys slept. Steam rolled up from pavement gratings. On the yellow disk of the illuminated City Hall clock, the hands swept round to three. Stark-lit by composing-room reflectors, typesetters' fingers flashed over the forms. Headlines took shape: MORE BLOODSHED! . . . PITTSBURGH SACKED . . . THE GREAT STRIKE EXTENDING . . . ALARM IN WASHINGTON . . . THE STRIKE ON THE ERIE. As darkness ebbed from the street, the waiting urchins scrambled and fought for their share of fresh-printed sheets. And presently their shrill voices shattered the Sunday morning silence with tidings of rage and terror. So it was in other American cities as the midsummer night retreated westward. Now all the people knew.

Sunday editions came out in almost every city that day, often for the first time or (in the *Baltimore Sun's* phrase) as "an expedient of rare occurrence." At Cumberland, Maryland, Pittsburgh papers brought fifty cents apiece, and the *Cumberland Daily News* itself sold out edition after special edition. Up and down the hilly streets

of Pottsville, Pennsylvania, where people still wore mourning for
the Mollies, newsboys cried out "Extra! . . . The strikers' war! . . .
Bloody battle in Pittsburgh!" and in one hour sold more than 2,000
copies of the *Chronicle's* unprecedented Sunday edition. The *Harrisburg Independent* rushed out with a single-sheet extra. So did the
Zanesville Courier, omitting its own place of publication in its haste
to report PITTSBURGH IN FLAMES.

Even these sketchy extras lagged hours behind events. And so
rumor sprouted rank and hardy in a thin soil of known truth.
People in Baltimore, for example, heard and believed that the Pittsburgh rioters had armed themselves from the United States Arsenal
and had killed 300 militia. "But we have no fear," wrote a Baltimorean to his vacationing wife, "as the town is full of U. S. troops.
It looks as though the North is now to get what we have had."

It looked that way to "the North" too. Only Baltimore, purged of
pent-up tensions, could count on immunity. Most other cities now
felt their turns coming. Still shaken by the Molly Maguire hangings
in June, the average American city dweller agreed with the *Nation*
that "the time has never been more propitious for a rising of the
worst elements." In Harrisburg as early as Friday evening, first reports of the Baltimore riot had set off wild rumors of open warfare,
of pitched battles in the streets, of a great conflagration.

In those days, startling news drew people into crowds about newspaper and telegraph offices, instead of pulling them indoors to radio
or television sets. Thus the apprehension of mob violence helped
to collect mobs. At Little Rock large crowds gathered in front of the
Arkansas state capitol, "discussing the situation." In Raleigh, North
Carolina, "the strikers' war is the all absorbing theme on the streets
now." In Kansas City, Missouri, "men gathered in groups on the
corners and discussed the situation of affairs in the East." A lady
visitor to Cincinnati complained that "the sidewalks and streets in
front and round the *Commercial* and *Enquirer* offices are so completely filled with anxious people that pedestrians, including ladies,
must make their way as best they can in the middle of the streets."

Early on Sunday evening, a crowd began to gather—no one knew
why—in front of the capitol at Wheeling. By dark it numbered 2,000,
mostly railroad and mill workers. After listening to a few impromptu
speeches counseling moderation, the crowd melted away. But the
B. & O. strikers were clearly heartened by the news of Pittsburgh's

temper. In Pennsylvania the atmosphere reminded many of "April 1861," "the stirring scenes of the civil war," "the news that Fort Sumter had been fired upon." Even in places less nearly touched, in Charleston, South Carolina, in Denver, in New Orleans, the outbreaks were "almost the exclusive topic of conversation upon the streets." At the fashionable resorts, the news induced severe visceral churnings. Alarm came early to Long Branch, New Jersey, a seaside resort favored by propertied Philadelphians. On Saturday, while whistles screamed and foghorns moaned through a heavy mist, the upper classes rocked nervously on verandas and talked of nothing but the "railroad war," of business obstructed, of acquaintances called to militia duty. On the hotel piazza at White Sulphur Springs, West Virginia, under the shade trees and on the plushy lawns, knots of "governors, congressmen, judges, merchants, farmers, and all classes representing wealth and intelligence" discussed the "frightful condition of affairs," speaking "in bated breath and with serious aspect."

Some newspapers claimed that the Pittsburgh upheaval turned public opinion abruptly against the strikers. This seems doubtful. On Monday street talk in Boston still ran strongly in their favor. Most Bostonians, like the Baltimoreans, distinguished between strikers and rioters, and condemned the destruction of property. Not all were so conservative. "Well," said one man, "of course the strikers must carry their point . . . I don't care how much railroad property they burn; it will teach those monopolists a lesson." In North Carolina that day, the *Raleigh Observer* noted that "everyone seems to sympathize with the railroad strikers." The same feeling pervaded Scranton, and the *Republican* expressed satisfaction "that the popular heart is sound. It is full of warning to the corporations to adopt a wiser and kindlier policy in their dealings with their employees."

Even the business community shared popular sentiment. On Wall Street during Monday, "a strong undercurrent of sympathy with the strikers, as far as their lawful demands were concerned, was observable among the brokers," though all denounced "outrages on life and property." At Cincinnati, "the general feeling among business men and others in favor of an advance to the employes, even at the public expense, is every day increasing." Many businessmen of Cincinnati said they would willingly pay higher freight rates, especially if the rates were stable, in order to give the men a decent wage.

Unquestionably the outbreaks of violence dismayed labor and its sympathizers, put them on the defensive, perhaps even turned a few coats. But the American people were less easily shocked by violence in 1877 than they had been a generation before or were to be a generation after. And the stress of riot exposed a growing fear of powerful corporations. Nicholas Biddle had felt the force of it a generation before. But since the Civil War the great business corporations had come into their own; and with every year that passed, Americans grew more uneasily conscious of a new power in their land. Foreigners gasped at it. "The power wielded by the Great Corporations in this country is almost incredible," wrote the British Minister in a confidential dispatch that July.

In 1877 these fears centered on railroad corporations, for the age of the great industrial corporation had scarcely begun (only three of these being capitalized at more than a million dollars). Even the railroad corporations had been an issue mainly in the Granger movement, where the term "monopoly" had already worn thin as a synonym for all corporate misdoings. Nevertheless, the Independent or "Greenback" Party of 1876 had adopted an antimonopoly plank. And the "National Anti-Monopoly Cheap Freight Railway League," with its crackbrained scheme of toll-supported public railways, was now ten years old. Below these surface straws a deep current moved. While press and politics kept mum, the cries and slogans of city mobs were now about to show how vigorously antimonopolism worked on the mind of the common man.

The newspapers had denounced the strike almost from the start and now only grew more strident. "It is not surprising," the *Iron Molders' Journal* had remarked some months earlier, "that the press of the country is against Trade Unions. It could hardly be expected that the newspapers of an enemy, in any conflict, would do justice to both sides." Just a week before the outbreak the *Journal* had flatly called the press "the worst enemy we have." A prolabor sheet, the *Irish World*, accused its contemporaries of selling their souls for free railroad passes for their reporters and canvassers. Tom Scott owned the *New York World*. The *New York Sun* referred to a noted competitor as "Jay Gould's *Tribune*." In a humbler sphere, the *Alleganian* of Cumberland, Maryland, charged its rival, the *Civilian*, with being "the advocate and organ of the Baltimore and Ohio Railroad Company"; this was stoutly denied by the *Civilian*. However that may have been, the papers of John W. Garrett yield such suggestive letters as one from the business manager of the *Baltimore American*: "Mr. Matthews, Assistant Editor . . . was not on duty last night, or the article to-day would not have appeared in the form it did. He regretted the occurrence, and promised to look very carefully into all matters hereafter pertaining to the Baltimore & Ohio, with a view of correcting any errors that might be made by indiscreet reporters." Speaker Samuel J. Randall of the House of Representatives—a Democrat—was advised by a knowledgeable correspondent that Tom Scott was the best man through whom to "reach the [*Cincinnati*] *Enquirer*."

Most editors, as men of education and social substance, had absorbed the views of Herbert Spencer, first- or second-hand. Furthermore, newspaper publishers and railroad presidents were brother employers. Even as the Great Strike spread, Whitelaw Reid of the *New York Tribune* gloated privately over his crushing of a compositors' strike: "it is the largest strike, and the most effective and prompt defeat of the strikers known in American newspaper history." "The expenses of my composing room for the previous weeks were $1860," he wrote; "for this week they were $1180." On July 24 Reid referred to "a young beggar who said he was employed on The World" as "a liar as well as a trades unionist." "In fact," he added, "the two things seem to go together." Even if Jay Gould had not controlled the *Tribune*, its editorial line toward labor would probably not have been much different.

And so one newspaper's views were much like another's. A composite editorial would have read about as follows: Strikes, though legal, are foolish and mischievous, at odds with the law of supply and demand, doing the strikers themselves more harm than good and seldom gaining their objects. Theory aside, the railroads are essential to public welfare, and so there is a question as to whether a general stoppage should be tolerated at all in that field. The pay cuts may or may not work some hardship, but hard times and fierce competition require them. The railroaders ought to accept them cheerfully, or at least with manful resignation, as others have had to do and as widowed and orphaned stockholders have borne dividend cuts. Thus far (the composite editorialist would have said) we speak of policy. But from the moment that the strikers trespassed on railroad property or kept a single strikebreaker off the job through force or intimidation, the issue became simply and wholly one of law. Only one question remains: how to crush the outbreak most effectively. Governor Mathews had no choice but to call the militia into action. That failing, he was justified in appealing for federal aid. We approve the calm but firm course thus far taken by President Hayes. The Pittsburgh horror proves that an organized and popular defiance of law in any form must lead to a general leap of unpropertied rabble at the throat of society. We must not be disarmed by weak pity for the misguided strikers. All citizens, including workingmen, should and must close ranks immediately against the peril.

Not all editors talked like that. Some conceded that the railroad men would have a hard time getting along on the new wages. A few thought that the cut might have been avoided by reducing dividends, and a still smaller number blamed reckless and greedy management. The latter group even urged concessions to the strikers. Yet almost all agreed that the strike had been a bad gamble from the start and was now doomed by the intrusion of the mob.

Pittsburgh's Sunday papers fell into a class by themselves. A *Globe* headline proclaimed THE LEXINGTON OF THE LABOR CONFLICT AT HAND. "The cowardice and imbecility of the railroad sharks, who sought to overawe all this community by imported bummers, [has] met its proper rebuke," announced that sheet. The *Leader* blamed everything on the Philadelphia troops. The *Critic* arraigned "before the board of public opinion General Pearson, Sheriff Fife, Thomas Scott, and Governor Hartranft, and their aiders and abettors for the murder of our fellow-citizens, who were slaughtered by the Philadelphia militia." The *Critic's* indictment covered the social order itself: "there is tyranny in this country worse than anything ever known in Russia. . . . Capital has raised itself on the ruins of labor. The laboring class cannot, will not stand this longer. The war cry has been raised . . . the principle that freed our nation from tyranny will free labor from domestic aggression."

Most of Pittsburgh's larger and stodgier papers could not or would not show themselves on "that awful Sunday." For that they were later thankful. Such a one, the *Telegraph*, congratulated itself on being the only paper in the city to stand firm throughout for law

and order. "Those incendiary sheets," it said, "that . . . fed the insatiable fury of the rioters and led to the destruction of millions of
valuable property . . . have an awful indictment to answer at the
bar of public judgment and returning reason."

No doubt editorial wind fanned the people's rage. Still, the
people raged before as well as after Sunday morning's gusts. As the
editor of the *Leader* himself stated: "at this writing the air is filled
with rumors of fire and war."

Emerging from the flaming complex of railroad buildings at ten
minutes to eight that Sunday morning, General Brinton's Philadelphia militia, though white-faced with fatigue and fear, shouldered
arms and marched with parade-like bearing in column of fours
down Liberty Street toward the Union Depot. Having been unable
to drag their fieldpieces through the cluttered carpenter shop or
past the blocked gates, they had left the heavy guns behind, spiked
and dismounted, with powder soaked and ammunition scattered.
But they brought out the lighter Gatling guns. These glittered in
the morning sun like deadly sewing machines, ready to stitch a hem
of blood across the front of any charging crowd. The eruption of
the troops frightened the crowd from Liberty Street into doorways
and alleys.

Seeing that Brinton did not mean to attack, some of the rioters
ran down toward the Union Depot, perhaps to cut the troops off. If
so, they mistook Brinton's aim. During the night Brinton had received orders from Latta to quit the roundhouse if necessary, go
east along Penn Avenue and join forces with Colonel Guthrie's men
out at Torrens Station. Brinton and his staff felt that the Union
Depot would have been a better goal. Still, orders were orders; and
so when the Philadelphians got down to Twenty-fifth Street, they
turned in, marched a block to Penn Avenue and headed back along
Penn, parallel to Liberty. Brinton's first objective was the Federal
government's Allegheny Arsenal, where he hoped to get ammunition
and food for his state militiamen. They had eaten nothing since the
coffee and sandwiches of Saturday noon, and they were down to
half a dozen rounds of ammunition apiece.

Brinton deployed a dozen men in a skirmish line across Penn
Avenue, put a squad of men on each side to watch buildings and
alleys and stationed the Gatlings between the two brigades to

cover attacks from front or rear. For a quarter of a mile no one molested them. As they passed Twenty-sixth Street on their way out of town, they caught a glimpse of the roundhouse, looking now like a great brick incinerator. Flames streamed from all its windows. The troops marched on steadily but slowly, so that the Gatlings could keep up. People began to line the sidewalks and venture out of alleys. Women leaned from windows and cursed the Philadelphians. Men waited impassively with navy revolvers sagging their coats. Troops at the head of the column met no opposition; but behind them they presently heard the surly bickering of rifles and pistols.

A little past Twenty-sixth Street, a tall middle-aged man, either in shirtsleeves or wearing a white linen coat, had begun to follow the retreating troops with a breech-loading rifle. From a white belt around his waist hung a black cartridge box. The lone attacker fired coolly and deliberately, now and then stepping into a doorway or alley to reload. One spectator claimed afterward to have overheard him muttering something about revenge for the shedding of his friends' blood. Occasionally his shots took effect. A soldier fell dead at Thirty-third Street, whereupon several of the troops paused to fire back at their grim pursuer. Splinters from a grazed doorway struck the man's face, but he kept on, unscathed otherwise. He seemed bent on following them, regardless of his own life, until he fell or ran out of targets. Never identified, he was to pass into Pittsburgh legend as "Pat the Avenger." Some believed him to be the man who had fired explosive bullets into the roundhouse the night before.

"Pat the Avenger's" fate, as well as his name, remained unknown because he presently merged with the mass of those who now began to follow his example. For a time the troops held their fire in obedience to orders, though pistols blazed at them out of doorways and windows, from behind corners, projecting signs, crates and boxes, from cellars and other sheltered places. A gang of assailants followed along parallel streets, sallying out of cross streets and firing from corners. Most of the shots came from the rear, the waiting crowds standing quiet until the troops had passed, then opening fire. At last, when the mob began using rifles, the Philadelphians shot back. Near Thirty-seventh Street a railroad man, just going home from servicing engines at the Allegheny Valley Railroad roundhouse, got a bullet in his ankle. His leg was amputated a day or two later, and shortly after that he died. Another bullet slammed into a saloonkeeper standing in his doorway at Butler Street; after breaking his left arm, the slug passed on through his body, touching his heart on the way and stopping it. A plasterer fell wounded a block further on. The troops sustained casualties also, their dead and wounded being carried into houses along the way.

On the porch of a stationhouse, several Pittsburgh policemen stood glowering at the Philadelphians. Put in mind of a reviewing stand, the troops broke into facetious yells: "Eyes right! Pass in review!" After they had gone by, pistol shots came from the vicinity of the police. Some militiamen swore later that they had seen at least one policeman fire at them. (The police swore to the contrary.)

A couple of blocks from the arsenal, the troops passed a row of two-story houses. A fusillade of shots poured from the windows down into the ranks of the rear brigade. Two men were killed and several wounded, one mortally. The harassed troops stopped and fired without orders into the windows, whence gunsmoke was curling from behind half-closed shutters. "Pat the Avenger" was last seen at this point, down on one knee in a front yard, taking aim as calmly as though at target practice. Rifle fire erupted from the crowd. The troops divided and one of the Gatlings opened up. Within seconds the street to the rear of the troops lay empty, except for a dead horse, some smashed signs and two or three dead or wounded Pittsburghers. The first brigade, not fully aware of the skirmish, had not halted; indeed, one of its officers just then ordered his straggling men to close up. Seeing their comrades scampering off, the rear brigade panicked briefly and charged pell-mell up into the front ranks.

Happily, the arsenal now seemed to offer a haven, and the men broke for it. Thirsty, hungry and bone-tired, they saw an oasis of peace in the broad, tree-shaded arsenal grounds. Major Buffington had been catching up on his sleep in the commandant's quarters, and Lieutenant Lyons had just dismissed the arsenal's twenty enlisted men from Sunday morning inspection. Jarred awake by the noise of gunfire, Buffington pulled on his pants, grabbed a coat and ran downstairs, stuffing his nightshirt into his breeches as he went. Before he got out the front door, he knew from the exclamations of his household that strange men were running through the grounds; and in all likelihood, he thought at first that the mob had come back upon him. As he stood bewildered on the porch, Lieutenant Lyons and a bleary-eyed young man in a military blouse and cap came up the walk. Brinton's shoulder straps were gone—one torn off, the other discarded—and Buffington failed to notice the two stars of a major general on Brinton's cap. But he gathered that Brinton was in command of the invaders, and Buffington's orders were peremptory. "You must take your men right out, sir," he barked fiercely; "there is no protection here for you!" "You have walls," said Brinton. "Yes, we have walls," replied Buffington sarcastically, raising his hand waist-high. But the major relented to the extent of offering to shelter the wounded, who were accordingly brought in. One of these, Lieutenant J. Dorsey Ash, died at the arsenal two days later. The others, some eight or ten, were mere skulkers (or so thought Buffington, who later charged that their wounds, so-called, had been sustained in climbing over the arsenal's picket fence).

Writing off the arsenal as a refuge and apparently giving up hope of reaching Guthrie at Torrens, Brinton led his weary troops on toward Sharpsburg. By now the crowd had given over the pursuit; they seemed content to have ushered the Philadelphians out of town. One of the militiamen wrote years later: "I recollect stopping at farm houses for milk, and resting at a stream where we bathed our feet and arose weak and dizzy from long marching and want of food." In Sharpsburg a few citizens consented to give (or sell, as one soldier claimed) some berries and buttermilk to the fugitives. Two Sharpsburg boys had been among the Pittsburgh militia wounded on the hill Saturday afternoon, and a chill in the town's attitude persuaded Brinton to push on. At last, about noontime, Brinton found a resting place for his men on a hill by the Allegheny County Workhouse, a dozen miles from town. The inmates yelled from the windows at the fagged-out troops, but the Philadelphians had got used to that. Later that day the workhouse officials let the troops have bread, coffee and such meat as could be spared.

Meanwhile, the mob had Pittsburgh pretty much to themselves. A score or so of the Philadelphia troops—the "Black Hussars"—had been left at the Union Depot on Saturday afternoon to guard the ammunition. Early Sunday morning a charitable Pittsburgher got some civilian clothes for them and sneaked the frightened men over the hill in two instalments, letting them hide in his house until the storm blew itself out. The ammunition was left to take care of itself.

Aside from Colonel Guthrie's men, waiting out at Torrens for trains to start coming, the only Pittsburgh militia left under arms by Saturday night were about 175 men of the Fourteenth Regiment. Their nominal commander, General Brown, still in civilian clothes, was seen roaming around talking to the rioters and making prom-ises—"the old gentleman was pretty well excited," recalled an un-sympathetic witness. At about eleven o'clock Brown ordered his men disbanded, feeling, he claimed later, that they were too few to do anything but exasperate the crowd.

Mayor McCarthy, sulking over the usurpations of railroad and state authorities, nevertheless began trying to restore order early on Sunday. Assuming that dawn would bring the Philadelphians out of the roundhouse to disperse the mob, he issued no orders to hold the night force of police, which went off duty at six in the morning. When he realized some time later that Brinton's men pro-posed to let Pittsburgh fry in its own fire, the mayor wired the central station to hold any night men still on hand. These few un-lucky stragglers, along with the regular day force, amounted to about eighty men. The chief of police had advertised in the Sunday papers for recently discharged men to volunteer for the emergency, and some forty or fifty eventually responded; but most of these showed up late in the day and then without enthusiasm. Of the eighty tired men on duty during the height of Sunday's turbulence, some were scattered through the city and most of the others were separated from one another in the huge mob. At any given moment McCarthy and his chief of police could get no more than fifteen or twenty together in a body. During the day the mayor drove up and down Liberty Street in a buggy, encouraging the firemen and prom-ising them police protection which never came. At one point during the afternoon he was seen leaning despondently against a lamp post at the corner of Twentieth and Liberty. Later he turned up on the platform at the Union Depot, where he addressed the crowd. Hoot-ing and jeering drowned out his counsels, and finally the crowd picked him up bodily, all 210 pounds of him, and dumped him on the street outside.

Sheriff Fife had last been seen shortly after the opening skirmish on Saturday afternoon, heading west along the tracks and "making pretty good time." During the night people came to his house and warned his family to leave before they were burned out or killed. Mrs. Fife sought refuge with her neighbors, but nobody on Washington Street would let her in. They blamed the sheriff for the killing and were afraid the mob would turn on them if they sheltered his family. Editor James P. Barr of the *Pittsburgh Post* wired the War Department at midnight: "Sheriff Fife's dead body just brought in." The bulletin went out over the nation; and in the rush of later news most people probably never did learn that Fife had in fact spent Saturday night and all day Sunday breathing with fair regularity in his office at the courthouse. His home and family likewise escaped harm.

During Sunday morning a Pittsburgh militia officer sought out Adjutant General Latta and urged him to reassemble the Nineteenth Regiment. Latta refused. He no longer trusted Pittsburgh troops. Having no other force at his command, he and the other state officials wandered about helplessly, watching Pittsburgh's carnival of arson until early afternoon, when they withdrew to new quarters at the Monongahela House. The desk clerk, observing a reddish glow in the direction of their previous accommodations, inked out their names and substituted aliases in the register of guests.

Since Friday afternoon Tom Scott had been putting pressure on Governor Hartranft to return from his western junket. Latta wired Hartranft that he need not end his vacation; but at nine Saturday night, word of the Pittsburgh slaughter reached Hartranft in Utah, and he took a special train east at midnight. Missouri Valley newspapers made much of the governor's dash for home in the manner of Sheridan's ride. By Monday morning he had reached Omaha, where another special train awaited him, courtesy of the Chicago & Northwestern.

Despite the example set by Mathews of West Virginia and Carroll of Maryland, Hartranft did not see fit to ask President Hayes for aid until Sunday night. The War Department's only official reaction to the Pittsburgh affair during Sunday, therefore, was to send a company of regulars from Columbus Barracks in Ohio, to protect the Allegheny Arsenal. These men, about fifty in all, did not even leave for Pittsburgh until 5:00 p.m.

Thus, on that day and in that place, law had no force. City

authorities were feeble in numbers and spirit. The county's chief officer cowered at his desk. State troops were disaffected or dispersed. The Federal government lacked official grounds for action. Like a staked-out pig, the Pittsburgh yards of the great corporation lay waiting in the sun for the tiger to spring.

As the morning sun swung up over the great ridge, it drove night shadows to the shelter of the hillside. Nevertheless, Liberty Street remained dark with immense crowds. From the Rush House to Seventh Avenue, thousands jammed the street so "you could hardly get through." Some came from the factory districts of the South Side. Passenger trains, still running to and from the West, brought others from a distance. Hundreds of miners from the surrounding region had come to town on Saturday to do their usual weekly shopping. Many returned on Sunday for the excitement. A party of 150 people came in from Beaver County as if on an excursion.

Women pitched in, some of them bringing hot coffee to smoke-begrimed looters and burners. If a harridan here or there made the day a witches' sabbath, imps and warlocks also abounded. More than one freight car held drink more warming than coffee, and a growing number of boozy men and incoherent boys showed that not all of it went to blazes.

Some claimed later that the Irish element predominated. "Most everyone that spoke to us about not playing on the fire was Irish, that is, had the brogue on the tongue," said a Pittsburgh fireman named Miller. Jane Grey Swisshelm, a feminist reformer and journalist, wrote in a Protestant periodical that she had talked with a score of witnesses and all agreed "it was an Irish Catholic mob." That same journal, the *Independent*, drew a moral from the Pittsburgh affair: "our mobs and riots are mainly carried on by foreign-born Catholics and their children, and we have the right to hold any religion responsible for the character of those who have been educated under it." Bishop Tuigg of Pittsburgh, on the other hand, denied that more than 5 per cent of the mob was Catholic, and a man named Campbell remarked that in the looting "the Germans carried the heaviest loads."

Since Pittsburgh was heavily Presbyterian and Methodist, the apparent prominence of Irish rioters doubtless indicated something, just as did the Irish majority in the New York House of Refuge.

Some businessmen would have seen proof in it that trade unions and strikes were the work of foreign agitators, and it was true that the *Irish World* had often expressed "full sympathy with the cause of labor." But the same paper, a month before the Great Strike, had also asserted that "if a workman does not choose to belong to the union no man has any right to persecute him on that account." And in the preceding ten years more and more industrialists had themselves imported foreign strikebreakers after the fashion set by Andrew Carnegie of Pittsburgh. Celtic abandon at Pittsburgh probably signified little more than that the Irish, being poor newcomers, lived nearest the tracks, had the greatest need of loot and bore the deepest grudge against the employing class. Their economic and social status, not their nationality or religion, determined their role.

Sectarian recriminations came later. At dawn on Sunday all men on the scene seemed to be brothers in arms against the great corporation, and they joined in cutting its substance to the measure of its soul. People on the outskirts of town woke early to the rumble of loot-burdened wagons heading for the country. All morning long the procession of plunderers moved past, and in the afternoon the same wagons went by again with new loads. In the yards hundreds of people spent the morning breaking open and looting freight cars. Some looters struck a grotesquely carnival note with little flags of all nations, 1,000 of which had been shipped from Philadelphia to adorn the Pittsburgh Exposition Building. Small crowds scrambled wildly for goods tossed from cars by their public-spirited comrades. Into the mob vanished corn in sacks, flour in barrels, cotton in bales, wool in bags, bread, crackers, fruit, sugar candies and confectioneries, hides, leather, shoes, queen's ware, glassware, clothing, hay, whisky, alcohol, tobacco, coal, coke, silks, jewelry, even assorted volumes of *Chambers' Encyclopedia* and a number of Bibles, evidently sent by Providence that he who ran might read. Women gathered up their dresses and filled their laps with as much flour as they could carry. During the afternoon, rioters co-operated in rolling flour barrels over the retaining wall and down planks to Liberty Street, one man sending and another receiving. A stout middle-aged woman without a partner lost three barrels to unchivalrous men below. On the fourth try she bounded grimly after her barrel, fell and rolled down the plank into the street, but jumped to her feet again and managed to grab the barrel as it struck the opposite curb. The crowd cheered.

During the morning the police collared about 130 looters and bundled them off in the Black Maria to the Central Station. Deputy Mayor Butler held hearings until noon, when he threw up his hands amid "terrible confusion." Most prisoners gave false names and no addresses. Some were plainly tramps, and almost all the rest evidently belonged to "the poorer class of people." Some were fined from three to five dollars, others were held for court, many were discharged for lack of room to hold them.

The overwhelming size of the mob seemed to demoralize the police. Mayor McCarthy led some twenty policemen up Liberty Street about noontime and sent them against the looters on the retaining wall. To his disgust he presently discovered one policeman throwing felt hats down to the mob and two others dispensing cigars broadcast. "The moral effect of their previous conduct was gone," recalled McCarthy later, "and the crowd mounted the hill like so many rats, and that was the end of that business."

Some of the active rioters believed that railroad detectives were watching them, though they did not seem inhibited by the notion. Perhaps they had heard the reports, later accepted as true by a noted writer on organized labor, "that a great many old freight cars which must soon have been replaced by new, were pushed into the fires by agents of the railroad company." "This," said Carroll D. Wright, first United States Commissioner of Labor, "was a novelty then, but it occurred in subsequent strikes, and of course the loss was included in claims on the county of Allegheny."

Fire followed looting. Now and then flames burst from an emptied car. Whenever there was a gap, the crowd carried brands to the next string of cars. Down toward the Union Depot thousands watched approvingly as a score or so of half-drunken men spread fire among the rolling stock. Billowing oil smoke shadowed the flushed and yelling mob. Up at Twenty-sixth Street firemen had begun playing their hoses on the roundhouse ten minutes after Brinton's command left it, but it was already doomed. They soon turned away to the burning frame shanties and lumber yards across the street, saving them without major damage. The firemen dogged the railroad conflagration down Liberty Street, wetting down the buildings opposite. At some points heat from burning railroad yards, especially from coal dumps and oil bins, grew unbearable. Nevertheless, the mob refused to let a drop of water fall on railroad property. Near the Union Depot a fireman who turned a stream on some burning cars was corrected by what seemed a twenty-one-pistol salute. Across the square at the big grain elevator someone cut the hose, and water sprayed over the crowd. No one seemed to mourn the railroad's losses except old Bobby Atchison, who lamented helplessly as flames swept over his beloved engine Number 281. It was wrong, he moaned, and he was sure that the railroad men had nothing to do with it.

The flood of fire lapped steadily toward the Union Depot. A hundred or so wild-looking men and boys urged it on. Some spread coal beneath the cars, broke oil barrels into it and touched off the mixture. One man, so drunk he could hardly stand, weaved and capered among the cars with a flaming brand, performing feats of agility a sober man would not have attempted. Here and there a boy sank down in a stupor from drink or sun, but others seemed as fresh as ever. "Champagne puzzled the finders of a case and they used it to wash their hot faces, delighted by the fuzzy impact, not knowing it was wine."

Around one-thirty fire burst from cars at Fifteenth Street, a jump of six blocks nearer the depot. A rumor of powder kegs among the flames started a panicky scramble for safety, spectators and looters tumbling headlong over barrels of flour being rolled along the street behind them. A few minutes later an exploding liquor car touched off another panic and sent a stream of flame thirty yards closer to the depot, now only four blocks from the fire. By two o'clock horses and carriages were clattering through the crowd about the Union Depot Hotel, taking out baggage and valuables to safer places.

A few minutes before three, fire broke out in a passenger car standing half under the depot train shed. Thousands of spectators cheered on the hillside near by as the huge roof of the platform blazed up. Simultaneously a gang of young men burst into the two-story frame office of the depot master on the other side of the platform. They smashed windows, pulled out desk drawers, scattered books and papers on the floor and touched a match to the debris.

Within minutes the building and the sheds were a roaring mass of flame. The Rush House, the St. James Hotel and other buildings across the street smoked from the heat, but a drenching by fire hoses saved them. At three-thirty the heavy gravel roof of the shed crashed down with a noise like a powder blast, setting off another panic. Children were knocked down, and horses ran off.

At that moment a cry went up: "The Union Depot is on fire!" Thousands swelled the huge crowd, indifferent to danger. People covered the hillside above the depot "thick as leaves upon forest trees." Scores climbed the high tower of the City Hall and found the view magnificent. As smoke rolled up, it drew public attention in Allegheny across the river, and crowds gathered on the bluff there. Hundreds, mostly children, watched from Observatory Hill. Nearer the scene, onlookers gasped as three men climbed out a window of the hotel, dropped to the shed roof and tumbled to safety. One other man presently made a similar escape. No one seems to have been trapped in the building. By four-thirty little remained of the depot and hotel but burning rubble in a ragged shell of brick.

During the Union Depot fire, looters broke into some freight cars on the track between the depot and the great grain elevator and found fresh stocks of wine and whisky. In a general rush for liquor the crowd smashed several barrels, spilling the contents over the track. Someone fired a car of liquor and sent it rolling down a grade toward the transfer depot of the Adams Express Company. Flames swirled fifty feet into the air and blossomed out along the whisky-soaked roadbed. Frightened men ran out of the Adams Company buildings, the Pan Handle freight depot on Seventh Street and a house on Fountain Street just above the track. Women screamed and children sobbed in terror. Within fifteen minutes a great sheet of fire shrouded the doomed buildings. Uneasiness ran through the mob. Here and there someone found his individuality again and ran home to evacuate his movable property before Pittsburgh could go the way of Chicago.

A wire drawer and a machinist from the Jones and Laughlin steel mill watched the Union Depot burn itself out. "I suppose they'll be satisfied when that's burned," said the wire drawer. "No," said his friend, "we won't be satisfied until this elevator is down. Everything in these monopolies has got to burn." "This isn't railroad property," said the wire drawer. "It don't make a damned bit of difference," said the machinist, "it's got to come down. It's a monopoly and we're tired of it."

Though rioters kept firemen from hosing it, the slate-sided grain elevator, 150 feet high and 80 square, had stood solidly all afternoon like a great gray promontory by a lake of fire. At about five-twenty the wind shifted and carried fire flakes from the Pan Handle property through a hole which a gang of young men and boys had knocked into the rear of the elevator. A single stream of water could have saved the structure, and firemen begged the mob to give them a chance at it. The secretary of the elevator company persuaded mob leaders that the railroad owned none of the property. But a brass-throated rioter yelled: "It's owned by a damned monopoly— let it burn!" Others took up the cry, and the elevator stood condemned.

From the roof came a curl of smoke, then a thick black cloud, then an orange tongue of flame, diaphanous and fleeting against the blue sky. A roar of exultation welled up from the crowd that packed Liberty, Grant and Washington streets. The towering edifice burned for three hours, firemen being permitted to throw water only on the houses opposite. From time to time patches of slate fell off and crashed into the street, after which flames would break out of the exposed wall. The great brick smokestack stood through it all.

Along with the Pan Handle buildings and the grain elevator went nearly everything in a triangle bounded by Washington and Bedford streets and Seventh Avenue. Firemen did their best, now aided rather than restrained by the mob. Nevertheless, the blaze lasted until seven o'clock, consuming twelve brick tenements, a chair factory, a blacksmith shop, a row of stables, a cooper shop and about a score of small frame houses, one being the home of Chief Detective O'Mara's mother.

During the afternoon a small group of substantial citizens made futile and occasionally comic efforts to restore order. At nine that morning Editor Barr of the *Pittsburgh Post* had found a number of gentlemen waiting "alarmed and dazed" at his office. With Barr's help they composed a call for a citizens' organization to be formed at the old city hall about twelve-thirty. The summons went up on newspaper bulletin boards and was read from several pulpits during morning services. A hundred or so gathered at the appointed

time and place, adjourned to the mayor's office and there formed a
Committee of Safety. The mayor seemed distracted and irresolute,
and no stronger leader emerged. Bishop Tuigg, the Reverend Syl-
vester Scoville of the First Presbyterian Church, an Irish-American
physician named Edward Donnelly and a couple of businessmen
were sent to reason with the mob at the Union Depot.

The peacemakers drew up in two carriages at the mob-be-
leaguered depot shortly after two o'clock. Bishop Tuigg attempted
to speak from a car platform, but found that his co-religionists were
not present in force. In Dr. Donnelly's words, the crowd "began
throwing iron ore and other missiles at the bishop's head, which no
good Catholic would do, unless he was an Orangeman." The doctor
tried his luck next. "Get down from here, Doctor," yelled a burly
rioter; "we're going to set fire to this." Said the doctor afterward:
"I considered it most prudent to get down." Anyway, a rioter just
then took out an engine with bell ringing and steam hissing, attached it to a burning car and ran it off the tracks four or five blocks
east, which commotion drowned out all oratory.

The dispensers of reason left the Union Depot to its fate, already
at hand, and set out to unite railroad strikers and officials against
the riot. At the suggestion of Mayor McCarthy, a Pittsburgh bank
official was already up at Twenty-eighth Street sounding out the
strikers. Most of these had prudently absented themselves after the
events of Saturday night, but the banker found a couple of apparently influential strikers who promised to help. This pair turned up
at a second citizens' meeting about three-thirty and were authorized
to organize strikers in behalf of law and order. Meanwhile, members of the peacemaking committee searched along Liberty Street
for strikers. The few who turned up professed their abhorrence of
the riot, and some showed up at the citizens' meeting. Old Bobby
Atchison and some other railroaders went down afterward to the
grain elevator, but were helpless against the huge mob there.

Scoville, Tuigg and a nail manufacturer named James Bennett
drove over to Allegheny to confer with railroad officials. On the way,
Bennett stopped off at the Monongahela House and found Alexander Cassatt, who decided to go along. Cassatt felt uneasy about
riding in an open buggy, but the streets turned out to be nearly
empty, everyone being up on the hills watching the fire. At the
meeting, attended on the Pennsylvania's behalf by Cassatt, William

Thaw, J. N. McCullough and John Scott, Bishop Tuigg urged a token concession to eliminate the strike issue from the riot. The railroad officials said no. It was plainly visible then and from there, they pointed out, that the Pennsylvania had nothing more to lose. Besides, any concessions would seem to register the triumph of the mob. Grievances might be discussed when traffic had returned to normal, not before. The committee gave up, returned to Pittsburgh and dissolved without reporting.

After the second citizens' meeting in midafternoon, Mayor Mc-Carthy authorized Dr. Donnelly to form a company of citizens as "special police." People were afraid to serve. It took Donnelly a couple of hours to scrape together and arm about sixty professional and business men. They marched to Western University for some old arms used by cadets, were refused them by college authorities, thereupon marched off and acquired some ax handles from a storekeeper, tried the university again, tried an armory, tried the university for the third time and at last were given some rusty old muskets without ammunition. By then, many had dropped out in disgust. Shortly after five the remnant marched wearily down to the elevator, wearing white handkerchiefs around their arms as badges. The elevator had already gone up in smoke. Dr. Donnelly persuaded some rioters to tear down a fence which threatened to carry fire to "private property." Otherwise, he and his force were helpless. Rioters even wrenched muskets from the hands of some. After a while Donnelly and his men went back to the City Hall, stacked arms and dispersed forever.

Out at Torrens Colonel Guthrie had wondered about the glow in the sky on Saturday night, but no direct word of events reached him until Sunday morning. That afternoon, dressed in civilian clothes, he made his way to the Union Depot, arriving as it began to burn. After sounding out some of the crowd, he concluded that even passive spectators would side with the rioters if the authorities used force. Guthrie at last found Latta fretting helplessly in the Monongahela House, and with Latta's approval he sent orders for his troops to march into the city. At dusk, after an unexplained delay of two hours, the Pittsburgh militia regiment tramped in via Fifth Avenue, Penn still being choked with crowds. No hostile demonstrations occurred along the way to the regimental armory, where the men remained on duty through the night.

Thus, in the end, the city's fury was left to burn itself out along with railroad property. Symptoms of disenchantment had first appeared in midafternoon, when some of the crowd at Twenty-first Street began amusing themselves by pitching rotten eggs at looters on the cars. Fears of a general conflagration increased mob misgivings after the Pan Handle fire had spread to private homes. When the fire reached the railroad tunnel at Seventh Street, someone yelled, "Now for the point depot." Fortunately, one final car of whisky, found behind the elevator, had made most of the arsonists dead drunk. (One died that night from whisky swilling.) Seven or eight stumbled down to the Duquesne Depot near the junction of the two rivers, broke open a car and started a fire inside. A half dozen spectators kicked out the blaze. The rioters rolled a keg of beer from a near-by store, split its contents among themselves and reeled back to work. One fuddled young man hammered ineffectively at the depot door. At last some citizens stepped in and arrested the troublemakers.

By nightfall quiet was returning to Pittsburgh. Besides being tired or drunk or both, the rioters had run out of targets. About then, some ex-policemen showed up at last for special service, bringing the total night force to nearly 150. At seven-thirty the police were able to stop looters from rolling away kegs of Milwaukee beer near the ruined depot. A few minutes later twenty-five police surrounded the waterworks, rumored to be next on the burners' program, and guarded it until daybreak. At ten that night a crowd of boys still hung about at Liberty and Grant streets, but the police had them under control. When that awful Sunday ended, the streets were almost empty and the night was troubled only by the songs of a few die-hards drinking beer in a vacant lot near the smoldering depot.

From across the river in Allegheny, Mayor Ormsby Phillips thankfully observed the subsidence of tumult in Pittsburgh. He had been braced for an assault by Pittsburgh rioters, rumored to be plotting the destruction of the Allegheny railroad shops and a jail delivery at the Allegheny penitentiary. All day police had guarded the bridges with muskets and artillery pieces, while citizen volunteers patrolled the streets. Throughout the city Phillips had placards posted announcing in black brush strokes that AT 10 TAPS OF BIG BELL THE MAYOR REQUESTS THE CITIZENS TO ASSEMBLE AT CITY HALL ARMED

TO PROTECT THEIR HOMES. The "big bell" in city hall, one of the largest bells ever cast in the United States, happily did not toll on this occasion, nor were the bridge guards challenged.

In the gray dawn of Monday the fifty United States regulars from Columbus arrived at Pittsburgh and marched out to the arsenal through drifting strands of smoke and fog. Along the way, from Grant Street to Thirty-third Street, lay nearly two miles of smoking ruins. In that bleak landscape of ashes and old iron rested the remains of 104 locomotives and 2,152 cars of all sorts—passenger, Pullman, officers' and emigrants' coaches, baggage, paymaster, express, postal, refrigerator and stock cars, gondolas, coal cars, boxcars and cabooses. If coupled into one ghostly train, they would have been strung out for eleven and a half miles. In the roofless roundhouses rods and straps of heat-twisted iron were draped over locomotives like seaweed on wrecks exposed by a marine upheaval. Along canted road beds and over charred ties, the iron rails dipped in curves and rose to graceful cusps. Everywhere lay a carpet of flaked and crumpled sheet iron, jumbled gears, distorted pipes, metal in all the shapes and figures geometry admits. The course of buried tracks could be traced by thousands of car wheels in neat files like soldiers on parade. Eventually 1,200 carloads of scrap were taken to Altoona.

Round about stood gutted brick buildings, eyeless and empty as calcined skulls. An occasional smokestack towered unbroken amid ragged scraps of brick wall. Near the ruins of the Union Depot a ponderous safe lay on its back with one corner sunk in cinders. In a ruined building squatted a potbellied stove with door agape. Besides the roundhouses, sheds, depot, offices and other railroad property, seventy-nine buildings, ranging from elevator to shanty, lay in ashes.

Not for reckoning were the ruins of human lives. The coroner reported twenty-four killed on Saturday and Sunday. Only three were railroaders. The roll included four Philadelphia soldiers, three of them workingmen. A fifth Philadelphian later died of wounds. The *Pittsburgh Post* noted on the tenth anniversary of that deadly Sabbath: "it has always been believed that persons were killed and buried without notice to the officials." In a tally of sorrows one must also count the maimed and the mourners. One fifty-eight-year-old blacksmith, for example, left a wife and four children.

As the sun rose higher, the day turned warm and sticky. The clouds drifted away, and the fog vanished; but smoke kept the air hazy. Nearly all business and manufacturing establishments remained closed, giving Pittsburghers a rare long week end. Once again Liberty Street filled up with people, this time peaceable sightseers and souvenir hunters. People in Sunday clothes stood around watching fire hoses play on the ruins of the grain elevator and Union Depot. Saloons along Liberty Street, despite evidence of rough treatment by Sunday's mob, did a business so thriving that mayor and council ordered them closed again. Photographers set up their tripods and drew crowds of volunteer posers, including a number of small boys. Men, women and children "of the poorer classes" picked their way through the rubble for what they might glean in scorched and smoky merchandise. Rumors circulated that a carload of bullion had been melted into the debris. A couple of boys, perched on a ruined locomotive near the depot, happily tolled the engine bell.

Elsewhere in the city, streets were crowded—some from curb to curb—with idle men, many of them miners, tramps and other strangers. There were alarms and a couple of excursions. When three fieldpieces being hauled for the committee of public safety were momentarily halted on Market Street, a bold onlooker spiked them and was promptly arrested. Word came from Elizabeth, a town some miles up the Monongahela, that several hundred miners had set out for Pittsburgh. Mayor McCarthy led a group of apprehensive citizens against the invaders, only to find that the miners had merely come to save the city from a rumored sacking by Philadelphia militia. On assurance that all was now calm the unarmed visitors went back home. That afternoon at Cumberland, Maryland, a gang of young men and boys took over a coach on a Pittsburgh-bound train, intending to see the ruins and have "a little sport." A brakeman warned them just before reaching Pittsburgh that a delegation of police and military awaited. Twenty or thirty of the skylarkers jumped out and escaped. The remaining forty-six were jailed, tried next morning before the mayor and given ninety days in the workhouse or a twenty-five-dollar fine. The *Pittsburgh Post* called them "the hardest looking set of villains which ever traveled." Some of the villains were released when their parents paid their fines.

Despite such embers of turbulence order reigned in Pittsburgh. The Pittsburgh militia reassembled Monday morning and paraded through the streets without incident. They remained on duty in Pittsburgh through the week, and most of them served in the mining districts until December. A new and more confident Committee of Public Safety was formed by the mayor and citizens. Nearly 300 volunteers came forward for patrol duty and were armed from the Allegheny Arsenal (after Mayor McCarthy had appealed over Major Buffington's head to Washington). Wearing blue lapel ribbons as badges, the volunteers stood guard on almost every street corner; and next morning a mounted patrol of fifty men extended their vigilance to the outskirts of town. When Monday evening brought rumors of a projected attack on the banks, bank officials found plenty of young men on the streets who were willing to stand guard.

And yet the return of order only underscored the doggedness of labor. The railroaders found that they were not alone. Scarcely noticed in the turmoil of Saturday night, a mob of 600 men from the mill of Everson and Macrum had stopped a through freight on the B. & O.'s Pittsburgh division and had forced the crew off; as a result, road officials suspended through freight service. Stirred by the events of Sunday in Pittsburgh, workers of the National Tube Works at McKeesport gathered together in the small hours of Monday morning and marched all over town to martial music, calling fellow workers from their houses. A general strike movement swept the area, first spreading to a rolling mill, then a car works, then a planing mill. The tube strikers demanded $1.50 a day for laborers and a raise of twenty-five cents a day for all, including boys. In mid-morning a thousand McKeesport strikers marched with a brass band to Andrew Carnegie's great Edgar Thomson Steel Works at Braddocks, calling out planing mill and tin mill workers en route. By midafternoon both the Carnegie workers and those in the Braddocks car works had joined the strikers. Over near Allegheny one mill force struck for $1.25 a day and settled within hours for $1.12½. At Castle Shannon 500 miners struck for four cents a bushel instead of two and a half. On the South Side, laborers struck at Jones and Laughlin and at the pipe works of Evans, Dalzell and Company.

Tuesday morning's papers carried a card from the railroad strikers to the public. They had been trying earnestly to settle with the company since before the riot, they assured the world, but had not been given the courtesy of an answer. Tom Scott could not or would not be reached. "If we are further ignored we know our last resort," they said mysteriously, "and Thomas A. Scott will continue to assume the responsibility." On Saturday, July 28, after a half-inch of rain, a West Chester militiaman found the ruins still hot underfoot. So were the strikers. "I talked to all the strikers I could get my hands on," wrote the militiaman, "and I could find but one spirit and one purpose among them: that they were justified in resorting to any means to break down the power of corporations."

CHAPTER 10

Chain Reaction

THE PITTSBURGH holocaust had meanwhile acted on the nation like a hot coal in a barrel of firecrackers. On Monday and Tuesday, July 23 and 24, nerves crackled, tempers smoked and glowed, violence burst forth in a score of cities from the Middle Atlantic States to the Mississippi Valley. City officials and militia commanders reacted in different ways to the shapes which rose before them in a smoke cloud of rumor and confusion. Some officials kept their heads and the peace as well. Some blustered and beat wildly at the air, some cowered and made gestures of endearment. And some moved with impeccable firmness and composure, only to be confounded by chance.

In Pennsylvania all ten divisions of the National Guard, comprising 870 officers and 9,000 men, were called out on Sunday. But at Lebanon one company and part of another mutinied and marched through town amid "great excitement." At Columbia strikers seized the roundhouse and blocked all traffic. At the other end of the state, two companies were held up in Meadville when railroad men took off their engine—though on that road, the Atlantic & Great Western, there had been neither a pay cut nor a strike. The same thing happened to seven companies at Chenango.

On Saturday Robert Ammon had prepared a hot reception at Allegheny for any state militia which might try to pass through to Pittsburgh. With Hartranft out of the state, Ammon concluded that the militia call must rest on shaky authority; and he therefore proposed to treat such troops as no more than a mob. The strikers got arms from sympathetic businessmen (said Ammon) or else stole them from the local armory (said Mayor Phillips). Ammon's men dug rifle pits and trenches at Strawberry Lane outside the Allegheny depot, set up patrols and warned civilians off the streets

184

and out of the probable line of fire. If the Seventh National Guard Division had not been delayed by the railroad tie-up, Allegheny would have witnessed an encounter as sensational as any in Pittsburgh.

By Sunday that danger had passed. Mayor Phillips himself opposed any outside meddling. General Manager Layng of the Fort Wayne acquiesced in young Ammon's control of the road. Already Ammon had possession of the telegraph and was sending orders to the strikers up and down the road. Now he took over as the road's manager pro tem. His dizzy rise to authority caught the nation's attention, and he became known to millions as "Boss Ammon." Passenger service ran smoothly. As for freights, the strikers went energetically to work moving them out of the yards and stringing them along the line for miles, the better to keep them out of the mob's way. Day and night, working regular reliefs, the strikers stood armed guard over the cars and their contents. On Monday Mayor Phillips recruited 100 special police, held 100 Civil War veterans in reserve, and (to the joint applause of strikers and management) closed the saloons. Thereupon the weary strikers asked for and received police reinforcements.

Altoona, ringed by the hills of western Pennsylvania, looked like the railroad town it was. Its unpaved streets were laid out in a huge grid, relieved in severity only by the steep climb of the cross streets. Drab wooden houses and stores crowded about the great shops of the Pennsylvania, on which the town depended. Westbound freights, as they lumbered heavily up the mountain, belched black smoke that spread over the town in a sepia pall. Ordinarily relations between the town and the company were calm, even cordial; but as early as Saturday, Altoona was hotly denying its creator. That morning Brinton's Philadelphia troops passed through on their fateful trip to Pittsburgh, unmolested except by shouted insults and some futile pulling of coupling pins. Later on, the strike took hold in Altoona. At five-thirty that afternoon sudden fury seized the mob at the arrival of another westbound militia train. A striker got a bayonet through his arm when he tried to uncouple the engine. A soldier was pulled off and beaten, but managed to get back on. Boys and members of what Altoona called the "gut gang" swarmed about the train, stoning it and exchanging shots with the troops.

Miraculously the train pulled out without serious injury to anyone.

On Sunday morning a westbound trainload of about 500 militia stopped at Altoona to eat breakfast and get a heavier engine for the mountain pull. The sound of church bells mingled with the tramp of marching feet, the rattle and squeal of drums and fifes, the shouts of the crowd and the shriek of train whistles. The rioters shut the roundhouse gates on the mountain engine and captured a detachment of troops sent to escort it out. The troops gave up their arms with the best of wills, though Captain Foresman, in trying to fend off the crowd with his sword, was laid low by a well-flung rock. More troops started marching toward the roundhouse; but when it became known that the mob had drawn the sand, water and fire from the available engines, had soaped the boxes and had taken off the driving rods, the officers gave up and marched the men back. At the depot they stacked arms and fraternized with the crowd, which blocked them from proceeding but gave them loud leave to go home. That evening one full company and fragments of others accepted the boon. "We were told," said some to a reporter, "that riot and murder, arson and rape, were being committed through this part of the State. We have found it different here, and are satisfied to return home." As they left, a quartet from an all-Negro militia company was making "some excellent vocal music."

At Harrisburg, the state capital, halfway back along the line to Philadelphia, people behaved pretty much as they did in Altoona, except that boys from fourteen to twenty years of age made up a larger, even a dominant element in the mob. These "half grown boys," as most witnesses called them, "bootblacks and all classes," did most of the pin pulling and catcalling in the inevitable depot mob scene of Saturday night. A number of the striking railroad men appealed to older citizens "to get this [passenger] train on, that it was not the orders that the passenger trains were to be stopped," that the strikers "had nothing to do with it." But the young hellions had their way, and the passengers spent the night in Harrisburg. Tramps had been thick thereabouts, many of them having been run out of Altoona a few days earlier. Only two days before, Harrisburg police had routed forty of them from the stockyards in a flurry of bullets, stones and billies. Nevertheless, all witnesses agreed that throughout the upheaval it was "the mob of boys and half grown men who were so prominent in the noise and confusion." The worried strikers pushed forward a prominent local Greenbacker and all-around orator, who tried to give the frenzy a more moderate turn. This proving futile, the strikers at last announced through the press that "we have been peaceable and will remain so." And they organized to guard railroad property.

The great danger at Harrisburg was that the mob might seize the State Arsenal just outside town. Fortunately Major General J. K. Sigfried of the Fourth National Guard Division had foresight enough to order the Harrisburg militia company into the arsenal on Saturday night. By Monday morning some 800 of Sigfried's militia had converged on and occupied the arsenal after dodging waiting mobs at various points.

On Monday afternoon Harrisburg spirit was rekindled by some Philadelphia militia straggling homeward from Altoona. They had been put off an express train Sunday and had sought sanctuary in an old church. Recognizing the lieutenant's Masonic sign, a passer-by fraternally advised him that York, his contemplated goal, was no better haven than Harrisburg eight miles down the Susquehanna. So the lieutenant, in civilian clothes, stole timorously downriver and across the covered bridge and sounded out some of the Harrisburg crowd. "I told them we desired to surrender and wanted protection," he later confided. Obligingly, even jovially, a crowd of 200 or 300, mostly "half grown boys" and Negroes, brushed aside the protesting tollgate keeper, shoved the gates flat and clattered across. The Philadelphia troops shook hands all around and gave up their guns. On the way back fife and drum filled the resonant bridge with a joyful noise, while the captive militia ambled along in a square of juvenile guards. Through the streets of Harrisburg the mob marched in a sort of Roman triumph to Boyer's Hotel, where the captives were fed and bidden godspeed. At Mayor Patterson's request the crowd, now swelled to 3,000, cheerfully deposited the captured breechloaders in the city hall.

Harrisburg factories and shops had been idled all day by strikes or mob intimidation. The workers and a growing number of tramps joined the mob, now emboldened by its success with the militia. The sheriff had only just returned from out of town; the citizenry was either sympathetic or afraid. After dark the mob pushed into Altmier's gun store and helped themselves to the stock. Mayor Patterson persuaded them to return most of the guns. A few minutes later another gun store and then a pawnshop were besieged. Since his arrival Sheriff William Jennings had been busy getting a posse together; and at midnight two taps of the city's fire bell, the mayor's prearranged signal for a turnout of citizens, brought out additional defenders of order (as well as a couple of fire engines and their bewildered crews). With the city's little police force as a hard nucleus the sheriff and the mayor led the posse in a successful charge against the mob, scattering it bloodlessly. After that, citizen patrols kept the streets in order through the waning night, and Harrisburg's moment of crisis was over.

The city of Reading was not so lucky. To begin with, it depended on Franklin Gowen almost as much as Altoona depended on Tom Scott. Reading's commercial pulse kept time to the rumble of Gowen's trains, freighted with the coal of Gowen's Philadelphia & Reading Coal and Iron Company. In the city lived 1,500 employees of the Philadelphia & Reading Railroad alone, not counting the Coal and Iron Company men. Yet, as at Cumberland and Altoona, dependence did not inspire devotion. The engineers' strike of April had left bitterness behind and men to nurse it—the beaten strikers, blacklisted and jobless, subsisting on an increasingly hard-spared dole from the Engineers' Brotherhood. Even those who still worked on the Reading had not been paid since May.

Gowen himself had been absent since then, seeking financial support in Europe. He got back to his Philadelphia office on the morning of July 16 at the very moment the Great Strike began in Baltimore. That day the Reading management laid off all passenger brakemen but one on each train. Gowen plainly felt that he had his employees securely under his thumb. Even after strikes broke out on the B. & O., the Pennsylvania and the Erie, Gowen's mouthpiece, the *Miners' Journal* of Pottsville, wrote: "The men have no organization, and there is too much race jealousy existing among them to permit them to form one."

In Pottsville, haunted by remembrance of the hanged Mollies, this may have been true. It was not true in Reading. As to race, 90 per cent of Reading was native-born and almost all the rest German, hence not wholly alien to Pennsylvania Dutch country. As to organization the Trainmen's Union had a flourishing branch there. To the great relief of local merchants, the Reading at last paid May wages on Saturday, July 21. At a little table behind bars sat Paymaster Wells with piles of bank notes and bags of silver before him. On his spindle rose a white tower of impaled vouchers as men filed up to the window and drew their tardy dues. The men were not effusively grateful. They remarked that they "wouldn't have it long, as every cent would have to be paid right out on their debts." If anything, they felt all the freer to strike.

A committee of the Engineers' Brotherhood afterward told the press "that in the proceedings of their meeting Saturday night not one word was mentioned officially regarding the strike." Later still, testimony in criminal court made this protestation seem disingenuous. Dark deeds were reportedly planned that midsummer night in Columbia Hall. The chairman suggested that it would not be a bad idea to do the same as had been done on the B. & O. "While it is hot," someone chimed in, "we can keep the ball rolling." Men volunteered to head off incoming trains. Hiram Nachtrieb prescribed a keg of powder for the Lebanon Valley railroad bridge to "blow it to Hell!" So, at least, ran the sworn testimony of prosecution witnesses.

On Sunday people clustered around the *Reading Eagle's* bulletin board, hungry for news of Pittsburgh. Among them were many jobless men, including railroaders fired after the April strike. Anger nourished anger, and Pittsburgh gave inspiration. That evening the Sunday quiet was broken by a blast from a tin horn at Seventh and Penn. As if on cue, a crowd assembled. Flames rose into the blue dusk from a carload of shingles; but the blaze was quenched, and an eerie quiet persisted until ten o'clock. Then came yelling, cheering, blowing of horns, a din that carried for a dozen blocks. Two thousand people "of the lowest calculation" crowded along banks, tracks and sidings near the new depot, bellowing and screaming fearfully. Amid the uproar twenty-five or fifty silent men in work clothes, their faces carefully blackened with coal dust, equipped themselves with crowbars, picks, sledges, cotton waste and coal-oil from a tool house and set about tearing up tracks and jamming switches. They hammered rocks and wooden blocks between the sliding rails of the switches, or wedged them with iron rails. Locks were broken off, staples torn out. Across the tracks were thrown timbers, rails, a hand truck with wheels upward. Near the bridge a loaded coal car was derailed, with one axle and a pair of wheels unshipped, so as to dump it. The railroad officials, taken by surprise, seemed paralyzed.

Shortly before eleven, the dark destroyers set two cabooses afire. Fire Chief Boyer and his engines were stopped by the crowd. "No use for you here, Howard, better turn right back," people called. Chief Cullen and the night police detail stood by helplessly. The crowd joked as the flames crackled. "Lightning must have struck them," "Pittsburgh on a small scale," "Where's them Baltimore fellers?" The crew of an incoming train prudently uncoupled and abandoned the cars. When the engine started off again, a volley of stones rattled against it, smashing windows and headlights. A Gowen policeman fired from it twice into the crowd; but no casualties were evident, and after falling back momentarily the crowd came up again and stood solid.

Then the mob turned to bigger game. Several hundred headed up the Lebanon Valley tracks with a big can of coal oil and a bundle of cotton waste. Hiram Nachtrieb and a couple of other Engineers' Brotherhood men led them to the near end of the Lebanon Valley Bridge. A score or so of the mob crossed to the western end, chased away the watchman and climbed down through a trapdoor into the body of the structure. The Lebanon Valley tracks rested on a four-span timber truss sheathed in iron, its sides about twenty feet high. The truss in turn rested on high stone piers rising from the bed of the Schuylkill. Thus a good draft sent flames roaring high into the air, their glare reflected in the dark waters below. The crowd that stood expectant at the eastern end could see the whole water front of the city and, beyond it, nearly to the bend at the sheet mill. The leaping flames turned harsh water-front shapes into a weird chorus, bending and swaying to a medley of moonlight and fire. Church steeples in the town rose like giant specters against a backdrop of black night, and from trees and housetops for blocks around shone the pale faces of a watching multitude. For an hour and a half the flames gorged noisily, and then the western end of the bridge collapsed, sending red-hot rails and sheet iron to hiss and bubble in the water seventy feet below. By two-thirty the smouldering ruins were all but deserted.

Morning found Fire Chief Boyer and his men guarding the depot against possible arsonists while the hated "Johnny" Wootten and other Reading officials telegraphed at length to Franklin Gowen in Philadelphia. Columns of smoke still rose from the huge timbers and the tangled ironwork in the river. A jam of boats waited on each side of the debris that choked the Schuylkill and Union canals. The piers still stood, as well as five brick arches on the eastern end, so that the bridge was not a total loss; repairs were thought possible for $50,000 or so, about a third of its original cost.

In the town many strangers were about, and rumor had 200 Baltimore men on hand "for special work tonight." The heavy tramp of feet resounded all day from the depot platforms, and a huge throng milled about the tracks from Walnut to Chestnut streets. Mayor Evans was vacationing at Ocean Grove; Sheriff Yorgey had been frightened into uselessness by the reported murder of Sheriff Fife at Pittsburgh; Chief Cullen and his handful of police were helpless against the crowds. In midafternoon 100 men boarded and stopped a coal train, uncoupled its cars and left them spread along the down track at Penn Street in the center of town. At four the Philadelphia express and mail train came in. On the advice of several former Reading Railroad engineers, the mob spared it for the sake of the mails. But in shifting to the unblocked up track, the express had to push back an eight-wheel coal car with bottom gates open. Big lumps of steamboat coal fell under the wheels of the express, which crushed and scattered them the width of Penn Street. When the rioters cleared Penn Street for traffic, they piled the coal in three-foot heaps on the tracks. At six o'clock the engineer of the evening express got up steam and charged through these at forty miles an hour, sending up clouds of black dust. Stones were thrown at him, one leaving his face smeared with blood. At the depot a crowd seized the train. The six-twenty accommodation squealed to a stop in the Court Street cut, and the passengers, including "a number of ladies," found themselves reduced to shanks' mare. Inside the train a gang of boys expressed themselves by slashing the plush upholstery. (Much of the day's uproar was later laid to "crowds of bad boys, led by two or three men.") And then, at seven-thirty, there arrived the Easton Grays and six other companies of the Fourth National Guard Regiment. They had been sent at the instance of the Reading's General Manager Wootten after consultation with Franklin Gowen in Philadelphia.

The Easton Grays were in a sour mood. A few weeks before, they had done duty at Mauch Chunk during the Molly Maguire execu-

tions, a lugubrious assignment, though uneventful. A week ago, all
thirty-eight of them plus the drum corps had left Easton for summer camp at Stroudsburg. Their encampment was to have been
climaxed by a "hop" this very night of July 23. But on Sunday
evening, just after parade, orders had come to break camp and entrain. The Grays marched to the depot in a drenching rain, mourn-
fully singing "Good Night Ladies." At three o'clock Monday morning
they piled out at Allentown, keeping their sodden uniforms on because orders were expected imminently. At three o'clock that afternoon, after twelve hours of waiting, Colonel Good took it into his
head to march them all over Allentown in the broiling hot sun.
Orders for Reading reached them in the Public Square; and off they
trudged, soaked with sweat, to the depot. And now here they were,
fagged out and resentful. At that moment, people back home in
Easton were reading the delayed dispatch of a Stroudsburg correspondent: "Our hop on Monday evening promises to eclipse anything of the kind that we have yet had. There will be a very large
attendance of the elite and fair."

At the request of a railroad official, Brigadier General Frank
Reeder moved out of the depot with the Easton Grays to clear an
obstructing car from the tracks. The car stood in a deep "cut" which
ran along Seventh Street. The people of that shabby neighborhood,
some of them jobless, the rest ill-paid, jammed the sidewalks overlooking the cut on either side. Tenement houses rose like a dark
red wall behind them. "Have you come to shoot us down?" they
yelled at the militia. "We don't care for your blank cartridges!"
Reeder halted his men for a moment, moved the musicians to the
rear, ordered muskets loaded and then advanced into the gloomy
defile to the cadence of drum taps. The crowd had been ready to
harass trains. Brickbats, rocks, even boulders, waited in heaps along
the sidewalks. Stones now began rattling down on the Grays. The
"hop" had opened. "Don't fire, men, quicken your pace," shouted
an officer. "Kill them! Kill them!" yelled the crowd. Rocks clattered
down as if "shoveled over the sides of a wall." Two wagonloads
were later hauled away. Men, women and boys hurled stones and
other objects, including chamber pots, from house windows. It
was said later that two straining men heaved a huge boulder over
the edge. One man fired a pistol several times. Miraculously none
of the troops were killed; but twenty were wounded by pistol shots

and missiles, at least three seriously. "Don't shoot," the officers begged their men vainly. A solitary rifle shot rang out, then an uneven volley, not up toward the stone throwers, but forward through the cut toward the Penn Street crossing.

The crowd fell silent, the stone throwing ceased. The Grays hurried on through the cut and emerged about fifty yards from the Penn Street crossing, where they saw another crowd forming. Bricks flew from the crowd, and the Grays replied with a deadly volley which left the crossing empty save for crumpled bodies. At Seventh Street the Grays, tired and thirsty, asked the police to open the fireplugs and give them water, but the police would not. So the Grays returned to the depot.

After the tragedy people told of narrow escapes. Some young ladies watching from the portico balcony of a Seventh Street restaurant saw bullets smash flowerpots alongside them. Other bullets tore one man's hat, another's coat and Police Chief Cullen's vest. A Reading tradition has the town drunk lying in the cut happily oblivious to it all.

Others, however, found luck against them. Six men lay dead in the twilight: a fireman and an engineer formerly employed on the Reading, a carpenter, a huckster, a rolling-mill worker, a laborer. The rolling-mill man had been two blocks beyond Penn on his way uptown. A policeman and another man lay at the point of death. A score or more were wounded, including five policemen guarding the crossing, a *Reading Post* reporter and a laborer named Lewis Alexander Eisenhower. The last-named bled to death in two hours, and two other wounded died some days later, bringing the final death toll to eleven. Few, if any, of the dead or wounded had been active rioters.

For a time that night it seemed as though Reading might indeed turn into a "Pittsburgh on a small scale." A crowd broke into the armory of the Reading Rifles and seized about sixty rifles, only to find the ammunition removed. One angry Reading citizen, walking the streets in his shirt sleeves in search of a fight, told a Pottsville reporter: "I'm ashamed of the working people of Reading. Now that the strike has begun, the workingmen and every fair-minded man ought to turn in and burn the company's shops and depots. The best thing to do first would be to go to the dispatcher's office and kill every damned Reading official there, beginning with Johnny

Wootten." The little group that had gathered about him seemed in full accord. A mob made a rush for the car shops to burn out the militia; but at the last moment some whim diverted the rioters and they turned instead to plundering freight cars and tearing up tracks. No more blood ran that night.

Next morning the Easton Grays and two other companies of the Fourth Regiment joined with five newly arrived companies of the Sixteenth to escort a construction train through the Seventh Street cut. This time the force divided and went along the sidewalks above the cut. At the Penn Street crossing, a crowd fraternized with the men of the Sixteenth and threw rocks at the hated Easton Grays. The Grays turned menacingly toward the crowd, whereupon the Sixteenth Regiment men called out: "If you fire at the mob, we'll fire at you!" The mob cheered lustily, and railroad officials called off the whole enterprise. On the way back, hooted and pelted, the Grays were restrained with difficulty by their officers. The Sixteenth Regiment men freely announced that they would not fire on the people. One remarked that he would "rather put a bullet through Frank Gowen." Some passed out ammunition to the crowds in the street. But the militia all left for home that afternoon; six companies of the First United States Artillery arrived shortly after, and order was ensured. Tracks were repaired under Coal and Iron Police guard, and by Wednesday all trains were running. That same day Coal and Iron men began roving the city with local police, arresting suspected rioters and arsonists.

Six miles from Allentown, the engineer of the Grays' train had refused to go further. The Grays walked to Allentown and hired an omnibus to take them home to Easton, where they arrived, footsore and exhausted, early Wednesday morning. The home folks received them sympathetically, and the *Easton Express* commented that "the citizens of Reading owe a debt of gratitude to the Fourth Regiment which they can never repay." Notwithstanding this, some Easton people may have feared a settling of accounts. At any rate, a lot of excited citizens turned out that very morning at the tolling of a bell. It proved to be the bell at Zion's Church, calling children to the annual Sunday School picnic.

The news from Pittsburgh on July 22 brought excited people into the streets of Philadelphia as elsewhere. From his office in the

Pennsylvania depot, Tom Scott heard crowd murmurings above the clatter of telegraph keys. Since the engineers had refused to sign a no-strike pledge, Scott prudently halted westbound freights. Police and detectives roamed through the crowd. Saloons across Market Street did a rush business, and a rowdy element began to show itself. By midafternoon Scott began to fear an outbreak even worse than Pittsburgh's.

But Philadelphia was not Pittsburgh. Railroads converged upon it, thousands of men, women and children labored in its factories, vagrants and criminals abounded. Still, pressures were lighter. Philadelphia's neat buildings of granite, red sandstone, freestone and fine red brick, its clean white marble doorsteps and broad streets, its clearer air, all tempered the oppressiveness of city life. Along the Schuylkill River stretched Fairmount Park, 1,500 acres of forest trees, grassy glades and ambling paths. Philadelphia, moreover, looked on the Pennsylvania Railroad as its own, not an absentee lord. Most important, Philadelphia's mayor was not William McCarthy, but William S. Stokley.

Stokley, a roughhewn businessman in his fifties, reputed to be one of the Pennsylvania's largest stockholders, had served as mayor of Philadelphia for six years. He had a way with mobs. Back in 1872 he led a police posse against 400 marching gasworks strikers, scattered them, arrested their leaders and broke the strike. Many people ascribed his re-election in February 1877 to his success against rioters and his effective reorganization of the police force. (Others laid it to a well-oiled political machine.) On July 21 news of the Great Strike had brought Stokley back from his Long Branch vacation. Now on July 22, he moved with speed and decision. When darkness fell, the mob stopped an oil train. Five hundred people yelled and hooted from an embankment by the track. Stokley scattered them with a well-directed police charge. By midnight he had the depot cordoned off; and moonlight, fitfully emerging from a heavy procession of cumulus clouds, gleamed from the accoutrements of police sentries along the bluff. Stokley had wired Washington for help, and Secretary of War George McCrary now replied: "Troops will be immediately placed in Philadelphia under command of General Hancock to meet any emergency, and the President will exert every Constitutional power to restore order and protect property."

Next morning the regular troops did not arrive when expected, and a rumor spread that strikers had blocked them. Emboldened, a crowd of 500 or 600, "a large number of them being young men and boys," gathered at the Callowhill Street bridge over the tracks. When they refused to disperse, about 300 police charged, swinging their clubs. Heads were bloodied, and the mob was scattered. Just then, dense smoke rose at the lower end of the city. Clanging fire engines arrived to find an oil and freight train afire. While thousands watched, some 400 police made a hollow square about the blaze to protect the firemen. All but six cars were moved off to safety. The rest burned like "a mountain of red flame." An exploding oil car sent burning oil fifty feet into the air, dousing three firemen and two bystanders with flame. Two of the firemen were badly burned.

Early in the afternoon 125 marines arrived, fresh from duty at Baltimore. These went on picket duty along the bluff. General Hancock and his staff arrived a few minutes later and rode about the area with Tom Scott in the latter's carriage. Hancock had already ordered all troops en route from the north and east to be stopped at Philadelphia. Scott took heart. That afternoon he stood firm in an interview with twenty engineers. The cut would stand; and if the engineers chose to leave their jobs, two or three men could be had for each vacancy. The force about Philadelphia built up steadily. Mayor Stokley organized a Committee of Safety and promised to do anything it authorized, regardless of law, in order to keep the peace. At once, the committee gave him leave to double the police force. At midnight the rest of Hancock's troops, 500 men of the First Artillery, stepped off their train fully accoutered and with their heavy blankets slung jauntily over their shoulders. By Tuesday afternoon Philadelphia's peace was being kept by 1,400 armed police, 400 armed firemen, 700 United States regulars, 125 marines, 2,000 special police and 500 men of the Veterans' Corps. This aggregation enabled General Hancock to send four batteries of regulars to Reading that afternoon, in answer to the pleas of Franklin Gowen. The depletion was more than made up by sundown with 1,500 members of the Grand Army of the Republic, armed and ready for orders. Nothing now prevented freights from running but stoppages at other points.

To Hornellsville on the Western Division of the Erie, July 22 brought more farce than tragedy. Barney Donahue and his Erie strikers, as quirky as their bedeviled road, still refused to let passenger trains run. The westbound "Pacific Express" came in at nine that morning, and Erie officials chose it for a test of strength. They had detachments of the Fifty-fourth New York Regiment placed at the Canisteo Street and West Street crossings and smaller guards posted at intervals further on. At ten the express started confidently west toward Dunkirk with a mail car and two passenger coaches, the latter carrying fourteen passengers and forty militia. Four men and a sergeant rode in the locomotive cab; two soldiers with fixed bayonets stood guard on each car platform, supposedly to repel boarders.

The strikers held a trump card: the long, steep grade that led to the summit of Tiptop Mountain. Tradition has it that the women of Hornellsville had stayed up all Saturday night making soft soap. In any event, 500 strikers waited with buckets of the stuff a quarter of a mile up the grade. From the bottom to where they stood, soft soap had been slathered liberally over the rails. The speeding train ran bravely up the slippery incline. Then its wheels began to spin and its momentum slacken. The strikers broke into deafening cheers. Dave Cary, the engineer, opened the sand pipe to its limit, and sand streamed out under the wheels. Torpedoes banged away on the tracks, and hundreds of spectators shouted wildly from trackmen's shanties and the Hillside House. Cary opened the throttle wide, but his train lost speed steadily from twenty miles an hour to fifteen, to ten, to eight. A crowd formed on the track ahead, one man waving a red flag. Cary kept on, and the crowd grudgingly parted. Fireman Matt Dewey leaned out of a cab window and called down, "I'll get out up here aways, boys!"

As the train slowed to five miles an hour, strikers began clambering aboard, scorning the half-hearted resistance of the militia. One burly brakeman swung himself up onto the lead coach, shoved the guard to one side and set the brakes. Shouting strikers pushed among the terror-stricken passengers. Someone uncoupled the coaches. The bell rope snapped, and one end coiled itself around the neck of a militiaman, who nearly choked before he could be extricated. Engineer Cary was allowed to go on with the mails. The passengers and militia were turned out of the cars, after which strikers unhooked the brake rods, bent them out of shape and smashed the brake wheels with axes. Then the cheering crowd sent the cars thundering back down the grade toward Hornellsville. A quick-witted engineer in the yards turned a switch in time to divert the cars away from a stalled train and out onto the ground.

A few minutes later, another troop-laden train set out for Buffalo. The strikers stopped it by opening a switch, then boarded it, expelled the militia, bent the sand pipe out of shape and sent the train back to the yards. One more train went out, this time east toward New York City. An ambush of strikers halted it, drove off the crew and guards and left it stranded half a mile east of town, its fire out and its boiler drained. Upon news of these setbacks, New York State authorities ordered the Seventy-fourth Regiment to Hornellsville eastward from Buffalo and the Twenty-third westward from Brooklyn. Pending their arrival, Erie officials gave up trying to move trains; and when darkness settled on the town, the strikers jubilantly counted the day theirs. From the high hills roundabout, strikers' signal lights flashed gaily; and Hornellsville women trudged up steep paths with baskets of food for the men on guard.

On Sunday afternoon the Seventy-fourth Regiment departed from the Erie's Buffalo depot without interference, arriving at Hornellsville that evening. Though the Erie strike was a day old at Buffalo and Sunday crowds filled the streets, Buffalo's first real trouble came not at the Erie depot, but at the roundhouse of the Lake Shore & Michigan Southern, a Vanderbilt road. Erie strikers had pressured thirty or forty Lake Shore brakemen and firemen into striking on Saturday night. With stores and factories closed on Sunday, 1,500 people, "a large percentage of whom were boys and young roughs," massed at the Lake Shore roundhouse, where they joined the strikers in blocking freights. The Lake Shore's enraged superintendent called on Company A, Sixty-fifth National Guard Regiment, to clear the yards. As the twenty-two militiamen marched from the roundhouse, a mob of several hundred followed them angrily. Presently the juvenile element let fly with a barrage of stones. Brigadier General W. F. Rogers, accompanying the little detachment, stopped and shouted something at the mob; but hundreds of voices drowned him out, the stoning continued and Rogers himself was swallowed up in the throng. At last a militia officer halted the men and faced them about. "Make ready to fire!" he shouted. In the hush that fell like a hammer, people heard guns being cocked. There was a wild yell: "Look out, they're going to shoot!" The crowd flew apart like

feathers in a whirlwind, dodging around freight cars and dropping
to the ground. One Fourth-of-July squib could have given Buffalo
its own major tragedy. But the moment passed, the troops held their
fire and presently their commander marched them back to the
roundhouse. Lake Shore officials suspended freight movements for
the day, and the troops quietly left the roundhouse by another door
, a couple of hours later.

That night an excited crowd took over the New York Central's
Buffalo yards. William Vanderbilt wired the superintendent an expression of confidence in "the good sense and stability of a large majority of our employes." With the unstable minority in mind, the
Central's officials decided to stop all train service at Buffalo for the
time being.

Monday, though a workday, did not bring the expected peace.
In the morning a crowd armed with cudgels and knives stormed
first into the Lake Shore shops and then into those of the Erie,
brushing aside militia guards and forcing shopmen to quit. The mob
took full possession of the Erie roundhouse and painstakingly bar-
ricaded it. A twenty-man company of the Sixty-fifth Regiment
marched out in the afternoon to recapture the property. A thousand
or more rioters blocked them, and in the inevitable retreat the
troops were manhandled. Some lost their muskets. Two officers
were beaten, one of them being held with his arms pinned while
rioters belabored him with sticks.

All day long, crowds rudely stopped such trains as were sent out,
uncoupling cars and pulling off crews. At dusk a "wildcat" passenger
train moved toward Buffalo along the Lake Shore line, bearing
forty passengers and a Westfield militia company sent to guard the
bridge over the Buffalo River. At the bridge a mob of 300 stopped
the train, cut off the engine and mail car and sent them on to the
depot. Captain J. H. Towle of the Westfield company stepped out
of the militia coach and tried to reason with the mob. For a moment
the rioters seemed impressed by his eloquence. Then a dozen of
them rushed the coach, swarmed in and, with pistols levelled at
soldiers' heads, seized several muskets. When Towle grasped the
situation, he bawled orders to clear the car, and a confused melee
erupted. While militia and rioters grappled and fought in the aisle,
the mob fired in through the windows. The troops fired back, managed to eject the intruders, disembarked and routed the mob with

another volley. Seven of the militia suffered more or less serious wounds, none fatal. As for the rioters, Towle and his men felt sure that at least half a dozen lay dead about the car. One militiaman later declared he "saw nine dead men, counted them, and felt some of them with his foot; of these four were at the front of the car, three at the right hand side, and two at the rear, one of these lying on the platform, the other hanging over the platform railing." Other soldiers gave similar, though not identical accounts. Several of the Westfield men fled beyond recall, two of them taking refuge in a haystack and turning up next morning a dozen miles away. The rest of the company headed for some near-by houses for succor. The returning mob pushed the car down the tracks, smashed it up and set it afire, driving Buffalo firemen away. A militia detachment sent from Buffalo found the site of the engagement unoccupied even by corpses. The only verified death was that of a striker, eighteen-year-old Michael Lyons, who died of wounds next morning. A dozen or more rioters were badly wounded, including a carpenter whose left arm had to be amputated.

Monday night was quiet, largely because most of the principal railroads—the Canada Southern, the Lake Shore, the Erie and the New York Central—had given up trying to move anything but local passenger trains. Only two Canadian roads—the Great Western and the Grand Trunk—ran as usual.

Tuesday brought the climax. Mobs composed, by all accounts, largely of tramps, toughs and teen-age boys roamed the city trying to bring about a general strike. Most workers were unenthusiastic, perhaps because trade unions had not fared well in Buffalo lately. ("Strike," said the *Workingman's Advocate* earlier that year, "is an obsolete word in the Buffalo workingman's dictionary.") But at planing mills, tanneries, car works, a bolt and nut factory, hogyards, coalyards and canal works, a display of pick handles and brickbats effectively stopped operations. At nightfall a mob boldly attacked an isolated militia company at a car works in an attempt to capture ammunition. The militiamen managed to escape with all but two muskets.

The sheriff swore in 300 deputies. Mayor Becker set up citizens' patrols and added special police. The G.A.R. formed a battalion of special troops and nostalgically shouldered Springfield rifles for picket and guard duty at the Erie yards. Mayor Becker wired Governor Robinson for more troops, and the governor obligingly started two militia regiments on their way. It was Buffalo's regular police force, however, that took the honors. Throughout the day's disturbances, squads of police had effectively broken up roving bodies of rioters. The showdown came at the New York Central's East Buffalo depot at dusk. An unruly mob of boys and tramps (but no railroad men) pelted the depot with stones and threatened to burn it. They did burn a freight car and dismantle a flagman's shanty. When they stoned and blackguarded the police detachment, Captain Philip Wurtz of the Eighth Precinct summoned a wagonload of reinforcements. A feint by a few policemen distracted the mob while Wurtz formed a line of seventy-five police across the wide street at the rioters' backs. "Now boys, slash 'em!" shouted Captain Wurtz, and the charge began. In the appreciative words of the *Weekly Courier*:

Like lightning the clubs descended and ascended. Every stroke hit a new head whose owner went solid to the ground or bowled in continued sommersaults. The officers seemed to put their whole souls into this commendable work . . . Those who did not get hit fled as fast as legs could carry them, and . . . a howling chorus of pain could be heard at the high trestle more than a mile away. The rout was complete and final.

Next day rioters made sporadic attempts to invade mills and shops, but were frightened off easily by the newly respected constabulary.

The men of the New York Central seemed slow to take fire. In this they resembled their employer, the stubborn, phlegmatic William H. Vanderbilt. That railroad baron had himself once known penury and rejection. A dull youth, held in contempt by a cold father, he and his wife had lived for a time, until his health broke, on a clerk's pay of $19 a week. Then he took over a lonely seaside farm on Staten Island, where he sat on the fence, read his newspaper and watched his hired hands work, getting his money's worth out of each or firing him. Money accumulated. He enlarged the farm, built a villa and began to indulge a passion for fine trotting horses. Prosperity notwithstanding, the younger Vanderbilt remained prudently submissive under his father's hectorings, perhaps fortified by hope of a hundred-million-dollar reward. He obeyed his father's whim and gave up smoking at the age of thirty. Year by year, the old commodore grew prouder of his son's crafty, methodical bent for business. William's influence spread through the father's enterprises. And the reward came. Now, with a confident smile on his good-humored Dutch face, his long English side whiskers fluttering in the breeze, William Henry Vanderbilt, aged fifty-six, could drive his smart trotters through Central Park as a free man (though he complained increasingly of a feeling of "suffocation"). Thanks to old Cornelius Vanderbilt's reliance on primogeniture as a prop to family fortunes, William had just come into $90,-000,000, mostly in the form of an 85 per cent interest in the New York Central. Within seven years he would more than double it.

Vanderbilt could be brusquely cynical under provocation (as when he blurted his famous remark "the public be damned"). But he was generally affable, democratic in manner, a kind and loving family man. The men of the Central did not dislike him as intensely as those of the B. & O. did John Garrett. If his messages to employees in the present crisis had a patronizing tone, a touch of the grand seigneur, surely no one had better warrant. He may well have been genuinely aggrieved, therefore, when his men at last joined the Great Strike, not under compulsion as at Buffalo, but of their own accord.

Elsewhere it had usually been the trainmen who took the lead. At West Albany it was the shopmen. During the noon hour on Monday, a man from the Western Division of the Central stirred them into calling a meeting at Capitol Park that evening. Most of them showed up, and the usual complement of idlers was sternly relegated to the fringes. Organized with some difficulty and never clearly led, the meeting at length called for a strike and a demand on Vanderbilt for a 25 per cent raise. Tuesday morning found the strikers hanging aimlessly about the park. "No leaders, no head and no concerted action," complained a machinist. "I'll be damned if I ain't sick of it." Some of the men finally started off for the shops at West Albany, picking up sympathizers along the way. A Central official "noticed many boys about the age of 16." A mob of 500 stormed through the shops and roundhouse, ejecting the men still at work, then emerged and began stopping freight trains.

From Albany westward, New York Central trainmen fell rapidly into line with the shopmen. They had no over-all leadership. Nevertheless, a pattern emerged. In Syracuse, in Rochester, in Albany, the brakemen, firemen and conductors met with grave composure to draw up demands, usually for a rescinding of the July 1 cut. The engineers generally stayed aloof, though sympathetic. Pains were taken to renounce force, keep clear of liquor and repel mischievous strangers. To some observers, the railroaders' self-discipline seemed ominous, and both state and municipal authorities mustered all their available forces at key points. Governor Robinson called out the entire state militia. Yet even though the usual gangs of boys and ne'er-do-wells roamed about, though switches were spiked and couplings pulled, no real violence troubled the Central.

Differing demands poured in on William Vanderbilt from a number of strike committees, and he cited that fact in avoiding a direct answer. He would discuss the complaints, he said, but only after work had been resumed and a committee had been chosen to speak for all employees. Meanwhile, he presented a genial and confident front to reporters who interviewed him on the porch of the United States Hotel at Saratoga. The road, he intimated, would not lose but save money by a suspension in the dull season. Anyway, the strikers were a small minority. If freight traffic had nearly stopped on the Central, it was by his orders for safety's sake, and not really because of a strike. "While some of my men may have succumbed to evil influences," he said, "I am prouder than ever of my men as a body."

So it may have seemed to Vanderbilt. But to most it was clear that the last of the four great trunk lines had caught the fever.

And still it spread.

Ohio got off lightly for two reasons. Tie-ups to the east made it pointless to break the freight blockade by force. And the examples of Baltimore, Reading, Buffalo and, above all, Pittsburgh made it seem wise not to try.

Newark, Ohio's first point of strike infection, profited from such considerations. With Pittsburgh making headlines, Governor Young chose not to press the stern measures he had promised for Sunday. Though B. & O. freights remained idle, so did the militia. Civic order was preserved by patrols of citizens and of strikers, both organized with the blessing of town authorities. The strikers themselves managed to pacify and turn back 600 angry miners from

Shawnee, who had started for Newark to "clean out" a militia
company used against them in a previous strike. This brief crisis
over, Governor Young returned to Columbus on Tuesday and left
Newark to itself.

Worse might have been looked for at Cleveland. Since the fifties,
with the coming of railroads and the exploitation of near-by coal and
iron, industry had increasingly lighted Cleveland's sky by night and
darkened it by day. Cleveland factories turned out sheet metal,
iron and steel goods, railroad cars, iron bridges, sewing machines,
ships, paint, paper, woolens—and smoke, visible from far out on
Lake Erie and all too palpable in town. "Clean linen becomes an
impossibility here; food and drink is impregnated with the coal
dust and smoke," complained a lady visitor from Arkansas that
July. More than that, Cleveland was the chief lair of what was soon
to be the antimonopolists' model monster, Standard Oil.

A large proportion of Cleveland's hundred thousand citizens lived
in the modest frame houses that lined side streets. But industrialism
had increased the number and magnificence of the fine homes along
Superior Street and Euclid Avenue even as it expanded the "Flats,"
a cluster of squalid, flimsy shacks along the Cuyahoga River in the
industrial heart of the city. Most inhabitants of the Flats were of the
foreign-born—German, Irish, Bohemian and Canadian—who made
up 40 per cent of the population, and who had joined an exotic
strain to the New England culture of the region. They had also
heightened the militance of Cleveland labor. Strikes had been almost a monthly occurrence during the past ten years. Violent and
disorganized, those ventures had generally run on the rocks of
stubborn management and desperate job hunters. The year 1877
had brought a climax, with the April strike of Standard Oil coopers
against a cut in pay to fifty-six cents a day. Led by two Bohemian
socialists, the coopers' strike had burgeoned into an attempted general strike of all Cleveland workers getting less than a dollar a day.
Sewer masons, bricklayers, cigar makers and others scored some
gains. But lack of discipline and staying power undid most of the
strikers. A subsequent attempt to organize rolling-mill men ended
in failure and mass discharges. July thus found Cleveland labor dis-
heartened, and the conservative Cleveland public both angry and
scornful.

Public hostility and the prudence of both city and railroad officials go far to explain the quiet course of events in Cleveland. On Sunday afternoon, crowds stopped Lake Shore trains at the freight yards in outlying Collinwood. The Lake Shore officials promptly suspended all business, including passenger and mail service, the last over the protests of the strikers. On Monday the strike reached the Cleveland, Columbus, Cincinnati & Indianapolis Railroad, known for somewhat involved reasons as the "Bee Line." After conferring with a strike committee, President J. H. Devereux countermanded the 10 per cent pay cut, and the men returned to work. A group of Bee Line men appreciatively serenaded Devereux that evening at his Euclid Street home. The Atlantic & Great Western, having made no cut, incurred no strike. The Cleveland & Pittsburgh management of its own accord stopped all operations, freight, passenger and mail. The Standard Oil refinery and the Cleveland Rolling Mill Company were shut down for a couple of days from lack of coal. At Collinwood, a "Sunday quiet" prevailed, at least until Wednesday, when the ladies of the neighborhood gave the strikers an "out-door dinner" (pronounced a "very enjoyable affair"). The Lake Shore strikers themselves closed Collinwood saloons and threatened to wet down the streets with the stocks of any violators. By Wednesday evening the business of "Happy Cal Wagner's" minstrels suffered less from strike excitement than from the competition of the Cleveland Club races and the evening concert at Haltnorth's Garden.

Cincinnati, the "Queen City," had a livelier time of it. The men of the Cincinnati, Hamilton & Dayton, the Ohio & Mississippi and the Dayton Short Line mutually agreed to strike at noon Monday unless the pay cut was rescinded. The officers and directors of the C. H. & D. met hurriedly Sunday night, canceled the cut (which had not been officially announced yet anyway) and called on the men to "avoid violence and passionate action." When the news reached Hamilton, "a large number of men, to give vent to their joy, discharged volley after volley of firearms." In contrast, the O. & M. held firm, blaming unrest on men it had fired for striking the year before. Consequently, as soon as the pay car went through on Monday morning, O. & M. men struck against freight traffic. The management thereupon cut out passenger trains as well. The Dayton Short Line rescinded its cut after the noon strike began, but its men decided to stay out until their brethren had won elsewhere.

Meanwhile mob spirit showed itself in Cincinnati. The police commissioners forehandedly called for citizens' patrols and asked the newspapers to discontinue their lurid extras and bulletins (not all the papers complied). Nevertheless, a mob varying from 300 to 3,000, and including a large proportion of teen-age boys, surged about the O. & M. depot Monday afternoon and night, shouting, jeering and cursing. At about ten-thirty the O. & M.'s wooden trestle bridge over Mill Creek blazed up. Someone had saturated it with oil from a near-by refinery. The mob assaulted firemen and cut hoses industriously, but two companies managed to preserve their hoses and save most of the bridge. On Tuesday afternoon several hundred rioters forced out the shopmen of the Indianapolis, Cincinnati & Lafayette, threatening them with clubs about the size and shape of baseball bats. When some boys stopped a train in the yard, an observer remarked: "Why don't the trainmen drive them off and make them go about their business?" "Well," said a striker, "just let anyone touch them boys, and they touch us. They're doing our work, you bet." Late that dark and sultry evening, however, drops from long-threatening nimbus clouds began to "touch them boys" and their protectors, and by midnight a slow, steady rain had cooled and dispersed Cincinnati's hotheads.

Though Ohio escaped bloodshed, it caught the same general strike fever that broke out at McKeesport, Harrisburg and Buffalo. In Ohio it began at Zanesville on Monday morning, when some 300 unemployed men halted construction work on the Clarendon Hotel. Thence the mob worked through the town, shutting down nearly every factory and foundry and sending horsecars to the barns. A meeting of bona fide workingmen on Tuesday morning recited labor's wrongs and drew up a schedule of acceptable wages for various classes of labor. It also disavowed violence and lawlessness. The police began making arrests, the mayor used the nine o'clock curfew against troublesome teen-agers, and a "White Ribbon Brigade" of citizen patrols appeared in force that afternoon. By Wednesday morning work had been resumed by all who had jobs.

The Great Strike reached Columbus on Sunday, July 22. Goodale Park "seemed to be literally covered with people" in the afternoon when brakemen and firemen of the "Pan Handle Road" (the Pittsburgh, Cincinnati & St. Louis) met there and resolved to strike for

1874 wages. Meanwhile the local division of the Engineers' Brotherhood took counsel near the rolling mill; and when all the trainmen met together that evening, strike plans went forward smoothly, each item of business being reported out by its own committee. To the railroaders' frank displeasure, Monday noon brought turbulence in the Zanesville style. A mob of 300, waxing eventually to 2,000, went through town forcing out workers at a rolling mill, pipe works, fire clay works, pot works, planing mill and other establishments. Of the four mob leaders, two had long criminal records and the other two were "as hard pills as the city affords." Their following, "the ragtag of creation," was "swelled to two or three times its genuine size by the army of boys who followed around cheering them on." "Shut up or burn up" was the mob's summation of alternatives, and everyone shut up.

Next day Bee Line freights began moving at Columbus, after news of the management's concession. Other lines made no effort to force an issue. A meeting of rolling-mill men endorsed the railroad strikers, urged labor to combine politically and legislate justice, but rejected mobbism as apt to destroy "the best form of republican government." The mayor appointed 350 special police, a citizens' meeting was held, and by Wednesday the only mills still closed were those deprived of coal by the railroad tie-up.

Lake Shore strikers at Cleveland firmly and effectively discouraged a mob which closed the Cleveland Screw Works on Tuesday. Further west on the Lake Shore line, however, Toledo produced the most purposeful and systematic of all the Ohio general strike movements.

Prodded by a committee of brakemen and firemen from the Cleveland Division, the Lake Shore men at Toledo struck on Monday. At a meeting of railroad men that night in Eversman's Hall, Police Commissioner Coyle told them: "You are not slaves, gentlemen, and I am glad to see you assert your manhood." Next morning the Canada Southern men struck for three months' arrears of pay and cancellation of the 10 per cent cut, and two hours later the men of the Wabash followed suit.

That evening another rally at Eversman's Hall drew 3,000 people and had to be moved out into the warm night. A breeze blew in from Lake Erie, and the moon hung bright and full in the summer sky. Major General James B. Steedman of Civil War fame gave the strikers fiery encouragement. An offshoot meeting of workingmen afterward resolved to call a general strike for a minimum wage of a dollar and a half a day.

On Wednesday morning a large crowd of laborers, grain trimmers, stevedores and other workingmen assembled in orderly fashion. A "Committee of Ten" drew up resolutions: co-operation with the strikers; $2.50 to $3.00 a day for skilled workers and $1.50 for laborers; saloons to be closed by the mayor; and, to prevent disorder, a committee of safety made up of one member of every trade represented in the movement. After an impromptu speech by Mayor W. W. Jones counseling moderation, 300 men formed in procession, four abreast, and marched through the manufacturing district. A committee called on the management of each factory. Some establishments already satisfied the pay demands. In others, workers joined the strike movement more or less willingly. Sometimes noisy but never violent, the march was over by midafternoon. Next day the sheriff assembled a large posse, citizen patrols tramped the streets, the local militia turned out, the leaders of the general strike were jailed and life in Toledo returned to normal—or as near normal as the railroad strike allowed.

CHAPTER 11

The Republic on Trial

THE WESTWARD sweep of the Great Strike, even in mid-course, had made it a national event. But beyond that, it now involved the prospects of mankind.

Since 1776 American leaders had recognized the experimental importance of the new nation. There, for the first time and perhaps also the last, men might test self-government on a grand scale. There they might try its fitness for a continent—or a world. Trials had thus far gone forward under varied conditions, most lately in "a great civil war, testing whether that nation or any nation so conceived and so dedicated can long endure." A fateful test remained: industrialism, the way of the future. Was the great ideal compatible with swollen cities? Jefferson had recorded his misgivings. Could it overcome class divisions, deepened and poisoned by economic and social injustice? Karl Marx thought not.

Now, suddenly, came the first such test, perhaps the most severe. If the American system failed it, when would men dare try again? And on what proving grounds?

In this new trial the Republic had at least one special advantage: a seat of government apart from its centers of industry and finance. Of Washington's 150,000 citizens, only 7,000 were industrial workers. The city therefore remained quiet, though apprehensive, on the week end of the Pittsburgh upheaval. Friday's bloodshed in near-by Baltimore set nerves on edge, and according to the *New York Sun* President Hayes stayed up all that night receiving dispatches. A few garrison troops were scraped together Saturday afternoon to strengthen the Washington Arsenal; and the Chief Signal Officer offered up thirty of his men, though he doubted that they could "handle the Gatling Gun."

Around midnight Saturday, Tom Scott intercepted General Hancock in the Philadelphia depot as the general passed through on his way to Baltimore. Scott wanted Hancock to go to Washington and urge that President Hayes call for volunteers as Lincoln had done in 1861, volunteers enough "to quell all these disturbances along the Railroad routes." Hancock listened politely and went on to Baltimore as planned, whence he wired Washington at dawn that "everything seems quiet here at this time."

Word of the slaughter at Pittsburgh had reached President Hayes late Saturday evening in his summer residence at the Soldiers' Home. However wakeful he may have been that moonlit summer night, he attended church in the city as usual Sunday morning. Afterward he met with his cabinet in the State Department.

The five cabinet officers on hand made an odd assortment, politically and personally. Secretary of State William M. Evarts, slender, nervous, witty, with a face like that of Punch and a skin like wrinkled brown parchment, represented New York and a break with the political past. He had been Andrew Johnson's Attorney General and had acted as counsel for Johnson in the impeachment trial. His present appointment had gravely affronted Senator Roscoe Conkling, boss of New York's Republican machine. Evarts' law firm did much business with railroads. On the preceding Tuesday, for example, Vanderbilt's Lake Shore road had paid the Evarts firm $2,500 for its services in a squabble with stockholders.

Secretary of the Treasury John Sherman, tall, thin and humorless, wearing a close-cropped beard, represented Ohio, hard money and practical politics. Without the fire and color of his famous soldier-brother William, Secretary Sherman had abundant political craft and staying power. Now more than two decades along on a career that was still only half over, Sherman fancied himself a man of unsatisfied business talents, and had compensated for his frustration by making a specialty of government finance. In the teeth of greenback ravings, he pressed doggedly on toward resumption of specie payments. A dozen years ahead, and as yet unimaginable, lay the time when this prosy conservative would lend his name to the first Federal antitrust law.

Secretary of War George W. McCrary, a stout, puffy, chin-whiskered ex-Congressman with saturnine eyes and a bald pate, represented Iowa and Tom Scott. He seems to have got his seat in the Cabinet on the recommendation of his close friend, General

Grenville M. Dodge, a henchman of both Scott and Gould and a leading go-between for Scott and Hayes during the election dispute.

Secretary of the Navy Richard W. "Uncle Dick" Thompson, his dark eyes set in a pallid, clean-shaven face surmounted by silky white hair, had a curiously old-fashioned look, as if he had stepped from a print of the Jackson era. He represented Indiana and machine politics, and his previous nautical experience had begun and ended on the banks of the Wabash. He was said to have remarked on his first official inspection of a naval vessel: "Why, the thing's hollow!" That was doubtless a joke; he and Evarts were the Cabinet comedians. Thompson's political experience ranged much further and longer than his naval activity. By the time he reached ninety, he would easily qualify as the nation's champion political name dropper, as demonstrated in his two-volume *Recollections of Sixteen Presidents*. For many years he had been chief counsel for the Terre Haute & Indianapolis Railroad. In 1873 Tom Scott wrote him: "Your letter of the 5th instant received, in regard to application for position for your son on the Texas and Pacific Railroad. I will take pleasure in referring it to Gen. G. M. Dodge, Chief Engineer, Marshall, Texas." In May 1877 the president of the Columbus & Hocking Valley Railroad wrote to express his joy that the President "had wisdom to put you where you can do the most good."

Attorney General Charles Devens of Massachusetts, an old bachelor whose heavy-lidded dignity barely skirted stuffiness, was the best-dressed man in the Cabinet, though always in sober black. He was a judge by nature, born to the robe, out of his element among mere politicians. Like Sherman and McCrary, he held his peace in Cabinet and left yarn spinning to the two chief jesters. He and Evarts had passed through Baltimore in one of Tom Scott's private cars on the very day the B. & O. strike began. They were setting out on a junket to the Pennsylvania coal regions, courtesy of the railroad companies. The night before Governor Mathews' call for troops, Evarts and Devens hobnobbed pleasantly with "Johnny" Wootten, the Reading's hated general manager, in Franklin Gowen's own private car.

Secretary of the Interior Carl Schurz happened to be in New Jersey that Sunday. That was unfortunate. The absent member could have discussed "insurrection" with particular authority, having first made a name for himself in the German revolution of 1848. In his own days as an insurgent teen-ager he had known Karl Marx. "I have never seen a man," he recalled later, "whose bearing was so provoking and intolerable." Within ten years after fleeing his homeland, young Schurz had mastered the English language, been admitted to the Milwaukee bar, campaigned for Lincoln, served as American minister to Spain and taken the field against a different sort of rebellion. Coming out of the Civil War a major general, Schurz plunged back into politics in St. Louis, served a term as Senator from Missouri and led the Liberal Republican political revolt of 1872. Even now, he constituted Hayes's most radical appointment, a genuine recognition of the reform element. Intense and intellectual, a competent pianist, expert journalist and brilliant talker, Schurz added a dash of red pepper to the Cabinet stew. With his shock of red hair and his pugnacious spade beard, Schurz looked, in the words of a contemporary, "very like Mephistopheles, except that Schurz wore glasses."

There was, however, one ex-rebel present: Postmaster General David M. Key of Tennessee, Southern Democrat and ex-Confederate colonel, a big, burly man, spade-bearded like Schurz and with a similarly determined cast of countenance. Hayes liked to think of Key's appointment as a daring gesture toward sectional reconciliation. No doubt it was. It also represented a payment to the Southern Democracy for their part in throwing the disputed count to Hayes.

The strike elsewhere kept freights at a standstill in Washington yards that Sunday. Prostrike crowds loitered about telegraph bulletin boards; newsboys for the *Critic* and the *Star* shouted their extras. The chief of police alerted all his reserves. But during the morning two batteries came in from Fort Monroe, and extra guards appeared at all public buildings. After the churches let out, the city began to relax in the July sun. Along the avenues shimmered the rich green of parks, made lush and verdant by recent rains. A warm breeze drifted the spray of fountains over beds of scarlet verbenas. In Lafayette Park, children romped, while grownups in their Sunday best strolled about or stood in the shade, quietly talking over the strike and the riots.

Quiet prevailed in the State Department building also, but little peace. The Cabinet listened grimly to President Hayes's outline of the situation. Grave but self-contained, Hayes fingered a sheaf of yellow telegrams from Signal Corps sergeants, who in those days were stationed as official weather observers in all the major cities. Already the Signal Corps had begun tracking the social storm; and before the day was out, the Chief Signal Officer would order his men to keep sending news reports from key points every six hours and when otherwise warranted. Hayes now read some of these dispatches aloud: Baltimore quiet, Hornellsville riotous, Philadelphia tense, Pittsburgh raging.

Pennsylvania was Hayes's immediate concern. A few days earlier, he had sent Federal troops into West Virginia and Maryland. But in those cases the constitutional formalities had been observed. In contrast, Pennsylvania's governor was now far away from his state, and the Pennsylvania constitution did not clearly provide for an acting governor in any case but death, disability or resignation. Should the President wait for a formal call from the junketing governor? Or should he, in the emergency, make use of a reconstruction statute which authorized him to send Federal troops directly against civil disorders?

Cabinet opinion was divided. The decision was left with Hayes after all. Everyone agreed, however, that the Federal power would likely be tested sooner or later. Discussion, therefore, turned to the practical question of just what the Federal power amounted to. Adjutant General Townsend, present for the purpose, summed up the Army's resources. In the Military Division of the Atlantic, encompassing all the current disturbances, only three thousand men were on hand, the rest of the Army being scattered over the Divisions of the Missouri and the Pacific. Only fifty United States troops were stationed in all of Pennsylvania.

How about a call for state militia, then? The Cabinet chewed on the question awhile. Militia behavior at Martinsburg and Pittsburgh suggested that state troops had better not be used in their own neighborhoods. But could units made up of workingmen, such as the Sixth and Ninth New York, be relied on anywhere? Hayes and his advisers decided to wait out the day before acting.

After the meeting broke up, Hayes rode out to the Soldiers' Home with McCrary. There the President found dispatches piling up. The hostile *New York Sun* (with knowing allusions to "railroad chiefs like Scott" and "the man they inaugurated") reported on the authority of "men well informed" that "Hayes grew more and more alarmed, and Tom Scott pelted him with dispatches, peremptory and dictatorial, as perhaps they had a right to be." However that may have been, the nation's excitement did not appear to be subsiding.

One of the dispatches came from General Hancock in Baltimore, endorsing a request by Governor Carroll that United States troops along the B. & O. establish their headquarters at Cumberland, Maryland. At 2:50 p.m., Adjutant General Townsend wired Hancock: "Your dispatch of 12:11 p.m. received. Colonel French, now at Martinsburg, has been instructed to act under your orders. The President thinks he had better be directed to change his headquarters to Cumberland." Thus casually, Hayes set in train a remarkable series of events.

Hayes could scarcely have fathomed the complex currents beneath Governor Carroll's innocent-sounding request. Some of those currents were personal. Colonel French of the regulars and Colonel Delaplain, Governor Mathews' aide, were alike in excitability and suspicion. They were alike also in detesting the B. & O. and its local representative, the overbearing Colonel Thomas R. Sharp, late of the Confederate States Army. Delaplain let Governor Mathews know just what he thought of "a certain large corporation always clamorous for protection and advantage at the hands of our State." "I have been in conflict with them," he told the governor, "since parting with you at Grafton. Their selfishness and indifference to interests more important than their own have impeded me from the start." General French took the same view, perhaps because he disliked Sharp, perhaps because he and his troops had been detained at Harper's Ferry at the outset.

Carroll of Maryland and Mathews of West Virginia were competing for the services of Colonel French's troops. Sharp, seconded by Governor Carroll's aide, Major H. Kyd Douglas, pressed for a concentration of troops at Cumberland, Maryland. Hundreds of people—railroad and canal strikers, sightseers and "a horde of vile looking tramps"—had milled around the Cumberland depot all day Saturday, and Sharp was worried about the nearly 200 cars of oil in the yards. By evening three companies of regulars had arrived and cleared the space before the Queen City Hotel. Sharp was still not satisfied. He wanted French to make Cumberland his headquarters and concentrate his forces there. In surviving telegrams, we can follow the slow advance of pressure through the channels of command: B. & O. Vice-President King first, then Governor Carroll, then General Hancock; finally, on Sunday afternoon, President Hayes. At four o'clock Hancock wired French to move his headquarters to Cumberland and remain there.

But before Hancock's order could reach him, French had begun carrying out a plan of his own: to work along the line westward from Martinsburg, dropping off troop detachments at key points, until Wheeling was reached and the line cleared. In a special train, along with two artillery companies, French and Delaplain reached Cumberland shortly before seven o'clock Sunday evening, still unaware of Hancock's order to go no further.

Through a heavy rain French walked across the depot platform to the Queen City Hotel and reported to Major Douglas. When Douglas told him to get Sharp's permission to proceed, French declared that the United States government, not Thomas Sharp, was master of troop movements on the B. & O. just then. He stalked back to his private car and gave orders to go ahead. Word came back that Colonel Sharp said otherwise, and that if Colonel French wanted to see Colonel Sharp he would have to come to Sharp's office. French refused. After a long wait, during which reporters and a large crowd gathered around the train, Sharp came in person and explained haughtily that the train could not go on without orders from Vice-President King. French, his mottled face getting redder by the minute, said excitedly that he did not care, that the train was going on anyway. Sharp turned on his heel and left. French bellowed after him in the hearing of the delighted crowd: "The train shall go, and if you're going to be an obstruction instead of cooperating, I'll order your arrest and send you to Baltimore!"

Flushed and shaking, French blurted to the reporters (and incidentally to the crowd): "I am not going to be under the control and orders of that man Sharp. He is a damned old rebel as he was during the war. I have telegraphed to the President of the United States to be relieved from duty here unless I am allowed to have entire command. If Sharp hadn't stopped me I would have been at the end of the line." Douglas and Sharp at last became aware that French by himself was likely to make more of a disturbance than all the strikers together. Orders were given, the train whistle blew, and in the middle of his remarks the furious old soldier was hauled away, troops and all, into the darkness.

In the highly public criminations and recriminations which followed, B. & O. officials charged French with having been roaring drunk. "The company," said their published statement, "had furnished three gallons of whisky and two dozen bottles of ale within the last twenty-four hours for use in General French's private car, and on arriving at Cumberland fresh supplies of ale were asked for." French disclaimed knowledge of any potables on the train save "a jug of seltzer and a bottle of claret," although, he confessed, "I have a peculiar kind of temper, and when I am aroused might create the impression that I had consumed thirty gallons of proof instead of three, as charged by the railroad officials." Major Douglas later disavowed the drunkenness charges. There was liquor on the train, apparently, but it was consigned to one "Mr. Woodside." Men aboard the train testified that French was not drunk, though roaring he certainly had been. The cause of French's death three years later—apoplexy—may explain his flushed face.

The charges against French had their effect on General Hancock, even though he acknowledged them to be *ex parte*. Around midnight Sunday, French angrily wired Hancock from Keyser: "If I cannot act independent of [B. & O. officials] . . . it would be preferable to have another officer who would be less objectionable to that corporation." Hancock relieved him of his command and turned it over to General Getty. The latter eventually adopted French's plan of posting troops at key points along the B. & O. It was a complete success. There were no further outbreaks in Maryland or West Virginia.

Early on Sunday evening, however, the B. & O. officials had not yet trumped up the drunkenness charge. On the contrary, King hastily ordered Sharp to "cultivate the most friendly relations with the federal officers in the interest of the road." Thus far, Hayes had only French's side of the story, and it was not calculated to inspire affection for railroad corporations. That evening a reporter for the *National Republican* managed to interview the President, who seemed cool toward the more extreme demands of embattled capitalists. Hayes expressed, to be sure, "the opinion that the most rigorous measures should be used in putting down the troubles, and thought it was greatly to be regretted that a larger force had not been thrown into Pittsburgh." Also regrettable, said Hayes, was Governor Hartranft's absence, especially in view of Hartranft's experience in dealing with labor riots. But Hayes threw cold water on any idea of summoning Congress into special session, and he told the reporter "that, as the matter now stood, he did not think that any further action would be taken by the National Government than to respond to any calls which might be made by States, as had been done in the cases of West Virginia and Maryland."

After nightfall a wire came from Governor Hartranft at Creston, Wyoming Territory:

I call upon you for troops to assist in quelling mobs within the borders of the state of Pennsylvania. Respectfully suggest that you order troops from adjoining states and prepare to call for volunteers as authorized by act of Congress.

Hayes reassembled the Cabinet at Evarts' house to consider this message. By ten o'clock all but Schurz were there. They agreed with Hayes that Hartranft's request was not in proper form, and the governor was notified that he must fulfill constitutional requirements. Mayor Stokley's alarums from Philadelphia, however, persuaded Hayes to order General Hancock there with Federal troops to protect United States property. "You had better see Mr. Scott," Hancock was told. Then Hayes showed the cabinet Tom Scott's telegrams.

These, according to newspaper reports, viewed the Federal government as obligated to keep interstate commerce moving, that is, to keep the trains running. Like Hartranft, Scott suggested a call for volunteers in the manner of 1861. When a wire arrived from Stokley seconding that motion, a pattern became evident. Tom Scott, it seemed, wanted a general showdown with labor; he wanted the United States government to fight for him; and he was now applying his formidable influence to that end.

All present, including Hayes, had strong political or business ties with railroads. But in this crisis their responsibility to the nation proved stronger. Colonel French's dispatch must have strengthened their resolution. At any rate, the half-dozen worried men who met in William Evarts' house that Sunday night passed their test. They agreed that whatever happened the United States government would do its duty and no more. The railroads would have to find their own men to run the trains. This settled, the need for a general call to action seemed less than obvious. A wire came in from the

Signal Corps weather station at Pittsburgh: "The situation is improving. The fire is now under control and the mob is becoming more quiet." The cabinet presently adjourned without further action. Afterward, according to a *New York Sun* reporter, one or two members remarked that "the railroads wanted to run the government."

Next morning, Monday, July 23, the Navy brought the twelve-gun *Plymouth* up to Alexandria and the eight-gun *Swatara* to the Navy Yard; 500 sailors and marines debarked for garrison duty; Major General John M. Schofield arrived from West Point to take charge of District defenses; and the city's mild unease passed away.

After sending Schofield to confer with Hancock in Philadelphia, President Hayes called the Cabinet together once more. Again they canvassed the reliability of state troops and found it wanting. New England and Southern troops might be dependable if used in the middle states, but then their use might bring on a sectional war. Someone suggested a suspension of habeas corpus, so that Federal troops might arrest rioters. The situation at that moment did not seem to justify so radical a step. Pittsburgh lay exhausted; Harrisburg, Reading and Buffalo had not yet begun to fight. At noon Hartranft's duly amended request for troops came in at last by wire from North Bend, Nebraska. Hayes and the Cabinet agreed to issue a proclamation commanding the Pennsylvania rioters to disperse by Tuesday noon. They themselves dispersed immediately for lunch. There is no record of another meeting that day.

Evarts found the British Minister waiting for him at the State Department. Minister Plunkett, aware of the situation, recorded with a touch of admiration that "Mr. Evarts received me very pleasantly." Hayes, too, remained self-possessed. With his son Webb, he dropped in on the Navy and War departments during the afternoon. An air of frenzy hung about the latter place, and understandably so. All night, clerks had been on special duty. The bewildering events of Sunday had snarled up troop movements. All New England troops had been dispatched to Baltimore on Sunday morning. Then, after the Sunday night Cabinet meeting, all southbound troops were ordered held at Philadelphia. On Monday morning the Fort Porter company was intercepted at Rochester and sent back to restive Buffalo.

That same morning Hancock transferred his headquarters from

Baltimore to Philadelphia, and Hayes wisely gave him authority over all troop movements in the Division of the Atlantic. During the day a company from Atlanta, Georgia, and two from Columbia, South Carolina, were hurried off to Jeffersonville, Indiana. Threatening developments in Indiana that evening led Hancock to alert the troops in the Department of the Gulf and to order two companies from the Department of the South to Newport Barracks, Kentucky, across the Ohio from Indiana. He also ordered the commander at Fort Mackinac, Michigan, to send all the men he could spare to Fort Wayne in Detroit. Tom Scott wanted troops for Harrisburg, and Franklin Gowen wanted some for Reading; but Hancock told them none could be spared at that moment. All this activity stirred up a maelstrom of telegraphic inquiry, clarification, protest and reassurance. But the comings and goings had their uses. Scarcely a major railroad center in the troubled areas but had a sobering glimpse of Federal troops in transit. In retrospect a few days later, Hancock observed: "We have not made much noise, it is true, nor did we emblazon our numbers—and that silence led to an exaggeration of the strength of the force at our disposal at whatever point the troops appeared; the troops moved steadily with calmness and celerity. The presence of the troops had a powerful effect."

That dividend was apparent later, but at the moment no one knew how Federal troops would fare. Notwithstanding the fearful lesson of the late war, the prestige of United States troops had already come close to direct challenge. At Baltimore on Saturday Colonel Abbott's men had been stoned. At Pittsburgh that same day Major Buffington's little force had been saved from the mob by a chance diversion. On Monday afternoon in New Jersey, where Governor Bedle had called out the state militia in anticipation of disorder, some 1,500 men and boys at Jersey City threatened a trainload of regulars passing through from New England. Police protection and some adroit maneuvering got the train through, and later detachments passed without hindrance.

If the spell of Union blue had once been shattered, the cost might have been enormous. In the files of the Adjutant General's Office lies a pensive memorandum, undated and unsigned but placed among papers of July 23 and 24, on the subject of Federal arsenals and their garrisons. Forty men guarded the Rock Island Arsenal with its "large quantity of arms and ammunition." Twenty guarded the

Allegheny Arsenal. Twenty guarded the Indianapolis Arsenal with its artillery battery, 25,000 rifles and 1,000,000 cartridges. Such garrisons were effective only as symbols of power. If Hayes had thrown a handful of troops into Pittsburgh while the riot still raged, he might have saved property. Or he might have achieved nothing more than the discrediting of those symbols.

The French-Sharp controversy touched indirectly on the question of Federal-state relationships. Once United States troops had been directed to aid a state, were they to be chief or auxiliary? The question seems to have been raised in the Cabinet meetings of Sunday and Monday, but not clearly met. The War Department had ordered Federal troops in Maryland and West Virginia to report to state authorities, and General Hancock assumed that to be a standing policy. When, contrariwise, Governor Hartranft on Tuesday directed some Pennsylvania militia commanders to report to Hancock, the general asked Washington for a ruling. Hancock himself respectfully suggested that Hartranft was right, that if state authorities could not keep order by themselves, the Federal authorities should take full command of the situation. After mulling over Hancock's suggestions, Hayes declined to lay down a general rule. "Under existing circumstances," however, he thought Hancock should command both state and Federal troops in Pennsylvania.

Notwithstanding Hayes's refusal to generalize on the matter of military command, a formula had already evolved for the initial use of troops. Regulars had been sent to various trouble spots with orders to protect United States property "and by their presence to promote peace and order." They were carefully instructed, however, not to aid in enforcing state law until a formal request was made by the governor and granted by the President.

Hayes's policy was conservative. Other grounds might easily have been cited for Federal intervention. Scott, Garrett and others urged Federal military action to protect interstate commerce, but they were ignored. Clearer and more pressing were the obligations of the postal service. A year before, labor trouble on the Lake Shore & Michigan Southern had blocked traffic, including mail. A special agent of the Post Office Department threatened the strikers with arrest by United States marshals, and the mail was then passed through. The present situation was more formidable and also more complicated. On Sunday, July 22, five loaded mail cars were stranded on the way to Pittsburgh; but no edict of the Federal government could move them into that city until the tracks had been repaired. On the same day Erie strikers wired Postmaster General Key that the Erie management was delaying the mails, not they. In Cleveland Monday morning Cleveland & Pittsburgh Railroad officials returned mail "with the message that no trains whatever will be run for the present." That morning a New York Central express came into Syracuse from Buffalo with the mail car at the end, contrary to custom. This was done, surmised the *Syracuse Journal*, "so that the train could not be cut without causing a detention of the mails . . . [upon which] the aid of the General Government will at once be invoked." On Tuesday Lake Shore strikers wired Hayes from Erie, Pennsylvania: "The Lake Shore Company has refused to let U. S. mail east of here. We would be pleased if you would in some way direct them to proceed with mails and also passengers." Next day both Vanderbilt and Scott refused to run trains made up solely of mail cars; and, in separate wires to Key, they insisted that mail would be carried only on regular passenger trains. (This implied that mobs or strikers were stopping passenger trains on their lines, which does not seem to have been true.) Other roads followed suit, despite public anger.

The stand taken by Scott and Vanderbilt was reported in that day's Cabinet meeting, but elicited neither discussion nor action. Key did what he could to find alternate routes, even to sending mail through Canada in charge of Canadian agents. The War Department furnished arms to railway mail employees for defense against pillage. On July 27, after mobs had stopped Chicago, Burlington & Quincy passenger trains in Iowa, the Chicago superintendent of the Railway Mail Service warned "Strikers, Rioters and Other Parties Whomsoever" that "all passenger trains carrying mails are mail trains . . . and parties delaying same will be rigorously prosecuted under United States laws." So far as the mails were concerned, this was the extent of Federal action during the Great Strike.

When accounts were settled after the strike, the "Other Parties Whomsoever" got off lightly. Postmaster General Key, indeed, praised the railroad companies for making "every reasonable effort to carry the mails during the disorderly period." Even the few

"Strikers" and "Rioters" who were convicted of obstructing mails fared reasonably well. Most drew fines ranging from $40 to $100 and costs. Few, if any, went to prison.

Monday, July 23, had brought disturbing news: slaughter at Reading, riot and the surrender of militia at Harrisburg, mobs and arson at Cincinnati and Philadelphia, menace to Federal troops at Jersey City, attacks on militia at Buffalo, an imminent strike on the New York Central at Albany, general strike movements at McKeesport, Harrisburg, Zanesville and Columbus. And the end was not in sight. By Tuesday noon, when the Hayes Cabinet met for the third time in as many days, the Great Strike had spread through Ohio, Indiana and Illinois into Kentucky, Missouri and Iowa.

At the Tuesday meeting all seven Cabinet members took their seats, Schurz having at last arrived from New Jersey. President Hayes waited in a heavy swivel chair at the head of the ponderous oblong table. On the wall facing him, General Washington gravely surveyed the scene from a full-length portrait. The nineteenth President may have found reassurance in this reminder of the first, who had put down an earlier "insurrection" in western Pennsylvania. At any rate, after reading Signal Corps dispatches from Cleveland, Buffalo, St. Louis and Philadelphia, Hayes pointed out that although the strike continued to extend, violence was diminishing. United States troops, moreover, were "everywhere respected."

New York City was the chief point of interest this day. One hundred million dollars lay there in the Custom House and Subtreasury, a fact which weighed on the mind of Assistant Treasurer Thomas Hillhouse. On Sunday he had written an anxious letter to Secretary Sherman, hoping that the government would not "draw too heavily on the few small detachments of U. S. troops at the forts in the vicinity for service elsewhere." Recalling the ferocious draft riot of 1863, Hillhouse warned that "the city is filled with the most inflammable materials for a riot, if an opportunity should occur." Hancock nevertheless swept the New York garrisons clean. On Monday Hillhouse begged the general to send a company or two back again, meanwhile gloomily writing Secretary Sherman that satisfaction was unlikely. Sherman backed up his subordinate, however, and that afternoon Hancock was ordered "to keep in view the danger of an outbreak in New York City, apprehended by some." Next day he

THE REPUBLIC ON TRIAL 223

agreed to furnish one or more companies on Hillhouse's requisition.

In Cabinet meeting, Navy Secretary Thompson now offered to send Hillhouse a monitor, which could "clear the streets around the Custom House." Secretary Sherman thought the streets were too crooked for that. "The big guns will straighten them," remarked Evarts wryly; and the monitor was duly dispatched.

Other problems emerged. The governor of Ohio had asked for arms, and a militia officer wanted blankets. Both requests, though irregular, were granted. Some matters had no bearing on the strikes. General Ord had arrested some Mexicans recruiting on United States territory for the Mexican civil war. The assistant treasurer at Chicago had failed to make his bond, and it was decided to appoint someone else. The Spanish Minister was ready to settle claims. But at the end, the Great Strike again pushed other matters aside. General Pope wanted to know if he was to use Federal troops at St. Louis before the governor called for them. The Cabinet voiced an emphatic no. Thompson had second thoughts. Suppose the case were desperate? "Can an officer move his men against the mob before the governor calls?" he asked. "It will be given him in that hour what he shall do!" said Evarts, and Hayes nodded agreement. After agreeing that Hillhouse might be furnished with muskets, and that 200 regulars might be sent to Reading if Hancock thought it best, the Cabinet adjourned until Wednesday noon.

As remarkable as anything mentioned in that day's meeting was the silence of Hayes and his Cabinet on a subject currently agitating the public, or at any rate the publicists. Late news from the West suggested to many that the rabble had at last found its long-anticipated revolutionary program and leadership, and that the Republic now faced a trial as fateful as in Lincoln's time.

As soon as the unparalleled intensity, speed and scope of the Great Strike became manifest, people had begun searching for explanations. What was at the bottom of it all? In the perspective of history, the answer seems manifold: endemic violence, cruel economic distress, employer arrogance or lack of understanding, the birth pangs of a new age, the organizational nuclei provided by local divisions of the brotherhoods and the Trainmen's Union, the precipitant of idle men and boys, the spreading of excitement by rail and by sensational news stories. Yet to many, especially among the gentry of letters and trade, such an explanation seemed both too complex and too unflattering to their world. They preferred to blame the trouble on a conspiracy. Who, then, were the conspirators?

Though individual members or even whole lodges of the three railroad brotherhoods took the lead in such places as Reading, the national leaders publicly washed their hands of the affair, some of them with compulsive vigor. The Order of Railway Conductors, which had begun the year with about 1,100 members, reaffirmed its purely fraternal, benevolent and temperance objects. "Our organization," declared its Grand Chief soon after the Great Strike, "nobly, grandly, stood the test, notwithstanding the powerful influences that were exerted by other organizations, individually and collectively, to induce us to unite with them in their unwise and desperate attempts to coerce their and our employers." A few conductors, he added with sorrow, "were so unwise as to permit themselves to be drawn within the whirlpool of folly and destruction," but these "are to us no more."

The Brotherhood of Locomotive Firemen stuck to its insurance business, though its national leaders expressed sympathy with their fighting brothers. Afterward a national officer declared: "Does the brotherhood encourage strikers? To this question we must emphatically answer, No, brothers. To disregard the laws which govern our land? To destroy the last vestige of order? To stain our hands with the crimson blood of our fellow beings? We again say, No, a thousand times No!" Thus spoke young Eugene V. Debs.

"They say the [Engineers'] Brotherhood is back of the strike," a *New York Herald* reporter remarked to Grand Chief Arthur of the Engineers on July 24. "Is it connected with it in any way?" "No," Arthur insisted, "it is not. In the first place, the Brotherhood has not been consulted in this movement at all. As an organization we are not participating in it. My advice to members of the Brotherhood has been not to jeopardize their lives nor to compromise their manhood." Most observers acquitted Arthur and his fellow officers of being prime movers in the strike. Those who saw it as the work of railroad men were more inclined to blame "Boss" Ammon's Trainmen's Union.

"The [Trainmen's] Union was oath-bound and secret, and, although its life was brief and stormy, its inner work has never been revealed," observed a Pittsburgh paper on the tenth anniversary of that city's worst day. Mystery, novelty and the dramatic rise of its young chief explain the union's fascination for the public. The union's size and extent were, however, exaggerated by some newspapers, like the *Harrisburg Independent,* which credited the Trainmen's Union with "almost two-thirds of the railroad employes throughout the country." Delegations of strikers occasionally traveled from their own cities to others along the line, and this was sometimes laid to the Trainmen's Union. But it could easily have been a spontaneous development.

A variation on the Trainmen's Union theory presently became popular: "It may be stated," wrote General Hancock to Secretary McCrary on July 27, "that it was not intended by the leaders that this outbreak should occur until the month of October, but certain events precipitated matters and the leaders were made to follow." A correspondent of the *Engineers' Journal* scoffed at such notions. "Managers claim," he wrote, "that [the strike] was the result of preconcerted action of the labor forces, and that the explosion took place prematurely. The *Journal* knows, the laboring men of the country know, I know, that none of the acts of last July were premeditated by the actors . . . and the explosion was as unexpected as would be a thunderbolt from a cloudless sky." Yet in 1894 the editor of the *Railroad Trainmen's Journal* quoted the premature outbreak story and by implication accepted it. And he must have known many of Robert Ammon's onetime followers. Probably the story was essentially true.

True or not, the hypothesis failed to satisfy those who longed to hiss a gaudier villain, preferably a foreign one. Almost from the start the press had referred to the strike as a rebellion, a revolt, a "direct and defiant war against society." Hayes's first proclamation against the West Virginia "insurrection" helped fasten the tag. This gave a cue, and the *National Republican* of Washington, D. C., took it brilliantly on July 21, the day after the Baltimore riot, with an editorial on "The American Commune." "The fact is clearly manifest," asserted the *Republican,* "that communistic ideas are very widely entertained in America by the workmen employed in mines and factories and by the railroads. This poison was introduced into our social system by European laborers." There were provocations, the editorialist conceded. The postwar boom had permitted "the sudden acquisition of wealth" through "the most unscrupulous means." Moreover, "the crimes of men who made haste to grow rich . . . were suffered to go unpunished." Nevertheless, the Great Strike "is nothing less than communism in its worst form . . . not only unlawful and revolutionary, but [also]anti-American."

In the *National Republican's* interview with Hayes on Sunday evening the dread hypothesis was put to the President with somewhat disappointing results. Hayes "said he did not regard the present disorders as any evidence of the prevalence of a spirit of communism, since their attacks had not been primarily directed against property in general, but merely against that of the railroads with which the strikers had had difficulties." This remark dampened the *Republican's* zeal. Other papers, however, caught up the falling banner and waved it as enthusiastically as they had heretofore flapped the bloody shirt of sectional animosity.

The Pittsburgh saturnalia confirmed the darkest suspicions of the editorialists. By Monday, July 23, Communist guilt was taken for granted.* The *Pittsburgh Commercial Gazette* referred to the city's travail as "this display of Communism." "War between labor and capital has begun in earnest," said the *New Orleans Times;* "America's first experience in communism is now the most significant episode of the most extraordinary year in our political history." The leading headline in Monday's *New York World* was RIOT OR REVOLUTION? The *New York Post* struggled for balance. It scoffed at talk of half a million American Communists and declared that "no educated workingman" would support a Communist revolution, "because he knows that he would suffer first, last and longest." Nevertheless, the *Post* was sure that the labor uprising was Communist-inspired. While freedom of speech would be untouched, the Communists "must not be surprised if, in the event of overt acts, things go rather hard on them."

By Tuesday, Grand Chief Arthur felt constrained to say: "Of course we [Brotherhood leaders] are in sympathy with the railroad men who are on a strike, but not with Communism."

The roots of the Red scare ran back to the spring of 1871, when the workers of Paris raised the red flag and defied the national government of France. Mostly the Parisians wanted freedom from a regime dominated by the conservative provinces. Out-and-out

* Since the public of that day, as now, called Marxian Socialists "Communists," they will be so called in this narrative.

socialists made up only about a fifth of the Paris "Commune's" governing body. But the American aristocracy of wealth saw the red flag, heard the socialist vauntings and shuddered at the "Bloody Week," when Paris weltered in blood and the Seine ran between two walls of fire. An upper-class New York diarist saw this "demonstration against capital" as "the first organized and violent move of any importance toward great changes." He only hoped that "any decomposition of our present social order will not be explosive, but gradual." Two years later, on the eve of the great depression, he had grown more doubtful: "after all our brag about modern civilization, it is capable of decomposing at any moment into anarchy, barbarism, and diabolism."

American employers almost at once began to slap a Red label on labor agitation. In 1872 the *Nation* saw red on the subject of the Federal eight-hour law, ineffective as it was. "This, disguise it as we may, is Communism," wrote the editorialist, "doubtless imperfectly developed and unorganized, but still Communism, and it is at the bottom of the movement which is now forcing the eight-hour system both on the capitalists and the soberer and more peaceable and industrious workmen." When a wave of strikes hit New York City that summer, a steam pump manufacturer told a meeting of 300 employers: "I see behind all this the spectre of Communism. Our duty is to take it by the throat and say it has no business here."

By then New York City itself had become the nominal center of world Communism. Karl Marx's International Workingmen's Association—the "First International"—moved its headquarters there in 1872 to escape control by Russian anarchists. At first the change put some life in the American branch of the movement. When the depression came along, American sections of the International began organizing mass meetings of unemployed. So much red-tinged parading and speechifying led the *Chicago Tribune* to wonder late in 1873 if "the cry of 'bread or blood' might be raised in our streets this winter."

In New York City on January 13, 1874, a Communist-inspired mass meeting assembled peaceably at Tompkins Square to demand a public works program, some emergency relief for the needy and a moratorium on evictions. The paraders, men, women and the inevitable crowds of children, filled the Square expecting to hear Mayor Havemeyer speak, not knowing that the mayor had changed his mind, that official permission for the meeting had just been withdrawn and that the police were awaiting the order to charge. Suddenly the onslaught began. Police clubs battered skulls indiscriminately as the screaming crowd struggled to escape. Many were trampled in the panic, others ridden down and clubbed by mounted police. John Swinton, chief editorial writer for the *New York Sun,* had come there to speak. What he saw from the platform made him an aggressive champion of labor for the rest of his life.

The same outrage, however, made most New York workingmen wary of mass meetings. That feeling, and the endless internal bickerings of the Communists, blighted the party's depression activities. The American branch broke into several splinters. The First International withered away and was officially pronounced dead by a wind-up meeting of eleven forlorn delegates at Philadelphia in July 1876. In the same city a week later, amid the festivities of the Centennial Exposition, the fragments of the American movement recovered some stature by reuniting as "The Workingmen's Party of the United States." But the newborn party had a combined national membership of no more than 3,000. This corporal's guard alone remained to carry the red banner of Marxian socialism in the United States.

The Marxist faction wanted to emphasize trade unionism and internationalism. The "Lassallean" faction, on the other hand, wanted political action and a national outlook. The new W.P.U.S. compromised on Marxist trade unionism and Lassallean Americanization, with electioneering put off until some hope of success could be seen. The compromise recognized the facts of life in 1876. The Workingmen's Party could not have elected a dog catcher just then, whereas any one member could join a union and any two could start one. On the other hand, 90 per cent of the party members were immigrants, mostly German. Many of them spoke no English. If the party was to get anywhere in American trade unionism, therefore, it would have to "Americanize" itself. But despite the good sense of the compromise, the old feud soon broke out again.

Disunited or otherwise, neither the party nor its program constituted the clear and present danger to American institutions that alarmists supposed in 1877. To be sure, the party now had perhaps 4,500 members, and some of these talked wildly. In a letter published by the *Workingman's Advocate* that May an Indianapolis man had announced: "Tyrants—if we cannot get our God-given rights by any other means we will get them by revolution." The *Labor Standard*, official organ of American Communists, headlined the Pittsburgh upheaval as "WAR!!! Plundered Labor in Arms." When the socialistic *Irish World* went to press that Sunday night, its lead editorial declared that "labor, wasted by hunger and battered, bruised and torn by bullets, wades through rivers of blood to destroy its enemy—Capital!"

But these were the ill-considered words of startled men, not the pronunciamentos of triumphant conspirators. "There was no concert of action at the start," the *Labor Standard's* editor, J. P. McDonnell, told a trade union rally in New York City on July 26. "It [the Great Strike] spread because the workmen of Pittsburgh felt the same oppression that was felt by the workmen of West Virginia and so with the workmen of Chicago and St. Louis." The *Labor Standard* itself denounced charges of Communist complicity in the riots as "base and wicked inventions."

More convincing than these disclaimers was the tone of uncertainty and improvisation pervading McDonnell's editorials during the strike. Still more convincing are the manuscript minutes of the Workingmen's Party's Hoboken and Philadelphia sections, the members of which showed not the slightest advance knowledge of the great labor uprising. Indeed, they seemed slower than the capitalist press to appreciate the sweep and power of the movement after it began—testimony, perhaps, to the rigidity of the Marxist mind. On the day after the B. & O. strike began, the Hoboken section actually voted to put off a proposed mass meeting until September. At that moment, half of the section's assets resided in United States Bond #47,157, valued at $570 and drawing 5 per cent interest.

Significant also, perhaps, is the fact that Philip Van Patten (who, as corresponding secretary of the National Executive Committee, was the party's national leader) received $4.61 for expenses during the Great Strike, over and above his regular weekly salary of $10. If this was revolution, it was certainly revolution on a shoestring.

Outsiders, however, could not know this. They only knew that the Marxists, in the second week of the Great Strike, were not only talking, but also acting. And this being so, there were those who trembled for the Republic.

CHAPTER 12

The Mobs and the Marxists

THE NATION'S press had already begun whooping up the Red menace when the Marxists' first official response to the Great Strike came on Sunday, July 22. After an executive committee meeting in Chicago, Party Secretary Van Patten sent a letter to all sections of the Workingmen's Party. This urged party members to aid the railroad strikers. It also spelled out the party's immediate demands: government ownership of railroads and telegraphs, and the eight-hour day in industry. All this seems tame enough against the lurid visions of editorialists. But Van Patten's muted call came late. Already the party's local leaders were improvising their own responses to the crisis. Even as Van Patten dispatched his letter, the process had gone far in Cincinnati.

The "Queen City" was as ripe for revolt as any other American metropolis. In January, the young Cincinnati reporter Lafcadio Hearn had seen

the same rickety room, the same cracked stove, the same dingy walls bearing fantastic tapestry of faded rags and grotesque shadow-silhouettes of sharp profiles . . . shadowy tenement houses and dilapidated cottages, and blind foul alleys with quaint names suggesting deformity and darkness. . . . A dream of reeling buildings of black plank, with devious corridors and deformed stairways; with interminable suites of crooked rooms, having sloping floors and curving walls; with crazy stoves and heavy smells.

Here lived people with a bent for riot. And Cincinnati also had its German district across the Miami Canal—"over the Rhine"—where street signs read "Bier Keller," "Tanz Boden" and the like. An English visitor that year found Cincinnati beer excellent and the business district suggestive of Teutonic solidity. Yet, for all its surface *Gemütlichkeit,* Cincinnati's German population nurtured a flourishing

Communist movement. Many German immigrants here, as elsewhere in America, regarded Marxist orations *auf deutsch* as a welcome breath of the fatherland. They loved the language, they relished the emotional appeal and so they tolerated and occasionally accepted the doctrine. A German community in or near a slum district stood somewhat in the relationship of blasting cap to dynamite.

In midafternoon on July 22, the German section of the Workingmen's Party, headed by the Eureka Band and carrying "the blood-red flag of the Commune," set out from Luebkert's saloon for the Court Street market place. There the marchers joined the English-speaking and Bohemian sections. The crowd of 3,000 or 4,000 included many curiosity seekers, but also a number of grim workingmen. Forty police waited for signs of trouble. The sunbaked crowd listened sympathetically to addresses from four speaking stands, two for English-speaking orators and two for German. "Now, workingmen," said the Bohemian Franz Hruza, "stand by the strikers, and if the other side employs force meet it with force." Here was a seed of mischief. But a Negro schoolteacher named Peter Clark outdid the other speakers in eloquence and also, fortunately, in moderation. "Let us finally not forget," said he, "that we are American citizens; that the right of free speech and a free press is enjoyed by us. We are exercising to-day the right to assemble and complain of grievances. The courts of the land are open to us, and we hold in our hands the all-compelling ballot. There is no need for violent counsels or violent deeds. If we are patient and wise, the future is ours." Clark's way prevailed. In the end, the gathering resolved "That we will use all *lawful* means to support the down-trodden, outraged railroad employes now on a strike." The meeting dispersed without blood or bruises. A second Communist-sponsored meeting that evening drew a mild and good-humored crowd of 2,000 which listened approvingly to Mayor R. H. Moore's advice against violence.

When Cincinnati railroaders joined the Great Strike next day, the Communists "seemed to talk as though they considered that a great opportunity had arrived, and they were going to make the most of it." A Cincinnati paper charged them with being "active among the men in the yards." Most accounts, however, showed teen-agers to be the chief troublemakers, and the late evening rain (as recounted heretofore) quenched the firebrands of Cincinnati for good.

In Boston on Tuesday evening, a turbulent W.P.U.S. rally began
in front of the Providence Station. Plagued by hecklers and noisy, sky-
larking boys, the speakers adjourned the meeting to Hampshire Hall.
The workingmen who jammed the hall (small boys having been
barred) grew impatient at the mildness of W.P.U.S. speakers. Toward
the end some fiery speeches erupted from the floor. But the party
leaders kept things generally in hand. While sympathizing with the
strikers, they opposed lawlessness and urged restoration of peace
and order "with the least possible use of military power." At last
the meeting endorsed the program suggested in Van Patten's letter: the eight-hour day and the peaceful nationalization of railroads.
At ten o'clock the meeting adjourned. Boston's only real excitement
during the Great Strike had already occurred outside. After the
outdoor fiasco the frustrated rowdies, 800 or 900 strong, had swirled
down Kneeland Street to the Boston & Albany depot. For a while
they milled about, yelling and joking. "Where are the strikers?"
they shouted as each train arrived. But the B. & A. men ignored
the crowd, the waiting police were wisely ordered to let it wear itself
out, and after the New York Express arrived uneventfully at ten-
forty, the roisterers drifted away. Two-thirds of them were boys
from twelve to sixteen.

Philadelphia authorities showed less forbearance. On Monday
the city's press made much of the Communist menace. The strikers,
said the *Inquirer*, "have declared war against society . . . They have
practically raised the standard of the Commune in free America."
The *North American* referred to the "riotously communistic workingmen." The *Bulletin* thought that a subsidy of Tom Scott's Texas
Pacific would have made the country prosperous and thus prevented
"this present rebellion of the Railroad Communists." The *Times*
quoted "a prominent official" of the Pennsylvania Railroad as saying: "We do not now fear trouble so much from the people out
here [at the depot] as we do from the Communists in town. I have
just heard of a meeting where inflammatory addresses were made
and where preparations were made for further meetings. I want
Mayor Stokley's attention called to that matter."

Mayor Stokley did his duty. On Tuesday evening police barred
Kelly's Hall to a W.P.U.S. meeting, clubbing a few heads for em-
phasis. Two mass meetings on Wednesday, one of 3,000 and the
other of 5,000, were broken up by police. About a dozen men were

arrested. Later that week the police confiscated all the copies of the *Labor Standard* they could find.

The tragic climax came on Thursday in Kensington, Philadelphia's most solidly working-class district. Warned of imminent trouble there, Mayor Stokley asked the police officer in charge if he knew the ringleader. The officer said he did. Stokley told him to have a good force on hand that night and, if a riot started, to see that the right man was killed. "The policeman seemed to understand the mayor perfectly," recalled a listening member of the Committee of Safety. The W.P.U.S. called two meetings that night. At one of the designated sites, the police broke up small crowds of young men as they gathered. By nine o'clock the street was clear. At the other site, 1,500 people assembled and began calling for the speakers. Ten minutes later 180 police charged into the crowd and drove it off in a contest of bricks against clubs. An hour later fifteen police did battle with a gang of young men. This time shots were exchanged. After the fracas an eighteen-year-old boy lay wounded on the street. He died a half hour later and was eventually identified as William McBride, an only child. Next morning the police officer in charge of the district reported that a riot had indeed started, but that the ringleader had been killed before it got out of hand. "The mayor thanked the police officer." On July 28, the Workingmen's Party tried one more meeting. After police broke it up, its leaders sent a committee to remind the mayor of their right to peaceable assembly. Stokley insisted, however, that no meetings could be allowed "for the present."

By then, perhaps, he had some warrant for his fears. The recent "Communist" disturbances in Philadelphia were as nothing to what the Workingmen's Party had just done (or been blamed for) in Chicago and St. Louis.

Even at the start of the troubles Chicago knew its vulnerability. From the ashes of 1871 it had risen as gusty and brawling as ever—more so, perhaps, for the Great Fire had consumed the last enclaves of peaceful village life. ("The tendency is to the metropolitan in everything," remarked the *Tribune* a little sadly as early as 1873.) The great new stone buildings along State Street and Michigan Avenue might be fireproof, but Chicago's half-million people were not. And all the social frictions of newly urban America heated their tempers. The palaces of the "Prairie Avenue set"–the Fields, the Armours, the Pullmans, the Hibbards and their peers–mocked the rear-lot hovels of the Fourteenth Ward, shacks without foundations or plumbing, where a whole family might live in one squalid room, where lodgers holed up in dank cellars or former clothes closets.

Not all of Chicago's working classes lived in such absolute squalor. Many, especially the skilled, had their own little wooden cottages. None, however, got a full share of the wealth heaped up by their skill and brawn. Hence the need of thousands of families for the wages of their women and children. More than 5,000 Chicago boys and girls between the ages of ten and fifteen were officially listed by the census report as wage earners. In dark, crowded firetraps, little girls averaged fifty cents a week for sewing on coat buttons or pulling basting threads. By the time they had risen to hand sewing at two dollars a week, they were bent and twisted in body like their elders. Children surrendered their youth to furniture factories, print shops, packing houses, drygoods stores. Half the children of Chicago died before they were five, and it is not clear which half were the luckier.

After the fire Chicago's building spree had drawn thousands of workers to the city, only to collapse and leave them stranded when the depression set in two years later. By late 1873 even skilled craftsmen could be hired for board alone. Resentment and despair brought strikes. Not a year of the seventies passed without them. After a bloody strike of lumber shovers in 1876, one of the strikers, August Hielank, killed himself. "No cause, except despondency, caused by poverty, is assigned," reported the Evening Journal; "the Coroner was notified."

Many others preferred Marxism as a cure for the blues. Chicago's heavy population of foreign-born citizens made it receptive to this exotic doctrine. Fifteen per cent of Chicago's population was German-born, supporting three German-language newspapers and a variety of societies. One of the papers, the Vorbote, became an official organ of the Workingmen's Party. The Bohemians claimed only one Chicagoan in forty, but they lived clannishly. Their most congested colony, between Halsted Street and Ashland Avenue, acquired the nickname of "Pilsen." Germans and Bohemians formed the backbone of the Workingmen's Party in Chicago.

Despite that fact, two of the party's principal leaders in Chicago came of old native stock. Philip Van Patten, the party's national secretary, was a draftsman by trade and a poet by appearance. A photograph taken of him at about this time shows a young man with an aquiline nose and a mass of glossy black hair worn long in the back. He is wearing the stock Victorian poet's open stand-up collar with flowing black necktie, and is gazing intently, perhaps a little anxiously, to the observer's left, as if at some dim, receding vision. Van Patten had received a good education, which may explain his sudden appearance in July 1876 as head of the first Marxist party organized on a national basis in the United States. One of the movement's persistent handicaps was its paucity of members who could write correct English.

Sharing the limelight with Van Patten during the Great Strike was Albert R. Parsons, whose American ancestry reached back to 1632. Born in Montgomery, Alabama, of well-to-do Yankee parents, Parsons was an orphan at five. His elder brother in Texas took him in charge until the Civil War broke out, when the thirteen-year-old boy joined a Texas militia company. At fifteen he became a scout in the Texas cavalry brigade commanded by his brother, who had risen to major general. After the war young Parsons rattled around in Texas for a while as a typesetter, newspaper editor and holder of political office under the Republican regime. His editorial stand for Negro civil rights, and perhaps also his marriage to a girl of mixed Spanish and Indian blood, made him unwelcome in Texas. In 1873 he became a typesetter on the *Chicago Times*. His affinity for radical causes drew him into the socialist movement in 1875, and in the spring of 1877 he made a creditable though unsuccessful run for alderman on the Workingmen's Party ticket in the Fifteenth Ward. In July 1877, at twenty-nine, Parsons had an alert bearing, a ready tongue and a handsome, intelligent face adorned with a luxuriant handlebar mustache. These assets helped make him one of the party's two most effective English-speaking orators in Chicago. The other, John McAuliffe, being an extremist, was trotted out only on "great special occasions."

Mindful of their city's social inflammability and unsurpassed rail connections, Chicagoans had little hope of escaping the Great Strike. To meet their nervous craving for late news from the East on Sunday, July 22, Chicago's newest paper, the impudent, sensational, one-cent *Daily News*, ran off frantic extras with the two inside pages left blank. In this crisis the young proprietors of the *News*, Victor Lawson and Melville Stone, saw the making of their paper. Whether out of conviction or calculation, they attuned their editorials to the ears of the masses. As early as July 20 the *News* called the strike of the B. & O. men "their only redress, unwise though it may be," and hoped that railroad companies would soon see the folly of paying "exorbitant prices to the genteel ornaments in the general offices, and starvation prices to the bone and sinew of the road." Sales on Sunday vindicated their tactics; and when on Monday morning a group of Chicago businessmen, including many *News* advertisers, called on Lawson and Stone to suspend their inflammatory sheet until calm had returned, the canny pair refused. Their paper was made; and knowing this, they were not concerned at standing alone among Chicago's English-language papers in support of the strikers.

While newsboys hawked the *News* extras, the Workingmen's Party of the United States made a bid for leadership of the strike movement. Chicago workingmen evidently hungered for some kind of guidance. A crowd of them gathered at the corner of Halsted and Twelfth that afternoon, and various individuals extemporized fiery but aimless speeches. The Workingmen's Party, in contrast, had an organization, a program and a string of practiced orators. An eager audience jammed Sack's Hall at Twentieth and Brown when the W.P.U.S. meeting opened at three o'clock. Moderate in substance, the speeches were bitter in tone. "If the proprietor has a right to fix the rates and say what labor is worth," cried Albert Parsons, "then we are bound hand and foot, slaves, and we should be perfectly happy; content with a bowl of rice and a rat a week apiece." "No! No!" yelled the crowd. After Parsons' speech, the chairman invited everyone to join the party and announced a mass meeting for Monday evening at the corner of Market and Madison, in the heart of the industrial district.

Railroad managers had meanwhile been making cheerful noises for the reporters. The Rock Island's deputy superintendent "was inclined to smile" at fears of a strike in Chicago. "There were a few chronic grumblers on the road who had hammered around considerably at the time the [June 1] reduction was made," he admitted, "but the majority of the men were inclined to accept the situation, knowing well that it was necessary* for the road to act as it did." So ran other managerial comments. Privately the officials talked differently. Vice-President Charles E. Perkins of the Chicago, Burlington & Quincy hurried back from Nebraska to his Burlington, Iowa, office. There he found a wire from General Superintendent William B. Strong in Chicago: "It is estimated we have thirty thousand idle men in Chicago. There is much excitement here over the riots, & the sympathy is with the strikers, it being talked of in street cars and streets as a bread riot. If matters in the East go on unchecked twenty-four hours longer, I fear serious trouble here."

Others had like qualms. Mayor Monroe Heath met in secret session on Sunday afternoon with members of the Common Council and National Guard commanders. Major General Arthur C. Ducat, commanding the two Chicago regiments, ordered all Chicago armories under guard, alerted the brigade and joined the conferees. Deputations of anxious citizens scurried from the police to the militia to the sheriff, pleading for preparedness. Field, Leiter & Company armed the employees of their wholesale store. Double guards appeared around the McCormick reaper works. And from Secretary McCrary in Washington word flashed to General Terry: six companies of the Twenty-Second United States Infantry, then en route from Bismarck, Dakota Territory, to join the rest of their command in the Division of the Atlantic, were to be held at Chicago when they reached the city.

On Monday, July 23, as "matters in the East" went on unchecked, tension grew in Chicago. The managers continued to force their public smiles. A sardonic reporter summed up their expressed views: "Everything lovely." But a tremor showed here and there. "When you have a regular communistic mob to deal with," said a B. & O. official, "there is no calculating on anything." The Fort Wayne freight agent conceded that the First National Guard Regiment was composed of "weak boys" and the Second "largely of working-men." A Rock Island Road boilermaker shared that view. "Why, we could just eat them up," he bragged to the reporter. "A crowd

---

* The Rock Island had ended up with a half-million-dollar surplus that spring after paying a 10 per cent dividend.

could grab the guns right away from them." Mayor Heath, however, thought the militia "far too loyal to permit any such result." Meanwhile he was looking up his legal authority over the two local regiments. The police were ready for anything. Some 250 muskets were said to be stocked at the Harrison Street station. Baseless rumors circulated of strikes at the North Chicago Rolling Mills and on the Michigan Southern. Superintendent J. C. McMullen of the Chicago, Alton & St. Louis summed up the feeling vividly: "Although quiet now, everyone might rise up like a flock of birds before night."

That night (the night of the Reading slaughter) the W.P.U.S. held its second Chicago rally. Under clear skies, with a cool breeze blowing in from the lake, 6,000 excited Chicagoans packed the intersection of Market and Madison. The circulars that called them together had charged a conspiracy by "the Money Lords of America" to restrict the ballot to property holders. "For the sake of our wives and children, and our own self-respect," said the broadsides, "LET US WAIT NO LONGER! ORGANIZE AT ONCE!!" The crowd was joined by a procession bearing banners: "Life by Labor or Death by Fight," "United We Stand, Divided We Fall." George Schilling, a well-known cooper, opened with a moderate speech. Albert Parsons followed in a warmer vein. John McAuliffe declared that if capital fired on labor's Fort Sumter, "he should raise his voice, thought and arm for bloody war!" So the speeches went. At last Secretary Van Patten took the chair, and resolutions were adopted calling for nationalization of railroads and support of trade unionism. Another rally was announced for Tuesday evening. Meanwhile, enrollment was to go forward at the *Arbeiter Zeitung* office on Market Street. Van Patten's moderation, and perhaps also the plain-clothes men who circulated through the crowd, helped to bring the meeting to a tame conclusion. But if nothing else, the Workingmen's Party had now succeeded in capturing the attention of the public, the press and the police.

Superintendent Strong of the Burlington also took note. "The speeches were full of blood or bread," he wrote Vice-President Perkins at midnight, "but they had less effect on the crowd than was expected." Strong felt more hopeful than before. "The Michigan Central reductions have been much more severe than ours," he wrote, "and everything is quiet east of Chicago on that line. If that line can carry its reductions, we certainly ought to. I am not in favor of receding."

It was Tuesday, July 24, which, in the phrase of the day, opened the ball at Chicago.

On Monday night, unknown to Strong, about forty Michigan Central switchmen had declared themselves on strike. On Tuesday morning they passed through their road's shops and freight houses, calling for a stoppage. After a show of protest, their fellow workers put on their coats and swarmed out of the buildings to the cheers of a waiting crowd. Excitement spread through the neighborhood and raised what the *Chicago Times* called "an uncombed, unwashed mob of gutter-snipes and loafers" numbering about 200, under the lead of John "Sandy" Hanlon, a husky switchman lately discharged from the Burlington.

Some roads, such as the Burlington, the Chicago & Alton and the Chicago & Northwestern, had anticipated this turn of events by refusing to accept freight and by moving their rolling stock to safer points along the line. The Northwestern, in fact, had gone so far as to rescind its recent wage cut. The mob now proceeded methodically to make the partial freight stoppage a general one. Joined by an indeterminate number of Michigan Central strikers, the crowd swept through the yards and buildings of the Illinois Central, the Baltimore & Ohio, the Michigan Southern and others. By noon the marchers numbered about 500. "Not ten per cent of them," said the *Times*, "were railway workmen. They were for the most part boys from 14 to 20 years of age, and as hard-looking a lot as could well be selected from any reform school or bridewell. The grown men were simply of the same sort, a little harder in looks because a little older."

At two o'clock, the mob reached the Burlington yards at West Sixteenth Street, announcing itself with "a series of yells and hoots in the sharp treble of adolescent boyhood." "Shouting wildly, displaying much more brass than beard, but making no attempts to harm anybody," the mob raced through the Burlington shops and freight houses. The Burlington men quit as directed. Thence the crowd rode out to the Rock Island shops on a commandeered freight train. Brandished laths and cries of "Quit, you —— —— ——!" brought the few contrary-minded into line there. At the

Fort Wayne yards, angry strikers had already arrived from the road's eastern divisions to stir up their brethren, the Fort Wayne having repudiated its reported concession of Sunday. There the mob had its way easily.

Passenger trains kept running. Some of them were crowded. But by sundown the rumbling freights had fallen silent nearly everywhere in the great railroad center of the mid-continent.

Though concentrating on railroads, the mob had paused at the stockyards and turned out the workers there, as well as at several packing houses. Smaller mobs meanwhile pursued the same course in several localities at once. Early that morning, "a gang of ragamuffins" called out 400 or 500 planing-mill workers and then, with their new-found allies, worked along Blue Island Avenue and Canal Street shutting down factories. At some the men quit willingly, at others reluctantly, at still others under orders from their Pittsburgh-conscious employers. On Canal Street, a husky newsboy, his bundle of papers still under his arm, spied an old man digging for a leaky gas pipe or drain. Grabbing a stick, the boy yelled, "Get out o' there, you old son of a gun, and come along." Without a word the old man climbed out and joined the crowd. Another crowd of men and boys, led by "a tall and lanky Irishman in shirt sleeves and a black slouch hat," worked south along Desplaines Street, closing every workshop and halting every construction job. This gang paused for refreshment at Fortune's brewery on Van Buren Street, carrying kegs and buckets of beer to a vacant lot and alley opposite, where the beer was consumed on the spot, "the youths and boys hanging over the beer longest of all, deliberately getting drunk." Then the picnickers returned to their serious business. So went affairs elsewhere in the city all that hot and hectic day.

The crews of several lake vessels struck for $1.50 a day. This development, combined with the rail tie-up, forced a number of unvisited establishments to stop work also. The North Chicago rolling mill shut down for lack of coke. Whether from mob threats, employer prudence or lack of shipping facilities, a great many Chicago workingmen now faced at least a day or two of idleness.

On that turbulent Tuesday, Chicago's social, financial and political elite seemed at loose ends. With business at a standstill, most of the city's leading merchants and businessmen loitered aimlessly about the financial district, swapping rumors and waiting for news-boys to cry the latest extra. Some may have girded themselves for combat. Gun stores reported brisk sales, and at least one establish-ment reserved its weapons for "the better class of citizens" (other classes being told that guns were out of stock). The martial spirit burned low, however, among the 1,800 members of the Board of Trade. When Mayor Heath sent an alderman to recruit a citizens' guard at the Board of Trade building, only twelve joined, of whom five were conscripted messenger boys.

Others of "the better class of citizens" contributed heavily to the confusion prevailing at City Hall. By early afternoon a milling crowd jammed the corridors, smoking, chattering and plaguing officials with free advice. About then they were herded out and a guard placed at the door. At the urging of one influential committee, Mayor Heath closed the saloons. The mayor also called on citizens to "organize patrols in their respective neighborhoods and keep their women and children off the public highways." In midafternoon the fire bells rang the military alarm, calling the militia to their armories; but few militiamen heard (or admitted hearing) the signal. By nightfall, however, about 500 had shown up. Simultaneously the Veteran Club held a meeting of all Civil War veterans at the Grand Pacific Hotel. Volunteer companies were formed, and the latest Remington breechloaders were passed out. "Generals and colonels were very thick," said the *Times,* "with a liberal sprinkling of ma-jors and captains."

Assistant Adjutant General R. C. Drum of the U. S. Army's Di-vision of the Missouri saw "serious trouble" ahead for Chicago. He so informed the War Department, meanwhile holding at Chicago a shipment of arms bound from the Rock Island Arsenal to Pittsburgh. Mayor Heath considered borrowing the arms for Chicago's police, but otherwise he shied from Federal help. As long as the Twenty-second Infantry had already been ordered to stop at Chicago on its way east, the mayor thought it might as well do so. But to order more regulars to Chicago would, he thought, "only aggravate ex-isting troubles." The War Department compromised by shifting six companies of the Ninth Infantry from Omaha to Rock Island, there to stand ready in case Heath changed his mind or the governor changed it for him.

Among all the champions of order, the police seemed keenest for combat—so keen, indeed, that Mayor Heath cautioned them to injure no one if they could possibly avoid it. At police headquarters in City Hall, clattering telegraphs kept Superintendent Hickey apprized of mob movements. Telegraph boys darted through the crowd outside Hickey's office. When "a prominent citizen" that morning made an offer to pay for extra policemen, Mayor Heath took him up on it. By evening, several hundred specials had been sworn in, invested with their stars and clubs and dispatched to the various stations, where they freed the regular force for emergency duty.

The authorities meanwhile followed the doings of the Communists with annoyance and suspicion. That morning Albert Parsons showed up for work at the *Times* office, only to find himself fired and blacklisted for his speech the night before. At noon, tired, disheveled, depressed, hoarse from oratory and a cold, he submitted meekly to an order from Mayor Heath to appear at City Hall. The wind flapped the coats of the two men sent to fetch him, and he saw that they carried pistols. In a room full of police, city officials and leading citizens, Superintendent Hickey catechized the seedy-looking Communist, browbeat him and lectured him on the iniquity of coming up from Texas to incite insurrection. Parsons' denials and defense were punctuated by cries of "Hang him! Lynch him!" from the solid citizenry roundabout. After two hours of this, Hickey escorted Parsons to the door. "Parsons," he said melodramatically, "your life is in danger. I advise you to leave the city at once. Why, those Board of Trade men would as leave hang you to a lamp-post as not." Turning the spring latch, Hickey pushed Parsons out into the hall. "Take warning," Hickey croaked, and slammed the door. "I was never in the old rookery before," Parsons later recalled. "It was a labyrinth of halls and doors. I saw no one about. All was still. The sudden change from the tumultuous inmates of the room to the dark and silent hall affected me. I didn't know where to go or what to do. I felt alone, absolutely without a friend in the wide world." The treatment had been effective. Parsons wandered gloomily about, watched the crowds, but no longer put himself in the forefront.

Despite the intimidation of Parsons, the Workingmen's Party remained a cynosure. The *Daily News* asserted positively that "the different crowds moving about the city to-day closing factories were committees of the Commune." "One of the principal hives for the gathering of the discontented," observed the *Times*, "was the office of the *Vorbote*, a dingy little den in the second story of a building on the west side of Market Street, near Madison Street. Up and down the narrow, dirty stairway leading to the hive, a constant stream of idle drones were passing, buzzing and snarling in their various languages. Not one of them bore the marks of a decent workingman. Sallow Bohemians and Poles, dirty and ragged renegade Frenchmen, stupefied by idleness, and Germans, outcasts from the society of their own nation, mingled in a filthy, snarling crowd."

The party's public statements did not bear out these imputations of ferocity. "Fellow Workers," the W.P.U.S. proclaimed that day, "Under any circumstances keep quiet until we have given the present crisis a due consideration." Even the fiery John McAuliffe, in a letter to the *Times*, denounced the roughs and troublemakers and urged the police to arrest them. The W.P.U.S., he insisted, was a force for peace. Still, the party was growing bolder in its aims. Van Patten called a meeting for that evening of trade union representatives. Sixty, representing twenty shops, showed up and chose a provisional committee. The committee in turn formulated the W.P.U.S. strike program: a nationwide general strike for the eight-hour day and for a 20 per cent increase in wages, the strike to be organized and conducted by "a permanent executive committee."

The impact of that heroic resolve was somewhat lessened by a rival meeting of the Chicago Labor League at the same time. Twenty-five trade unions were represented. After denouncing the *Chicago Tribune*, whisky, railroad authorities and "the money lenders," the meeting proposed two sovereign remedies: repeal of the resumption act and free coinage of silver.

Nevertheless, the W.P.U.S. rally that evening drew 1,000 enthusiastic listeners. It also drew 140 police, who formed a wedge and plunged into the yelling crowd. During the day, the police had acquired a taste for the sport of crowd busting. Heretofore the work had been easy. This evening there was sporadic resistance. One man was locked up for firing a revolver. It took the police an hour to disperse the crowd completely.

On Wednesday the lines of battle hardened, and contact was made at several points.

The day had scarcely broken, cool for July but oppressively humid, when gangs of from fifty to 200 began ranging up and down Canal Street, armed with clubs and stones. More violent and determined than on Tuesday, they extended and tightened the shutdown of mills and shops. Streetcars and even wagons and buggies were stopped, sometimes by "mere boys, but the hardest little devils that it is possible to find in the lowest slums of the city." Roving mobs on the North Side closed up tanneries, stoneworks, clothing factories, a large distillery and other places; but police turned them back from the gasworks, much to the relief of the city, which dreaded a night of darkness in riotous times. On the West Side squads of rioters fanned out to enforce and extend the strike in factories and lumber yards along the river. A mob of 1,500 men and boys streamed down "the Black Road," as Blue Island Avenue was called, taking care of brickyards, furniture factories, lumberyards and other establishments. A score of police confronted them at the United States Rolling-Stock Company. Stones from the mob drew shots from the police. In the ensuing skirmish the police were saved from rout only by the arrival of reinforcements. This encounter blocked the mob's drive on the great McCormick reaper works, but the mob had shown its temper.

The railroad blockade likewise tightened. The Chicago & Alton replied to strikers' demands by abandoning all traffic—freight, passenger and mail. The Burlington had been delivering grain to elevators, but a mob of several hundred now stopped that. Any illusion that the Burlington men had quit only under duress was dispelled when at 9:00 A.M. the trainmen and switchmen struck at Galesburg and in Iowa. Their demands were precisely and elaborately worked out for a score of different jobs and classifications. President Harris promptly closed the shops and discontinued all but passenger trains. Vice-President Perkins went him one better in Iowa and cut off passenger service also. "I made up my mind to strike myself," he recalled somewhat bitterly, ". . . and try the effect of my medicine here in Iowa, leaving Harris and Strong to manage it their own way in Illinois." By so doing, Perkins boasted, the strikers at Burlington, Iowa, were cut off from the rest of the line and deprived of a chance to test their strength.

Tempers and thermometers rose together that Wednesday afternoon. Squads of police, tired but still full of fight, rushed from place to place doing battle with roving gangs of rioters. A mob of North Side teen-agers, for example, having visited and closed a number of establishments, had reached the Michigan Central yards when a frightened cry arose: "The peelers are coming!" Catching the mob in a narrow alley blocked at the far end by freight wagons and horses, the police charged the panicky mass and laid about them with their billies. "The sound of clubs falling on skulls was sickening for the first minute," reported the *Times*, "until one grew accustomed to it. A rioter dropped at every whack, it seemed, for the ground was covered with them. Some dropped their clubs and begged for mercy. In less than five minutes there was not a rioter in sight, except those who were disabled or in custody."

While the police warmed to their work, 600 Civil War veterans drilled with their breechloaders, and 400 men of the First National Guard Regiment waited impatiently in their armory. In midafternoon several hundred dispirited citizens gathered at the Moody and Sankey Tabernacle for a sort of law and order revival meeting. "Do you know, fellow-citizens," declaimed the Reverend Robert Collyer, pastor of Unity Church, "as God lives and as my soul lives, I would rather die in twenty minutes in defense of order and of our homes, against these men, than to live twenty years of as happy life as I have lived all these fifty years. [Loud cheers.]" The meeting resolved that Mayor Heath should call for 5,000 volunteers. Lawyer Leonard Swett, a long-time intimate of the late Abraham Lincoln, closed with a plea that the mayor ask for Federal troops. As the audience flowed out into the sticky air, they heard shouts and cheers from several blocks away: two companies of the Twenty-second Infantry had at last arrived. Weary from long service in the Indian country and a 400-mile march to Bismarck, clad in patched and threadbare uniforms, unpaid for more than three months, the regulars nevertheless looked bronzed, hardy and well disciplined as they marched up Madison Street, impervious to both cheers and cat-calls. A mob of rioters pushed into the regulars' bivouac area in the Exposition Building, but were ejected swiftly, efficiently and without casualties. The regulars' timely arrival, and the summer shower that thinned out the crowds soon after, revived the appetites of those Chicagoans who could afford a good meal that evening.

But while good citizens supped, the plebeian squall blew up again. At about six o'clock, soon after the shower, hundreds of

railroad strikers, lumberyard men, onlookers and the usual complement of boys converged from several directions on the Burlington
switchyards near Sixteenth and Halsted, apparently to check on
compliance with the strike there. After much shouting and club
waving, the crowd satisfied itself that all was in order; and it was
beginning to disperse when an omnibus rattled up and eighteen
policemen piled out. The crowd drew together again, yelling insults and pelting the "peelers." The police drew their revolvers.
And the battle was on. The police banged away at the advancing
crowd, but only four of the hundred or so shots took effect, and
those not fatally. Undismayed, the mob pressed forward. On Halsted Street, thousands of excited spectators gathered amid a hopeless jam of drays, wagons, stockyard trucks and streetcars. The
Halsted Street viaduct over the tracks was packed with people.
These saw the police start to retreat, at first slowly, then on the
dead run up Union Street with the mob pounding after them. Intercepted by another crowd, the fugitives turned out onto Halsted
Street, made a brief stand at the viaduct, were chased back to the
switchyards, in and out of the machine shop and once again to
Halsted Street. There they met reinforcements. The augmented
force now took the offensive, finding most of the mob happily
stoning the railroad buildings and an incoming passenger train.
(Others were busy sacking a gun store and two hardware stores
on Halsted Street.) After a fusillade of police bullets, the fleeing
mob left nine of its number lying wounded in the yards. A Burlington switchman had been killed instantly by a bullet in his chest.
Two other men were later reported dead.

Night closed in soon after, and torches flared at Market and
Madison, where the W.P.U.S. was holding another rally. Philip
Van Patten, calling at police headquarters that morning to declare
the party's peaceful intentions, had been given the Parsons treatment complete with threats of a lamppost hanging. But its effect
had worn off by the time of the meeting. He had just begun ad-
dressing a large crowd when a picked squad of police, shoulder to
shoulder, came at the audience from behind "at a sharp double
trot." In its flight the crowd brought down the flimsy speakers'
stand, Van Patten, torches and all. Knots of resistance kept the
police engaged. Van Patten was reported to have fallen on his
knees and begged for mercy, but this he later denied. Just then

a procession of 1,000 workingmen marched up, with fife squealing and drum pounding. They had come to hear the speeches, but the police supposed them to be joining the fight. A warning volley in the air sent the newcomers scampering. Most ran down La Salle Street and collided with twenty-five police reinforcements, who took them for a new mob and commenced another skirmish. The wonder of that whole torchlit Donnybrook was that there were no serious casualties—at least, none left lying after the streets were cleared of rioters.

In that respect, Chicago's luck had less than a day to run.

That night the First National Guard Regiment waited tensely in its Lake Street armory, the Second at the Rock Island depot. The lately arrived Federal troops stayed at the Exposition Building, at the other end of which Theodore Thomas and his symphony orchestra were giving a summer-night concert. The little band of Indian fighters, so lately lulled by the yipping coyote, drifted off that Wednesday evening to the strains of Strauss. So far there were only seventy regulars on hand, but more were on the way. The swelling turbulence of Wednesday afternoon had at last moved Mayor Heath to seek Federal help. He appealed to Governor Shelby Cullom, who in turn that afternoon formally requested military assistance from President Hayes. "Great danger of an outbreak any moment," Cullom wired Secretary McCrary soon after. Colonel Drum at Chicago went ahead and ordered six companies of infantry from Rock Island. President Hayes seemed oddly hesitant. But at last, an hour or two before dawn Thursday, he authorized Drum to use his regulars against the Chicago rioters.

Meanwhile the home guard had sprung to arms. "The property-owners of the city," said the *Times*, "are at last thoroughly aroused." Such houses as Field, Leiter & Co. and John V. Farwell & Co., having already loaned their wagons to the police and their horses to the cavalry, now organized their employees into armed companies. A hundred Illinois Central men and as many Chicago & Northwestern men were sworn in as special police and given arms to guard their companies' property. Civil War veterans were out in force, and most of the city's wards (but not the Fourteenth) organized citizen patrols. Veterans in the Fourth Ward formed six companies,

300 strong, "most of whom [had] marched with Grant from Donelson to Vicksburg."

It was the police, however, who were to take the lead in the coming showdown. Wednesday's hors d'oeuvres had whetted their appetite for combat, and the enrollment of hundreds of "specials" for routine service had freed the regular force for an all-day feast. It began at the Halsted Street viaduct in the vicinity of Wednesday's worst outbreak.

Word had been given out Wednesday night that the combined militia and regulars would occupy that area at daybreak. For some reason they did not. Instead, a large and belligerent mob gathered there in the sultry dawn, presumably as a reception committee. Rioters began cutting telegraph lines, stoning and stopping street-cars and terrorizing citizens who looked suspiciously prosperous. The midsummer sun rose higher, and the wind blew hot from the southwest. In midmorning a squad of thirty or forty police charged the crowd, and battle was joined. The shock of the police charge scattered the vanguard of the mob, and the police chased it across the viaduct and down the far slope, south toward Sixteenth Street. Then the tide turned. At Sixteenth Street the little squad of police ran into 5,000 enraged rioters. Some of the mob made a dash to re-cross the viaduct and cut off their adversaries. The attempt was blocked by free use of clubs and revolvers. But the police found themselves in an uncomfortably hot spot. Swarms of boys stoned them "with deplorable vigor and accuracy" until driven off by a pistol volley. Answering shots came from the crowd. The older rioters surged closer, shouting furiously. Police bullets dropped man after man in the crowd, each casualty being dragged off by his friends. Still the crowd pushed nearer. With only one or two rounds left of their original sixteen, the police turned and fled, and the mob came howling after them. "I tell you," said Sergeant Butler later, "I never was in such close quarters in my life before, and I don't want to be again."

Then, with dramatic timeliness, the tide turned once more. A block from the viaduct, Sergeant Butler's unhappy few met fifty more police and a company of mounted militia coming up full speed. Falling in behind these, Butler's men faced about; and the combined force struck the onrushing mob, "shooting and cudgeling without mercy." A club crushed in the back of one man's skull.

"The blood and brains were oozing down his neck, but buoyed by the unnatural excitement he managed to continue with the others for quite a distance without falling. When he did fall he was borne away by his comrades." A teen-age boy was said to have stood with a pistol in each hand, blazing away at the police until a shot brought him down. A leader of the mob likewise stood his ground with a revolver. "He fell with a bullet through the base of his uncultivated brain, and lay like a log upon the pavement." This sight broke the mob's spirit, and off it ran, south on Halsted, scattering into side streets on the way until only a determined few remained—determined and designing, it appeared. For they led the advance elements of the police across the bridge near Archer Avenue, whereupon several of their confederates turned the bridge in order to isolate the police. But a boy of ten or eleven, left on the bridge, went to work and swung it back again. "The policemen who were rescued by the little one's pluck cheered and patted him, and threw in a collection of a nickel each for his benefit." A young baker was just then shot in the act of firing a pistol at the police; he died that afternoon.

At this point, the police felt the need of companionship. In response to their appeal, the Second Regiment was sent out along Archer Avenue with a battery of fieldguns, the Stars and Stripes and a banner emblazoned with "the Harp of Ireland." The militiamen found all quiet at Archer and Halsted, but they had not been there long when a new alarm sent them up Halsted to Twelfth Street, where a shocking melee had just erupted.

A few minutes earlier, a squad of regular police had charged to the rescue of some specials battling a crowd near the corner of Halsted and Twelfth. Thus reinforced, the police drove the crowd back until it merged with a smaller crowd standing outside the Vorwärts Turner Hall on Twelfth Street. Inside the hall, 200 or 300 members of the Harmonia Association of Joiners, a cabinetmakers' society, had gathered peaceably to discuss the eight-hour question. The uproar outside broke into their discussion. Suddenly a number of frightened men ran up the stairs and into the hall, closely pursued by club-swinging police. The proprietor of the hall tried to keep the intruders out, but was laid low by a well-aimed club. Without making any effort to learn the nature of the meeting, the cursing police attacked everyone in sight. A few in the hall tried to fight back with chairs and table legs; but this only incited the police to open up with pistol fire, wounding many of the cabinet-makers and killing at least one. Most of those who fled were hurt in jumping from windows or clubbed by waiting police who lined the stairs. "Sometimes, in the confusion," reported the *Chicago Times*, the victims "would lie struggling, kicking and cursing, a most unsavory mess, piled five or six deep, upon the stairs." Outside, Sergeant Brennan fired his pistol indiscriminately at passers-by and at men emerging from the hall. At last the Second Regiment charged up the street with bayonets leveled and drove everyone in the neighborhood indoors, including women and children.*

While all this went on, crowds in the Burlington yards stoned and fired on the ten-thirty Dubuque express and derailed the incoming Mendota accommodation. Passengers from the latter stole safely away on foot while the thirsty mob "irrigated their nasty thoraxes" with the contents of milkcans found in one car. Later that day a mob of boys stoned out all the windows in the Burlington's freight house and tried to tear off the slate roof. Some passenger service continued through the day, but little or no freight moved.

All that afternoon, Halsted Street swarmed with thousands of people, most of them in knots of 100 or more. Police and mounted militia patrols harried them indefatigably. Now and then came brief, ugly little scuffles, some of which lengthened the list of dead and wounded. Often a crowd would scatter at the approach of a mounted patrol, then reassemble as the troop cantered past. Half of the First National Guard Regiment and several hundred regular and special police established a base near Twelfth and Halsted, whence detachments now and then sallied out to points of real or rumored violence. At three o'clock the police and cavalry broke up a mob on Canal Street, two or three rioters being badly, perhaps mortally wounded.

Amid all the street fighting, Chicago's factories were not forgotten by the mobs. At the stockyards and the gasworks, mobs forced the officials to sign papers promising to raise wages to $2 a day for the next eighteen months. The officials signed cheerfully, knowing the pledges to be unenforceable. Lake vessels swung at anchor

* In a test case months afterward, the Harmonia Joiners preferred charges against the police for this attack. Declaring the meeting to have been orderly and legal and the police action a "criminal riot," Judge William K. McAllister fined Sergeants Brennan and Householder, the leaders, six cents each.

for lack of dock workers. Mobs swept through the lumberyards; and even after they passed, the lumberyard workers refused to return to their jobs—the strike there, at least, was voluntary. Some factories, previously closed, managed to reopen. Internal Revenue Collector Harvey, in the name of the United States government, took the distilleries under his wing on grounds that the government had a lien for taxes on the products thereof; and G.A.R. men armed with wagon spokes, if not bung starters, assumed the job of guarding them. But the tanneries on "Goose Island," the rolling mills and, indeed, every factory from Chicago Avenue to North Avenue, stood idle. Though the McCormick Works had not been bothered by the mob, its manager decided that "being through all the work on the fifty," it might as well stop "to clean up & take account of stock."

Turbulence lingered into Thursday night. At dusk police charged and scattered a Goose Island crowd. Later on, harassed by stones and pistol shots, the Second Regiment fired a couple of random volleys at the dark switchyards below their bivouac on the Halsted Street viaduct. Thick clouds hid the moon, and people still roamed the streets apprehensively, startled by an occasional shot. In the Exposition Building the undaunted Theodore Thomas led a grimly Wagnerian program, including the *Flying Dutchman* overture, the "Bacchanale" from *Tannhäuser*, "Siegfried's Death" from *Götter-dämmerung*, and the "Ride of the Valkyries," now and then augmented by the hoofbeats of passing patrols. A vague sense of imminent calamity still hung in the air, and one of the Burlington's detectives reported talk in the mob of burning freight depots and roundhouses. Some thought the whole city would be put to the torch.

Yet more and more signs appeared that the crisis had passed. Afternoon trains from the West had brought six companies of the Ninth United States Infantry and two more companies of the Twenty-second, all of them rugged veterans of the late campaigns against the Sioux and the Cheyenne. Colonel Drum put them at the mayor's disposal at once. On Kinzie Street a gang of young hoodlums stoned a detachment of the Twenty-second until one soldier, hit by a pebble, turned and fired his Henry rifle reprovingly at the miscreant. He missed, perhaps intentionally, but the course of the bullet was later traced through two frame saloons and into a third building. That pacified the crowd, and at five o'clock Colonel Drum was able to inform the anxious War Department that the regulars had not engaged the mob, had merely guarded property and were at the moment resting in their quarters.

Dejected prisoners accumulated in the police stations, while their hosts remained "full of war," roused by the day's successes to "the highest pitch of excitement." All day long volunteer "specials" streamed into police headquarters and were sworn; by nightfall there were said to be 5,000 on duty. The old Ninety-sixth Illinois had a reunion under arms—Remington breechloaders—and even the Board of Trade drummed up 100 volunteers for its own patrol. City Hall furnished the best barometer. Thickly infested for three days past by the curious, the fearful and the meddlesome, its dark, low-ceilinged corridors by eight o'clock in the evening heard only the purposeful tread of incoming and outgoing messengers and "specials." Chicagoans seemed to agree with Vice-President Ackerman of the Illinois Central. "If we get through without a fire," he wrote that night, "I think the backbone of the movement is broken."

Broken—but at what a price! The people who had made a mob took time now in the warm night to sit on doorsteps and gather at corners along Halsted Street, weighing the cost. "John Weinert, aged 19, living on South Canal Street, shot and instantly killed . . . J. Wallace aged about 18, instantly killed . . . A man whose name was not learned, living on Archer Avenue, shot through the lungs and died almost immediately of hemorrhage . . . Joseph Cooley, shot through the head and killed . . . Edward Phillips, aged about 17 years, was shot dead in the morning and taken to the morgue, where he now lies . . . Harry Collins, shot in the thigh; a dangerous wound which may result in amputation. . . ." The list ran on. At least eighteen men and boys, some of them mere onlookers, were dead, and scores were wounded. This is a minimum; many others were carried off by companions and never reported.

Did the movement actually have a "backbone," that is to say leadership, organization, a concrete program? For a time Van Patten and the Workingmen's Party had struggled to meet that need. But the police cut short the party's development before it passed the gristle stage. Frank Norbock, leader of the party's Bohemian section, was shot through the head and instantly killed at the corner of Sixteenth and Canal Thursday morning. Otherwise, in the explosion of Thursday the word "Communist" appeared in the press only as a casual epithet. A *Post* reporter looked in on the *Vorbote* office that afternoon and found everything quiet. No more meetings were planned at present. "We don't think it advisable," said his informant. The mob remained invertebrate.

There was one great city, however, where the Workingmen's Party held the center of the stage from first to last; and that was Chicago's long-time rival, St. Louis.

The Great Strike found St. Louis as vulnerable as its northern competitor. Sprawled along eighteen miles of Mississippi shore opposite Illinois, the city still hoped to catch and pass Chicago as the commercial center of the Midwest. Though steamboats, some of them palatial, lined St. Louis levees, the great days of river traffic had passed. Industrial smoke now hung in the sky like a banner proclaiming the city's new allegiance. Flour mills, smelting works, rolling mills, foundries, packing houses, machine shops, lead, zinc and sugar refineries gave work to a growing proportion of the city's 300,000 people. Breweries were especially plentiful, the concomitant of a large German population.

As a distributing center, St. Louis was making up through its railroads for what it had lost by the decline of steamboating. The great Eads bridge, an engineering milestone completed in 1874, shifted St. Louis' commercial polarity from a north-south to an east-west axis. The city became a gateway of trade, with a large population of transients. Now, in July 1877, these gains became dangers. The strike impulse was bound to reach St. Louis via one railroad line or another; and when it did, it would be felt. Beginning with the Missouri Pacific, most of the St. Louis roads had gone along with the spring fashion of low-cut wages. The Ohio & Mississippi's cut rankled most, for a costly strike in 1876 had wrung from the management a promise of no further slashes. The promise had been broken as of July 16. O. & M. brakemen charged that their earnings now averaged $30 a month, just enough to buy them meals at a quarter apiece and a twenty-five cent lodging. The company claimed that pay averaged $42. Forty-two or thirty, it was clear that faith had not been kept.

The railroad men were not alone in their distress. Far back in old French days the region had been nicknamed *"Pain Court"*—"short of bread"—and there were grounds in 1877 for reviving the title. The depression cast its shadow over the hundreds of dingy, crowded tenements in the center of town, over the slums of Castle Thunder, the Cross Keys, Clabber Alley, Wild Cat Chute, even over the wealthy sections of town. The collapse of the city's oldest and strongest bank had touched off a string of bank failures in mid-July.

Besides their grievances, the unemployed and underpaid of St. Louis also had potential leadership. The Workingmen's Party of the United States had a firm foothold there. The *St. Louis Times* estimated local membership at nearly 1,000: 600 in the German section, 200 in the English, 75 in the Bohemian and 50 in the French. Only a month before, the party had given a successful picnic in Lindell Park to help finance a projected daily newspaper. Significantly, the picnickers included members of the bakers', coopers', cabinet-makers', cigar makers' and brewery workers' unions—a federation in embryo.

All these things considered, St. Louis citizens received the news of railroad strikes in the East with surprising detachment. On Saturday evening, July 21, railroad men across the river in East St. Louis, Illinois, held a wildly enthusiastic meeting and appointed committees of three each from various roads "to consider what is best to be done." A Wabash brakeman, later if not then a W.P.U.S. member, presided; and one speaker compared the meeting with the First Continental Congress. Yet on Sunday St. Louis citizens read the news of Pittsburgh's ordeal with more interest than apprehension. Mayor Henry Overstolz passed the day quietly at home, then went for an evening drive. The poor swarmed out of their alleys, the rich forsook the parlor for the porch, but that was the rule on a summer Sunday in St. Louis. Except for the *Missouri Republican*, which cried havoc, St. Louis newspapers felt secure enough to view eastern antics with indulgence. "GIVE US RIGHT—THE CRY OF THE WORKINGMEN IN HAMLETS AND CITIES" read a *Times* headline. "The right of revolution is inherent in all people," said the *Journal*, which even promised not to condemn the laboring men "if they prefer war to starvation."

At least one man in St. Louis took matters more seriously. James Harrison Wilson, not quite forty, had behind him a brilliant Civil War record. He had, indeed, become one of the outstanding cavalry commanders of the war's later days, and had come out of the war a major general. Young, self-confident, quick in temper and intelligence, he turned after the war from destruction to building; and he was proudest of having built up the St. Louis & Southeastern Railroad. He had been one of its original promoters, had been a partner in the contracting firm that built it, had been a director or vice-president almost continuously ever since. The road went bankrupt in 1874; and in September 1876 a United States circuit court appointed Wilson one of its two receivers. Pride, a sense of duty, innate pugnacity, all made Wilson a jealous guardian of his road's well-being. Perhaps there was something else, too. On July 19, 1877, he wrote Jacob Schiff of Kuhn, Loeb & Co. that the road was in finer shape than ever, that business was picking up and that he wanted Schiff to buy him some St. Louis & Southeastern first mortgage bonds in the amount of $20,000 par value, but at a 65 per cent discount. Wilson sent $2,000 margin, furnished him by the other receiver. Schiff was to put up the balance at 7 per cent. Wilson would put up nothing, but would split the profits with his fellow receiver. A lovely arrangement—but where would it be if a bitter strike cut into the road's business?

No wonder, then, that Wilson began goading the Federal Government to take action. He addressed himself to Carl Schurz, who was an ex-general, a St. Louis man and a Cabinet member. "My dear General," wrote Wilson that Sunday, ". . . the strike seems to be traveling westward, and our men may be forced into it. . . . The fight might just as well be made *now* as at any time, and should the General Government be called upon to intervene in this region, it can command my services unreservedly." Pointing out his responsibility as a receiver for the United States courts, Wilson added testily: "I shall certainly not permit my employees to fix their own rate of wages, nor dictate to me in any manner what my policy shall be."

That afternoon all four sections of the Workingmen's Party met, proclaimed solidarity with strikers everywhere and then set out, 500 strong, to join a mass meeting of railroad men just getting under way in East St. Louis. Shunning the bridge as a monopoly, the crusaders took a ferry across the Mississippi and on the way lustily sang the "Marseillaise" (with some assistance from the French section). Word of the approaching W.P.U.S. delegation raised tremendous cheers from the railroaders, and they adjourned their meeting from their packed hall to the yards of the Relay Depot, the better to receive their allies.

Under a blistering sun 1,000 railroaders and East St. Louis citizens waited for the W.P.U.S. marchers to arrive. A sidetracked coal train became a grandstand, and a flatcar waited to serve as speakers' platform. Off-duty telegraphers lounging near the telegraph office windows listened to news dispatches clicking in from the East, and they reported the latest to the crowd. Cheers arose at news of the Philadelphia militia's retreat from Pittsburgh. Then the W.P.U.S. men marched up two by two, hats and handkerchiefs waving madly; and the speech-making commenced, hot as the afternoon sun. Like their counterparts in a dozen other cities, the sweating orators pounded away at capitalist oppression, the venality and bias of the press, the subservience of government to the railroad kings. Said one W.P.U.S. speaker: "All you have to do, gentlemen, for you have the numbers, is to unite on one idea—that the workingmen shall rule the country. What man makes, belongs to him, and the workingmen made this country." Another speaker reminded the railroaders that they had friends, "good, warm friends, and the fact is exhibited in the strong delegation from the St. Louis party of working men present at the meeting. (Cheers.)"

The reminder hardly seemed necessary, for W.P.U.S. speakers clearly dominated the meeting. There was Henry F. Allen, sign painter and self-taught physician, an odd little man with a large head crammed full of nostrums for the ills of the body, the soul and the world. There was Laurence Gronlund, a young Dane who had assumed the name of "Peter Lofgreen," vigorous, intelligent, well read, a graduate of the University of Copenhagen, an ex-school teacher, a student of law, currently doubling as financial secretary of the local W.P.U.S. and clerk on the St. Louis Globe-Democrat. There was Albert Currlin, aged twenty-four, not long over from Germany, by trade a baker, by avocation the head of the W.P.U.S. German section. Slight and unathletic, marked by the stoop and pallor of the scholar, a halting speaker in English, Currlin nevertheless had a habitually pleasant expression and a ready smile; and in German he spoke both well and often.

Despite the heat, the crowd did not soon tire of hearing its hopes and fears set to oratory. After six o'clock, evening trains disturbed the closing speakers, "but sympathy oozed out of the windows of all the passing cars in atonement, and handkerchiefs were waving in all directions, expressive of the sympathy of the traveling public." Before the open-air meeting was well over, East St. Louis railroad men began assembling at Traubel's Hall. Once in session, the meeting quickly plumped for a strike at midnight. Representatives of six railroads, including the Vandalia, the Ohio & Mississippi and James Wilson's St. Louis & Southeastern, committed themselves and their fellow workers to the strike; and a committee of one man from each line was set up to direct it. Afterward the new-made strikers marched about the streets to the music of fife and drum. At news of the East St. Louis strike excitement ran ominously high in Carondelet, the southernmost district of St. Louis and the site of the city's heaviest industrial concentration. Excitement, in fact, was everywhere. "Are there any troops at the Arsenal here?" Receiver Wilson wired Secretary Schurz. "My services are at the disposal of the government." Schurz being out of town, the acting Secretary of the Interior passed Wilson's wire along to Secretary of War McCrary, who ordered Brigadier General John Pope to send what force he could spare to St. Louis, and to go there himself from his headquarters at Fort Leavenworth, Kansas, if he deemed it necessary.

As a railroad town, East St. Louis—like Altoona or Martinsburg—belonged to the strikers. Their "executive committee" ran the strike with efficiency and self-assurance. Mayor John Bowman could not have challenged them if he had wanted to, since by a recent twist of the city's tangled politics the legal right of his dozen policemen to arrest anyone at all was then in question. As it happened, he did not want to. He himself, as a boy of seventeen, had been an active revolutionist in both Austria and France. More to the point, he depended on the railroaders' votes. So on Monday he closed the saloons, swore in a dozen strikers as special police and then consented to serve as the strikers' emissary to the railroad managers. All the managers except General Wilson spoke softly, but none would yield. Therefore, while passenger and mail trains ran as usual, freight traffic ceased. Little else happened in East St. Louis for several days thereafter.

On the Missouri side of the river St. Louis had a livelier time of it. Mayor Overstolz timidly suggested to the railroad companies that withdrawal of the wage cuts might be both just and wise. After a day of haggling the Missouri Pacific management elated strikers by caving in and restoring wages to the levels of 1876—a 25 per cent increase which wiped out the two most recent cuts! That Monday evening the Missouri Pacific strikers accepted the agreement, and next day the M.P. announced that freight would be received for shipment. But a force of 300 men, sent across the river by the East St. Louis strike committee, kept the M.P. men off the job after all.

The stubbornness of other managements clouded the splendor of the M.P. victory. On Monday morning General Wilson called off his cherished bond deal, and the pill did not sweeten his temper. He told a reporter that it was "out of the question to talk of making any concessions to the strikers. If this were done, there would be no end to their demands, and the railroads would have to submit to being controlled by their employes." That afternoon Secretary Schurz sent the War Department another pointed message from Wilson, who complained about the weakness of local authorities and insisted that "no U. S. marshal, unless backed by Federal troops, can restore order or protect men willing to work. . . . The presence of Federal troops will form a rallying point and do much to restore order." A few hours later, General Pope wired the War Department: "Your dispatch received. Six companies of Twenty-third Infantry leave for St. Louis in three hours. . . ."

Wilson's allusion to the United States marshal presaged a development of immense importance to American labor: the emergence of the Federal judiciary as a potent agency for the breaking of strikes. It may not have been unknown to Wilson that on that day Judge Thomas Drummond of the Eastern Illinois District, which included East St. Louis, had ordered the marshal to identify those who obstructed railroads in Federal receivership, with a view to later punishment.

At the moment neither the strikers nor St. Louis citizens at large could see these gathering forces. They fixed their eyes instead on the astounding rise of the Workingmen's Party.

An open-air mass meeting held by the Workingmen's Party Monday night at Lucas Market established the party as the directing force of the strike in St. Louis. The meeting had been heralded by no advertisements, no marching bands, no banners; and yet, as the *Globe-Democrat* observed, "no political meeting in the great Cen-

tennial campaign was by any means so large or so enthusiastic."
Torchlight flickered over the eager faces of perhaps 5,000 people as
the W.P.U.S. orators held forth. More people came. A second
speakers' stand was set up, then a third, so that three meetings were
going at once. The crowd's enthusiasm led some of the speakers to
talk more boldly than they had probably intended. "The workingmen," said one, "intend now to assert their rights, even if the result
is the shedding of blood. . . . They are ready to take up arms at any
moment." "Capital has overridden the Constitution," said another;
"capital has changed liberty into serfdom, and we must fight or die.
Which shall we do?" The crowd shouted, "We'll fight, we'll fight!"
Still another speaker called for nationalization of railroads, mines
and industry. Henry Allen urged speedy organization. The party
rolls would be open for signatures at Turner Hall next day. "We
workingmen," said Allen, "can present such a force that even the
government itself must and will comply with our demands. We will
take such steps as that the old and the young, the sick and the
healthy, will be provided for."

Next day, Tuesday, July 24, the St. Louis, Kansas City & Northern
followed the Missouri Pacific's lead in rescinding its cut. "The railroads must yield," said the *St. Louis Times*, "because they are in the
wrong." But the East St. Louis men who shut down the M.P. also
blocked the Northern. Other railroad managements took the offensive and discontinued passenger service. "The railroad officials
say," reported the *Times*, that "the roads were not making any
money anyhow, and can well afford to . . . starve the employes into
submission." The move would have the further advantage of "in-
commoding the public so as to produce a revolution in the sentiment
which now seems to be in favor of the strikers."

St. Louis' militia forces were weak, and its 325 police remained
strangely inert during the upheaval. But that afternoon Mayor Overstolz met with leading citizens and formed plans to organize a
citizens' guard. And at six o'clock six companies of the Twenty-third
United States Infantry arrived at Union Depot from Fort Leavenworth under the command of Colonel Jefferson C. Davis—300 men,
"all bronzed and hardy looking," with Springfield breechloaders
and two "very cold and suggestive looking Gatling guns." They
marched without incident to their quarters in the old Federal
arsenal two miles south of the business district; and Colonel Davis

announced, as instructed by the War Department, that he and his troops were there "merely to protect government and public property," not "to quell the strikers or run the trains."

General Wilson was not satisfied. He thought at least 1,500 regulars were needed to support U. S. Marshal Roe, who had been ordered to open up the Southeastern. Furthermore, Wilson wired Schurz, the troops ought to be kept in the center of town, and arms ought to be sent from Rock Island "so well disposed people can defend themselves."

On the other side of the battle line, St. Louis coopers struck. So did coal stackers at the gas works, newsboys for the *Dispatch* and boatmen on the levees, some of the latter winning increases. The greenbackers met and descanted on the fiscal cause and cure of national woes. But again, as on Monday, the W.P.U.S. held the center of the stage.

Early Tuesday evening, delegates from trade unions and workshops met with the W.P.U.S. at Turner Hall and appointed a five-man "Executive Committee" to take charge of the strike movement. "Nobody ever knew who that executive committee really was," says a noted historian of American socialism; "it seems to have been a rather loose body composed of whomsoever chanced to come in and take part in its deliberations." But from their public prominence in the movement, we may safely guess that Allen, Currlin and Lofgreen "chanced to come in" as often as any.

Meeting done with, off they all marched to Lucas Market. The turnout there on that sultry night eclipsed Monday's in size and enthusiasm, and the speakers took up the same refrain. One new note sounded after Albert Currlin's speech: someone suggested "that the colored men should have a chance." A Negro steamboat man mounted the stand and spoke for the men of the levees and steamboats. "We work in the summer for $20 a month," he said, "and in the winter can't find the men we worked for. . . . Will you stand to us regardless of color?" And the crowd shouted: "We will!" Henry Allen cautioned against violence. Then, in the name of the Executive Committee, he called for "a general strike of all branches of industry for eight hours for a day's work . . . and the nonemployment of children under fourteen years of age."

The stage had been set for the climax.

Reverberation

CHAPTER 13

Climax and Collapse

SOME EASTERN cities — Baltimore, Pittsburgh, Buffalo, Reading—had passed their crises. Chicago's was yet to come. But taken as a whole, the Great Strike reached its climax on Wednesday, July 25, 1877. By then all but two regions of the United States had succumbed to the strange contagion.

One of the two immunes was New England. Only at New York City and Albany did New England roads touch the fever, and New England's February inoculation had taken well. "Not one of the men who voluntarily left us on the 12th of February is now in our employ," reported the Boston & Maine at the end of the year. "Very few of them have been able to obtain any employment since." The B. & M. justifiably doubted that "another similar conspiracy could be organized in New England."

The other largely exempted area was the South. After that region's late ordeal under military rule, its smugness was pardonable. "What a comfortable reflection it is to Southern people," remarked the *Arkansas Gazette,* "that nearly all of the mob violence . . . has occurred north of the Ohio River." "The Southern people are not as the Northern people," said the *Raleigh Observer;* "person and property, life and liberty are alike safe where Southern men hold sway. Will Mr. Hayes and Northern people generally please make a note of this?"

A few Southern cities had their moments. On the night of July 25, encouraged by the withdrawal of Federal troops for northern service, a gang of about twenty rowdies—not railroaders—shot up the freight depot of the St. Louis, Iron Mountain & Southern at Little Rock, Arkansas. No one was hurt, and the jolly strangers explained that they merely "intended to have a little fun." This, or perhaps the blockade further north, led the road to discontinue freight service for about four days.

At New Orleans, where Negro dock workers had rioted a few months before, the roustabouts met in fruitless protest against a recent pay cut. A rumor spread that the men of the New Orleans, St. Louis & Chicago were about to set off a railroad strike. And on July 28, a brief Communist scare kept Police Chief Boylan and his plainclothes men circulating through the city. All was serene, however, and when evening came, "the city enjoyed itself al fresco, hundreds pouring into the suburbs in every direction."

In the Southeast the nearest approach to a railroad strike came on the Georgia Central, which had announced a 10 per cent cut for September 1. Encouraged by local newspaper support, the Central men sent grievance committees to the managers, who grudgingly consented to put off the cut until November. For this an employees' mass meeting expressed thanks and voted to continue work.

Several explanations were advanced by Southerners for their region's quiescence. "A genial climate and fertile soil makes the Southern man less exacting than his Northern neighbor," said the *New Orleans Times,* "and he submits to impositions that would never be tolerated in a colder climate." Communism, moreover, was "an innovation he would instantly crush." The South had fewer city dwellers, and tramps were seldom seen on the South's rough and lonely roads except in winter. Most Southern railroads had done their heavy cutting a year or two earlier and hence had not joined in the more recent Northern wage experiment. "We might strike if there was any possible chance of doing good, but there isn't," said a New Orleans brakeman. "There are too few railroad men in this section, and besides they are not organized." Race divided both the public and the railroad workers. Except for engineers and conductors, most Southern railroad men were Negroes. The newly "redeemed" state governments were even then encouraging a vigorous revival of militia activity, and Southern militiamen were not apt to hold their fire against Negro rioters.

In two cities on the fringes of the South, nevertheless, Negro workers touched off Northern-style disturbances.

The strike caught the workingmen of Galveston, Texas, in a restive mood. On the day before the B. & O. strike began, they had met and resolved to petition Congress for a law "making it a penal offense for any corporation or firm to advertise for men, either laborers or mechanics, when the supply is equal to the demand in their own localities." After the Pittsburgh outbreak, tension mounted. On Tuesday, July 24, Texas & Pacific hands struck at Marshall, Texas, for back pay and the rescinding of the 10 per cent cut. Popular sympathy with the strikers led the *Galveston News* to trim its antilabor sails and gave Negro longshoremen courage to strike for—and win—the same pay as their white fellow workers. The new self-confidence of Negro labor survived the lame ending of the Texas & Pacific strike on July 30, when the railroaders settled for back pay and the empty promise of a pay-raise recommendation to Tom Scott. On that day about fifty Negro workers marched down the Strand in Galveston, inducing construction men, track layers and others to strike for $2 a day. The marchers listened respectfully to the mayor's address and gave the watchful police no occasion for action. Later, however, the growing crowd scuffled with some reluctant draymen and incurred a dose of police clubbing. Two arrests were made. But organization proceeded, committees circulated next day, the white workers joined in, and when peace returned to Galveston, $2 a day had become the rule.

On the other edge of Dixie, Louisville had a shattering experience. On Monday, July 23, at the plea of a workers' committee, Chancellor H. W. Bruce canceled the 10 per cent cut announced for August 1 by the receiver of the "Louisville Short Line" (Louisville, Cincinnati & Lexington). In the evening the men of the Louisville & Nashville met and demanded the rescinding of that road's July 1 cut, as well as an additional raise for brakemen, switchmen and laborers. Dr. E. D. Standiford, president of the L. & N., withdrew the cut on Tuesday morning but balked at the laborers' raise. That same warm and misty morning Negro workers began asserting themselves. A number of them, led by a Cincinnati man called "Buffalo Bill," made the rounds of the sewers then under construction throughout the city and persuaded or forced the workers to strike for $1.50 a day. At noon sewer workers quit everywhere in town.

By evening the mist had stopped, and 2,000 people had gathered at the courthouse, excitedly but without purpose. The mayor tried to soothe and disperse them, but they howled him down. Someone at last suggested a procession. Some 500 or 600 people started off aimlessly. Then a cry went up: "Let's go to the Nashville Depot!" The yelling marchers turned down Seventh Street. Someone hurled a rock through the large plate-glass window of a sewing-machine shop. The tinkling and crunching of glass came to the ears of the mob as Christmas candy to the teeth of a child. Ammunition lay at hand near the street excavations, and rocks began flying in all directions. Street lights suffered first, windows next. Few houses along Seventh Street to Broadway escaped without a broken window. By now the more responsible citizens had withdrawn and left the enterprise to 200 or 300 of "the bummer element and boys who love to throw rocks." That hard core of vandals grew ferocious outside the Louisville & Nashville depot at Ninth and Broadway, leaving not a pane unsmashed, even breaking wooden sashes. Turning, the mob bombarded houses across the street and then went raving up Broadway. Huge rocks crashed through windows, frightening the householders. Corner stores, subjected to enfilade, were all but demolished. Down Third Street to Walnut went the idiot mob, rocking every house on either side. At Dr. Standiford's house, the mob paused for a special effort. While the attackers riddled the house with rocks and bricks, breaking plate-glass windows and damaging parlor furniture, the Standiford family took refuge in the upper rooms and escaped injury, though a spent rock now and then bounded in among them. The mob had now dwindled to fifty, of whom about half went on down Walnut toward the Short Line depot, smashing windows all the way. A squad of police and a few militiamen waited in the depot for the little band, which paused uncertainly and then turned tail. Onlookers dodged into doorways as the running police fired briskly at the fugitives. No one, innocent or otherwise, was known to have been hit, however; and the streets were quiet by midnight, except for patrols of volunteer militia. Young Louis D. Brandeis, fresh out of Harvard Law School, returned from a party that night and found the big front window smashed in his family's home at Walnut and First.

Next day, Wednesday, July 25, Standiford offered to pay Louisville & Nashville laborers 5 per cent more than the other Louisville roads. His men accepted the compromise and by nightfall were voluntarily serving as special guards on the company's property. Meanwhile most of Louisville's factories were shut down by roving gangs. There was mild scuffling, and the police made thirty or forty arrests; but Louisville's excitement that day came mostly from mounted citizen patrols galloping about the streets. For some reason, Louisville's militiamen were younger than in other cities; and one citizen wrote indignantly to the *Louisville Commercial* about "striplings who know no more the use of a gun than a Chinaman does of an English spelling book. One might as well be maltreated by a mob as killed by a stray bullet from a gun in the hands of a careless boy." One of those boys was young Brandeis, who recalled many years later that his parents were much relieved when he presently "turned in his munitions unused and himself unharmed." Thursday brought a rash of strikes among coopers, textile and plow factory workers, brickmakers and cabinetmakers; but the walkouts were both orderly and voluntary. Otherwise, Louisville industry was back to normal by the end of the week.

Westward the course of uproar took its way. The Northern Pacific had not yet got around to cutting wages, and so it escaped. The men of the Missouri, Kansas & Texas struck in sympathy with the movement elsewhere and stopped freight traffic after Tuesday morning, July 24. A prompt restoration of former rates failed to save the four Kansas City roads which had cut pay, chief among them being the Missouri Pacific and the Atchison, Topeka & Santa Fe. At Kansas City on Tuesday noon, the men of the four wage-cutting roads struck, closed all the packing houses, elevators and machine shops in "the bottom," marched off to Armstrong and shut down the shops of the Kansas Pacific (which had made no wage cut). Freight traffic ceased, saloons were closed by the authorities, streetcars were stopped and Kansas City experienced something like a midweek Sabbath. Despite much excitement, no vandalism occurred. Citizens organized patrols, and the railroaders themselves stood ready to keep order.

The strike impulse had leaped cross-country to Omaha at a surprisingly early date. On July 18, even before the strike began in Pennsylvania, someone left a notice for insertion in the next morning's *Omaha Republican* that Union Pacific shopmen would meet in the evening "to consider the matter of the reduction of wages." The meeting, large and spirited, sent a committee to Superintendent Clark, who insisted politely but firmly that the U.P. wage cut would stand. On Sunday, July 22, however, the company's nerve cracked. Iowa engineers were in town stirring up the local Brotherhood men, fearful dispatches came in from the East, the U.P. men threatened to quit, and U.P. President Sidney Dillon anxiously wired Secretary of War McCrary: "What protection can the Government afford our property against a lawless mob which, judging from actions at Pittsburgh and elsewhere, is likely to follow the strike?" That afternoon, Superintendent Clark rescinded the cut. Instead of a "lawless mob," therefore, Omaha saw only a meeting of U.P. men on Wednesday pledging themselves to stand by the company and protect its property.

Denver got by without a strike, though the tie-up at Kansas City forced the Kansas Pacific to close its Denver shops and suspend all train movements. It was beyond the Rockies and the Sierras, on the very edge of the continent, that the western string of squibs ended with a cannon cracker.

California was then suffering from its worst drought in a quarter of a century. Because of it, the grain crop failed, cattle died and the placer mining yield fell off. Tom Scott's inability to run his Texas & Pacific road into California had brought disaster to speculators, especially at San Diego. A wild boom and collapse in mining stocks a couple of years earlier had enriched a few and impoverished many. These troubles were piled upon the sufferings of the depression, and those in turn upon long-standing economic and social grievances. A few rich men monopolized land and held it for high prices. Farm labor was seasonal, and at best poorly housed and fed. Tramps abounded. The "Big Four" rulers of the Central Pacific Railroad—Huntington, Hopkins, Crocker and Stanford—had lately perfected what a historian of their activities has called the era's "choicest example of a complete and sustained monopoly."

Demagogues, scornful of logic, blamed all of California's woes on a single helpless and conspicuous scapegoat: the Chinese population. More than 50,000 Chinese, no longer needed for the drudgery of railroad building, had painfully made their way into farming, fishing, domestic service, laundry work and some factory labor, especially shoes and textiles. Most of them chose to retain their exotic dress, diet and culture. Choose or not, they lived in rookeries as crowded and squalid as any in the East. Their sins and follies of gambling, opium addiction and prostitution were played up sensationally by white detractors. And whether from necessity, traditionally low standards or freedom from family expenses, they worked long and hard for perhaps three-fifths of white men's pay.

It was on these peaceable folk, especially the 12,000 in San Francisco, that mob fury now fell—not on the wealth-glutted "Big Four," who on July 18 had forehandedly rescinded the Central Pacific's 10 per cent wage cut. And it was the Workingmen's Party of the United States that unwittingly sounded the signal for the onslaught.

On the afternoon of Sunday, July 22, the two San Francisco sections of the W.P.U.S. met, expressed sympathy with the eastern strikers, deprecated violence and called for a mass meeting next evening on the vacant "sand-lots" before City Hall. The sentiments were innocuous, but the call was ill advised. San Francisco's "mercurial people" had been charged with high excitement that day by exaggerated reports of mass murder and citywide conflagration at Pittsburgh. Excitement persisted through Monday, and National Guard regiments were assembled under arms at their respective armories to await a possible call by authorities.

For a time, apprehension seemed groundless. Between 7,000 and 8,000 people gathered on the sand lots in the summer twilight, a crowd so large that two speakers' stands were set up some distance apart. Delegations of San Francisco's notorious "hoodlum" element occasionally made themselves known by jeers and catcalls from the fringes. But the crowd remained orderly. James F. D'Arcy, the "chief organizer" of the local W.P.U.S., took the chair, denounced the Democrats, the Republicans, the monopolists and the "money ring," counseled against violence and called for an effective eight-hour law. The moon climbed higher in the cool night sky; transparencies were raised—"Workingmen, Protect Your Families," "Self-preservation Is the First Law of Nature"; and a band struck up a tune. More speeches followed, all temperate. Someone shouted for the appointment of a committee to demand the discharge of the Central Pacific's Chinese workmen, but D'Arcy explained that this was a discussion of the broad question of capital and labor, not an anti-coolie rally. Then came more speeches and finally resolutions denouncing various economic and social injustices and demanding the eight-hour day and government operation of strike-bound railroads. D'Arcy closed by urging the crowd to go home quietly.

But the fatal spark had already been struck. At nine o'clock a young rough knocked down a Chinaman at the near-by corner of McAllister and Leavenworth Streets. Collared by an alert policeman, the hoodlum was freed again by a gang of his comrades. The scuffle drew hundreds from the edges of the sand-lot meeting; and at the cry of "Chinatown, boys, let's go for Chinatown," about 200 rowdies headed up Leavenworth Street, yelling like madmen. Diverted and sometimes daunted by an occasional club-waving policeman, the mob ranged erratically up and down the streets demolishing Chinese laundries or "wash-houses." It also broke into Edwards' liquor store and cleaned out the stock. The streets of Chinatown proper grew suddenly dark and quiet as the inhabitants put out their lamps, barred their doors and improvised defenses. The mob confined itself, however, to wrecking a score of isolated laundries. At one of these a rock smashed a kerosene lamp and started a fire which destroyed both the washhouse and an adjacent two-story home. A woman hurt herself badly in jumping from an upper window of the house, while hoodlums gleefully cut firehose. No Chinese were injured. But as the police gathered their forces, nightsticks beat in rising tempo on hoodlum skulls until midnight at last brought quiet. Meanwhile, W.P.U.S. leaders had hastily promised the mayor that they would call no more meetings and would do their part to keep order.

Next morning a Chinaman, who had been employed in one of the demolished washhouses, surrendered to fear and despair and killed himself with an overdose of opium. During the day, Tuesday, July 24, San Francisco's leading citizens assembled at the Merchants' Exchange for a renascence of the city's famous vigilante organization, now, as twenty years before, under the lead of William T. Coleman. The vigilantes of 1877 called themselves the "Committee of Safety," but acquired the nickname of "the pickhandle brigade" from the weapons they wielded. Unfortunately, night closed in before the Committee of Safety was well organized. Once again, therefore, gangs of young hoodlums carried on their senseless guerrilla war against isolated washhouses, though prudently heeding every cry of "Cheese it, cullies, here's the cops!" Most of the "hoods" were teen-agers, but it was a gang of grown men that swooped down at eleven o'clock on an isolated Chinese laundry and bunkhouse at Greenwich and Devisadero streets. Storming in with pistols blazing, the gang ransacked the place of everything valuable, poured kerosene on the ironing tables and set the building afire. Most of the dozen Chinese occupants managed to escape, but the charred body of one was later found in the ruins.

On Wednesday the chief of police summoned and swore in a large *posse comitatus* at City Hall. Chinatown perfected its defenses and took in refugees from outlying washhouses. All day long, recruits streamed through the Committee of Safety rooms, and by evening the enrollment had grown to about 3,000. At dusk, William Coleman organized some 1,500 vigilantes into companies, and these in turn chose officers. With white cloth badges in their lapels and pickhandles in their hands, the Committee of Safety men were ready—and not a moment too soon.

Being an adjunct of the great Central Pacific monopoly, the Pacific Mail Steamship Company wharf had seemed a likely target of the mob. The fire that blazed up at eight o'clock Wednesday night, however, began in a lumber pile on the great Beale Street wharf, a block to leeward; and for that reason, many people doubted that the fire had been set. At any rate, there it crackled; and before firemen arrived, it had spread to several warehouses crammed with oil, shingles and lumber. Hose carts rattled up to find a sea of fire raging on the wharf, lighting up the whole of Rincon Hill as bright as day, clearly defining every window in buildings roundabout, every rope and spar in ships near by. Thousands of people watched the waving masses of flame and smoke reach into the sky. Now and then the full moon appeared dimly through the shifting veil, as though struggling in a net of black and gold. The crews of near-by ships fought embers that strewed decks and lodged in riggings, until three tugs at last steamed in and towed the vessels to safety. On the wharf firemen battled valiantly, rolling burning barrels into the bay, tearing down the lumber pile, dragging hose over burning planks.

But a growing number of hoodlums barred the wharf entrance, shouted at the firemen and began to impede operations generally.

Suddenly the crowd let out a yell, and a strong detachment of Coleman's vigilantes marched up with pickhandles at the ready. After a brisk scuffle, the hoodlums were cleared out of the immediate area. But for some time they staged occasional forays. Exasperated at last by the attempted firing of a rigging loft, the Committee of Safety men chased their tormenters clear up the hill, speeding the hoodlums' ascent with pistol fire. The latter's effect on the lawless element could not be determined; but several professedly innocent bystanders were hit, none mortally. In the excitement a Committee of Safety man dropped his pistol, which went off and fatally wounded a comrade in arms. Shots from the mob on the bluff killed one fireman on a hose cart and wounded his companion. Gradually and laboriously, after $100,000 worth of property had been consumed, the fire was brought under control. At ten-thirty, one last, lively brawl commenced after a crowd of hoodlums on the bluff responded to someone's shout of "Charge the cops!" Law and order took the palm, however, and the crisis was past. The evening's work had cost at least three lives, including that of a sixty-year-old man run over by a hose cart on its way to the fire.

Elsewhere in the city that night, an inflammatory anti-coolie meeting was held on the sand lots without interference from vigilantes or police, though the mayor had prohibited such gatherings. This touched off a last round of wash-house sacking. Only three or four establishments were attacked before a handful of special police broke up the mob and dragged off several prisoners. Along the streets south of Market, mounted militia patrols galloped up and down, dispersing crowds in their front and collecting others in their rear; but for all the noise, the surgings, the hoodlum catcalls and the occasional arrests, there was neither bloodshed nor vandalism. Next day vigilante patrols guarded almost every block, Union and Confederate veterans united in a "Veterans' Brigade," and 200 United States Marines joined with an equal number of police and vigilantes to guard the Pacific Mail dock. That evening San Francisco relaxed and settled back to normal.

On Wednesday, July 25, 1877, the last spreading ripple of the railroad strike reached Michigan. Detroit authorities had expected it for days and prepared accordingly. On Tuesday the governor of Michigan had asked the War Department to let him use the Federal troops stationed near Detroit, but Secretary McCrary insisted that such an appeal must rest upon evidence of an insurrection actually in progress and too formidable for the state to suppress. Officials of the Michigan Central maintained that their men were content and would not strike. Their men did not agree. The Michigan Central had joined other Vanderbilt properties in a 10 per cent pay cut on July 1; and the stubbornness of its officials was emphasized on Tuesday, when the Great Western, a Canadian road entering Detroit, yielded to employee demands. Later that day Canada Southern men went on strike at St. Thomas, Ontario; and on Wednesday night at ten o'clock, notwithstanding inspirational addresses by two high railroad officials at a trainmen's meeting, the men of the Michigan Central at Jackson fell into line with their brothers elsewhere.

On that momentous Wednesday, therefore, the Great Strike stood at its full. Here the precise mind looks for a tidy summation. How many roads were on strike, how many men, how many miles of track? But history can make no answer, for this reason: in too many cases, it is impossible to distinguish a strike from a lockout, or a lockout from simple lack of business, or mob intimidation from either. If train service stops, and some of the men claim to be on strike and others claim they are not, who is correct? Michigan Central firemen and engineers met and resolved to strike, for example; trains stopped running; and yet the company's annual report stated:

With but very few exceptions the employees of the Company were its staunch friends, and remained at their posts discharging their duty. The trains and business of the Company were not interrupted for a single day.

This is not the only such case.

So we can only say that of the nation's 75,000 miles of track, about two-thirds lay in areas affected directly by the strike; and that on these roads, most freight trains and some passenger trains had stopped running.

Much as the nation depended on train service, inconvenience had not yet become disaster. Only nine days had passed since the Great Strike began at Baltimore. The cities had at least a week's food left, most of them two or three, while boats and wagons helped ease the pinch. In rural areas, harvest time lay weeks ahead for most crops. To the farmer, big city riots seemed as remote as the Russo-Turkish War, and the railroad tie-up thus far meant only quieter times along the tracks. Even in business circles, concern developed slowly. Railroad stocks scarcely wavered. "The roads are just where they were," said a Boston broker on July 22; and he predicted that after the strike, "business will be rushing for weeks to come." At Long Branch that day a group of tycoons including George Pullman and Russell Sage discussed the Pittsburgh outbreak with professional equanimity. Since full damages would be paid and the roads were in a slack season anyway, observed one man, Scott and Garrett could not have done better if they had hired the rioters. "In fact," he added jovially, "I am inclined to think the whole thing a bull movement." In Washington on Monday, Secretary of the Treasury Sherman wondered if the outbreak might not actually help the sale of government bonds by turning some nervous investors against railroad securities.

By Wednesday, however, doubt had set in. A buying rush drove gold up to 106⅛—quite a rise, considering Secretary Sherman's commitment to resumption. "The distressing, if not alarming situation of affairs is increasing the demands on us," wrote an official of Drexel, Morgan & Company to John Garrett; "the news this morning is far from reassuring, and we fear that the worst is not over yet." At Philadelphia bank transactions fell to about half of normal, while food prices rose.

Show people were thankful that the theater season had not opened yet. Most actors were on vacation. The riots certainly made formidable competition for productions then on the boards. Theodore Thomas' doggedness paid off, however. A young man who heard one of the Thomas concerts in Chicago during the riots came away so deeply impressed that years later he took the lead in organizing the Chicago Symphony for Thomas.

Traveling shows suffered most. The Harrigan and Hart troupe cut short its western tour at Buffalo and headed back to New York City via the Erie Canal. Circuses were hard hit, since itineraries were made out weeks in advance and bills and advertisements prepared accordingly. The tours of Barnum, Forepaugh, the Metropolitan Olympiad and the Great London were all interrupted. An alligator and two horses, consigned to Adam Forepaugh's show at San Francisco, had to wait out the strike at the Fourth Street crossing in Altoona, Pennsylvania. At Elgin, Illinois, the Lake Shore strike forced "P. T. Barnum's New and Only Greatest Show on Earth" to lay over an extra day in "Three Monster Special Trains of Its Own Solid Steel Cars," thereby causing woe and desolation among the small fry of Laporte, Indiana, the omitted stop. Women and children, including Mlle. Dumas (the European Empress of the Dens) and Tony (the Centaur Child Wonder), went ahead on a passenger train. The men strapped on six-shooters (a derringer, perhaps, for Admiral Dot), and off went the circus train at midnight, with a U. S. marshal aboard and the locomotive displaying placards: THIS TRAIN IS UNDER THE PROTECTION OF THE UNITED STATES GOVERNMENT. After a daring and circuitous run through riot-torn Chicago, the train reached Elkhart and the show went on.

At least one line of business made money from the strike. "The newspapers of America have stood manfully to their duty," said one of them, "have vigorously urged the necessity of maintaining order, and have condemned with the bitterness that it deserves the lawless assault upon society and trade." At the same time, and with equal vigor, they turned the "lawless assault" to their own account. Most journalists lived up to their responsibility. The *Springfield* (Mass.) *Republican* did much to steady the nerves of New England. William Henry Smith, general agent of the Western Associated Press, wired his excitable young Chicago correspondent to "hold his horses." Others, however, welcomed the worst, including reports of cannonading on the streets of Chicago. In several cities officials or citizens urged the abandonment of inflammatory newspaper bulletin boards, and Receiver Wilson of the St. Louis & Southeastern went so far as to exclude all newsboys and newspapers from his trains. It was not surprising that in city after city the newsboys themselves caught the spirit of their wares and struck for better terms.

The importance of Wednesday, July 25, as the turning point of the Great Strike could only be reported in retrospect. Nevertheless, the day presented journalists with recognizable sensations enough to keep the pennies coming: more railroads on strike, rioting in San Francisco and Chicago, the closing of factories by mob action in half a dozen cities. One of the choicest items was the apparent domination of St. Louis by the Communists.

The sheriff of St. Louis took steps that day to raise a posse of 5,000 men. At the Four Courts building, the newly organized Committee of Public Safety worked busily at forming a citizens' militia by wards, and Mayor Overstolz and the Merchants' Exchange urged a suspension of business so that employees might join. Governor John S. Phelps dispatched arms and ammunition (including two fieldpieces) from the state arsenal at Jefferson City and promised to come in person as commander in chief of the campaign. Yet the hand of authority was stayed. St. Louis police continued in their strange torpor, so unlike the spirit of their Chicago counterparts. And when Wednesday night came, only about 600 of the citizens' militia had acquired weapons. The Workingmen's Party thus remained unchallenged, and it made conspicuous use of its latitude.

A Signal Corps weather station telegram from St. Louis to the authorities at Washington had summed up the prospect as of midnight Tuesday: "General strike in all branches of industry is requested in favor of eight hour law, which seems now to be as much an object as a return to former wages." As forecast by the Army's weather station, Wednesday brought the nation's first formal general strike of the new industrial era—not the mob improvisation of other cities, but the deliberate undertaking of an established organization.

Admittedly the Workingmen's Party found its team a little hard to manage. Confusion marked the morning. The party called off a nine o'clock rally at Lucas Market, and an impatient crowd gathered outside Turner Hall headquarters while the shadowy "executive committee" conferred. Hastily printed handbills at last appeared throughout the city, reaffirming the eight-hour general strike call and summoning St. Louis labor to show its strength in a noontime procession from Lucas Market. Meanwhile, Negro labor began testing the support promised it by the crowd at the Tuesday evening rally. Under a scorching midday sun, about 400 steamboat men and roustabouts "of all colors" marched noisily along the levee, led by a fife and drum band and waving a huge American flag. On boat after boat the crowd extorted written promises of higher pay. Then, cheering triumphantly, it headed for Lucas Market.

The throng at the assembly point grew larger minute by minute. Six hundred or more factory workers marched up behind a brass band and waved a huge transparency: No MONOPOLY—WORKING-MEN'S RIGHTS. A company of railroad strikers arrived, bearing emblems of their calling: coupling pins, brake rods, red signal flags. At two o'clock the great procession started off in a cloud of dust along "the miles of stone-built streets and red-brick walls . . . heated only to a less degree than Nebuchadnezzar's furnace." Four abreast and stretching for nearly four blocks, the sweating marchers moved down Locust Street while the band played the "Marseillaise." Spectators crowded the sidewalks. No red flags were raised, excepting the railroaders', but someone ran into a bakery, emerged with a loaf of bread, stuck it on a flagstaff and bore it aloft to the cheers of the crowd.

At the Four Courts building, headquarters of the developing opposition, the paraders confined themselves to jeers and threats. The Workingmen's Party handbills had passionately disavowed violence, and the party's parade marshals succeeded remarkably well in preventing it. Their chief objects were to show their strength and to close factories. The latter activity proceeded much as in other cities: to the tune of shouts, cheers, threats, expostulations and an occasional chorus of shrieks from excited factory girls. No one was hurt; and aside from some broken windows and some pilfering in a cracker factory, no property loss was suffered. Midway in the march Negro roustabouts began taking the lead, and this seems to have given Albert Currlin and other party leaders some anxiety lest the cause thereby suffer in the eyes of white labor. But when the parade at last got back to Lucas Market and its participants dispersed for supper, the afternoon was put down as a whopping success.

The Workingmen's Party rode high that evening. Currlin and two other members of the executive committee called on Mayor Overstolz, who accepted with thanks their offer to furnish several hundred men to keep order. He would call for them, he added smoothly, if he needed them. At Turner Hall the English section chose a committee to negotiate with employers. Meanwhile, strike committees were detailed to call out workers next day at factories not reached by the afternoon procession.

The grand finale of the day came at Lucas Market, where an estimated 10,000 people gathered that evening for still another W.P.U.S. rally. After "a few airs" from Angerstein's Centennial Brass Band Peter Lofgreen took the chair. Hoarse from past oratory, the speak-

ers nevertheless exulted. The general strike must go on until the
eight-hour day triumphed. In the name of Lincoln, who freed 4,000,-
000 black slaves, labor must unite behind the Workingmen's Party
to free 9,000,000 white slaves. "The people are rising up in their
might and declaring they will not longer submit to being oppressed
by unproductive capital," said one speaker. "This great movement is
rapidly increasing in intensity," said another, "and is now so strong
that no state, and not even the United States Government can peaceably put a stop to it." He demanded that Congress pass an effective
eight-hour law, recall the charters of all national banks, institute a
public works program to relieve unemployment and purchase all
railroads with an issue of greenbacks. "I propose," he said, "that we
make an appeal directly to the President of the United States."

The latest from St. Louis had not yet reached European Communists. Nevertheless, they had heard enough to share the elation
of their American comrades. From Switzerland that day the Federal
Board of the International Workingmen's Association wrote the
editor of the *Labor Standard*: "The events now taking place in the
United States have awoken to the highest degree the attention and
sympathies of your brethren from the I.W.A. in Europe." The Board
also wrote the W.P.U.S. National Executive Committee for "as much
as possible of detailed information as to the struggle undertaken
now . . . for the rights of the workingmen." Likewise on that day,
Karl Marx wrote his apostle Friedrich Engels in a strain of jubilation tempered by experience: "What do you think of the workers of
the United States? This first explosion against the associated oli-
garchy of capital which has occurred since the Civil War will naturally again be suppressed, but can very well form the point of
origin of an earnest workers' party. . . . A nice sauce is being stirred
over there, and the transference of the center of the International to
the United States may obtain a very remarkable *post festum* opportuneness."

St. Louis would be no mean prize for Marxism; but it was New
York City, the metropolis of the New World, to which the nation
looked that Wednesday night for a crucial test of Communist
strength. "The evil tendencies and examples of European Communists are potential with tens of thousands of men in this city," warned
the *New York Evening Mail*, adding that at least 5,000 United States
regulars were needed in the city.

On Monday a committee representing Communist groups in New York City had asked permission of municipal authorities to hold a mass meeting in Tompkins Square on Wednesday. The proposal stirred unhappy memories. "You mustn't make such a disturbance as you made there in 1874," cautioned the park commissioner. "Mr. Commissioner," said Justus Schwab, a German saloonkeeper, "*you* mustn't make the trouble *you* made in 1874. *We* didn't make any trouble." Officials conferred nervously and decided to grant permission. "I think such a meeting ill-timed," Mayor Ely told a reporter, "but we concurred in the opinion that there was no reason for interfering with a peaceable assemblage of any portion of our citizens who want to express their opinion of any public matter." The *New York Times* denounced Mayor Ely's action as "a direct attack on the peace and safety of the city . . . all the more despicable that it proceeds from the cowardice of the political demagogue."

The authorities braced themselves for trouble. All police leaves and passes were canceled. Two hundred police were assigned to attend the meeting, and 600 were held in reserve near by. A number of N.Y. Central railroad men were sworn in as special police to guard the Central's roundhouse and depot. Assistant Treasurer Hillhouse garrisoned the Subtreasury with seventy-five volunteers, barred the massive iron doors and shutters and threw up barricades inside. The cadet engineer class from the training ship *Mayflower* was stationed with two Gatlings just inside the Wall Street and Pine Street entrances. Chief Signal Officer Albert Myer alerted Secretary McCrary: "If there be any organized conspiracy underlying present disturbances, tonight may be a serious night, an outbreak in New York being the signal for violence elsewhere."

The War Department already had plenty to worry about that day. With the great upheaval now grown continental, the little United States Army had been spread disturbingly thin. Mexican rebels, Indian chiefs and railroad presidents seemed in league with strikers and Communists to embarrass McCrary's overworked department. When General Pope urged that two regiments be sent to Chicago, the department replied that "keeping in view Indian relations it is not known from whence they can be drawn without danger." That same afternoon brought another wire from Pope: "Efforts are making by [the Union Pacific] Railroad Company to prevent Ninth [Infantry] being sent away from Omaha, and I have directed [Colonel] Williams to act at once and have the regiment sent to Rock

Island without delay." But U.P. Superintendent Clark, Mayor Wilbur of Omaha, Governor Garber of Nebraska and finally even Colonel Williams all joined in the answering howl, and in the end six companies were permitted to remain—unnecessarily, as it turned out. Meanwhile, the Mexican government was complaining about General Ord's arrest of Mexican recruiters in Texas.

At noon General Hancock reported matters very quiet in his command. "It may be the lull before the storm elsewhere," he wired, "or that the backbone of the disorder within these limits is broken." At any rate, he felt that his limited force had now been disposed as well as possible "at the most important points for service, and along the great centre line of this division from the Mississippi to the Atlantic seaboard, and where they can be readily moved on railroad lines or by water communication."

Wednesday's cabinet meeting opened in good spirits. Hayes began by noting "a better feeling as to riots." From New York City, Assistant Treasurer Hillhouse wired that he felt safe. The Army had only ninety men there, fifty of them recruits, but the Navy had 1,000 men on hand—1,100, counting the cadet engineers. As dispatches were read from Chicago, Omaha and Pittsburgh (where there seemed to be "danger of a revival of riots"), the eight men at the long table grew more somber. Even Secretary Evarts refrained from his usual witticisms.

Through the dispatches and letters ran an urgent refrain: the President must call for volunteers! The cry had been raised as early as the Pittsburgh riot—probably emanating, suggested the *New York Herald* cynically, "from men who would like contracts." Hard-pressed railroad officials must have liked the idea; Perkins of the Burlington did, for one. Henry W. Slocum, who had commanded the Union right wing at Gettysburg, wrote Hayes on Monday, perhaps a little hopefully, that 30,000 to 50,000 volunteers should be called, and that "each state where these disorders exist could be declared in 'insurrection'—made a military department and placed under command of our experienced officers."

Now came resolutions from the merchants of Milwaukee, Baltimore and other cities urging an immediate increase of the armed forces—that is, a call for volunteers. Most of the pressure, however, came from Philadelphia. The newspapers, the mayor, leading citizens, even the Army Signal Corps officer seemed all of one mind.

Two frantic letters from Tom Scott were read, one addressed to Hayes and the other to Secretary Thompson. Governor Hartranft himself joined the cry early that morning.

Inasmuch as Philadelphia had got off much more lightly than some other cities, this obsession might seem strange, were it not that Tom Scott had set up his headquarters at the Philadelphia depot. The origin of the force behind Philadelphia's unanimity may be inferred from its direction, but it scarcely need be. Emerging from an all-day conference with Tom Scott on Sunday, for example, City Solicitor Collis had told the press as a fact "that President Hayes would call for 75,000 volunteers." On Tuesday or Wednesday House Speaker Samuel J. Randall was asked to see Scott at the depot. "I accepted," wrote Randall privately, "because I supposed him in trouble . . . I soon found why I was wanted. After usual salutations and further conversation generally as to strikes, Colonel Scott asked me to write or telegraph 'President' Hayes to call out by proclamation a further force. . . . I abruptly and pointedly said I could not and would not do so."

Thus, on Wednesday, July 25, Hayes and his Cabinet were put to their last great test. And they passed it triumphantly. What a failure might have meant, we cannot know for sure; but there is a chilling tone of conviction in the telegram John Sherman received from a Cincinnati citizen: "Tell the President a call for volunteers will precipitate a revolution. Tell him I speak advisedly." There was to be no revolution. Hayes and his Cabinet did nothing—perhaps the bravest and certainly the wisest course.* One of Hayes's closest friends wrote a few days later: "They were not seduced by the

---

* Readers familiar with Hayes's notes on that Cabinet meeting, as published in the *American Historical Review* for January 1932 (XXXVII, 288), will wonder about the following passage: "Evarts suggests that the U.S. may put these rioters in the position of levying war against the U.S.—I advise a proclamation to be issued soon . . . The Proclamation is to be prepared, but as to its issue the decision is to be postponed. *Subject passed.*" This has nothing to do with a call for volunteers or anything so sensational. It arises out of a letter from General Hancock, referred to earlier in the meeting, on the subject of Federal-state relations in handling the disturbances. Hancock felt that Federal authority should be paramount; and to make that plain, he suggested that when a state found itself unable to suppress disorder and therefore called in Federal troops, "from that moment commences a state not of peace but of war." (Adj. Gen.'s Off., Letters Received, 1877, #4328). The "proclamation," sounding so portentous in Hayes's hasty notes, was only meant to clear up an administrative ambiguity.

promises of Eastern Democrats interested in the great corporations to support him if the President would call on adjacent states for 100,000 militia to guard railroad property." And on Wednesday night, Charles Nordhoff, the best-informed and most influential Washington correspondent of his day, wrote to Carl Schurz: "I am greatly delighted that the President takes so little hand in the riot. . . . Nothing would be less prudent than any positive action by the Administration, such as calling out volunteers. . . . If you should call for troops there are signs that you would only get a lot of riffraff who would mutiny on your hands."

That night, as if a spell were broken, the Great Strike began to collapse.

The Tompkins Square meeting in New York City called the turn for the Communists. The night was warm and fair. A bright calcium light at each corner of the square and two flaring gasoline torches over the main speakers' platform shone over a crowd of several thousand, while hundreds more looked on from near-by roofs and windows. Over the railing of the main platform was draped an American flag, borrowed from the Park Department with assurances that it would be returned without stain. Tense at first—there was a frightened stir when a calcium light fizzed and went out— the crowd presently relaxed. At the second stand, erected for German speakers, someone raised cheers and laughter by passing a huge stein of beer up to the arriving spellbinders. The Germans brought their women and children, and a spirit of bantering good nature infused the scene. But everyone felt the quiet presence of 200 police in the shadows, with hundreds more at near-by stations.

John Swinton of the *New York Sun* presided as well as he could amid the interruptions of a beer-logged comrade. The speeches, at least, were temperate. Indeed, some of the crowd lost interest and began drifting away. The resolutions proclaimed sympathy with the railroad strikers and hostility to corporations and their political hirelings. Workingmen throughout the nation were called upon to unite in "a party based upon the natural rights of labor" and to achieve "a political revolution through the ballot box." Perhaps the shadowy police dampened the speakers' ardor; perhaps the pitch of the last nine days simply could not be sustained. About the German speeches especially there seemed to float an aura of nostalgia for the past, mixed with hope for the future. "If you will unite," said one speaker, "we may have here within five years a socialistic republic. . . . Then will a lovely morning break over this darkened land."

At nine-fifteen, less than two hours after it began, the Tompkins Square meeting was quietly adjourned. The last-recorded words were: "Whatever we poor men may not have, we have free speech, and no one can take it from us." Regardless of that, the police were clearly spoiling for a fight. They charged and clubbed a departing crowd without apparent provocation. Even reporters hostile to the speakers angrily denounced police attacks on solitary citizens walking home—and, in one brutal case, on a middle-aged German standing quietly in his own front yard. But the people did not fight back, and by nine-thirty Tompkins Square was as quiet and uncrowded as it had ever been on a moonlit summer night. "New York," said the next day's *Tribune*, "breathes freer this morning."

After that, the specter of a bloody Commune uprising *à la française* passed rapidly away. Everywhere now the W.P.U.S. walked softly. In Louisville, it politely asked Mayor Jacobs' permission for a meeting in Phoenix Hill Park, meanwhile condemning lawlessness and pointing out plaintively that Tuesday's mob had smashed windows in the home of M. J. Nolan, secretary of the W.P.U.S. English-speaking section. At Milwaukee the same inoffensive spirit prevailed.

At St. Louis sheer momentum carried the W.P.U.S. through Thursday before the inevitable collapse. A procession of some 5,000 men set out from Lucas Market Thursday morning and brought the total of closed factories to at least sixty. The W.P.U.S. Executive Committee requested Governor Phelps to call the legislature and help put through a child-labor and an eight-hour law. Yet, despite these brave proceedings, many signs foretold defeat. The proprietors of Turner Hall suddenly evicted their radical tenants, and the executive committee had to shift its headquarters to Schuler's Hall near the worst slums in town. The committee itself disavowed some of the morning paraders' work and even sent 200 men to reopen and guard Belcher's sugar refinery. News from the East brought gloom and uncertainty to party leaders. That night a crowd collected at Lucas Market—for the last time, as it turned out. When no W.P.U.S. speakers showed up, part of the angry crowd marched to Schuler's Hall and shouted their disgust. Others remained at the scene and heard wild speeches by self-appointed and half-drunk orators. Shocked by the incendiary talk, Henry Allen of the W.P.U.S. got permission from the police to arrest the troublemakers; but they had gone by the time he returned. In sum, the St. Louis Workingmen's Party that day lost confidence in itself and contact with the people.

Meanwhile, the city and state authorities had grown more powerful, confident and aggressive. St. Louis police roused themselves at last. Here and there they turned crowds back from factories and made arrests. St. Louis merchants raised $18,000 to arm citizen militia, while enrollment, organization and drill went forward at the Four Courts building. Fifteen hundred rifles arrived from the state arsenal, and General Pope ordered 500 stand of small arms shipped by river from the Federal arsenal at Rock Island to arm citizens. Three more companies of United States infantry came in from Kansas. "Time has come," wired Receiver Wilson to Secretary Schurz, "when President should stamp out mob now rampant. . . . The law can be found for it after order is restored."

The President did no such thing. Having been well briefed on administration policy, Colonel Jefferson C. Davis of the regular troops insisted that local authorities must "deal with these difficulties themselves & not call on me for aid until their whole resources are exhausted." The local authorities did nobly by themselves. On Friday afternoon thousands of the sympathetic or curious jammed the streets outside the Schuler's Hall headquarters of the W.P.U.S. to see the grand assault that was known to be imminent. At three o'clock the shout went up: "Here they come!" First came a squad of mounted police, then fifty dismounted police, then 600 citizen militia, the hot sun flashing from their bayonets. Up the narrow stairs and into the crowded third-floor hall charged the dismounted police. The huge crowd outside went wild with excitement, but not a shot was fired nor a stone flung. Many Communists and fellow travelers clambered out of windows and onto adjacent roofs or shinned down balcony pillars, but seventy prisoners were marched off. Currlin and Lofgreen got away, but were arrested later. And so fell the mighty executive committee.

The railroad strike, like the Red scare, began running out of steam on Wednesday evening.

It had come close to success—closer, indeed, than the strikers knew. Even on the surface, signs had been encouraging early that week. Some roads—the Long Island, the Union Pacific, the Central Pacific, the Louisville Short Line and others—had narrowly forestalled a strike by rescinding their wage cuts. Other roads, such as the Missouri Pacific, the Chicago & Northwestern, the Louisville & Nashville, the Atchison, Topeka & Santa Fe, the Great Western, the Texas Central, had quickly conceded the strikers' demands. Beneath the surface, private correspondence reveals a near cave-in all along management's lines.

Management post mortems on the Great Strike, public and private, are not hard to find. The shifting views of management *during* the strike are not so well preserved. Fortunately, complete files of both the Illinois Central and the Burlington have survived mice, mold, fire, flood and housecleaning, and, best of all, have been opened to historians. The Burlington records are especially revealing, since that road's management was divided between Chicago, Burlington and the board of directors at Boston, and hence its vacillations were committed to paper hour by hour.

On Monday morning the four top Chicago officials of the Burlington, including President Robert Harris, had "a long session" and agreed that "the only question is whether or not to concede all demands." One of them, Treasurer George Tyson, wrote Vice-President Perkins: "The wages question is now a small affair & if by yielding it we could ward off the enormously greater danger of a riot & save our property, it would be cheaply bought. . . . While we were all willing to take the risk of an ordinary strike of employes, we, I am sure, never contemplated facing this tiger of mob rule . . ." The board of directors in Boston showed signs of backtracking on Tuesday. If such an outbreak had been foreseen, wrote one, "I should not have been in favor of cutting . . . those who receive $2.00 a day or less." Since the Northwestern had given in, "we may have to yield so far as to pay the same rates which the other western roads pay."

Vice-President Ackerman of the Illinois Central felt much the same. On Tuesday he wrote: "We may have to yield 10 cents per day to the laborers, and put the switchmen back to the wages they were receiving last month. There appears to be a general disposition to concede small and reasonable demands during the day by the different companies."

If any further confirmation be needed that management had been severely shaken, it is given by the letters and telegrams of Burlington Vice-President Charles E. Perkins, the sternest of antilabor doctrinaires before and after the strike. On Monday: "I see nothing but to give in & restore pay or tie up everything. . . . Since several lines have given in there is more money in long run to follow suit—unless things look brighter tomorrow." On Tuesday, after the Northwestern's concession: "I think tomorrow will see others going and if so is there any other practicable course open to us?" On Wednesday morning: "If the troubles continue all over the country, I still think it is the part of wisdom for us to make some kind of a settlement of the difficulty & get to work . . . Public opinion even now inclines to say we ought to fix it up."

An inclination developed that day, not only among strikers but also among businessmen and newspapers, to have President Hayes mediate a compromise. But the golden moment had already passed. Even in management's darkest hours, some officials had been seized with spasms of rigidity often enough to delay a general surrender. They felt that a principle was involved, and that they were in the right. To yield now would be to yield again later, and eventually to surrender control of their (or their stockholders') property. That would be pure Communism. And so, like the cynical tycoons at Long Branch, they reminded themselves that business was slack in that season anyway, that damages for property loss were recoverable from city or state governments, and that since "all other roads are in the same fix, we lose no business, as it must all stay packed up till the roads can carry it." Besides, Tom Scott was holding out—perhaps, as Charles Nordhoff suggested, "because being already bankrupt, he can only gain from being 'damaged'," but holding out nevertheless, an inspiration to all.

As a clincher, the managements who resisted observed with "some gratification" that those who yielded got no benefit after all, partly because of tie-ups elsewhere, partly because the strikers absurdly insisted that all roads must be blocked until all roads yielded. This, perhaps, was the deciding factor. The sight of the Northwestern or the Bee Line or the Missouri Pacific in full and profitable operation might well have turned management's vacillation into rout. But the strikers missed that chance because (notwithstanding all dark hints) they had no central leadership.

By Wednesday management had developed a formula: grievances
would be fairly and patiently discussed, but only when lawlessness
and insubordination ceased—that is, when all those men had returned whom the company chose to take back.

When the strikers saw management digging in along a common
line, their hearts sank. The public remained sympathetic, but that
did not help. Except in Chicago the riots had spent themselves; the
authorities now could turn to the protection of strikebreakers. Strikers began recalling the fate of the B. & M. and Reading engineers.
Even if strikebreakers were not brought in, lack of money handi-
capped the strikers in a waiting game. From the start, their only
real hope had been in stampeding management into surrender; and
they had not quite done it.

On the warm moonlit Wednesday evening of the Tompkins
Square meeting, breaks began appearing in the ranks of the railroad
strikers. At Rochester strikers on the New York Central voted to
resume work and sent a committee to notify their comrades in Syracuse, who followed suit immediately. At Albany and Buffalo, however, New York Central strikers held out stubbornly. The decisive
break that night came on the Erie.

The men of that road had a weaker case than did others: even
after the July 1 cut, their pay was higher than that of most roads
had been before. Furthermore, on Monday they had suffered two
blows. A thousand state troops had arrived at Hornellsville; and
little Barney Donahue, leader of the strike, had been arrested for
contempt of a New York State court, the Erie being in receivership.
Next day the strikers near Hornellsville doggedly tore up rails before
and after troop trains, yet the militia on a couple of trains managed
to replace the rails and get through. All day Wednesday a strikers'
committee haggled with Erie officials. At last it agreed to what the
younger strikers angrily called a surrender: the company promised
to let trainmen stay on their little patches of land without rent, to
prosecute only those who had destroyed property and to let the rest
come back to work. At midnight Wednesday, exactly six days after
it began, the Erie strike ended. Early next morning the militia left
Hornellsville, and trains began running.

On Wednesday afternoon Governor Hartranft had at last come
out of the West to Philadelphia. On his way through Pennsylvania,
he had heard disturbing reports that food might run out within a

week at some points. In conference at Philadelphia with Generals Hancock and Schofield, Hartranft proposed to run a strong force of militia and regulars along the main line of the Pennsylvania to Pittsburgh. A victory at the latter point, he felt, would settle the matter for the whole state. General Hancock agreed. If coal ran out and factories had to shut down, thousands of men would be idle and perhaps ready for more devil's work. "This insurrection," Hancock told the War Department, must be stifled "by all possible means." Militia were gathered, and regulars drawn in from Baltimore (over the protests of Maryland officials who still feared trouble). Hartranft and several hundred militia set out from Philadelphia on Thursday afternoon in two special troop trains. That evening more than 500 regulars followed.

Hartranft, noted for his prudence, moved slowly and carefully. At Harrisburg he took on more troops and ammunition, and Gatling guns were mounted on flatcars at the head of the procession. The mob at Altoona, sullen but dispirited, gave way to a garrison of 500 militia, and the rest of the expedition pushed slowly around Horseshoe Curve and into the mountains, preceded by walking skirmishers. Meanwhile Major Hamilton and his regulars ran into difficulty back at Altoona, not from the mob but from Pennsylvania railroad officials. The latter, while never actually refusing, delayed hour after hour in putting on the necessary extra engines; evidently they wanted the regulars to stay in town. After fuming for a couple of hours, Hamilton seized an eastbound train, but released it on the officials' "word of honor" that an engine was coming in. Back from "a fool's errand" to see the mythical engine attached, Hamilton furiously seized a large eastbound passenger train. "Do you want to hold up the United States mails?" asked the depot master self-righteously. "Yes!" said Hamilton. At last the engine was attached, and off went the regulars. Just outside Johnstown the train was stoned and derailed, and cars piled up in a wreck. Miraculously the only injury was Hamilton's broken rib. A hundred bystanders were scooped into custody, but only fourteen were finally held. The regulars set out again Saturday morning, arriving at Pittsburgh early next day.

Hartranft and his troops had already arrived and gone quietly into camp, slightly annoyed by crowds of good-humored sightseers. They had found Pittsburgh in a state of unwonted calm because of the business shutdown. Since the preceding Monday, the Pittsburgh Committee of Safety had kept things well in hand. On the morning of Sunday, July 29, a double-header freight pulled out of Pittsburgh with thirty-four cars of cattle and two of troops. More freights left, and others came in. Pennsylvania Railroad officials set Tuesday morning as the deadline for reporting to work. By Monday night the roll book was full.

The coup de grâce in the Midwest fell on Thursday, July 26, and it was delivered by an arm of the Federal government. The instrument, however, was suggested early, if not first, by Receiver James H. Wilson, who had shown in the Civil War that he knew a good new weapon when he saw one. On Sunday (it may be recalled) Wilson had pointedly reminded the Hayes administration that his road, the St. Louis & Southeastern, was in receivership—that is to say, in the custody of United States courts—and hence entitled to Federal protection against strikes. Sweet are the uses of adversity.

In his view of the law Wilson soon acquired two notable supporters. One was United States Circuit Judge Thomas Drummond of Chicago, a cultivated and opinionated gentleman of whom it was once said: "God rules in Israel, but Thomas Drummond in the Seventh Circuit." The other was Walter Quintin Gresham of Indianapolis, a former Union general and currently United States District Judge for Indiana. In their jurisdictions were a number of roads in receivership, including Wilson's. Wilson kept up a steady pressure on both judges to break the strike with the power of the United States government.

Drummond promptly decided that to obstruct roads in receivership was in contempt of court. Never before had it been suggested that a judicial command could be disobeyed except by a person to whom it was addressed. Gresham went along with the notion, however, Drummond being not only his senior in appointment and superior in office, but also his mentor in legal matters. On Monday Drummond ordered his U.S. marshals to identify obstructors of trains for future contempt charges, while Gresham wired President Hayes for regular troops to sustain the courts. The War Department replied only that Captain Arnold's troops at the United States Arsenal in Indianapolis might be so used, if the captain saw fit. There were twelve of these.

The strike wave had meanwhile rolled through Indiana much as through other Midwestern states. It reached Fort Wayne on Sunday, July 22, via the Pittsburgh, Fort Wayne & Chicago and was followed by the usual crowd excitement, mayoral proclamations, a strike at the Olds spoke factory and a belated and somewhat perfunctory committee of safety. Indianapolis railroaders succumbed on Monday afternoon, first on the Vandalia and the Indianapolis & St. Louis, then on the Bee Line and the Pan Handle, finally (under ostensible compulsion from a roving crowd of strikers) on every other line in the city.

Much of the credit for preserving the peace in Indianapolis seems due to Mayor John Caven, a burly bachelor with scholarly tastes and kindly impulses. The city had been hit late but hard by the depression; and when a legal dispute halted work on the municipal belt railroad early in June, a mob of jobless men threatened violence. Caven hurried to the scene, promised that work would resume next day, led the mob to the city's largest bakeries, distributed bread and then arranged a settlement of the legal deadlock within a day. Strengthened by this recent triumph, Mayor Caven now soothed the strikers, enlisted them as special police and organized a committee of citizens to hear strikers' grievances and present them to managements. A W.P.U.S. meeting meanwhile fell flat, and no threat developed to the weakly held United States Arsenal.

Governor James D. Williams of Indiana, politically shrewd but farmerish in appearance, was nationally known as "Blue Jeans" Williams, because he wore blue jeans on all occasions, including inaugural ceremonies. Like Caven, he hung back from stern measures against the strikers. Judge Gresham grew steadily more impatient with the Caven-Williams approach. The judge had United States Marshal Benjamin Spooner warn Indianapolis strikers of their liability to contempt charges, but this proved to be no open sesame for rail traffic. Gresham assembled a group of distinguished gentlemen and urged them to form a committee of public safety, which they did. He proposed to make them special United States marshals and assign them to opening the court-operated roads. Yet very few undistinguished citizens showed up to fill the ranks. Word came from Attorney General Devens on Tuesday that no regular troops could be spared to help Marshal Spooner. And all the while Wilson and other receivers clamored for action.

On Wednesday, therefore, Gresham methodically set about

frightening the Federal authorities into sending more troops to Indianapolis. General Benjamin Harrison and others of Gresham's cronies sent an urgent appeal to the President. Gresham himself sent an extraordinary letter, which might be called hysterical if it were not so clearly calculated. The situation at Indianapolis, Gresham announced, was "most critical and dangerous." The state authorities were inert, and "the mob is the only supreme authority." Though committing no actual violence, the mob "sheep together" and thereby, in some occult fashion, "stop all business." Few would join the citizens' militia, and the town was "full of idle mechanics and laborers." Ergo, "there may be an outbreak at any moment." Next day Gresham egged Captain Arnold of the arsenal into asking for at least 200 troops.

It is not likely that Hayes and the Cabinet were deceived. Newspaper and Signal Corps dispatches gave the lie to Gresham's letter. Sergeant Wappenhans at Indianapolis reported "not the least sign of mob violence." But Gresham and his allies were men of weight. And Thursday's cabinet meeting showed signs of a reaction against the grave burdens just now being lightened. Evarts laughed at a request from Governor Ludington of Wisconsin that 300 residents of the Old Soldiers' Home at Milwaukee be mustered in to save the city from "the laborer insurrection." "The Old Home men had better be called out to keep open the drives in the parks," suggested Evarts. There were still only 3,140 regulars east of the Mississippi. "Well," said Evarts blithely, "as the rioters kill none of them, that may be enough." In that lighthearted, if not lightheaded mood, Hayes and his Cabinet casually decided to send troops to Indiana and to order Marshal Spooner to open and keep open the railroads in the custody of Federal courts.

Next day Secretary Evarts wrote privately: "It looks now as if our expectation of getting through without extraordinary measures would not be disappointed." He did not realize how extraordinary Thursday's decision had been, if not legally, then at least historically. It pulled the lanyard, of course, on management's biggest gun in the Midwest. But beyond that, the first round set a whole battery of such guns roaring down the decades, until the threat of contempt charges became one of the most formidable weapons organized labor had to face.

On the evening of July 27, 200 regulars arrived in Indianapolis.

They found no mob beleaguering Captain Arnold's doughty dozen at the arsenal, but the presence of the regulars ended the strike on court-operated roads, including Gresham's share of the St. Louis & Southeastern. United States marshals arrested a number of strikers, one of them the national secretary-treasurer of the Locomotive Firemen's Brotherhood. Gresham sent Marshal Spooner with a posse of fifty regulars to Terre Haute and Vincennes, but the strikers fled before them. The expedition proved useful, nevertheless. Though the Vandalia was not in receivership, Judge (formerly General) Gresham saw fit to oblige its president by sending Spooner's force back to Terre Haute once more, thus frustrating an attempt to block Vandalia trains.

Receiver Wilson's final triumph came at East St. Louis, Illinois. There the strikers had been in quiet but firm possession all week. With the administration's new attitude plain, pressure now developed from the Federal courts, Mayor Overstolz, Governor Phelps and others for Colonel Davis to send regulars across the river into East St. Louis as a marshal's posse. Davis gave way. On Saturday morning his laconic report from East St. Louis reached the White House: "Occupied this place early this morning with U.S. troops without the least opposition. Everything very quiet. This ends all trouble in this vicinity." Receiver Wilson wired Judge Gresham: "Our campaign here has ended in complete victory. I think all trains will be regularly at work by Monday." A week later Wilson revived his bond speculation with Jacob Schiff.

The end came quickly now. In some places, the strike was snuffed out clean. The Michigan Central strikers gave in on July 26. Where the flames of anger had burned hardest, the strike smoked and sputtered awhile. The Vandalia engineers at St. Louis, for example, struck on July 29 against the July 1 cut; next day the company advertised for "competent and reliable locomotive engineers." On the last day of July the strikers turned briefly stubborn again at points along the Fort Wayne road. And the Lake Shore men at Cleveland held out until August 3.

On the Baltimore & Ohio, a freight moved out of Cumberland with an escort of regulars at midnight, July 27, and reached Martinsburg without interruption. There were flareups at Keyser on July 29 and 30, and 100 regulars had to be sent out. On August 2 someone took a shot at the conductor of a freight coming into Baltimore; and that same day "a large mob, principally composed of half grown boys," stopped another at Bellaire, Ohio. Otherwise, the B. & O. was back to normal all along the line. The strikers had surrendered unconditionally.

The New York Central strike had faded gracefully away by the end of the week. "I am rejoiced," proclaimed William Vanderbilt on July 26, "that the men in the service have stood up manfully against the outside mob." Most roads which had not already resumed operations set Monday, July 30, as a deadline for their men to return with no questions asked. Very few passed up the chance.

Among those observers who rejoiced from afar was General William T. Sherman, the man who by a stroke of chance or intuition had forecast a great mob frenzy if the Army were reduced. On the climactic afternoon of July 25, though holding out against the warmongers, President Hayes had nervously called back Generals Sherman and Sheridan from a trip through the West. Sheridan reached Chicago on July 29 in his usual dashing style and found an exciting "revolution in public sentiment on army and other matters." He thought Sherman ought to come back, too. But Sherman considered it all a tempest in a teapot. He delayed, and on August 2 gratefully received word in Montana that he might resume his trip.

Tom Scott's hopes died hard. "Please do not be misled by any news of peaceable settlement of existing troubles," he wired President Hayes on July 31; "the removal of the military in all probability will be followed by renewed outbreaks." But Hayes paid no attention. The summer days were passing, each one more peaceful. On August 5 came the last Signal Corps strike report, like a benediction or an epitaph:

Pax Semper Ubique.

CHAPTER 14

Shock Waves

BUT THERE was no peace. Reverberations followed, and sympathetic detonations. Then, after the dust settled and the debris was cleared away, came the work of building anew. Meanwhile, fissures had been started and forces released, the ends of which were not to be seen by that generation.

Even at the moment of Chief Signal Officer Myer's valedictory telegram, peace was not "everywhere." Though Carnegie's steel mills and others resumed operations by the end of July, the men of Jones and Laughlin's American Iron Works at Pittsburgh stayed out eight weeks before settling for their old wages. On August 8, 200 United States regulars helped the sheriff of Washington County, Maryland, arrest nine canal strikers for burning a boat; but the Chesapeake & Ohio Canal boatmen kept on with their strike nevertheless. And long after these had surrendered, the miners of Illinois and Pennsylvania held out desperately.

One of the ugliest and most tragic struggles in that violent year was the miners' strike at Braidwood, Illinois. Some dark glimpses of life at Braidwood were given in testimony before an Illinois legislative committee two years later. The miners worked from twelve to fourteen hours a day. In winter they saw no daylight from one Sunday to the next. One hundred and fifty children worked in the mines because their fathers' wages could not feed them. In the black depths, where there was no ventilation, a lamp could hardly burn. The mineowners skimped on timbers, and so cave-ins were frequent and deadly. Yet the owners paid nothing to men who were injured or to the families of those who died. If the miner lived through a cave-in, he had to clear out the rock and debris—one or two weeks' work—without pay. This was because he was paid by the ton of coal mined. About 150 pounds of "nut coal" was sifted out of every ton and not counted, though the owners sold it at two thirds of the regular price. In summer the men averaged only about three days' work a week. They were paid monthly, half in non-transferable scrip good only at the company "truck" store, known also as a "pluck-me store" because of its heavy markups over regular prices. Those who made trouble were fired and blacklisted.

Superintendent Alanson Sweet of the Chicago, Wilmington & Vermillion Coal Company at Braidwood prided himself on being the champion wage cutter of the region. Back in 1862, he had been hired by the Michigan Central as superintendent of motive power on the strength of his promise to make the railroad men take a cut. He did so, firing those who protested and replacing some of the firemen with Negroes. This had led to the founding of the Brotherhood of Locomotive Engineers in 1863. Now he tried his hand with the Braidwood miners.

In 1876 Sweet cut wages from $1.20 a ton to $1.10 and then to $.95. In the spring of 1877 he announced a further cut to $.70 in summer and $.80 in winter. On April 1, 1877, 1,500 miners struck for $1.05 a ton. After assembling a force of armed guards, Sweet announced that he would not pay the strikers for their last month's work. The company stood by his policies. "To take any other course," wrote the general solicitor, "would simply be destruction to the property, and we had better make an assignment and give it away at once. We expect of course to succeed in breaking the strike." That was late in April, and already the men were going hungry. In June Sweet imported Negro miners from Kentucky and West Virginia. Writing from Cambridge, Massachusetts, a director recommended putting in "half or two-thirds colored miners, if not all." He was sorry to hear that the July dividend would be omitted, but not surprised. In three months the strike had cost the company $15,000. There were consolations, however, as pointed out in a circular to stockholders: "With the mines filled with colored men, it is believed that the Company will not be burdened with the expense of another strike for many years."

"Our coloured miners are doing nicely," Sweet bragged to a director in July. "I became so disgusted with my white men [strikebreakers] that I was trying to learn to mine that I discharged them all in a lump and sent for coloured men . . . They are no expence only for their fair to this place & that they pay back to us. We had to feed the other men & pay them $1.00 per day and they eat like a lot of Hogs & then lazed around for two months and slept and did no work." The Negro miners "say they have found the Land of Promise."

The promise was not one of peace. On July 27, excited by the Great Strike, Braidwood strikers forced 400 Negro strikebreakers to leave town with their families. The *Chicago Times* suggested that "the whole power of the government should be put in motion to send the Braidwood savages straight from the mouths of cannon to the infernal regions." And in fact, two regiments of regulars and a Gatling gun were requested for service at Braidwood. Colonel Drum refused to send them. But a couple of Illinois militia regiments did the trick; and on July 29 the Negroes returned, singing hymns. The strike dragged on dismally until November 8, when several hundred miners came back to work on the company's terms.

The nation at large took more notice of the anthracite miners' strike in eastern Pennsylvania. Working conditions there were much the same as at Braidwood. A *New York Sun* reporter investigated the miners' pay and shocked thousands of complacent readers with his findings. For example, one Delaware, Lackawanna & Western Coal Company miner had earned $28.40 in June. Out of that he had paid $9.40 for blasting powder, oil and other working materials, leaving $19.00 on which to support himself, his wife, his three children and his seventy-four-year-old father. Their meals consisted of corn-meal mush and a few potatoes from their little garden patch. Once every month or two, he managed to buy two pounds of fat pork and, more rarely, some wheat flour and a pint of molasses; but the family had not seen beef for half a year. A laborer with a family of five had averaged $14.00 a month over the past year; the company owed him for fifty-nine cars of coal. A miner with a wife, six children and a dependent mother averaged $18.00 a month, out of which came $6.00 for rent. His noon meal in the mine was cold mush or a slice of bread. These stories were typical. Thousands of men, women and children struggled to live on equally pitiful earnings. For those who did not succeed, the "pluck-me stores" had recently put in an undertaking service and a coffin department at not much more than regular prices.

The miners and their families lived in "clap-board sheds, built on trestles, painted with the storms and dust of years, fences unknown, floors uncarpeted, windows without shutters." Improvements made by the tenant generally brought an increase in rent. In July 1877 miners near Cumberland, Maryland, were living on dried roots, berries and a little corn meal. At Shamokin, Pennsylvania, where most mines were closed for lack of work, "ten families in one row of houses have been without food for the last two weeks, and have been living on green peas and cabbage, which they have raised in their little gardens, which are about run dry in their supply."

The Delaware & Hudson Canal Company, one of the five principal anthracite railroads, reported the coal trade "never so thoroughly depressed and demoralized" as in that year. Through 1876 and 1877, six collieries of the Delaware, Lackawanna & Western remained closed entirely, and the other twelve worked less than half time, except for a few weeks in the fall. In September 1876 D. L. & W. wages were cut 10 per cent. This, according to the manager of the company's mines, gave the men "a bare subsistence." In March 1877 wages were cut another 15 per cent. The men remained submissive. They seemed to have learned the grim lesson of the "Long Strike" in 1875, when Franklin Gowen and his allies destroyed their union.

But the breaking point was near. A Lehigh Valley wage cut on June 1 touched off a brief, useless strike of 1,100 miners. Another strike broke out in a colliery near Wilkes-Barre when the management demanded "cleaner" coal without extra pay. Then, after pay cars had gone through on the anthracite railroads, the Great Strike reached the anthracite regions. At Easton, early on the morning of July 24, firemen and brakemen struck on the Lehigh & Susquehanna Division of the Central Railroad of New Jersey. At Scranton later that day firemen struck on the Lackawanna and the Delaware & Hudson. Finally, on the evening of July 26, the strike spread to the men of the Lehigh Valley Railroad at Easton.

The people of the region took the spark like tinder. At Allentown a yelling mob marched about behind a brass band, defied the mayor, stoned the police and dispersed only after the arrival of a militia regiment. At Shamokin, a mob of unemployed miners stormed through the streets shouting for work or bread. After sacking the Reading's warehouse, they ran into an armed posse and were dispersed by gunfire, leaving several badly wounded. At Scranton the *Republican* sold out its largest issue since the Avondale mine

disaster. When the noon gong sounded on July 24 at the Lackawanna rolling mills and steel works in Scranton, a thousand men
struck against the recent 10 per cent cut. Two days later, the miners
struck for a 25 per cent increase. The mining strike spread to other
towns and other companies, and by the end of July it was general
throughout the Wyoming region.

The storm centered around Scranton, chief city of the anthracite
coal region. Its 35,000 people depended utterly on the shops, mills
and mines of the anthracite railroads, especially the Lackawanna.
While organizing and arming a posse, Mayor Robert H. McKune
worked desperately to soften the bitterness of the miners' strike.
For the first time in Scranton's history striking miners prevented
the manning of pumps, thus threatening to put some mines out of
operation for many months. But McKune at last persuaded the
strikers to let superintendents, foremen and civil engineers start the
pumps up again; and thanks to unusually light rainfall that season,
the skeleton crews managed to prevent flooding. The railroad
strikers gave in tamely at the end of July; and since everyone agreed
that the mine strike had been inspired by the railroad strike, Mc-
Kune felt that matters were on the mend. "Send no more troops until
you hear from me," he wired Governor Hartranft on July 29; "am in
hopes of a peaceful settlement." On July 31 a committee of mine
strikers met in McKune's office with the Lackawanna's legal adviser.
Giving up the wage demand, the committee offered to settle for
the right to send future grievance committees directly to the board
of directors. The company spokesman welcomed the proposition,
and the strike seemed virtually over. When rumors spread of a mass
meeting to be held next morning in an open space near the silk
works, most people in Scranton assumed that it would bring formal
ratification of the settlement.

Others were not so sure. The miners had fiercely resented the railroaders' surrender. They had a far greater score to settle with their
own employers. When the crowd came together near the silk works
on the morning of August 1, it included men embittered by suffering and bent on revenge. Others, members of a secret but peaceable
organization named the Knights of Labor, sensed trouble ahead
and hoped to prevent it. Several thousand people, mostly miners,
steelworkers and craftsmen, milled around for half an hour
waiting for developments. There seemed to be general uncertainty

about who had called the meeting, if anyone, and what its object was. Before much had been done, someone got up on a little stand and read a letter signed "Working Man." (Its author was never identified.) It reviewed the miners' sufferings and asserted that Superintendent William W. Scranton of the Lackawanna works had promised to have the men working for fifty cents a day or bury himself in a culm pile. With a roar the crowd turned into a mob. Three Knights of Labor men quick-wittedly led parts of the mob off in different directions in order to divide it. Most of it, however, headed for the Lackawanna shops.

Fifteen hundred or 2,000 rioters, mostly young men and boys, raged through the shops, attacked a small force of men still on the job, stopped engines and drew fires. Armed with sticks, they beat the fleeing workmen, knocked down a boiler tender in his late sixties, stoned another worker as he ran through the shops with his shirt torn off and his back bloodied. Mayor McKune hurried to Lackawanna Avenue, where he encountered a gang of about 100 men coming out of the shops with pickhandles and clubs in their hands. They were unknown to McKune and he to them; but from the aspect of the group around him, they guessed him to be an official of some sort. "Who's that?" cried the leader; and on being told, he bellowed, "Kill the son of a bitch! He's got no business here!"

The gang broke through a handful of citizens who tried to shield the mayor. A rioter gave him a thump across the back that started one lung bleeding. With blood dribbling from his mouth, Mayor McKune called for the posse. Stones and blows rained upon him. As he stumbled away, Father Dunn of the local Roman Catholic parish took his arm and tried to ward off the attackers, but one of them struck McKune on the cheek with a club and fractured his upper jaw. Carrying Father Dunn along with them, the mob surged past the mayor toward the Lackawanna's company store. McKune heard someone yell, "Let's clean out the town!" Then he saw about fifty of his posse coming down Lackawanna Avenue. Motioning them to come on, he turned toward his office; but as he started, he was put out of action by a heavy blow on the back of his head.

A considerable part of the posse had gathered at the company store after the mob began attacking the shops. When word reached them of the mayor's summons, they had set out behind William

Scranton, who called upon them to shoot to kill if attacked. At the corner of Washington Street and Lackawanna Avenue the mob closed in on them from three sides. "I never saw men more like devils in my life," recalled one of the posse later. Someone yelled, "Come on, boys, they've got blank cartridges!" Stones and sticks pelted the posse, and a rioter fired a pistol. The posse stopped, raised their rifles and fired. The racket lasted only a minute. When it ceased, three of the mob lay dead or dying on the street. The number of wounded was never settled, but there were many. Father Dunn comforted the fallen while the crowd fled in panic. Some broke into barred stores in their frenzy to escape. "In all my life I never ran so fast," recalled a chance spectator named Jacob Riis, a young newspaperman not long over from Denmark.

That tragedy put a stop to serious rioting in the Wyoming region. It also ended any chance of a quick and amiable strike settlement. The miners returned to their demand for a raise. On the afternoon of his ordeal, still bleeding profusely, Mayor McKune called upon both Governor Hartranft and President Hayes for military aid. Troops converged on the coal country. General Brinton's now-famous Philadelphia militia, increased to 3,000 by those who had previously missed the train to Pittsburgh, arrived next day and served for three months with admirable firmness, tempered by restraint. General Pearson led 1,000 of his notorious Pittsburgh militia to Luzerne County with equal success.

On August 2 McKune wired Hayes: "The Governor has rendered me all the assistance I require. If any U.S. troops are on way here, please stop them." But the troops came nevertheless. Even before the Scranton riot Judge Drummond's new formula had been applied to certain Lehigh Valley properties in United States receivership. Franklin Gowen and others also demanded Federal protection. Troops moved toward Pennsylvania from Michigan, Kentucky, Illinois, Indiana, New York, Maryland and West Virginia. By August 6 there were 112 Marines at Reading, 287 Army regulars at Easton, 300 more at Mauch Chunk, 510 at Wilkes-Barre and 315 at Scranton. General Hancock saw hope for a short stay in the fact that at least 150,000 people in the Luzerne district were living on potatoes, blackberries and whortleberries.

Hancock did not know the miners. The strike dragged on. In mid-August Hancock returned to his permanent headquarters in New

York City, and some of the regulars were sent elsewhere. Many remained, however, and Governor Hartranft called for state militia volunteers to serve three months in the mining country. Late that month, only 250 out of 3,500 miners voted to accept one company's offer of work at the July rates. Some operators in the Lehigh Valley settled for compromise increases in September. Though Lehigh and Schuylkill County miners contributed what they could to the support of their striking brethren, some hungry miners in the Lackawanna Valley began raiding farms for food. Fall came on. "The nights are cold," wrote Lieutenant Colonel Otis of the regulars at Wilkes-Barre, "and considerable shivering is going on about the camp." On October 15 a Pinkerton agent attended "a convention of the Molly Maguires" near Scranton. But the end was at hand. Next day the miners of that region voted overwhelmingly to resume work at the July rates. On October 19 Governor Hartranft formally notified President Hayes that "all reasons for the presence of United States troops in Pennsylvania have ceased to exist." One Wilkes-Barre politician wrote another a few days later: "Those who gave the advance are going to rescind it & take it off the 1st of Nov., but I don't apprehend much difficulty will result." And none did.

Like most of the mining companies, the Lackawanna refused to grant strikers "the privilege of returning to their old places without question, as several dozen of the more prominent radical leaders, agitators and terrorizers found to their cost." Fifteen of the marked men, not only jobless but also blacklisted, wrote Congressman Hendrick Wright of Wilkes-Barre for help in getting railroad passes to Chattanooga. Despairing of any work in the anthracite region, they dreamed of opening a mine of their own in Tennessee. "We have in our proposed colony miners, carpenters, blacksmiths, machinists, engineers—in fact every kind of colliery labor," wrote the leader. But Wright could not get the passes; and the result of the dream is not recorded, though it may be guessed.

While these afterclaps rumbled through the mining regions, the effects of the Great Strike itself began to ramify.

Some ordinarily sensible observers wildly overestimated the cost of the Great Strike to the railroads. The *New York Journal of Commerce*, for example, put the loss at $26,250,000 for five trunk lines alone. In arriving at this, it set property damage to the Pennsylvania and B. & O. at $15,000,000 instead of the actual $2,500,000, allowed $1,000,000 for five days' lost business and threw in an unexplained $10,000,000 for good measure. Investors took a calmer view, and railroad stocks hardly fluttered throughout the excitement. The wise and well-informed paid more heed to the bumper crop already in prospect. Stimulated by crop shipments, the railroads presently started up from the valley of shadows. After that violent summer both revenue and net earnings rose steadily throughout the rest of the decade.

Of all the roads, the Pennsylvania suffered most. "I've been ten days with T.A.S.," wrote one of Tom Scott's cronies on August 2. "His roads have been fearfully injured. The Federal Government could have crushed it at the start, but for the imbecile policy of Hayes & Co." Eventually the state supreme court held the Pennsylvania not liable for freight stolen or destroyed at Pittsburgh. For the $2,000,000 loss of the road's own property, a somewhat peculiar state law made Allegheny County responsible. But the county fought hard—so hard, indeed, that the Pennsylvania joined it in an attempt to change the law and make the state responsible. This fell through when five of their lobbyists went to prison for bribery of legislators. At last, in 1880, Allegheny County settled with the Pennsylvania for about $1,400,000 plus interest (raised through a bond issue not fully retired until 1906). Because of its riot losses, therefore, the Pennsylvania had to omit its usual dividends in August and November, 1877.

Humiliating as that necessity was, far worse afflicted Tom Scott. His dream of a Texas Pacific subsidy was dead. "Get to your hole, Tom Scott," exulted the *Iron Molders' Journal*, meanwhile reminding its readers to vote against prosubsidy Congressmen. "Between us," wrote the knowledgeable Washington correspondent Charles Nordhoff to a friend, "I think [the Great Strike] finishes Tom Scott, and I shall not be sorry." Accused of supporting the subsidy, Speaker Samuel Randall wrote scornfully: "Few men in Pennsylvania have received more hard knocks from this power ... than I have, and few have been more steady in hitting back ... Why should I now compromise with a crippled power and lean upon their broken staff?"

Almost as much of a blow, and far more ironic in the light of history, was the victory of Standard Oil over Scott's rival Empire

Transportation Company. No longer could the hard-pressed Pennsylvania afford to back the Empire in its titanic struggle. In October 1877, with a stoic smile, Scott signed the papers which sold his Empire to John D. Rockefeller. The Pittsburgh mob had cleared the way for the greatest monopoly of all.

Scott's death in 1881, according to historians of the Pennsylvania, was "probably caused or aggravated by the troubles of 1877."

Fate also dealt harshly with three of Scott's fellow tycoons. Despite talk of John W. Garrett's resignation after the Great Strike, he remained president of the B. & O. But he had to abandon his dream of seeing his son Robert take over and build up the road as he had done, for Robert had little inclination toward the work. The elder Garrett died in 1884, disappointed, unhappy and prematurely old. Failing in appetite, plagued by dyspepsia and insomnia, William H. Vanderbilt died of a cerebral thrombosis in 1885. "Pleasure had lost its zest," writes a historian of the Vanderbilt family; "in eight years he had lived twenty." Franklin Gowen, who had gloried in his fame and power, went down to ruin and obscurity; and at sunset on Friday, December 13, 1889, he walked into his Washington hotel room and put a bullet through his head.

History has heretofore written off the Great Strike as a failure, and for some of the strikers it certainly was. The Burlington, for example, fired 131 men specifically for being strikers (including 96 brakemen and 24 conductors), and other roads did much the same.

Yet the *New York Times* of that day saw it as "a drawn battle." Many of the companies had carried their point, the *Times* admitted. Still, "the workmen have here and there compelled compliance with their demands, and in other instances they have attracted popular attention to their grievances, real or alleged, to an extent that will render future indifference impossible." In fact, the *Times* thought, "the balance of gain is on the side of the workmen." Other contemporary newspapers agreed, and a closer examination should induce history to join them.

Even on the roads where pay was not raised, what had the men lost? The universality of the strike prevented reprisals against more than a small fraction of strikers. The rest lost only one or two weeks' wages. But since they were paid by the trip or the mile, most made up at least part of those wages in the subsequent rush of business. And had they gained nothing? "The material smitten proves to be very explosive," observed the *Commercial and Financial Chronicle* thoughtfully. "We have seen," wrote President Harris of the Burlington, "that a reduction of pay to employes may be as expensive to the Co. as an increase of the pay." "One point is probably settled for the present at least," concluded *Iron Age*, a manufacturers' journal, "the reduction in the wages of labor has reached its lowest point. . . . It would be a bold step in a wrong direction to give notice of a decrease in wages." If the railroad wage-cutting experiment had succeeded, it would probably have been repeated as pitilessly as among the miners. The Great Strike put a stop to that, not only on railroads but elsewhere. And in so doing (as *Iron Age* duly and gratefully noted) it also put a floor under prices, thus helping to break the spiral of deflation and depression.

In many cases, the gains were more than hypothetical.

Derision had followed William Vanderbilt's pious statement just after the strike: "Our men feel that, although I . . . may have my millions and they the rewards of their daily toil, still we are about equal in the end. If they suffer I suffer, and if I suffer they cannot escape." Derision also interlarded gushing praise when Vanderbilt distributed $100,000 among his men for their "loyalty and faithfulness during the strike." Charles Francis Adams likened the gratuity to a shilling thrown to a tramp. It is true that Vanderbilt spent slightly more than $100,000 to have an Egyptian obelisk put up in Central Park and three times as much for his own tomb. Still, the gift more than made up for the week's wages lost by his men. And something better followed. In October the Central restored half of the July cut, and in February 1880 it restored the rest. Other roads followed suit, including the Pennsylvania.

John Garrett went no further in largesse after the Great Strike than his usual annual donation of $100 to the Railroad Y.M.C.A., even though the Y.M.C.A.'s secretary pointed out that its visitor had done "a good work at Martinsburg" that year. Yet the B. & O. moved quickly to remedy certain grievances. Beginning in August 1877, its men were given passes home during layovers, were given regular runs with reasonable assurances of full time, were not called up more than an hour before leaving and were guaranteed a quarter day's pay when called, whether the train left or not. Late that month the Michigan Central began "equalizing" wages, which meant increases of from 4 to 12 per cent. The Central of New Jersey paid off half the back wages due its men. The Illinois Central gave all its men full pay for July. And in November the Pennsylvania Railroad, in spite of everything, set aside $3,000 for distribution to employees who had been loyal during the strike; if realistically apportioned, the average payment must have been considerable.

Top management now realized that labor policy could not be left to lesser officials. The consequences of Tom Scott's airy faith in Superintendent Pitcairn had made that plain. Railroad builders learned at last that their men were more than blocks and stones, that employee morale had to be considered. As the *Railroad Gazette* put it at the end of the year: "There is a feeling that the troubles may be repeated, and that it will be wise to provide a closer connection between the companies and their men."

Here, as in other matters, the Burlington Archives reveal managerial soul searching. President Robert Harris thought hard about the problem. "The men have real grievances which deserve consideration," he wrote. To begin with, he urged giving up Sunday freight service, except for stock in transit, since—religious duties aside—unremitting labor was "barbarizing our trainmen." More fundamentally, he questioned management's "moral right" to "discharge every person without notice" or to cut pay arbitrarily; and so he proposed to hire men under written contracts running for a period of one or more years. These agreements would spell out admissible grounds for discharge, would guarantee a set rate of pay and a minimum annual wage, and would require ninety days' notice for both firing and quitting. The leading directors thought well of this.

Director John Murray Forbes decided that now was the time "to fight the battle with Communism," and he proposed therefore to promise the men all the company's surplus earnings after an 8 per cent dividend had been provided for. Harris and others doubted the practicability of this. There would be no workable guarantee that management would not choose to spend such a surplus (if it ever came) on debt reduction or capital investment, and the men would know this and complain endlessly.

The most common morale-building proposals were those for relief or insurance. The Lehigh Valley set up a relief fund and matched employee contributions. The Central Pacific opened a hospital for sick or injured employees. Charles Francis Adams kept on campaigning for company insurance plans to outdo those of the Brotherhoods; and many roads studied the idea, including the Burlington, the Illinois Central, the Kansas Pacific and the Michigan Central. None got around to adopting it until the eighties.

This was not surprising. The upper echelons of most roads included men like Vice-President Perkins of the Burlington. The shock of the Great Strike at first drove him into a doubtful and temporary neutrality toward some sort of pension plan. But his instincts soon reasserted themselves. He agreed that morale was important. But it was to be maintained only by strict discipline and the rewarding of individual merit. He had nothing but contempt for Harris' proposals. "Harris," he observed disgustedly on August 9, "wants now to advance the wages of brakemen, when we are overrun with applications for work from competent men at current rates." "I don't know whether he thinks the laws of supply & demand are not up to the occasion or not," wrote Perkins. "But . . . I suppose there is no safe anchorage for the C. B. & Q. or any other employer of labor except in those old laws, and this is a good time to hammer that into the public mind & to try to divest the subject of a sort of sentimental fog which surrounds it." As to an insurance plan, Perkins felt by December that nothing would "do more to destroy in the end all zeal and esprit de corps than to adopt any plan of giving to our employes something for nothing." Shortly before Christmas, he opposed a pay raise "before the excitement of the strike has wholly died out." About then Harris gave up all his fine plans. They would have no chance to prove their value, he wrote wearily, unless all the chief officials were in sympathy with them; and Perkins was opposed to doing anything at any time.

In Pennsylvania, some managements turned to a less sentimental and perhaps less expensive means of keeping order: the "Coal and Iron Police," already used by Franklin Gowen's Reading during the Long Strike of 1875. During the summer of 1877, as authorized by Pennsylvania law, Governor Hartranft commissioned scores of such police, hired by and serving the Reading, the Pennsylvania, the Lehigh Valley, the Central of New Jersey and other roads. There were doubts about the judgment of these men. Some railroaders were shot at in the course of their regular duties, and one was seriously wounded. One guard even rested the muzzle of a loaded gun on his own foot and toyed with the trigger; the wound was "painful but not serious." Nevertheless, they were effective during the Great Strike. Hartranft thought the system should be generally adopted, and eventually it was. In June 1878 the Pennsylvania organized a standing force of 100 such men, with another hundred as inactive reserves. By 1902 the Coal and Iron Police had largely supplanted the regular police system of Pennsylvania in industrial disturbances.

Amid their strange new perplexities railroad leaders may have found solace in the disappearance of the Trainmen's Union and the disengagement of its notorious leader. The Lackawanna took the trouble as late as December 1877 to include the Trainmen's Union in the list of organizations it required its men to forswear, and on Washington's Birthday 1878 Robert Ammon testified under oath that his union still existed. But by then no one else seemed to care.

On July 24, 1877, Boss Ammon had grandly wired Governor Hartranft a guarantee of safe passage over the Fort Wayne road. When the governor paused at Allegheny that evening to change engines, Ammon introduced him to the cheering strikers and stood by while Hartranft made a brief and noncommittal speech praising their peaceable demeanor. On Tuesday Ammon thus walked with the mighty; on Thursday he fell, deposed in mid-career by his own mistrustful men. They said he had betrayed them.

On July 30 Ammon was arrested for inciting to riot and for violation of the new law against obstructing railroad operation. He loudly charged the railroad officials with ingratitude, claiming that he had saved their property and kept open their passenger and mail service; and perhaps he convinced them. Jailed for a time, he was released on bail and (though indicted) was never brought to trial. His activities for some years thereafter are obscure, though a family tradition places him briefly in California, working with the anti-Chinese movement.

In 1887 he came to live in New York City, joined a business firm and was admitted to the bar. Presently he acquired an estate, "Fair Acres," on Staten Island, next to the home of Jacob Vanderbilt, first cousin to the late William H. Vanderbilt. He voted Republican and had no dealings with union men. In 1902, when old "Squire" August Ammon died (in the West Penn Hospital on the hill overlooking the Twenty-eighth Street crossing), Robert Ammon's presence contributed to the strongly plutocratic atmosphere of his father's funeral. Two of his brothers were then prominent members of the Pittsburgh bar; and another, Walter, was one of the wealthiest businessmen and bank directors of Jersey City, as well as a member of the Union League Club. In 1904, however, Robert Ammon went to Sing Sing for his part in a Wall Street swindle; and in 1908 his brother Walter was shot dead in the Pennsylvania Railroad depot at Jersey City by an oleomargarine manufacturer who claimed to have been wronged by him. Robert Ammon later returned to Wall Street and lived to see at least one member of the family triumph over the Pennsylvania Railroad. His sister-in-law, Mrs. Samuel Ammon, as leader of the Pittsburgh Daughters of the American Revolution, saved a historic Pittsburgh landmark, the Block House, from condemnation proceedings brought by the Pennsylvania. (Another landmark, the Roundhouse, also survives today, still bearing the scars of battle; but the Ammons had no interest in that war memorial.) Robert Ammon became mortally ill on a railroad train and died in Green Cove Springs, Florida, on April 19, 1915, the hundred and fortieth anniversary of the Battle of Lexington. Like some who took part in that earlier disorder, he was not a great man but he was the agent of a great change.

While Robert Ammon's bizarre destiny thus lifted one burden from railroad managers, they settled down under another: the Brotherhood of Locomotive Engineers. Many railroad leaders had felt certain during the Great Strike that the Brotherhood was the real instigator and director of the affair. Their first impulse, in Charles Perkins' words, was to "make a clean sweep. . . . Men will leave it if we say so." Their second thought was to watch their step. In mid-August, freight conductors struck against the Philadelphia & Erie because one of them had been summarily discharged. That strike failed, but a trainmen's strike in early September against certain changes made by the Cincinnati, Hamilton & Dayton led to a compromise. All through August and September 1877 the railroad industry shuddered at recurring rumors of a nationwide engineers' strike; and while the engineers did not choose to strike after all, management seemed equally indisposed to provoke them.

That winter, management caught eagerly at reports that men in New England or in other sections were deserting the Brotherhood, and Grand Chief Arthur himself admitted a decline in membership, which he blamed partly on the Great Strike and partly on the defalcation of the treasurer with some of the insurance funds. But the Brotherhood lived on and, with the return of railroad prosperity, began growing again. While avoiding strikes, the Brotherhood pressed steadily for recognition as a collective bargaining agent; and the early eighties brought it more and more contracts. The firemen's brotherhood adopted the same course in 1885, and the conductors' in 1890. All three won acceptance and achieved much with surprisingly few strikes.

The effects of the Great Strike had meanwhile spread beyond the railroad world to the nation at large.

First of all, the law took its course. Somewhat disconcertingly General Pearson at Pittsburgh and the mayor's posse at Scranton were charged with murder and manslaughter, respectively; but a Pittsburgh grand jury ignored the bill against Pearson, and a Wilkes-Barre jury acquitted the posse at the judge's direction. All that was palpable horseplay. The law's chief concern was to punish rioters and strikers, and spokesmen for the established order demanded that punishment be swift, sure and severe.

At Baltimore thirteen rioters drew jail terms ranging from three to eight months. Hundreds were arrested at Pittsburgh, but many were discharged at preliminary hearings and most of the rest given short terms in the workhouse. Seventeen prisoners, including Andrew Hice, received long sentences. A boy of seventeen drew three years for having stolen goods in his possession. A man was fined $1,500 and given eighteen months in prison for diverting a switch. Thomas McCall drew a year in prison and a $1,500 fine for striking David Watt. The heaviest sentence went to Matthew Marshall for firing coke cars: a $5,000 fine, plus six years and ten months in the penitentiary.

At Reading Franklin Gowen trod the boards again as prosecutor; and again there were impassioned speeches and courtroom sensations, including the swoon of a witness. The Brotherhood of Locomotive Engineers was bombarded at long range by Gowen's heaviest rhetoric. Of the eight men indicted for burning the Lebanon Valley bridge, two were convicted and sentenced to five-year prison terms and $1,000 fines. Fourteen others were tried for inciting riot, and one was convicted. Forty-one were indicted but never tried. As a vehicle for Franklin Gowen, the affair fell grievously short of the Molly Maguire melodrama.

The ringleader in an attempt to interfere with mine pumps near Scranton drew twenty-one months at hard labor and a $5,000 fine; three accomplices got three months apiece in the county jail. In another mining case ten men were given from one to three months each. Elsewhere in the nation sundry rioters drew like terms. At Chicago, however, all of the 400 or so prisoners taken during the riots were let out two or three days later in a sort of general amnesty. At St. Louis a nolle prosequi was entered in the case of the notorious "Executive Committee," who consequently walked out of the Four Courts building "in triumph." And at Philadelphia everyone arrested for rioting was acquitted or discharged. (A member of the printers' union must have set the line of type in the *New York Times* which said that the Philadelphians "deserved some sort of punishment, but escaped scott [*sic*] free.")

After serving thirty days for contempt of court Barney Donahue, leader of the Erie strike, was tried on a charge of conspiracy, convicted and given three months in the county jail. This, and similar cases, revived the old doctrine of "malicious conspiracy" as applied to labor unions, and state legislatures presently began to confirm and extend the doctrine by statute.

Still more fateful were the doings of Judge Thomas Drummond and his colleagues. In Chicago Drummond sentenced one man to four months and eight others to two months each for contempt of court: they had obstructed a railroad in United States receivership. On the same charge, Judge Samuel Treat of the Southern District of Illinois gave thirty-seven strikers three months each. At Indianapolis Judge Gresham disqualified himself because of having led the citizens' committee during the strike. However, he invited his old friend Thomas Drummond to do the needful, sat beside Drummond on the bench and put in an oar now and then. Drummond dealt out three months apiece to fifteen strikers. At the end of August a United States circuit judge at Pittsburgh sentenced three men to three months each on the same grounds. "I dislike this mode of punishment," wrote Drummond, but the strikers had "carried things with a high hand." He thought it "absolutely necessary to impose some penalties—& not merely nominal—both to punish the offenders & to prevent interference hereafter with the property of the court."

Drummond probably did impose sentence with reluctance. At any rate, after a month had passed and the lesson had been learned, he and Treat released their sixty-one prisoners. But the strikers were not the only parties edified. The doctrine introduced by Drummond and his colleagues had turned all receivership orders into standing injunctions against strikes—indeed, the very language of such orders bore a close resemblance to the dread labor injunctions of later years. In such cases, strikers could now be swept up and deposited in jail without the inconvenience of jury trials. Companies not in receivership would have to get injunctions issued first in order to turn strikers into criminals, but the courts came to be admirably compliant and prompt in such cases.

Drummond and Gresham had made their decisions, but it had been the United States Army that enforced them. Few in number, overworked and unpaid, it had restored order without shedding a drop of blood—partly, no doubt, because the rioters sensed it would shed all the blood required. "Now," said some Pittsburghers to a sentry, "if there was another row, you wouldn't shoot us, would you?" "Not shoot!" said the regular. "Why, damn ye, I'm paid to shoot." At Wilkes-Barre some Irish miners asked an Irish soldier if he would fire on his countrymen. "That," he said thoughtfully, "would depend upon the Captain's orders." Reassured, the champions of law and order clamored for a larger Army. Hayes himself remarked sarcastically at the height of the upheaval that he did not know whether to recommend "that the Army should be 'reduced' to 50,000 or 100,000 men." And he called a special session of Congress for October to put through an Army appropriation bill. Most people expected Congress to enlarge the Army at that time.

It did not. The Army got its pay and no more. The advocates of an increase prudently talked only of the Indian and Mexican threats, though their opponents accused them passionately of seeking to subjugate American laboring men. Congressman Hendrick B. Wright of Wilkes-Barre spoke with quiet anger:

Troops were introduced into my district at the solicitation of the men who controlled the mines and the manufacturing establishments. . . . There was no necessity or occasion for it. . . . It only stirred up [the labor] element. And now, since that has been done, that element has shown its power and its strength, a power and strength that cannot be resisted, that will work its way out . . . You cannot suppress a volcano.

General Sherman fumed at congressional perversity. "Last week," he wrote home, "Congress took open ground that the Army must not be used to suppress labor riots. You had better overhaul all the muskets and pistols in the attic, for a time will come soon when every householder must defend with fire-arms his own castle. . . . The country will soon conclude that Congress is a nuisance to be suppressed."

Sherman was only relieving his temper in a private letter. Jay Gould had sounded the same note loudly and publicly during the Great Strike. On the Sunday afternoon of the Pittsburgh holocaust, Gould told reporters that the strikes were the beginning of "a great social revolution, which cannot be arrested until it has led to the destruction of the republican form of government in this country and the establishment of a monarchy." He added that he "would gladly give $1,000,000 to see General Grant in the White House to-day." "In spite of these doleful views," noted the *World* man, "Mr. Gould was in very good spirits, and seemed to contemplate the coming of the general conflagration as serenely as if he had a complete monopoly of the trade in lucifer matches and petroleum."

Gould's remarks raised a storm, and his friend Ben Butler urged him to come along on a cruise down the Maine coast. "You had better be away in case of trouble," warned Butler. But Gould was not seeking popularity. He had probably aimed at making the trouble worse, so as to depress certain railroad stocks which he had been selling short. The only trouble he encountered personally came on August 2, when a burly and recently betrayed associate dangled him over an areaway, rapped him on the head a few times and let him drop. "Gould landed on his feet as usual, more's the pity," wrote an unsympathetic Wall Streeter.

The Gould pronouncement seemed no more than a characteristic piece of sinister buffoonery. Yet it had disturbing echoes. "Many people I met," wrote a Brooklyn lady a few days later, "would shake their heads, and say it looked as if we were going to have another French revolution &c, and wish Grant were here." In London a month later Grant himself wrote that the strike "should have been put down with a strong hand and so summarily as to prevent a like occurrence for a generation." And certain unsavory but powerful politicians began puffing Grant for a third term as "an invincible barrier against Communism and currency inflation."

Grantism aside, certain influential newspapers began calling for a stronger central government. "The United States government is a fraud," announced the *Rocky Mountain News*. "That hoary old relic of antiquity, the constitution, is hardly worth the paper it is written upon when any extraordinary emergency arises . . . We are not so much afraid of the bugbear of 'centralization' as to hesitate about calling for a government that will be worth something when it is needed." Other organs chimed in—the *Railway World*, the *National Republican*, the *New York Graphic*, even the *Cumberland News*. Still others, equally as influential, fiercely disagreed. "The experience," insisted the *Boston Advertiser*, "will in the end exalt the prestige of our institutions." It did. And as the fever passed, the ugly dreams faded.

Grant was not crowned, the Constitution was not scrapped, Congress was not suppressed, the Army was not increased. Instead, those who wanted a stronger prop for the social order contented themselves with strengthening state militia. Governor Hartranft and his legislature thoroughly reorganized the Pennsylvania National Guard, improved its equipment, mustered out a number of major generals (including Alfred Pearson) and relegated fancy uniforms to the museums. Other states followed suit. In several large cities battlemented armories rose, complete with loopholes for guns with which to "prevent the approach of a mob." In April 1878 Governor Anthony of Kansas used state militia with heartening success in breaking a strikers' blockade of the Atchison, Topeka & Santa Fe. Governor Mathews of West Virginia sent a Gatling gun to Colonel Faulkner's militia company at Martinsburg, and Mathews used militia to break a miners' strike two years later.

Some newspapers noted the universal role of boys in turning demonstrations into riots, but all they could suggest was "a more rigid family discipline" and perhaps the restoration of corporal punishment in schools. As for tramps, certain western newspapers urged them to go south where the living was easy; and a good many did, much to the annoyance of Southerners. But tramps swarmed north again in the following summer.

In the summer of 1877 a San Francisco printer and free-lance writer took his family across the Golden Gate to Sausalito, between the mountains and the sea, where he studied and loafed and thought. The Great Strike filled his mind. Here was barbarism sprung from civilization, beggars on gaslit streets, more hideous Huns and fiercer Vandals in the shadow of college and library. The tramp had come with the locomotive. For years the tragic paradox had haunted Henry George. Now, in the fiery light of the Pittsburgh railroad yards and the San Francisco docks, he saw it in clear out-line. On September 18 he began a magazine article. It turned into a book, which he called *Progress and Poverty.*

Everywhere the shock of the Great Strike broke old patterns of thought and crystallized new ones. The nation put away childish things, the lead soldiers and toy drums of Reconstruction politics, and, for a season at least, faced a living issue. "The youth of the American Republic is over," wrote Goldwin Smith with the per-spective of an adopted citizen; "maturity, with its burdens, its dif-ficulties, and its anxieties, has come."

Henry Ward Beecher found that out shortly after his sermon of Sunday, July 22, 1877. He had been casting about recently for a theme which might take the public's mind off the adultery charges so nearly proved against him, and he had seized on the current depression. After immersion in the essays of Herbert Spencer he rose up a disciple of Social Darwinism and began spouting that merciless doctrine in a lecture called "Hard Times": the depression is ordained by natural economic law and must be borne by those strong enough to bear it; the rest are better extinct. Came the Pittsburgh riots, and the Reverend Mr. Beecher upended his brimming mind over the congregation of Plymouth Church in Brooklyn. After running through his lecture on political economy, he condemned the strikers for "tyrannical opposition to all law and order."

It is true [he said] that a dollar a day is not enough to support a man and five children, if the man insists on smoking and drinking beer. Is not a dollar a day enough to buy bread? Water costs nothing. [Laughter.] Man cannot live by bread, it is true; but the man who cannot live on bread and water is not fit to live. [Laughter.] ... A family may live on good bread and water in the morning, water and bread at midday, and good water and bread at night. [Continued laughter.] ... The great laws of political economy cannot be set at defiance.

At the end of the sermon the congregation applauded.

Beecher's point of view came naturally to him, to his propertied congregation and to the portly clericalism he represented. The *Congregationalist*, the *Presbyterian Quarterly*, the *Christian Union* all saw one lesson in the riots: that this was no time for mercy. The *Independent*, a Congregational journal closely identified with Beecher in the past, now spoke for all:

If the club of the policeman, knocking out the brains of the rioter, will answer, then well and good; but if it does not promptly meet the exigency, then bullets and bayonets, canister and grape . . . constitute the one remedy . . . Napoleon was right when he said the way to deal with a mob is to exterminate it.

Why, then, should Beecher have expected censure from anyone who mattered?

He may have guessed that the rabble would howl. The *Iron Molders' Journal* called him a "sanctimonious hypocrite." Mobs shouted, "God damn Beecher!" Crude jokes were made about his girth, his peccadilloes and his salary of $20,000 a year with matching lecture fees. For years afterward allusions to the "bread and water" sermon cropped up in the labor press. At Detroit in 1880 trade unionists held a "Workingmen's Banquet à la Henry 'Water and Bread' Beecher."

Beecher must have been surprised and dismayed, however, by the reaction in the camp of his benefactors. The sermon, said the *Commercial and Financial Chronicle*, did not "show either a wise head or feeling heart." The *New York World*, Tom Scott's own, called Beecher's remarks "suicidal and the part of a lunatic." Next Sunday, July 29, Plymouth Church was packed with worshippers, including thirty plain-clothes men. Beecher's efforts to explain himself succeeded all too well. He sank deeper into Spencerian quicksand. After a righteous assault on foreign Communism, he revealed the intentions of God. They were, he said, for "the great to be

great, and the little to be little." It was no man's design but God's
will that the poor must "reap the misfortunes of inferiority." The
fuller explanation did not help, however, and so Beecher gave it all
up and came out instead for the abolition of Hell.

Beecher and his comfortable colleagues did not realize how wide
a crack the Great Strike had started in the foundations of Social
Darwinism. "Whatever else the disturbances have done," said the
New York Times, "at least they have opened the eyes of the American people to the order of things which has grown up among them
so gradually as to be unobserved. . . . Beneath the vicious elements
which produced the riots, the country traces evidence of hardship,
of suffering, of destitution to an extent for which it was unpre-
pared." Middle-class people began at last to realize what "survival
of the fittest" implied, and to reject it. More than that, they began
to question its corollary of rugged individualism. "The laissez-faire
policy has been knocked out of men's heads for the next generation,"
said the *New York Graphic*. "It is the business of the State, that is,
of the people," said *Harper's*, "to prevent disorder of the kind that
we saw in the summer, by removing the discontent which is its
cause." The *Minneapolis Tribune* blurted shamelessly: "We want
the assistance of Uncle Sam."

Many favored compulsory arbitration as a solution. As an advocate thereof, Grand Chief Arthur found himself in strange company:
the *St. Louis Journal, New York Times, Cleveland Leader, Christian
Advocate,* Governor Hartranft of Pennsylvania and Senator Stanley
Mathews of Ohio, one of President Hayes's closest friends. As organized labor came to know the courts, however, it shied away from
government meddling. In 1888 Congress provided for Federal
financing of voluntary arbitration in railroad labor disputes, but
the device was never used.

The Great Strike renewed interest in Congressman Nathaniel P.
Banks's answer to the labor problem. Banks, a Massachusetts man
who had once worked in a textile factory, proposed before the strike
that Congress provide government loans on easy terms to prospective homesteaders, so that penniless workers and their families could
get a start in farming. Pathetic, misspelled letters now came to
Congressman Banks from hopeful workingmen; newspapers and
magazines endorsed the Banks idea; and "colonization societies"
were actually organized in Baltimore and St. Louis. But the Banks

bill never passed, and anyway there were few good homesteads
left in the West and even fewer good farmers among the urban
unemployed.

A demand grew for some kind of Federal regulation of railroads.
During the Great Strike Garrett, Scott, Sidney Dillon of the Union
Pacific, Robert Harris of the Burlington and others had talked and
written a great deal about the duty of the Federal government to
protect interstate railroad traffic. Afterward Scott himself wrote an
article on the subject for the *North American Review*. "Possibly he
does not see that the law desired would be a precedent for quite
another kind of interference," remarked the *New York Journal of
Commerce*. "If Congress makes such a law to please the railroads it
will probably try to balance the account with the people by regu-
lating freight on the lines." The *New York Times, National Republican, Philadelphia Inquirer* and other newspapers began to call for
exactly what the *Journal of Commerce* had warned they might.

Even President Hayes and his Cabinet played with the idea of
railroad regulation. In their meeting of July 31, 1877, John Sherman brought it up by pointing to the magnitude and importance
of railroad traffic as shown by a recently published government
study. This, he suggested, indicated the "need of national action."
Thompson thought any difficulties could be taken care of by agreements among the railroads; but Evarts, for all his railroad associa-
tions, denied this. It was a case for government, not contract, he said.
McCrary, in his days as an Iowa Congressman, had been strong for
Federal rate regulation. He suggested now that the interstate commerce power of Congress covered it. "The country," said Evarts,
"is ready for an exertion of its power."

Hayes was impressed. "The strikes have been put down by *force*;
but now for the real remedy," he wrote in his diary on August 5.
"Can't something be done by education of the strikers, by judicious
control of the capitalists, by wise general policy to end or diminish
the evil? The railroad strikers, as a rule, are good men, sober, intelligent and industrious." A few days later, he wrote to a friend:
"If anything can be done to remove the distress which afflicts
laborers, and to stimulate enterprise, I am ready and not afraid to
do my share towards it." He steered clear of the subject in a series
of speeches in New England that August. But John Sherman dared
to speak out for railroad regulation in a speech at Mansfield, Ohio,

on August 18; and as a supposed administration spokesman, he thereby converted many doubters. The Interstate Commerce Act, though still a decade away, was drifting into sight on the political horizon.

"The party that succeeds for any length of time in this country," said the *Chicago Inter Ocean* that August, "will not be the party of a few thousand selfish autocrats, but the party that strikes hands with toil, that makes common lot with busy workers." And being a Republican newspaper, the *Inter Ocean* begged "the thinking and reflecting men of the Republican party" to "lag not in their recognition of the workingman's claims." The Democrats, too, cocked an ear to the march of events. "It will require all the wisdom we have to deal with this labor question," wrote Editor Barr of the *Pittsburgh Post* to Speaker Randall on August 6.

In Ohio the bidding grew spirited. Meeting in Columbus on July 25, the Democratic state convention came out for currency inflation as a panacea. The Republicans met at Cleveland on August 1. They fondly recalled the Reconstruction issue. A delegate reported "a sort of low, mournful expression of regret at the loss of so good a card for campaign purposes as that old thing was . . . But everybody agreed that it is dead . . . and so we set about inventing something to take its place." The "something" was a platform calling for "statutory arbitration," Federal regulation of railroads and a "National Bureau of Industry," along the lines of the later Department of Labor. Ignoring charges that he was a Communist, the Republican candidate for governor made the labor issue his chief theme. But James Garfield and other key Ohio Republicans were cool toward the platform, and the Republicans lost. (If the votes cast for two small labor parties had gone to the Republicans instead, the Republicans would have won.) After that, Republicans seemed to agree with the *New York Tribune* that the labor movement and the Republican party had nothing in common.

The Democrats likewise saw the risk in such experiments, and the two major parties thereupon resumed their safe and easy shadowboxing with dead issues. Meanwhile labor jumped into politics on its own.

The upper classes had feared something like that. Even before the Great Strike, they had talked of limiting suffrage through poll tax, property, literacy and educational qualifications. After the strike an undercurrent of disillusionment with democracy ran through the private correspondence of such leaders as James Garfield the politician, Emory Upton the military historian and soldier, and Jacob Schiff the financier. "All honest, thoughtful men know that the ballot must be restricted," wrote Judge Walter Gresham to a close friend, "and I suppose that can be done only through blood. . . . Our revolutionary fathers . . . went too far with their notions of popular government. . . . Democracy is now the enemy of law & order & society itself & as such should be denounced. I wish Grant was president." George Vest of Missouri, later a Senator famous for his eulogy on dogs, said in a speech that "universal suffrage is a standing menace to all stable and good government. Its twin sister is the commune with its labor unions, etc." The *St. Louis Post* applauded this, adding that "universal suffrage is played out."

These were vain dreams, of course. Suffrage remained unimpaired. And so in Altoona on July 31, "the faces of the merchants, lawyers, and business men of the city generally wore a look of unutterable woe" at news that a "labor reformer" had won the election for city recorder. The great sensation, however, came from Louisville, where on August 6 the Workingmen's Party of the United States elected five out of seven candidates for the state legislature and won 8,850 votes out of 13,578 cast. Inspired by the news from Louisville, "Workingmen's Parties" sprang up that month in city after city, especially those in which ground had been broken by the Great Strike. "The political striker has taken the place of the railroad striker," said the *Martinsburg Independent*. Some of the local groups were generated by the W.P.U.S., some by the greenbackers, some spontaneously. Local elections in the fall showed the strength of the movement. In December the newly hopeful W.P.U.S. reconstituted itself into the Socialistic Labor Party; in February 1878, at Toledo, labor and greenback elements organized the "National Party," popularly known as the Greenback-Party of California." In other places, hack politicians bored from demagogue Denis Kearney, who set up his own "Workingmen's Labor Party.

The W.P.U.S. or Socialistic Labor Party faced deadly competition for the labor vote. In California, it lost out to the anti-Chinese demagogue Denis Kearney, who set up his own "Workingmen's Party of California." In other places, hack politicians bored from within. The Greenback-Labor Party hurt it most. A million Greenback-Labor votes were cast and fourteen Greenback-Labor congressmen were elected in the fall of 1878, while the Socialistic Labor Party lost momentum. Many of its members begun to suspect that Communism was a hopeless cause in the United States. Some of its leaders went one way, some another. Philip Van Patten and Albert Currlin quit the party and became prosperous capitalists, Van Patten as a merchant and contractor in Little Rock, Arkansas, Currlin as owner of a small newspaper chain in California. Albert Parsons, on the other hand, turned anarchist; and when Chicago police (led by a captain who had been beaten by a mob in 1877) brutally provoked the Haymarket bomb throwing of 1886, Parsons was one of the four men hanged—essentially by the "Board of Trade men" who had threatened him with hanging in 1877. The Red scare of 1877 flared up again in America as it would at intervals for generations.

The greenbackers' victory in the contest for labor votes proved to be a futile one. Greenbackism had an inscrutable attraction for some workingmen, but its greatest appeal was for the farmers. As they had shown during the Great Strike, farmers had little interest in labor's woes; and labor had no craving for higher food prices. The two groups had little in common but their enemies. Inherently weak, the coalition of malcontents rapidly collapsed after the return of prosperity in 1879. The movement had injected some live ideas into American politics, ideas which eventually prevailed. But it did nothing for labor.

Labor in the end took care of itself. "The railroad strike of 1877 was the tocsin that sounded a ringing message of hope to us all," remembered Samuel Gompers nearly fifty years afterward. After the uprising of July, labor knew its strength; and gradually, painfully, it learned how to use it. Existing trade unions, like the brewers and the cigar makers, were stirred into action. "The grand lesson is, however," said the Labor Standard, "that nothing can be accomplished by the working people without a system of perfect national organization"; and in August 1877 the national convention of the iron and steelworkers urged "a federation of trades unions." The Knights of Labor began eight years of phenomenal growth with their first national assembly at Reading, Pennsylvania, on January 1, 1878. But public hysteria after the Haymarket Riot cast them down to destruction from a dizzy peak of 700,000 members, and Samuel Gompers' conservative American Federation of Labor succeeded to their primacy in the American labor movement. The unskilled workers, who had sent up such a shout of rage and pain in 1877, would have to look to a new century for succor.

No one can weigh or even isolate the indirect consequences of the Great Strike. From time to time, however, it echoed clearly in the course of events. In the summer of 1878, as its first anniversary approached, rumors spread of a recurrence. A few Communist groups armed and drilled, tramps grew pestiferous, miners struck in Illinois and West Virginia. In Quebec that June a small-scale repetition did occur, complete with roving mobs, broken windows, a blockaded railroad and a clash with militia which took one life. In a magazine article that July, James Harrison Wilson sounded an alarm and beat the drums for a larger army. The only formal observance of the anniversary, however, was an excursion up the Schuylkill by the "Roundhouse Veterans" of the Philadelphia militia.

Now and then someone talked of "another '77," either in fear or hope. Parsons said much about it in his fatal Haymarket speech. The Great Strike found its way into fiction, ranging from Paul Leicester Ford's *The Honorable Peter Stirling* (1894) to an 1881 volume in Beadle's Dime Library: *Nemo, King of the Tramps; or, The Romany Girl's Vengeance; A Story of the Great Railroad Riots.* Lee Harris' *The Man Who Tramps* (1878), T. S. Denison's *An Iron Crown* (1885), Martin Foran's *The Other Side* (1886) and George T. Dowling's *The Wreckers* (1886) all drew on the Great Strike for plot and character. Most famous was *The Bread-Winners*, a snobbish and fiercely antilabor novel published anonymously in 1884. Its author, John Hay, had once been Abraham Lincoln's private secretary but was now the son-in-law of Amasa Stone, the Cleveland millionaire who had forced a faulty design on the builders of the Ashtabula bridge. Henry F. Keenan tried to answer *The Bread-Winners* with his *The Money-Makers* (1885), nearly as fierce on the other side; but it was *The Bread-Winners* that became a best-seller.

His antilabor expressions in '77 were used against Benjamin Harrison, a spirited leader of Walter Gresham's Committee of Safety, when Harrison ran for President in 1888; but they did not prevent him from being elected, nor from being the first President since Hayes to use Federal troops in a labor dispute (the silver miners' strike at Coeur d'Alene, Idaho, in 1892).

With the outbreak of the Pullman Strike in 1894, memories of '77 came rushing back. Many of the old ingredients were there: railroaders on strike in twenty-seven states and territories; a call for a general strike at Chicago; tramps, hoodlums, depression unemployed and teen-agers stirring up trouble; fine July weather bringing out crowds; dozens killed in rioting. Familiar names reappeared. Eugene Debs, who as a Firemen's Brotherhood official had condemned the 1877 strike, led this one as the 1894 equivalent of Robert Ammon. (Like George Bernard Shaw and others, Debs had been given a turn toward socialism through reading *The Coöperative Commonwealth* by Laurence Gronlund—the "Peter Lofgreen" of the St. Louis W.P.U.S. Executive Committee.) President Grover Cleveland and his attorney general sent Federal troops against the strikers over the protests of the governor of Illinois; and they based their authority on the precedent of Indiana and Missouri in 1877, the troops being sent to enforce Federal court orders. Ex-judge Walter Q. Gresham, who happened now to be Secretary of State, intervened to make sure that the Army (commanded by General John M. Schofield) kept up to the mark.

If Rutherford Hayes had been alive that July, he would have seemed as changed since 1877 as did Eugene Debs. In the middle eighties ex-President Hayes had begun asking himself strange questions: "Shall the railroads govern the country, or shall the people govern the railroads? . . . This is a government of the people, by the people, and for the people no longer. It is a government of corporations, by corporations, and for corporations. How is this?" And he came to the conclusion that "the governmental policy should be to prevent the accumulation of vast fortunes; and monopolies, so dangerous in control, should be held firmly in the grip of the people." By 1894, John Sherman's antitrust act was on the books. Its first great triumph was now at hand—sending Eugene Debs to prison.

No one noticed another tragic irony of that hectic July, though it involved the man who had started the greatest strike of all seventeen years before. Dick Zepp of Martinsburg had not gone back to the B. & O. in 1877, of course, nor to railroading. With his wife and eight children, he moved about from job to job and town to town through the eighties, at last settling down to help work his brother's farm in Maryland. In the spring of 1894 he happened to meet some

B. & O. men, among them the road's chief detective. A few days later he was offered a job as one of the extra detectives the B. & O. was taking on to guard against "Coxey's Army" of unemployed. At last he could come back to the life he loved. He accepted and worked the Rockville-Washington run for a while, disguised as a tramp. Then came the Pullman Strike, and Zepp was sent to Chicago. As he left, he said casually and characteristically to his son Tom: "If I'm going to die, I'll die with my boots on." At five o'clock on the afternoon of July 6, 1894, Dick Zepp fulfilled his prophecy. While he sat in the B. & O.'s Chicago depot awaiting orders, one of a stack of loaded riot guns fell against a radiator and discharged its load into his heart, killing him instantly.

A crowd gathered for a while, but dispersed after the body was removed. More exciting things were happening elsewhere. The Illinois Central yards were burning—the work of tramps and half-grown boys, the papers said. That night, flames swept over 700 cars in the Pan Handle yards. The man who lay dead in a Chicago undertaking parlor would have guessed the end of such a battle: another seeming defeat for labor. He would also have foreseen that, after the battle, labor would fight on.

Notes, Bibliography, Acknowledgments and Index

Notes

TEXT to which the notes refer is indicated below by page and paragraph, the number of the page followed in parentheses by the *final word* of the paragraph. When a paragraph carries over from one page to another, the number of the second page is given here.
Notes referring to passages longer than a single paragraph are located by the numbers of all pages involved and by the final words of all paragraphs covered.

CHAPTER 1

9 (suffered): J. S. Ingram, *The Centennial Exposition* (Philadelphia, 1876), pp. 290, 697, 705-706, 760.

10 (that): Ellen Elizabeth Guillot, *Social Factors in Crime As Explained by American Writers of the Civil War and Post Civil War Period* (Philadelphia, 1943), pp. 70-71. Ellis P. Oberholtzer, *A History of the United States Since the Civil War* (5 vols., New York, 1917-1937), III, 415.

10 (Year): Samuel Hazard, *et al.*, eds., *Pennsylvania Archives* (9 series, 138 vols., Philadelphia and Harrisburg, 1852-1949), Fourth Series, IX, 543-544. Guillot, p. 47.

10 (Irish): Works Progress Administration, comp., *Annals of Cleveland, A Digest and Index of the Newspaper Record of Events and Opinions* (59 vols., Cleveland, 1937-1938), LIX, 230; LVIII, 254 (hereinafter WPA, *Annals*). William A. Dunning, *Reconstruction, Political and Economic*, (New York, 1907), pp. 219, 278-279.

11 (bribery): Guillot, p. 101. Don C. Seitz, *The Dreadful Decade* (Indianapolis, 1926), pp. 200-233. Oberholtzer, *History of the U. S. Since the Civil War*, III, 75, 148-150. Dunning, *Reconstruction, Political and Economic*, pp. 192, 287-290.

11 (cases, purpose): *Ibid.*, pp. 229-233, 259, 292-293.

11 (cash): Quoted in William Graham Sumner, "What Our Boys Are Reading," in *Scribner's Monthly*, March 1878.

12 (Sing Sing): Quoted in Guillot, p. 103.

12 (robbed): *Ibid.*, pp. 67, 107. Ray Allan Billington, *Westward Expansion* (New York, 1949), p. 632.

13 (police): Guillot, pp. 60-63, 65, 67. WPA, *Annals*, LIX, 1229.

13 (1877): New York Society for the Reformation of Juvenile Delinquents: *Fifty-first Annual Report* (New York, 1876), pp. 34-35; *Fifty-fourth Annual Report* (New York, 1879), p. 23.

13 (forth): W. G. Marshall, *Through America; or, Nine Months in the United States* (London, 1881), pp. 268-271.

13 (old): E. J. Kahn, Jr., *The Merry Partners* (New York, 1955), p. 45. Guillot, pp. 68-69.

14 (thoroughfare): WPA, *Annals*, LIX, 1176. Scranton (Pa.) *Republican*, 7/23/77.

14 (literature): Guillot, pp. 31-35. New York Society for . . . Delinquents, *Fifty-second Annual Report* (New York, 1877), p. 37.

14 (afterward): Sumner.

15 (nation): John R. Commons and associates, *History of Labour in the United States* (4 vols., New York, 1921), II, 3-5, 43, 47-48, 71, 74, 76, 81. Bureau of Census, *Historical Statistics of the United States, 1789-1945* (Washington, D.C., 1949), p. 63.

16 (jungle): Richard Hofstadter, *Social Darwinism in American Thought* (Boston, 1955), pp. 31-50.

16 (elsewhere): *Iron Molders' Journal*, XIV (2/9/78), 37-40. *Proceedings of the Second Annual Convention of the National Amalgamated Association of Iron and Steel Workers of the United States* (Pittsburgh, 1877), p. 92 (hereinafter *Proceedings of Iron and Steel Workers*). Massachusetts Bureau of Statistics of Labor, *Tenth Annual Report* (Boston, 1879), p. 124.

16 (got): *Cigar Makers' Journal*, May 1877.

17 (job): Mass. Bureau, *Tenth Annual Report*, pp. 107-108, 135-136.

17 (normal): Commons and associates, II, 103-109.

17 (valor): *Proceedings of the National Forge of the United Sons of Vulcan* (Pittsburgh, 1875), pp. 11-12 (hereinafter *Proceedings of Nat'l. Forge*). Commons and associates, II, 176-177. *Cigar Makers' Journal*, March 1876.

18 (currency): Commons and associates, II, 195-196, 201-202. Philip S. Foner, *History of the Labor Movement in the United States* (New York, 1947), p. 440.

18 (humors): Edward W. Emerson and Waldo E. Forbes, eds., *Journals of Ralph Waldo Emerson* (9 vols., Boston, 1909-1912), VI, 450.

18 (disputes): Hazard, *et al.*, eds., Fourth Series, IX, 426-428, 476-481, 542.

19 (Police): *Ibid.*, 304, 481-482. Hyman Kuritz, "The Pennsylvania State Government and Labor Controls from 1865 to 1922" (unpub-

lished Ph.D. dissertation, Columbia University, 1953), p. 310. Samuel
W. Pennypacker, *The Autobiography of a Pennsylvanian* (Philadelphia, 1918), p. 530.

19 (unemployment): WPA, *Annals*, LIX, 70. Mass. Bureau, *Tenth Annual Report*, p. 88. Bureau of Census, p. 231. 45th Congress, 3rd session, House Document 29, p. 601.

19 (nationally): Arthur G. Auble, "The Depressions of 1873 and 1882
in the United States" (Ph.D. dissertation, Harvard University, 1949),
pp. 28-33. Bureau of Census, p. 64. Mass. Bureau, *Tenth Annual
Report*, pp. 4-6, 9. *The Census of Massachusetts: 1875* (3 vols.,
Boston, 1876-1877), II, 397, 399, 445-446, 518-521, 579-580, 615.

19 (times): O. V. Wells, "The Depression of 1873-1879," in *Agricultural
History*, XI (1937), 243.

20 (month): Overseers of the Poor of the City of Boston (hereinafter
Overseers of Poor), *Eleventh Annual Report* (Boston, 1875), p. 6.
Leah H. Feder, *Unemployment Relief in Periods of Depression* (New
York, 1936), pp. 39-40, 64-66. David M. Schneider and Albert
Deutsch, *The History of Public Welfare in New York State, 1867-
1940* (Chicago, 1941), p. 37. Frank D. Watson, *The Charity Organ-
ization Movement in the United States* (New York, 1922), pp. 89,
173, 176-180, 187.

20 (1,000,000): WPA, *Annals*, LIX, 1212. Foner, p. 443. Guillot, pp.
108-109. *New York Times*, 12/30/77, p. 6.

20 (passage): Allan Pinkerton, *Strikers, Communists, Tramps and Detectives* (New York, 1882), pp. 52-55. Paul Fisher, "A Forgotten
Gentry of the Fourth Estate," in *Journalism Quarterly*, Spring 1956,
pp. 167-169.

21 (assistance): In *Iron Molders' Journal*, XIII: (2/10/77), 238-239;
(3/10/77), 261. *Proceedings of Nat'l. Forge*, p. 11. *Cigar Makers'
Journal*, April, June and December, 1876.

21 (march): *Altoona* (Pa.) *Evening Mirror*, 7/24/77. Pinkerton, p.
60. WPA, *Annals*, LIX, 967.

22 (jails): *Ibid.*: LVIII, 808; LIX, 1032. *Frank Leslie's Illustrated
Newspaper*, 7/21/77. *Cigar Makers' Journal*, March 1877. *New
York Times*, 12/30/77, p. 6.

22 (Less): WPA, *Annals*, LIX, 1172. *Seventh Annual Report of the
State Board of Charities and Reform of the State of Wisconsin* (Madison, 1878), p. 25. *Wheeling* (W. Va.) *Intelligencer*, 6/21/77.

22 (where): WPA, *Annals*: LVIII, 807-808; LIX, 718, 1163. Worcester
(Mass.) Overseers of the Poor, *Annual Report for the Year Ending
November 30, 1877*, p. 6. Guillot, pp. 109-110.

23 (Park): James B. Whipple, "Cleveland in Conflict: A Study in Urban Adolescence, 1876-1900" (unpublished Ph.D. dissertation, Western Reserve University, 1951), pp. 20-21. Henry H. Vivian, *Notes of a Tour in America* (London, 1878), p. 52. John Leng, *America in 1876* (Dundee, Scotland, 1877), pp. 218-219, 224. Jacob A. Riis, *How the Other Half Lives* (New York, 1890), p. 183 (hereinafter Riis, *Other Half*).

23 (table): *Ibid.*, pp. 19, 301. Whipple, p. 20. David Burbank, *City of Little Bread: The St. Louis General Strike of 1877* (St. Louis, 1957), p. 4. Allan Nevins, *The Emergence of Modern America, 1865-1878* (New York, 1927), p. 320 (hereinafter Nevins, *Emergence*). Overseers of Poor, *Thirteenth Annual Report* (Boston, 1877), p. 8.

24 (contemporaries): Jacob A. Riis, *A Ten Years' War* (Boston, 1900) pp. 19, 31-32. Kahn, p. 47.

24 (numbers): *Ibid.*, p. 57. Riis, *Other Half*, pp. 35, 301.

24 (smallpox): Riis, *A Ten Years' War*, pp. 75-76. Riis, *Other Half*, p. 43. Sam B. Warner, Jr., "Public Health Reform and the Depression of 1873-1878," in *Bulletin of the History of Medicine*, November-December 1955, pp. 503, 506-507, 514. Nevins, *Emergence*, pp. 320-323.

24 (recognize): Allan Nevins and Milton H. Thomas, eds., *The Diary of George Templeton Strong* (4 vols., New York, 1952), IV, 96-97.

25 (publicans): Riis, *Other Half*, pp. 11, 13.

25 (theme): Leng, p. 221. Vivian, p. 50. John A. Kouwenhoven, ed., *The Columbia Historical Portrait of New York* (Garden City, 1953), p. 23.

25 (fortune): *Iron Molders' Journal*, XIII (2/10/77), 230.

25 (eighteen): Irvin G. Wyllie, *The Self-Made Man in America: The Myth of Rags to Riches* (New Brunswick, 1954), *passim*. Arthur M. Schlesinger, Jr., *The Crisis of the Old Order* (Boston, 1957), p. 96. Frances W. Gregory and Irene D. New, "The American Industrial Elite in the 1870's," in William Miller, ed., *Men in Business: Essays in the History of Entrepreneurship* (Cambridge, 1952), p. 204.

26 (air): *Iron Molders' Journal*, XIII (3/10/77), 270. Overseers of Poor, *Thirteenth Annual Report* (Boston, 1877), p. 16. Goldwin Smith, "The Labour War in the United States," in *The Contemporary Review*, XXX (September 1877), 537.

27 (classes): C. Vann Woodward, *Reunion and Reaction* (Boston, 1951), pp. 111-112. Samuel J. Randall to Hendrick B. Wright, 2/22/77, in Hendrick B. Wright MSS.

CHAPTER 2

28 (wreckage): Charles Francis Adams, Jr., *Notes on Railroad Accidents* (New York, 1879), pp. 100-104 (hereinafter C. F. Adams, *Railroad Accidents*). *Railroad Gazette*, 5/11/77.

28 (confidence): Tyler Dennett, *John Hay* (New York, 1933), p. 101. *Railway World*, 1/6/77.

29 (strike): *Engineers' Monthly Journal*, XI (February, 1877), 65-78; (June 1877), 263. Massachusetts Railroad Commission, *Ninth Annual Report*, pp. 43-45.

29 (it): *Engineers' Monthly Journal*, XI (June 1877), 258.

29 (wondered): Wayne Andrews, *The Vanderbilt Legend* (New York, 1941), pp. 175-180.

30 (beauty): Walt Whitman, "To a Locomotive in Winter," *Leaves of Grass*.

30 (rhythm): Stewart Holbrook, *The Story of American Railroads* (New York, 1947), pp. 2-3. William Taylor Adams (Oliver Optic, pseud.), *Lightning Express* (Boston, 1870), p. 247.

31 (fed): William B. Sipes, *The Pennsylvania Railroad, Its Origins, Construction and Connections* (Philadelphia, 1875), p. 138. Robert J. Casey and W. A. S. Douglas, *The Lackawanna Story* (New York, 1951), p. 3. William B. Catton, "How Rails Saved a Seaport," in *American Heritage*, February 1957.

31 (1877): George L. Davis, "Greater Pittsburgh's Commercial and Industrial Development, 1850-1900" (unpublished Ph.D. dissertation, University of Pittsburgh, 1952), p. 133. David M. Ellis, "Rivalry Between the New York Central and the Erie Canal," in *New York History* (July 1948), pp. 286-293.

31 (property): Bureau of Census, p. 9.

32 (1871): Rendig Fels, "American Business Cycles, 1865-79," in *American Economic Review*, XLI (June 1951), 326-328.

32 (barons): *Ibid.*, 326. Edward Stanwood, *A History of the Presidency* (Boston, 1906), pp. 336, 344, 347, 350. Solon J. Buck, *The Agrarian Crusade* (New Haven, 1920), pp. 19, 22-23, 43, 47-50. Charles Francis Adams, *Railroads: Their Origin and Problems* (New York, 1878), pp. 128-129 (hereinafter C. F. Adams, *Railroads*).

32 (net): Fels, "Business Cycles," pp. 336-337.

33 (alone): Bureau of Census, pp. 200-201. *Poor's Manual of Railroads for 1878-79*, pp. 1, v. *Philadelphia Inquirer*, 7/16/77.

33 (Railroad): C. F. Adams, *Railroads*, pp. 148-150, 156-157. "Pang-

330   1877: YEAR OF VIOLENCE

born's Chronology," p. 169, in Baltimore & Ohio Railroad Archives. Edward Hungerford, *Men and Iron: The History of the New York Central* (New York, 1938), p. 271 (hereinafter Hungerford, *Men and Iron*). C. F. Adams, *Railroads*, p. 166. Paul E. Felton, "The History of the Atlantic and Great Western Railroad" (unpublished Ph.D. dissertation, University of Pittsburgh, 1944), p. 210.

34 (resort): *Poor's Manual of Railroads for 1877-78*, p. vii. *Railway World*, 3/17/77.

34 (effects): *Idem*. Atchison, Topeka and Santa Fe, *Annual Report*, 1877, pp. 6, 25. T. F. Oakes to C. S. Greeley, 2/8/77, Box 8, in Henry Villard MSS. Chicago and Alton, *Annual Report*, 1877, p. 17. Central Pacific, *Annual Report*, 1877, p. 23.

34 (men): W. H. Osborn to W. K. Ackerman, 4/14/77, in Illinois Central Archives. In Villard MSS.: C. S. Greeley to H. Villard, 2/10/77; T. F. Oakes to C. S. Greeley, 2/8/77.

34 (foreclosure): "Pangborn's Chronology," in B & O Archives. *Wheeling Intelligencer*, 7/18/77. J. S. Morgan to J. W. Garrett, 2/7/77 and 3/21/77, in John W. Garrett MSS. *Railway Age*, 7/12/77.

35 (public): *Engineers' Monthly Journal*, XI (June 1877), 263-264. *Boston Transcript*, 2/13/77. *Boston Advertiser*, 2/13/77. *Railway World*, 2/24/77.

35 (Boston): *Boston Advertiser*, 2/14/77.

35 (strike): *Ibid.*, 2/14/77, 2/15/77.

35 (later): Boston & Maine, *Annual Report*, 1877, pp. 5, 8.

36 (mind): Charles Francis Adams, *Charles Francis Adams, 1835-1915: An Autobiography* (Boston, 1916), pp. 170-173.

36 (prison): *Ibid.*, pp. 174-175. Diary of C. F. Adams II, entry for 2/23/77, in Adams MSS. Mass. Board of RR Commissioners, *Ninth Annual Report*, pp. 155-156. *Railroad Gazette*, 3/30/77.

36 (Illinois): *Engineers' Monthly Journal*, XI (August 1877), 363, 365. *Railroad Gazette*, 3/30/77. U. S. Commissioner of Labor, *Sixteenth Annual Report* (Washington, D.C., 1901), pp. 994-995, 1016, 1022-1023.

37 (bond): Diary of C. F. Adams II, entries for 3/8/77 and 3/9/77 in Adams MSS., Massachusetts Historical Society. Daniel C. Haskell, comp., *The Nation, Volumes 1-105, New York, 1865-1917; Indexes of Titles and Contributors* (New York, 1953), p. 64. *The Nation*, 3/22/77.

37 (*Gazette*): Franklin B. Gowen, "To the Public" (Philadelphia ?, 1877), pp. 1-4. *Engineers' Monthly Journal*, IX (July 1877), 310. *Railroad Gazette*, 4/6/77.

37 (Gowen): *Ibid.*, 4/20/77.

37 (judgment): Marvin W. Schlegel, *Ruler of the Reading: The Life of Franklin B. Gowen, 1836-1889* (Harrisburg, 1947), pp. 7-8, 222-224, 264-265.

38 (years): Jules I. Bogen, *The Anthracite Railroads* (New York, 1927), pp. 51-56.

38 (unions): Schlegel, pp. 21, 63, 76. Gowen, p. 12.

38 ($4,000,000): Schlegel, p. 76. Bogen, p. 54.

39 (*Fear*): Schlegel, chapters VII-XI, *passim*.

39 (Reading, law): *Ibid.*, pp. 151-152, 158.

39 (bread): *Ibid.*, pp. 158-161. Gowen, p. 12.

40 (it): C. F. Adams, *Railroads*, pp. 150-169.

40 (less): J. W. Garrett to J. S. Morgan, 3/9/77, in Garrett MSS.

41 (over): *New York Times*, 4/6/77, 4/30/77, 5/20/77, 6/9/77.

41 (immediately): *Railroad Gazette*, 4/27/77.

41 (turns): *Ibid.*, 3/30/77, 4/20/77. *Pittsburgh Post*, 7/22/87.

42 (proven): *Report of the Committee Appointed to Investigate the Railroad Riots in July, 1877* (Harrisburg, 1878), pp. 928-929 (hereinafter *Report of Riots Committee*). Allan Nevins, *Study in Power: John D. Rockefeller, Industrialist and Philanthropist* (2 vols., New York, 1953), I, 386-387 (hereinafter Nevins, *Study*).

42 (quietly): *New York Times*, 4/9/77. In Illinois Central Railroad Archives: W. K. Ackerman to W. H. Osborn, 4/28/77; Ackerman to J. W. Wootten, 6/8/77. J. E. Wootten to W. B. Strong, 5/8/77, in Chicago, Burlington & Quincy (hereinafter Burlington) Railroad Archives. *St. Louis Times*, 7/24/77.

42 (Panic): *Report of Riots Committee*, p. 697.

CHAPTER 3

43 (Jackson): H. W. Schotter, *The Growth and Development of the Pennsylvania Railroad Company* (Philadelphia, 1927), pp. 170-171.

43 (scope): Sipes, pp. 23, 251-253. George H. Burgess and Miles C. Kennedy, *Centennial History of the Pennsylvania Railroad Company, 1846-1946* (Philadelphia, 1949), pp. 318-319.

44 ($330): *Easton* (Pa.) *Express*, 7/25/77, 7/27/77, 8/3/77. Gowen, p. 11. *Wheeling* (W. Va.) *Intelligencer*, 6/25/77. *Railroad Gazette*, 7/20/77. *Wheeling Register*, 7/31/77. United States Bureau of Labor Statistics, Bulletin No. 604, *History of Wages in the United States from Colonial Times to 1928* (Washington, D.C., 1934), p. 430. George Stark to the Board of Directors, 7/1/77, in Northern Pacific Railroad Archives. Illinois Railroad and Warehouse Commission: *Seventh Annual Report 1878*, p. ix; *Eighth Annual Report 1879*, p. xii.

44 (cheaper): Holbrook, p. 267. *Railroad Gazette*, IX (7/20/77), 328. Edwin P. Alexander, *The Pennsylvania Railroad: A Pictorial History* (New York, 1947), p. 93.

45 (death): *Wheeling Intelligencer*, 7/20/77. C. F. Adams, *Railroad Accidents*, p. 243.

45 (conduct): Sipes, p. 255.

45 (none): Emory R. Johnson, "Railway Departments for the Relief and Insurance of Employes," in *Annals of the American Academy of Political and Social Science*, November 1895, p. 69. *Engineers' Monthly Journal*, XI (February 1877), 75.

46 (bricklayers): Sipes, pp. 261-262, 264. U.S. Bureau of Statistics of Labor, pp. 432. Ill. RR. and Warehouse Commission, *Eighth Annual Report*, p. xii. Gowen, p. 11.

46 ($493): U.S. Bureau of Statistics of Labor, p. 441. *Wheeling Register*, 7/31/77. *Railroad Gazette*, 6/1/77, 7/20/77. *Easton Express*, 7/25/77, 8/3/77.

46 (firemen): *Wheeling Intelligencer*, 7/20/77. Sipes, pp. 267-268.

46 (road): U.S. Bureau of Statistics of Labor, p. 438. *Railroad Gazette*, 6/1/77. *Easton Express*, 7/25/77. Gowen, p. 11. *Wheeling Register*, 7/31/77. In Burlington Archives: R. Harris to J. Griswold, 7/9/77; R. Harris to J. Forbes, 8/2/77. Ill. RR. and Warehouse Commission: *Seventh Annual Report*, p. ix; *Eighth Annual Report*, p. xii.

47 (plumbers): R. Harris to J. M. Forbes, 7/31/77, in Burlington Archives. U.S. Bureau of Statistics of Labor, *passim*.

47 (money): Thomas A. Scott, "The Recent Strikes," in *North American Review*, CXXV (September 1877), 354. *Report of Riots Committee*, pp. 345, 498-499, 581.

47 (grievance): *New York Times*, 5/24/77. *Report of Riots Committee*, pp. 60, 74, 558, 579.

48 (strike): *New York Times*, 5/24/77, 5/25/77, 5/29/77. *Pittsburgh Post*, 6/7/77.

48, 49 (Scott-free, president): Burgess and Kennedy, pp. 341-347, 349.

49 (legislatures): Quoted in Henry D. Lloyd, *Wealth Against Commonwealth* (New York, 1894), p. 147, and in Woodward, p. 69.

49 (car): Harry Barnard, *Rutherford B. Hayes and His America* (Indianapolis, 1954), p. 403 (hereinafter Barnard, *Hayes*). My summary of Scott's role in the disputed election is based on Woodward, *passim*.

50 (all): Barnard, *Hayes*, p. 410.

50 (abolished): *Pittsburgh Post*, 6/7/77, 7/8/77. *Report of Riots Committee*, p. 925.

51 (again): *Ibid. Railroad Gazette*, 5/4/77.

51 (reductions): *Wheeling Intelligencer,* 7/3/77. *Railroad Gazette,* 7/13/77. *Engineers' Monthly Journal,* XI (July 1877), 316.

51 (call): *Pittsburgh Post,* 6/7/77.

52 (worth): *New York Times,* 6/2/77, 6/3/77, 6/5/77.

52 (hour): *Irish World,* 6/30/77.

52 (trains): *New York Times,* 5/24/77, 5/25/77. *Easton Express,* 7/27/77. *Bethlehem* (Pa.) *Daily Times,* 6/1/77, 6/2/77.

52 (futile): *New York Times,* 6/29/77, 6/30/77, 7/2/77. Memorandum from H. B. Ledyard, 6/30/77, in James F. Joy MSS. *Omaha Republican,* 7/1/77.

53 (know): Hungerford, *Men and Iron,* pp. 290-291. *Poor's Manual of Railroads for 1878-1879,* p. xiv. New York Central and Hudson River Railroad, "Minutes of Directors and Executive Committee," II, 110-112, in New York Central Railroad Archives.

53 (Central): Edward N. Mott, *Between the Ocean and the Lakes: The Story of Erie* (New York, 1901), pp. 238, 485. *Poor's Manual of Railroads for 1878-1879,* p. xiv. *Railroad Gazette,* 7/20/77.

53 (bill): *New York Times,* 6/29/77. Edward Hungerford, *Men of Erie* (New York, 1947), p. 203. *The Catholic Union,* 8/23/77. James D. McCabe (Edward W. Martin, pseud.), *The History of the Great Riots* (Philadelphia, 1877), p. 231.

54 (salary): Mott, pp. 231, 470. Hugh J. Jewett, *Speech of Hon. H. J. Jewett to the Muskingum County Democratic Club . . . July 5, 1867,* leaflet in the Library of Congress, *passim.*

54 (dollars): *New York Times,* 6/29/77. *Buffalo Commercial Advertiser,* 7/30/77. Mott, pp. 437-438.

54 (nation): *New York Times,* 5/26/77, 6/29/77. Mott, p. 231. *New York World,* 7/2/77.

55 (militia): *The Catholic Union,* 8/23/77. "Minutes of the Board of Directors," p. 179, Secretary's Office, Erie Railroad Company, Cleveland. *New York World,* 7/2/77.

55 (inexpedient): In No. Pac. Archives: George Stark to the Directors of the Northern Pacific, 7/1/77; "Minute Book of Board Meetings," 7/18/77.

55 (20%): J. N. A. Griswold to R. Harris, 6/14/77, in Burlington Archives.

55 (men): In Burlington Archives: R. Harris to J. N. A. Griswold, 6/21/77; R. Harris to C. E. Perkins, 6/21/77; W. B. Strong to C. E. Perkins, 6/21/77.

56 (leave): In Burlington Archives: W. B. Strong to C. E. Perkins, 6/21/77; R. Harris to J. N. A. Griswold, 6/26/77; J. N. A. Griswold to R. Harris, 7/7/77.

334 1877: YEAR OF VIOLENCE

56 (railroad): Thomas C. Cochran, *Railroad Leaders, 1845-1890* (Cambridge, 1951), p. 220. Sanford D. Gordon, "Public Opinion as a Factor in the Emergence of a National Anti-Trust Program, 1873-1890" (unpublished Ph.D. dissertation, New York University, 1954), pp. 23, 80-81, 379.

57 (paper): In Cunningham-Overton Collection (Letterbook III, 387-388, 397-399, 466-468): an essay, "Supply and Demand," 8/6/77; C. E. Perkins to W. Dexter, 10/1/77; memorandum by C. E. Perkins, c. July 1877.

57 (again): *Scranton Republican*, 7/16/77. Cochran, pp. 179-180. *Wheeling Intelligencer*, 7/20/77. 48th Congress, Senate Committee on Education and Labor, *Report of the Committee of the Senate upon the Relations Between Labor and Capital* (5 vols., Washington, D.C., 1885), I, 115, 154, 317. Robert E. Carr to Henry Villard, 8/2/77, in Villard MSS.

57 (men): J. West to F. P. Howland, c. June 1877, CBQ 33 1870 8.31, in Burlington Archives.

58 (spring): Allan Pinkerton to George Bangs, 3/30/77, in Pinkerton MSS.

CHAPTER 4

59 (labor): *Report of Riots Committee*, pp. 671, 673-674. *Pittsburgh Post*, 7/22/87.

60 (birthday): Roscoe A. Ammon, Swarthmore, Pa., son of Robert Ammon, to author, January 12, 1958. Mrs. W. K. (Freda A.) Boger, Cliffside Park, N. J., daughter of Robert Ammon, to author, January 7, 1958. *The Biographical Encyclopedia of Pennsylvania of the Nineteenth Century* (Philadelphia, 1874), p. 536.

60 (down): *Report of Riots Committee*, pp. 684, 829, 953. *Biographical Encyclopedia of Pennsylvania*, p. 536. "Student Record Book, 1865-1881, in Pitt Archives, Darlington Library, University of Pittsburgh. "Register of Enlistments, 1868," Records of the Adjutant General's Office, Record Group 94, National Archives.

61 (domesticity): *New York World*, 8/1/77. *Record of Riots Committee*, p. 682. *Pittsburgh Post*, 7/26/77.

61 (history): *Record of Riots Committee*, pp. 207, 683-684, 952.

61 (union): *Engineers' Monthly Journal*, XI (July 1877), 316-317.

62 (papers): *Record of Riots Committee*, pp. 75, 106, 138, 952. *Pittsburgh Post*, 6/7/77. *Pittsburgh Chronicle*, 6/23/77, 6/26/77.

62 (there): *Report of Riots Committee*, p. 951.

62 (reply): *Report of Riots Committee*, pp. 672, 952. *Pittsburgh Chronicle*, 6/27/77.

63 (away): *Ibid.*, 6/27/77, 6/28/77.

63 (ever): *Ibid.*, 6/28/77. *Report of Riots Committee*, pp. 206, 672-673.

63 (I): *Wheeling Intelligencer*, 7/4/77. J. Sherman to J. A. Garfield (date missing but filed with letters of 7/24/77), in James A. Garfield MSS.

63 (1877): Edward Hungerford, *The Story of the Baltimore & Ohio Railroad, 1827-1927* (2 vols., New York, 1928), II, 131-132. "Pangborn's Chronology," 3/30/77, in B & O Archives. *Ibid.*, range of B & O stock, 1877.

64 (you): In Garrett MSS.: J. W. Garrett to J. S. Morgan, 3/9/77, 5/2/77; J. S. Morgan to J. W. Garrett, 6/16/77, 6/28/77, 6/30/77.

64 (obliged): *Tiffin* (O.) *Tribune*, 12/17/74. In John W. Garrett Letters, B & O Employee Library (Baltimore): J. W. Garrett to William P. Smith, 9/2/63, 9/4/63; J. W. Garrett to W. H. Emory, 8/1/65; J. W. Garrett to W. C. Quincy, 8/1/65. (Copies of the foregoing were generously furnished me by Mr. William B. Catton.)

64 (vacation): *Wheeling Register*, 7/18/77, 7/20/77. "Minute Book J," p. 306, in B & O Archives.

65 (bridge): *Ibid.*, pp. 289, 305-306, 312. *Wheeling Register*, 7/18/77.

65 (fired): *Wheeling Intelligencer*, 6/15/77, 7/19/77, 7/20/77. *Wheeling Register*, 7/21/77.

65 (command): *Wheeling Intelligencer*, 7/18/77. *Baltimore Evening Bulletin*, 7/16/77. Notation on an envelope containing the key to a cipher, c. July 1877, in Garrett MSS.

65 (peak): Schneider and Deutsch, pp. 41, 44-45.

66 (earlier): *Wheeling Intelligencer*, 7/4/77. *Workingman's Advocate*, 5/5/77.

66 (sick): *Cigar Makers' Journal*, May 1877.

66 (Gowen): *Labor Standard*, 6/30/77. A. Pinkerton to G. Bangs, 3/30/77, in Pinkerton MSS.

67 (before): U.S. Commissioner of Labor, pp. 761-763. *Wheeling Intelligencer*, 6/12/77, 6/21/77, 6/25/77. *Iron Molders' Journal*, XIII (1877), 227, 239-240, 336, 386-387, 546-547.

67 (gallows): *Workingman's Advocate*, 5/19/77. *Pittsburgh Chronicle*, 6/21/77.

67 (you): *New York World*, 7/6/77, *Irish World*, 6/30/77.

68 (side): *New York Times*, 7/13/77. *Philadelphia Record*, 7/16/77. Robertus Love, *The Rise and Fall of Jesse James* (New York, 1926),

pp. 293, 295. *New York Sun*, 6/26/77. *New York World*, 7/6/77, 7/14/77. *Martinsburg* (W. Va.) *Independent*, 6/16/77, 6/30/77. *Pittsburgh Chronicle*, 6/30/77.

68 (patrols): *Chicago Post*, 7/18/77. *Pittsburgh Commercial Gazette*, 7/12/77. *Pittsburgh Chronicle*, 6/15/77, 6/25/77. *Harrisburg Independent*, 7/20/77. *Wheeling Intelligencer*, 7/26/77.

68 (seriously): *Iron Molders' Journal*, 7/10/77. Harry Barnard, *Eagle Forgotten: The Life of John Peter Altgeld* (Indianapolis, 1938), p. 54. *Indianapolis Sun*, 8/4/77.

69 (society): *Harrisburg Telegraph*, 7/19/77. *Wheeling Intelligencer*, 6/30/77, 7/14/77. *Pittsburgh Commercial Gazette*, 7/12/77. *Pittsburgh Chronicle*, 6/15/77. *Philadelphia Record*, 7/16/77. *Philadelphia Inquirer*, 7/23/77. *New York Times*, 7/10/77, 7/18/77. *Buffalo Commercial Advertiser*, 7/19/77.

69 (one): Bureau of Census, pp. 9, 29, 63.

69 (gratefully): Wells, pp. 243, 245. *Railroad Gazette*, 1/4/78.

70 (share): *New York Times*, 7/20/77.

70 (summer): *Wheeling Intelligencer*, 5/16/77, 7/4/77. Johannsen, *Beadle and Adams*, I, 62. *Pittsburgh Chronicle*, 6/19/77. *New York World*, 7/5/77.

71 (all): Pinkerton, pp. 140-141. *Report of Riots Committee*, p. 684.

71 (amusements): *Martinsburg Independent*, 6/30/77, 7/7/77.

71 (cut): Work Projects Administration, *Calendar of the Henry Mason Mathews Letters and Papers* (Charleston, W. Va., 1941), p. 30 (hereinafter WPA, *Mathews Papers*).

71 (day): *Martinsburg Independent*, 7/14/77. Diary of Louis P. Gratacap, entry for 7/27/77, New York Library MSS. room. "Jackson" to S. Cameron, 8/5/77, Simon Cameron MSS., Library of Congress.

72 (song): *Rochester* (N.Y.) *Evening Express*, 7/16/77. *Syracuse Journal*, 7/16/77. Gratacap diary, entry for 7/27/77.

72 (commissioner): *New York Times*, 7/12/77, 7/16/77. George Campbell, *White and Black, the Outcome of a Visit to the United States* (New York, 1879), p. 257. *Wheeling Intelligencer*, 5/28/77, 6/18/77. Marshall, p. 32. WPA, *Annals*, LIX, 1043.

73 (July 25): *New York Times*, quoted in *Wheeling Intelligencer*, 7/4/77. *Philadelphia Inquirer*, 7/17/77. *Pittsburgh Commercial Gazette*, 7/4/77, 7/14/77, 7/18/77. *New York World*, 7/12/77. *Easton Express*, 7/20/77.

73 (enviously): *Pittsburgh Post*, 7/19/77. *Rocky Mountain News* (Denver), 7/26/77. *Report of Riots Committee*, pp. 593-594.

73 (crops): *New York Times*, 7/14/77.

CHAPTER 5

74 (necessary): F. Vernon Aler, *Aler's History of Martinsburg and Berkeley County, West Virginia* (Hagerstown, Md., 1888), pp. 301-304.

74 (July 11): *Report of Riots Committee*, p. 684. *Martinsburg Independent*, 7/21/77.

75 (led): Conversations between the author and Mr. T. Raymond Zepp of Washington, D.C., son of Richard Zepp, December 1957. Joseph A. Dacus, *Annals of the Great Strikes in the United States* (Chicago, 1877), pp. 49-50.

75 (filled): *Baltimore Evening Bulletin*, 7/16/77. *Baltimore Sun*, 7/16/77. Clifton K. Yearley, Jr., "The Baltimore and Ohio Railroad Strike of 1877," in *Maryland Historical Magazine*, LI (September 1956), 194.

75 (point): Aler, p. 303. *Wheeling Register*, 7/20/77. *Wheeling Intelligencer*, 7/20/77.

76 (had): Aler, p. 303.

76 (day): *Ibid.*, pp. 303-305. *Wheeling Register*, 7/17/77.

76 (life): T. H. Garrett to J. W. Garrett, 7/16/77, in Garrett MSS. *Baltimore News*, 7/17/77.

77 (in); *Wheeling Intelligencer*, 7/18/77. WPA, *Mathews Papers*, pp. 30-32. Aler, p. 306.

77 (up): *Baltimore News*, 7/17/77. U.S. Army Signal Service meteorological report for Baltimore, July 1877, in the Records of the Department of Agriculture, National Archives: hereinafter, allusions to weather conditions—temperature, humidity, wind force and direction, cloud formation and coverage, rainfall and other weather phenomena —may be assumed, unless otherwise stated, to come from similar reports of the Signal Service for the localities involved.

77 (orders): Aler, pp. 307-308. Pinkerton, pp. 149-150. Hungerford, *B & O RR*, II, 135.

77 (family): Aler, pp. 308-309.

78 (cartridges, arm): *Wheeling Register*, 7/19/77.

78 (fire): *Martinsburg Independent*, 7/28/77, 8/4/77.

79 (orders): *Wheeling Register*, 7/19/77.

79 (Guards): WPA, *Mathews Papers*, p. 34. James M. Callahan, *Semi-Centennial History of West Virginia* (Morgantown ?, 1913), p. 237. *Wheeling Register*, 7/19/77.

79 (glory): *Wheeling Intelligencer,* 5/29/77, 6/18/77, 7/9/77, 7/13/77, 7/17/77, 7/18/77.

80 (mill): *Wheeling Register,* 7/18/77, 7/24/77. *Wheeling Intelligencer,* 7/18/77.

80 (1865, insufficient): WPA, *Mathews Papers,* pp. 36-37.

80 (press): *Ibid.,* p. 37. *Wheeling Register,* 7/18/77. *Wheeling Intelligencer,* 7/18/77.

81 (reporter): *Wheeling Register,* 7/18/77, 7/19/77.

82 (Wheeling): *Ibid.,* 7/19/77.

82 (Grafton): National Archives, Adjutant General's Office, Letters Received, 1877, #8035 (enclosure 80).

82 (then): *Wheeling Register,* 7/18/77. *New York World,* 7/18/77.

82 (troops): *Wheeling Register,* 7/18/77, 7/19/77. *Baltimore Sun,* 7/18/77.

83 (aid): *Wheeling Register,* 7/19/77. *Wheeling Intelligencer,* 7/19/77.

84 (whispers, already): *Baltimore Sun,* 7/19/77. *Wheeling Register,* 7/19/77.

84 (requirement): *Ibid.*

85 (West. Va.): *Martinsburg Independent,* 7/21/77. *Wheeling Register,* 7/19/77.

85 (times): *Ibid.*

86 (ferocious, intelligence): Barnard, *Hayes,* pp. 41, 73, 83, 91, 138, 156, 219, 233, 237.

87 (sun): *Ibid.,* pp. 45, 113, 234, 246. Vernon L. Parrington, *Main Currents in American Thought* (3 vols., New York, 1927), III, 74.

87 (courts): Diary of John Bigelow, entry for 6/13/77, in John Bigelow MSS. John Bigelow, *The Life of Samuel J. Tilden* (2 vols., New York, 1895), II, 119. Barnard, *Hayes,* pp. 439, 467.

88 (wreck): *New York Sun,* 6/25/77. *Wheeling Register,* 7/18/77.

88 (war): *Pittsburgh Post,* 5/16/77, 5/21/77. *Baltimore Evening Bulletin,* 5/8/77, quoting the *New York Tribune. Appletons' Annual Cyclopedia and Register of Important Events of the Year 1877* (New York, 1878), p. 38. Major General Philip Sheridan, *Annual Report of the Military Division of the Missouri for 1877,* printed copy in Philip Sheridan MSS., Library of Congress.

89 (anyway): *New York World,* 7/7/77. AGO, Ltrs. Rec'd. 1877, #4690. *Cumberland* (Md.) *Civilian,* 7/29/77.

89 (it): *Iron Molders' Journal,* XIII (3/10/77), 275.

89 (votes): Charles R. Williams, ed., *Diary and Letters of Rutherford Birchard Hayes* (5 vols., Columbus, 1922-1926), III, 314, 319. WPA, *Annals,* LIX, 729.

90 (it): Barnard, *Hayes,* pp. 310, 412.
90 (familiar): Richard B. Morris, "Andrew Jackson, Strikebreaker," in
   The American Historical Review, LV (October 1949), 54-68 *passim.*
   Marlin S. Reichley, "Federal Military Intervention in Civil Disturbances" (unpublished Ph.D. dissertation, Georgetown University,
   1939), pp. 119-120, 181-186, 196. *New Orleans Times,* 7/24/77.
91 (him): *Wheeling Register,* 7/19/77.
91 (out): AGO, Ltrs. Rec'd., 1877, #4064.
91 (baiters): Diary of John Bigelow, entry for 7/27/77, in Bigelow
   MSS.
91 (together): Williams, p. 427. Reichley, pp. 181-186, 196.

CHAPTER 6

93 (insurrection): *Wheeling Register,* 7/19/77.
93 (say): *Ibid.,* 7/19/77, 7/20/77.
94 (did): National Archives, Records of U.S. Army Commands, Military
   Division of the Atlantic, Register of Letters Received, 1877, #3734,
   3815. *Wheeling Register,* 7/19/77. Clarence C. Buel and Robert U.
   Johnson, eds., *Battles and Leaders of the Civil War* (4 vols., New
   York, 1887), II, 182, 645, 684; III, 108; IV, 88-91.
94 (order): *Wheeling Register,* 7/19/77. AGO, Ltrs. Rec'd., 1877,
   #4064, 4096. *New York World,* 7/20/77.
94 (opposition): *Wheeling Register,* 7/20/77.
95 (out): *Ibid.* Conversation on December 12, 1956, with Mrs. E. G.
   Lemaster, daughter of George Zepp, at her home in Martinsburg,
   West Virginia.
95 (ended): *Wheeling Register,* 7/20/77, 7/21/77. AGO, Ltrs. Rec'd.,
   1877, #4127.
96 (ceased): A. Brown & Sons to E. Ballinger, 7/25/77, General Letter-
   books, Alexander Brown and Sons MSS., Library of Congress. "Pangborn's Chronology," 6/14/77 and p. 170, in B & O Archives. *Cumberland Civilian,* 6/17/77, 6/24/77, 7/1/77.
96 (Martinsburg): *Wheeling Register,* 7/20/77, 7/21/77, 7/24/77.
   Cumberland Civilian, 7/22/77.
97 (brakemen): *Wheeling Register,* 7/20/77.
97 (said): *Ibid.,* 7/20/77, 7/21/77.
97 (Grafton): *Ibid.,* 7/19/77, 7/20/77, 7/21/77.
97 (interruptions): *Wheeling Intelligencer,* 7/21/77, 7/23/77,
   7/24/77. *Wheeling Register,* 7/21/77.
98 (molestation): *Wheeling Intelligencer,* 7/23/77. *Cumberland Civilian,* 7/22/77.

98 (here): *Wheeling Intelligencer*, 7/21/77, 7/23/77. *Wheeling Register*, 7/21/77.
99 (city): *Ibid. Wheeling Intelligencer*, 7/21/77, 7/23/77. *Cumberland* (Md.) *Daily News*, 7/14/77, 7/16/77, 7/17/77, 7/18/77.
99 (mob): *Wheeling Intelligencer*, 6/22/77, 6/25/77, 7/17/77, 7/21/77, 7/23/77. *Wheeling Register*, 7/21/77. *Cumberland Daily News*, 7/11/77, 7/19/77, 7/21/77. *Cumberland Civilian*, 7/22/77.
100 (Road): *Ibid.*
100 (enough): Charles Hirschfeld, *Baltimore, 1870-1900: Studies in Social History* (Baltimore, 1941), pp. 32, 40, 54.
101 (raise): *Ibid.*, pp. 41, 42, 66. *Baltimore Sun*, 7/16/77, 7/19/88. *Baltimore Evening Bulletin*, 7/16/77. *Baltimore News*, 7/16/77, 7/17/77.
101 (repressed): *Philadelphia Inquirer*, 7/23/77. *Baltimore Evening Bulletin*, 7/17/77, 7/18/77.
101 (July 20): *Baltimore Sun*, 7/21/77. Yearley, p. 202.
102 (o'clock): *Baltimore Sun*, 7/21/77.
102 (citizens): *Ibid.*, 7/19/77, 7/21/77.
102 (hack): *Ibid.*, 7/21/77, 7/31/77.
102 (call): *Ibid.*, 7/21/77.
103 (killed): *Baltimore American*, 7/21/77. *Baltimore Gazette*, 7/21/77.
104 (fruit): *Baltimore Sun*, 7/21/77, 7/31/77. *Baltimore Evening Bulletin*, 7/21/77.
104 (nerve): *Baltimore Sun*, 7/21/77.
105 (bruises): *Baltimore Gazette*, 7/21/77. *Baltimore Sun*, 8/2/77.
105 (shots): *Baltimore Gazette*, 7/21/77.
105 (fear): *Baltimore American*, 7/21/77. *Baltimore Gazette*, 7/21/77. *Baltimore Sun*, 7/31/77.
106 (corner): *Baltimore Daily News*, 7/21/77.
106 (then): *Baltimore American*, 7/21/77. *Baltimore Gazette*, 7/21/77.
106 (stoned): *Ibid.*
106 (replying): *Baltimore American*, 7/21/77. *Baltimore Gazette*, 7/21/77.
107 (funeral, thighs): *Baltimore Daily News*, 7/21/77.
107 (march): *Baltimore Gazette*, 7/21/77. *Baltimore American*, 7/21/77. *Baltimore Sun*, 7/21/77.
108 (side): *Baltimore Gazette*, 7/21/77. *Baltimore American*, 7/21/77. *Baltimore Sun*, 7/31/77, 8/2/77. *Baltimore Daily News*, 7/21/77.
108 (strikers): *New York Times*, 7/21/77, 7/22/77. *Baltimore Daily News*, 7/21/77. *Baltimore Evening Bulletin*, 7/23/77.
108 (haven): *Baltimore Sun*, 7/21/77. My remarks about Camden Station, which still stands, and about other buildings of the time are

based in part on contemporary drawings and in part on a retracing on foot of the routes taken by each regiment.

109 (down): *Baltimore Gazette*, 7/21/77. *Baltimore American*, 7/21/77. *Baltimore Sun*, 7/21/77.

109 (Baltimore): *Baltimore Gazette*, 7/21/77. *Baltimore American*, 7/21/77. J. King to J. Garrett, 7/20/77, in Garrett MSS.

110 (before): *Baltimore Sun*, 7/21/77. *Baltimore American*, 7/21/77.

110 (Harbor): Yearley, p. 205. T. Vincent to W. Barry, 2:35 A.M., 7/21/77, in William F. Barry MSS. National Archives, Records of U.S. Army Commands, Division of the Atlantic, Register of Letters Received, 1877, #3783-3787.

110 (rear): *Baltimore Sun*, 7/21/77. AGO, Ltrs. Rec'd., 1877, #4167.

111 (campaign): *Baltimore Sun*, 7/22/77. AGO, Ltrs. Rec'd., 1877, #3797.

112 (Yard): J. King to J. Garrett, 7/21/77, in Garrett MSS. In Barry MSS.: W. Clements to W. Barry, 7/21/77. J. Carroll to W. Barry, 7/21/77. AGO, Ltrs. Rec'd., 1877, #3783-3787, 4148. In Barry MSS.: J. King to W. Barry, 7/20/77; J. Thomas to W. Barry, "Midnight" (no date) and 7/21/77.

112 (anticlimax): *Baltimore American*, 7/23/77. *Baltimore Sun*, 7/22/77, 7/23/77.

112 (attention): *Baltimore American*, 7/23/77.

113 (dispersed): *Baltimore Sun*, 7/23/77.

113 (bloodshed): *Baltimore American*, 7/23/77. *Baltimore Sun*, 7/23/77. AGO, Ltrs. Rec'd., 1877, #4192. Diary of Henry L. Abbott, entry for 7/22/77 (Houghton Library, Harvard University).

113 (unbroken): AGO, Ltrs. Rec'd., 1877, #4155. *Baltimore Sun*, 7/23/77.

114 (boys): Cornelius B. Hite to Mrs. Hite, 7/27/77, in Cornelius Baldwin Hite MSS. Talbot Albert to Alexander Bliss, 7/26/77, in George Bancroft MSS., Library of Congress. *Baltimore American*, 7/21/77.

114 (responsibility): *Philadelphia Inquirer*, 7/23/77. *Baltimore American*, 7/23/77.

114 (Company): W. H. Joliffe to J. W. Garrett, 7/22/77, in Garrett MSS. H. R. Riddle to Thurlow Weed, 7/27/77, in Thurlow Weed MSS.

CHAPTER 7

115 (1877): William B. Wilson, *History of the Pennsylvania Railroad Company* (2 vols., Philadelphia, 1895), II, 116, 118. Andrew Carnegie, *Autobiography of Andrew Carnegie*, pp. 42, 66, 189.

115 (buildings): *Ibid.*, pp. 44, 49.

116 (brakemen): *Pittsburgh Commercial Gazette*, 7/20/77. *Report of Riots Committee*, pp. 59-60, 104, 696.

116 (later): *Ibid.*, pp. 60, 106, 138, 444, 581.

116 (times): Pinkerton, p. 217. *Pittsburgh Commercial Gazette*, 7/16/77.

117, 118 (all, good, New Jersey, back): *Report of Riots Committee*, pp. 50, 60, 98, 180, 183-184, 189, 219, 231, 439-440, 502, 661, 695, 925.

118 (double-header): *Ibid.*, pp. 75, 577. *Pittsburgh Commercial Gazette*, 7/19/77.

118, 119 (history, developments, leave): *Report of Riots Committee*, pp. 75-77, 85, 92, 95, 104-106, 120-121, 139, 250, 409, 464, 579-580.

119 (Baltimore): *Ibid.*, pp. 97, 105, 143, 145-146, 440.

120 (1876): Davis, pp. 114, 181, 188. Vivian, p. 63. *Railway World*, XXI (March 1877), 248.

120 (July 19): *Vulcan Record* (1875), pp. 12-16, 32-33. *Proceedings of Iron and Steel Workers*, pp. 46-47. *Report of Riots Committee*, pp. 393, 510. *Railway World*, 3/13/75. *Pittsburgh Commercial Gazette*, 7/19/77.

121 (discrimination): *Pittsburgh Post*, 6/6/77.

121 (corporation): Vivian, p. 66. Henry O. Evans, "Notes on Pittsburgh Transportation to 1890," in *Western Pennsylvania Historical Magazine*, September 1941, pp. 171, 175. Samuel H. Church, *A Short History of Pittsburgh, 1748-1908* (New York, 1908), p. 61. *Pittsburgh Post*, 6/6/77. *Pittsburgh Post-Gazette*, September 26, 1936. *Pittsburgh Commercial Gazette*, 7/10/77 and 7/11/77 to 7/21/77 passim. *Report of Riots Committee*, pp. 273-274.

122 (Company): *Pittsburgh Gazette-Times*, December 7, 1913. *Report of Riots Committee*, p. 76.

122 (men): James H. Thompson, "A Financial History of the City of Pittsburgh, 1816-1910" (Ph.D. dissertation, Pittsburgh University, 1949), pp. 191-192, 214, 219. *Report of Riots Committee*, pp. 153, 388, 512. *Pittsburgh Post*, 5/16/77.

122, 123, 124, 125 (detective, Wilkinsburg, police, said, Torrens, guidance, trouble): *Report of Riots Committee*, pp. 76-78, 96, 108, 115, 139-141, 143-144, 146-147, 156, 158, 162, 200-205, 224, 389, 491, 566-567, 578.

125, 126 (particular, railroad): *Pittsburgh Dispatch*, 7/20/77.

126 (Union, yards): *Report of Riots Committee*, pp. 116, 662-663.

127 (men): *Ibid.*, pp. 460, 464-465, 663-664. Pinkerton, p. 287.

127 (support): *Ohio State Journal*, 7/20/77. *Zanesville* (O.) *Daily Courier*, 7/20/77. *Newark* (O.) *Advocate*, 7/20/77.

127 (yards): *Zanesville Daily Courier*, 7/19/77, 7/20/77. *Newark Advocate*, 7/27/77. *Columbus Dispatch*, 7/19/77.

128 (cheers): *Newark Advocate,* 7/27/77. *Ohio State Journal,* 7/20/77.
128 (boys): *Newark Advocate,* 7/27/77.
129 (adversity): *Columbus* (O.) *Dispatch,* 7/20/77, 7/21/77. *Ohio State Journal,* 7/20/77.
129 (hour): *Ibid.,* 7/21/77. *Columbus Dispatch,* 7/21/77. *New York Times,* 7/22/77.
129 (expired): *Elmira* (N. Y.) *Daily Advertiser,* 7/21/77. *New York Times,* 7/21/77.
130 (Jewett): *Ibid.,* 7/22/77.
130 (handcars): *New York Sun,* 7/21/77. *New York Times,* 7/22/77.
130 (mustered): *Ibid.*

CHAPTER 8

131 (Watt): *Report of Riots Committee,* p. 170.
131 (lines): *Ibid.,* p. 78. *Pittsburgh Dispatch,* 7/20/77.
132 (on): Daily Journal of the U.S. Weather Bureau, Postoffice Building, Pittsburgh, entry for 7/19/77, reporting a "fair weather sunset." *Report of Riots Committee,* p. 189.
132 (upon): *Ibid.,* pp. 617, 924.
132 (visitors): Alexander K. McClure, *Old Time Notes of Pennsylvania* (2 vols., Philadelphia, 1905), II, 225-226. *Pittsburgh Gazette-Times,* December 13, 1913. *Report of Riots Committee,* pp. 51, 176, 285, 292.
133 (jump): *Ibid.,* pp. 60, 79, 176, 180-181, 374. Daily Journal, U.S. Weather Bureau, Pittsburgh, 7/19/77.
133, 134, 135 (walk, act, Sunday, Thursday, man): *Report of Riots Committee,* pp. 52, 61-64, 99-101, 113, 123, 176-178, 181, 185-186, 374-375, 377, 440, 485, 618, 926.
136 (communist): Quoted in *ibid.,* pp. 798-800.
136, 137, 138 (departed, Street, Street, troops, standing): *Ibid.,* pp. 53, 70, 87, 353-354, 375-377, 387, 510, 519, 581, 620-621, 699, 906, 963, 968, 993.
138 (stress): Joseph S. Clark, Jr., "The Railroad Struggle for Pittsburgh," in *Pennsylvania Magazine of History,* XLVIII (1924), 9.
139 (possible): *Report of Riots Committee,* pp. 87, 377, 605.
139 (bottom): *Pittsburgh Gazette-Times,* November 30, 1913.
139, 140 (charge, crossing, tracks, them): *Report of Riots Committee,* pp. 117, 191, 218, 299, 328-329, 334-335, 360, 367, 377-378, 459, 634, 800-801, 814-815.
141 (men): *Ibid.,* pp. 621, 907. *Pittsburgh Dispatch,* 7/23/77. *Pittsburgh Gazette-Times,* December 7, 1913.

141 (coffins): *Pittsburgh Dispatch,* 7/21/77.
142 (home, finality, it): *Report of Riots Committee,* pp. 378, 474, 694, 907.
142 (behind): *Ibid.,* pp. 68, 293, 378, 395, 941. Scrapbook I, p. 65, in Edward S. Sayres MSS.
143, 144, 145, 146, 147 (handsomely, like, troops, back, troops, back, seventeen): *Report of Riots Committee,* pp. 68-69, 88, 101-102, 117, 134-135, 188, 214, 218, 295, 368, 379, 385, 425, 446, 449, 469, 482, 524, 526, 543, 546, 571, 586, 588, 907, 992.
146 (reflexes): *Ibid.,* pp. 68, 88, 469, 471-472, 531, 907-908. *Pittsburgh Dispatch,* 7/20/77.
146 (hillside): *Report of Riots Committee,* pp. 215, 470, 472.
147 (workingmen): *Pittsburgh Commercial Gazette,* 7/23/77, 7/25/77, 7/31/77. Clarence E. Macartney, *Right Here in Pittsburgh* (Pittsburgh, 1937), p. 112n.
147 (ugly): *Report of Riots Committee,* pp. 214, 519. *Pittsburgh Commercial Gazette,* 7/23/77. *New York Times,* 7/22/77.
147 (uncertain): *Pittsburgh Commercial Gazette,* 7/27/77, 7/31/77.
148 (silence, train): *Report of Riots Committee,* pp. 68, 80-81, 114, 123, 213, 216, 295, 555, 958, 983.
149 (then): *Ibid.,* pp. 71, 380, 692-693. George T. Fleming, ed., *History of Pittsburgh and Environs* (4 vols., New York, 1922), IV, 236.
149 (Liberty): *Report of Riots Committee,* pp. 303, 327, 368, 380, 470, 943. *Pittsburgh Commercial Gazette,* 7/27/77.
150 (Hotel): *Report of Riots Committee,* pp. 81, 118, 217-218, 478, 582, 943, 972. *Pittsburgh Dispatch,* 7/23/77.
150, 151, 152, 153, 154, 155, 156, 157, 158 (anyway, riot, morning, ourselves, Pearson, stage, lumber, out, penitentiary, way, stint, job, cannon, property): *Report of Riots Committee,* pp. 118, 124-126, 155-156, 163-164, 173, 193-198, 208-212, 219-221, 225-228, 230, 232-236, 238, 241, 248, 251, 253-254, 380-382, 386, 400, 405, 434-435, 448, 450-454, 493, 521, 573, 581-582, 624, 849-850, 909, 911-912, 918, 938-939, 943-944, 964-965, 978-979.

CHAPTER 9

159 (knew): *Harper's New Monthly Magazine,* LVI (December 1877), 43-46. *New York Sun,* 7/22/77. *New York World,* 7/22/77.
169 (FLAMES): *Cumberland Daily News,* 7/22/77, 7/23/77. *Wheeling Intelligencer,* 7/22/77, 7/23/77. *Pottsville (Pa.) Evening Chronicle,* 7/22/77, 7/23/77.
160 (had): Cornelius B. Hite to Mrs. Hite from Baltimore, 7/22/77, in

Cornelius Baldwin Hite MSS. David Hutzler to Mrs. Hutzler 7/21/77, 7/23/77, in Hutzler MSS., Maryland Historical Society.
160 (conflagration): *The Nation,* 7/26/77. Carroll D. Wright, *The Battles of Labor* (Philadelphia, 1906), pp. 112-113. *Harrisburg Telegraph,* 7/21/77.
160 (streets): *Daily Arkansas Gazette,* 7/24/77, 7/28/77. *Raleigh* (N. C.) *Observer,* 7/22/77. *Wyandott* (Kans.) *Herald,* 7/26/77.
161 (aspect): *Wheeling Intelligencer,* 7/23/77. *Scranton Republican,* 7/23/77, 7/24/77. *New Orleans Times,* 7/24/77. *Charleston* (S. C.) *News and Courier,* 7/24/77. *Daily Rocky Mountain News* (Denver), 7/24/77. *Philadelphia Inquirer,* 7/23/77. *Wheeling Register,* 7/27/77.
161 (employees): *Ibid.,* 7/24/77, 7/28/77. *Pittsburgh Commercial Gazette,* 7/28/77. *Boston Globe,* 7/24/77. *Raleigh Observer,* 7/23/77. *Boston Republican,* 7/24/77.
162 (wage): *New York Times,* 7/24/77. *Cincinnati Enquirer,* 7/25/77.
162 (July): F. R. Plunkett to the Earl of Derby, 7/31/77, Public Record Office, London, Foreign Office 115, vol. 618 (microfilm in the Library of Congress).
162 (man): Gordon, pp. 23, 80-81, 83-86, 379-380. Alvin E. Harlow, *The Road of the Century: The Story of the New York Central* (New York, 1947), p. 281.
163 (*Enquirer*): In *Iron Molders' Journal,* XIII: (5/10/77), 321; (7/10/77), 385. *Irish World,* 8/11/77. *New York Sun,* 6/26/77. *Cumberland Civilian,* 6/24/77. Edward Potts to J. W. Garrett, 1/12/77, in Garrett MSS. C. W. Woolley to S. J. Randall, 6/10/77, in Samuel J. Randall MSS.
163 (different): In Whitelaw Reid MSS., Library of Congress: Whitelaw Reid to Roger Phelps, 7/6/77; to Samuel Seton, 7/24/77; to Leander Teas, 8/1/77.
163 (peril): My generalizations about the editorial opinion, here and later, are based in part on various newspaper files and in part on four volumes of clippings on the Great Strike, including about 600 editorials, gathered for President Hayes from all sections of the country. This present analysis, for example, is based on a breakdown of opinion in about ninety editorials published between July 20 and July 24 (Rutherford B. Hayes Scrapbooks, XCVII, 1-111, Hayes MSS.).
164 (aggression): *Report of Riots Committee,* pp. 802, 806-807, 817-819.
165 (reason): *Pittsburgh Telegraph,* 7/23/77.
165, 166, 167, 168 (war, alleys, apiece, pistols, before, way, contrary, ranks, fence): *Report of Riots Committee,* pp. 199-200, 225, 230, 239, 246, 449, 455-459, 541-542, 544, 789-790, 851-853, 855-856, 909-

910, 914-916, 939-941, 945, 955, 965-966, 970-971, 974-975, 981, 985.

168 (spared): *Ibid.*, pp. 500, 910-911. "Reminiscences of Edward S. Sayres," in Scrapbook I, 65, Sayres MSS.

169 (itself, crowd, outside): *Report of Riots Committee*, pp. 165-167, 235, 242, 251, 271, 276-279, 327, 337-341, 369-371, 373, 380, 398, 402, 410, 416, 418, 491, 575, 627.

170 (harm): *Ibid.*, pp. 179-182, 966-967. AGO, Ltrs. Rec'd., 1877, #4161.

170 (guests): *Report of Riots Committee*, pp. 136, 503, 611, 630.

170 (Northwestern): *Ibid.*, pp. 594, 600, 926. *Daily Rocky Mountain News*, 7/27/77.

170 (5:00 P.M.): McCabe, pp. 125-126. AGO, Ltrs. Rec'd., 1877, #4207.

171 (excursion, blazes): *Report of Riots Committee*, pp. 82, 226, 235, 244, 251, 254, 264, 275, 289, 318, 991.

171 (loads): *The Independent*, 8/16/77, 9/6/77. *Report of Riots Committee*, pp. 245, 323.

172 (role): N. Y. Society for . . . Delinquents, *Fifty-second Annual Report*, pp. 20-21. Morrell Heald, "Business Attitudes Toward Immigration, 1861-1914" (Ph.D. dissertation, Yale University, 1951), pp. 91-92. *Irish World*, 6/16/77.

172 (cheered): *Report of Riots Committee*, pp. 103, 136, 142, 166. *Pittsburgh Telegraph*, 7/24/77. *Pittsburgh Dispatch*, 7/23/77. *Pittsburgh Commercial Gazette*, 7/23/77.

172 (them, business): *Report of Riots Committee*, pp. 167, 174-175, 413.

173 (Allegheny): *Ibid.*, p. 103. Wright, p. 122.

174 (it): *Report of Riots Committee*, pp. 103, 195, 234, 235, 242, 254, 324, 325.

174 (wine): *Ibid.*, p. 225. *Pittsburgh Dispatch*, 7/23/77. Thomas Beer, *Mark Hanna* (New York, 1929), p. 89.

174 (places): *Report of Riots Committee*, p. 259. *Pittsburgh Dispatch*, 7/23/77.

175 (off): *Ibid. Pittsburgh Commercial Gazette*, 7/23/77.

175 (brick): *Ibid. Pittsburgh Telegraph*, 7/23/77. *Pittsburgh Dispatch* 7/23/77.

175 (Chicago): *Pittsburgh Post*, 7/23/77.

176 (it): *Report of Riots Committee*, p. 260.

176 (condemned): *Pittsburgh Commercial Gazette*, 7/24/77. *Pittsburgh Dispatch*, 7/23/77.

176 (all, mother): *Ibid.*

177, 178 (Depot, oratory, there, reporting, forever, night): *Report of*

Riots Committee, pp. 54-55, 91, 269-272, 286-291, 305-307, 356-357, 402-403, 436, 442, 475-476, 506, 511, 513.
179 (troublemakers): *Ibid.,* pp. 251, 357, 497, 504-505. *Pittsburgh Commercial Gazette,* 7/23/77.
179 (depot): *Report of Riots Committee,* pp. 165, 549, 576. *Pittsburgh Dispatch,* 7/23/77.
180 (challenged): *Report of Riots Committee,* pp. 297, 461. The big bell now stands outside the Historical Society of Western Pennsylvania, Pittsburgh, which also preserves one of Phillips' posters.
180 (Altoona): *Pittsburgh Telegraph,* 7/23/77. Daily Journal, U. S. Weather Bureau, Pittsburgh, entry for 7/23/77. Map of burned district, from fire commissioners' report, in "Pittsburgh Newspaper Clippings," Carnegie Free Library, Pittsburgh. *Railway World,* VI (October 10, 1880), 941-942. Davis, pp. 118-119. Photographs of the ruins in the Office of the Secretary, Pennsylvania Railroad, Philadelphia, and in the Historical Society of Western Pennsylvania, Pittsburgh.
180 (ashes): *Railway World,* VI, 942.
181 (children): *Report of Riots Committee,* p. 789. *Pittsburgh Commercial Gazette,* 7/25/77, 7/28/77. *Pittsburgh Post,* 7/22/87.
181 (bell): *Pittsburgh Telegraph,* 7/23/77. *Pittsburgh Commercial Gazette,* 7/24/77.
182 (fines): *Report of Riots Committee,* pp. 175, 439, 476, 494. *Cumberland Civilian,* 7/29/77, 8/5/77. *Pittsburgh Post,* 7/24/77.
182 (guard): *Report of Riots Committee,* pp. 132, 217, 437, 454, 503, 519. *Pittsburgh Post,* 7/24/77.
182 (Company): *Ibid.,* 7/21/77, 7/24/77, 7/25/77.
183 (corporations): *Ibid.,* 7/24/77. C. B. Sheppard to "My Dear Aunt," 8/13/77, in "Sheppard, C. B.," Society Miscellaneous Collection, Pennsylvania Historical Society.

CHAPTER 10

184 (Chenango): Hazard, *et al.,* eds., Fourth Series, IX, 590. *Philadelphia Times,* 7/23/77.
185 (Pittsburgh, reinforcements): *Report of Riots Committee,* pp. 304, 347-348, 350, 462-463, 465, 666-670, 677-678, 681, 793, 797, 826-832.
186 (anyone): Edgar A. Custer, *No Royal Road* (New York, 1937), pp. 2-3. James H. Ewing and Harry Slep, *History of the City of Altoona and Blair County* (Altoona, Pa., 1880), pp. 73-74. *Altoona Evening Mirror,* 7/23/77.

186 (music): Ewing and Slep, *Altoona*, pp. 78-79. *Altoona Evening Mirror,* 7/23/77.

187 (property): *Harrisburg Telegraph,* 7/23/77, 7/24/77, 7/25/77. *Harrisburg Independent,* 7/22/77. *Harrisburg Patriot,* 7/20/77, 7/25/77. *Report of Riots Committee,* pp. 636, 640, 642-643, 645, 660.

187 (points): George B. Stichter, "The Schuykill County Soldiery in the Industrial Disturbances in 1877, or the Railroad War," in *Publications of the Historical Society of Schuykill County* (Pottsville, Pa., 1905), I, 197-199.

187 (hall): *Harrisburg Independent,* 7/24/77. *Report of Riots Committee,* pp. 636-638, 641, 651-652.

188 (over): Stichter, "Schuykill County Soldiery," pp. 201-202. *Report of Riots Committee,* pp. 641-642, 645-648. *Harrisburg Patriot,* 7/24/77.

188 (May): *Pottsville Chronicle,* 7/18/77. *Reading* (Pa.) *Eagle,* 7/21/77.

188 (one): *Baltimore Evening Bulletin,* 5/9/77. *Philadelphia Inquirer,* 7/16/77. *Easton Express,* 7/16/77. *Miners' Journal,* 7/23/77.

189 (strike): Francis A. Walker, *A Compendium of the Ninth Census* (Washington, D.C., 1872), p. 448. *Reading Eagle,* 7/21/77, 7/26/77.

189 (witnesses): *Ibid.,* 7/23/77. *New York Times,* 10/4/77.

190 (paralyzed): *Report of Riots Committee,* p. 866. *Reading Eagle,* 7/23/77. *Reading* (Pa.) *Times and Dispatch,* 7/24/77.

190 (solid): *Reading Eagle,* 7/23/77.

190 (deserted): *Ibid. New York Times,* 10/3/77. Pinkerton, pp. 315-318.

191 (cost): *Reading Eagle,* 7/23/77. *Reading Times and Dispatch,* 7/24/77.

191 (Philadelphia): *Reading Eagle,* 7/23/77. *Pottsville Chronicle,* 7/24/77. *Reading Times and Dispatch,* 7/24/77. *Report of Riots Committee,* pp. 867, 871, 873, 883-884, 879.

192 (fair): *Scranton Republican,* 7/20/77. *Easton Express,* 7/17/77, 7/23/77, 7/25/77.

193 (crossing): *Ibid.,* 7/25/77. *Reading Times and Dispatch,* 7/24/77. *Reading Eagle,* 7/27/77, 7/31/77.

193 (depot): *Easton Express,* 7/25/77.

193 (all): *Reading Times and Dispatch,* 7/24/77. The story of the town drunk elicited by my request for information, October 15, 1957, broadcast from Station WHUM, Reading, Pa.

193 (rioters): *Reading Times and Dispatch,* 7/24/77. *Report of Riots Committee,* pp. 869-870.

194 (night): *Reading Times and Dispatch*, 7/24/77. *Pottsville Evening Chronicle*, 7/25/77. Pinkerton, p. 323.

194 (arsonists): *Pottsville Evening Chronicle*, 7/24/77. *Easton Express*, 7/25/77. *Report of Riots Committee*, p. 886. *Reading Eagle*, 7/25/77, 7/26/77. AGO, Ltrs. Rec'd., 1877, #4325.

194 (picnic): *Easton Express*, 7/25/77.

195 (Pittsburgh's): *Philadelphia Times*, 7/23/77.

195 (Stokley): Vivian, pp. 56, 59.

195 (property): Ellis P. Oberholtzer, *Philadelphia, A History of the City and Its People* (4 vols., Philadelphia, 1912), II, 399, 401, 416. *Pittsburgh Leader*, 3/13/78. *Philadelphia Times*, 7/23/77. Office of the Secretary of War, Letters Sent, 1877, Secretary of War to Mayor of Philadelphia, 7/22/77.

196 (burned): *Philadelphia Times*, 7/24/77. *Philadelphia Telegraph*, 7/23/77.

196 (points): *Philadelphia Times*, 7/24/77, 7/25/77. AGO, Ltrs. Rec'd., 1877, #4326, 4255, 8134, 8135. McClure, II, 455-457.

197, 198 (boarders, boys, ground): *New York Sun*, 7/23/77.

198 (guard): *Idem. Buffalo Commercial Advertiser*, 7/27/77. *Buffalo Weekly Courier*, 8/22/77.

199 (later, being): *Buffalo Evening Republican*, 7/23/77.

199 (sticks): *Buffalo Commercial Advertiser*, 7/23/77. *Buffalo Evening Republican*, 7/23/77. *Buffalo Weekly Courier*, 7/25/77.

200 (amputated): *Idem. Buffalo Commercial Advertiser*, 7/24/77.

200 (usual): *Idem. Buffalo Weekly Courier*, 7/25/77.

200 (muskets): *Buffalo Commercial Advertiser*, 7/24/77, 7/25/77. *Buffalo Weekly Courier*, 7/25/77. *Workingman's Advocate*, 1/20/77.

201 (constabulary): *Buffalo Weekly Courier*, 7/25/77. *Buffalo Evening Republican*, 7/26/77.

202 (it): William A. Croffut, *The Vanderbilts and the Story of Their Fortune* (Chicago, 1886), pp. 40-42, 58-60, 64, 68-69, 75, 80, 99, 125, 150, 202, 231, 239, 248.

202 (trains): *Albany* (N.Y.) *Evening Journal*, 7/24/77.

203 (Central): *Syracuse* (N.Y.) *Journal*, 7/24/77, 7/25/77. *Rochester* (Pa.) *Express*, 7/23/77, 7/24/77, 7/25/77. *Rochester* (Pa.) *Union and Advocate*, 7/23/77, 7/24/77, 7/25/77. *Albany Evening Journal*, 7/25/77.

203 (body): *Syracuse Journal*, 7/24/77. *Rochester Express*, 7/25/77. McCabe, p. 277.

204 (itself): *Newark* (O.)*Advocate*, 7/22/77. *Cincinnati Enquirer*, 7/25/77.

204 (oil): Whipple, pp. 7, 14-15, 20-21. *Arkansas Daily Gazette*, 7/29/77.
204 (scornful): Whipple, pp. 18-20, 85, 87-90.
205 (Garden): *Cleveland Herald*, 7/23/77 to 7/26/77. *Cleveland Plain Dealer*, 7/23/77 to 7/25/77.
205 (elsewhere): *Cincinnati Star*, 7/23/77. *Cincinnati Enquirer*, 7/23/77, 7/24/77.
206 (hotheads): *Ibid.*, 7/24/77, 7/25/77. *Cincinnati Commercial*, 7/24/77, 7/25/77.
206 (jobs): *Zanesville Courier*, 7/24/77. *Zanesville* (O.) *Sunday Times Signal*, October 16, 1955. J. Hope Sutor, *Past and Present of the City of Zanesville and Muskingum County, Ohio* (Chicago, 1905), p. 60.
207 (up): *Columbus Dispatch*, 7/23/77, 7/24/77. *Ohio State Journal*, 7/23/77, 7/24/77.
207 (tie-up): *Columbus Distpatch*, 7/24/77, 7/25/77.
207 (movements): *Cleveland Herald*, 7/25/77.
207, 208, 209 (suit, day, allowed): *Toledo* (O.) *Commercial*, 7/24/77, 7/25/77, 7/26/77, 7/27/77, 7/28/77, 8/1/77, 8/2/77, 8/3/77.

CHAPTER 11

209 (Gun): George E. Waring, Jr., comp., *Report on the Social Statistics of Cities* (2 vols., Washington, D.C., 1887), II, 27, 51. *New York Sun*, 7/22/77. AGO, Ltrs. Rec'd., 1877, #4146, 4208.
210 (time): *Ibid.*, #4186.
210 (Department): *Ibid.*, #4162. *National Republican*, 7/23/77.
210 (stockholders): Thomas C. Donaldson Memoirs, entry for 4/28/77, transcript copy in Hayes Library. *Pottsville Evening Chronicle*, 7/18/77. Barnard, *Hayes*, pp. 414-415. C. S. Greeley to H. Villard, 6/5/77, in Villard MSS. Minute Books of the Lake Shore & Michigan Southern Railroad, VIII, 322.
210 (law): Theodore E. Burton, *John Sherman* (Boston, 1906), *passim*.
211 (dispute): Donaldson Memoir. Barnard, *Hayes*, p. 417. Dodge's close relations with McCrary are indicated by Dodge to McCrary, 6/5/76 (two letters), 4/16/77, 4/21/77, 5/2/77, 5/4/77, 5/12/77, 9/29/77, 11/28/77, 12/7/77 (letterbook copies), in Box 384, Grenville M. Dodge MSS., Iowa Historical Department, Des Moines.
211 (good): Donaldson Memoir. Richard W. Thompson, *Recollections of Sixteen Presidents from Washington to Lincoln* (2 vols., Indianapolis, 1894), *passim*. *Railroad Gazette*, IX (3/30/77), 144. In Richard W. Thompson MSS., Lincoln National Life Foundation, Fort Wayne,

Indiana: T. Scott to R. Thompson, 3/24/73; J. Janney to R. Thompson, 5/12/77.

211 (car): Donaldson Memoir. *Baltimore Evening Bulletin*, 7/17/77. *Harrisburg Telegraph*, 7/19/77. *New York Times*, 7/17/77.

212 (glasses): J. Cochrane to C. Schurz, 7/26/77, in Carl Schurz MSS. Barnard, *Hayes*, pp. 414, 417. Carl Schurz, *The Reminiscences of Carl Schurz* (2 vols., New York, 1907), I, 139. "Ben: Perley Poore," *Perley's Reminiscences* (2 vols., Philadelphia, 1886), II, 343.

212 (Hayes): Donaldson Memoir. Barnard, *Hayes*, pp. 417-418.

212 (riots): *Boston Globe*, 7/23/77. *Toledo Weekly Blade*, 8/2/77.

213 (raging): *Boston Globe*, 7/23/77. Daily Journal, U.S. Weather Bureau, Pittsburgh, entries for 7/22 to 7/31/77. A bundle of about eighty such dispatches is filed as #4509 with #4042, AGO, Ltrs. Rec'd., 1877.

213 (disorders): *New York Sun*, 7/23/77. *New York World*, 7/24/77. Bennett M. Rich, *The Presidents and Civil Disorder* (Washington, D.C., 1941), pp. 85-86.

213 (Pennsylvania): *Annual Report of the Secretary of War for 1877*, pp. 4, 98.

213 (acting): *New York Sun*, 7/23/77. *National Republican*, 7/23/77. *Boston Globe*, 7/23/77.

214 (subsiding): *New York World*, 7/24/77. *New York Sun*, 7/24/77. *Boston Globe*, 7/23/77. *National Republican*, 7/23/77.

214 (events): AGO, Ltrs. Rec'd., 1877, #4178.

214 (outset): WPA, *Mathews Papers*, p. 52.

215 (there): AGO, Ltrs. Rec'd., 1877, #4178, 4185, 8133. *Wheeling Intelligencer*, 7/23/77, *Cumberland Civilian*, 7/22/77. *Cumberland Daily News*, 7/23/77.

215 (further): WPA, *Mathews Papers*, pp. 50-53.

215 (Baltimore): *Baltimore Sun*, 7/23/77. McCabe, pp. 38-39.

215 (darkness): *Baltimore American*, 7/23/77.

216 (face): In the Personal File of William H. French, AGO: J. Rodgers to W. French, 7/28/77. W. French to J. Carroll, 7/26/77; W. French to E. Townsend (Adjutant General), 8/1/77. McCabe, pp. 37, 39.

216 (West Virginia): AGO, Ltrs. Rec'd., 1877, #4187, 4203. McCabe, p. 42.

217 (Maryland): AGO, Ltrs. Rec'd., 1877, #4023. E. Townsend to Secretary of War, Dispatch 8, 7/22/77, Hayes MSS. *National Republican*, 7/23/77.

217 (telegrams): Hartranft to Hayes, received 7:00 P.M., 7/22/77,

Hayes MSS. *New York World*, 7/23/77. *New York Sun*, 7/23/77, 7/24/77. AGO, Ltrs. Rec'd., 1877, #4211.

217   (end): *New York Sun*, 7/23/77, 7/24/77. William Stokley to Hayes, received 9:26 P.M., 7/22/77, in Hayes MSS.

218   (government): *New York World*, 7/24/77. *New York Sun*, 7/24/77. Sgt. Hay to Chief Signal Officer, 9:45 P.M., 7/22/77, in Hayes MSS.

218   (day): AGO, Ltrs. Rec'd., 1877 #4197. 45th Congress, 2nd session, House Executive Document 1, pt. 1 (report of the Secretary of the Navy), pp. 40-41. *New York Sun*, 7/24/77. *New York World*, 7/24/77. Hartranft to Hayes from North Bend, Nebraska, 7/23/77, in Hayes MSS.

218   (Buffalo): F. R. Plunkett to Earl of Derby, 7/24/77, confidential dispatch #218, vol. 618, Foreign Office 115, Public Record Office, London (microfilm in Library of Congress). *New York World*, 7/24/77. HQ, Military Division of the Atlantic, Letters Received, 1877, #3880 (National Archives Record Group 98). Elwell S. Otis, "The Army in Connection with the Labor Riots of 1877," in *Journal of the Military Service Institution of the United States*, V (1884), 298-299. AGO, Ltrs. Rec'd., 1877, #4254.

219   (effect): Otis, pp. 299-301. AGO, Ltrs. Rec'd., 1877, #4247. W. S. Hancock to J. M. Schofield, 7/30/77, in John M. Schofield MSS., Library of Congress.

219   (hindrance): McCabe, pp. 328-331.

220   (symbols): AGO, Ltrs. Rec'd., 1877, #4272. Rich, pp. 85-86.

220   (Pennsylvania, President): AGO, Ltrs. Rec'd., 1877, #4261, 4328, 4397.

221   (anger): Rich, pp. 82-83. James E. White, *A Life Span and Reminiscences of Railway Mail Service* (Philadelphia, 1910), p. 17. *New York Sun*, 7/23/77, 7/26/77. *Cleveland Plain Dealer*, 7/23/77. *Syracuse Journal*, 7/23/77. "Firemen, brakemen & citizens" to Hayes, 1:53 P.M., 7/24/77, in Hayes MSS. *Easton Express*, 7/26/77.

221   (Strike): Hayes's notes on cabinet meeting of 7/25/77, in Hayes MSS. Rich, pp. 82-83. Off. Sec. War., Ltrs. Sent, 1877, Secretary of War to Postmaster General, 7/24/77. White, *A Life Span*, pp. 17-18.

222   (prison): *Railway World*, III (12/8/77), 1164-1165. *Easton Weekly Argus*, 9/7/77. *New York Times*, 11/8/77.

222   (respected): Notes on cabinet meeting of 7/24/77, in Hayes MSS. Group portrait of the Hayes cabinet in session, in John Sherman, *Recollections of Forty Years in the House, Senate and Cabinet* (Chicago and New York, 1896), p. 530.

223   (requisition): Notes on cabinet meeting of 7/24/77, in Hayes MSS. In National Archives Record Group 56: T. Hillhouse to J. Sherman,

7/22/77, 7/23/77, 7/24/77, Assistant Treasurer's Correspondence; J. Sherman to R. Hayes, 7/23/77, Letters to the President. AGO, Ltrs. Rec'd., 1877, #4263.

223 (dispatched, noon): Notes on cabinet meeting of 7/24/77, Hayes MSS.

224 (more): *Proceedings of the Grand Division of the Conductors' Brotherhood at the Ninth Annual Session* (Omaha?, 1876), p. 183. Edwin C. Robbins, *Railway Conductors, A Study in Organized Labor* (New York, 1914), p. 20. *Proceedings of the Grand Division of the Order of Railway Conductors . . . 1868-1885* (Cedar Rapids, 1888), p. 205.

224 (Debs): Ray Ginger, *The Bending Cross* (New Brunswick, N. J., 1949), pp. 22-24.

224 (Union): *New York Herald*, 7/25/77.

225 (development): *Pittsburgh Post*, 7/22/87. *Harrisburg Independent*, 7/25/77. *Scranton Republican*, 7/21/77, 7/23/77. *Scranton Times*, 7/23/77, 7/27/77.

225 (true): AGO, Ltrs. Rec'd., 1877, #4787. *Engineers' Monthly Journal*, XII (April 1878), 165. *Railroad Trainmen's Journal*, XI (September 1894), 778.

226 (anti-American): Hayes Scrapbooks, XCVII, 1-70, *passim*, in Hayes MSS. *National Republican*, 7/21/77.

226 (animosity): *Ibid.*, 7/23/77.

226 (them): All quotations are from issues of 7/23/77.

226 (Communism): *Philadelphia Evening Bulletin*, 7/25/77.

227 (diabolism): Nevins and Thomas, eds., IV, 351, 490-491.

227 (here): M. R. Werner, *It Happened in New York* (New York, 1957), pp. 223, 233.

227 (winter): Morris Hillquit, *History of Socialism in the United States* (New York, 1903), pp. 182-183. Feder, pp. 51-53.

228 (life): Commons and associates, II, 220. Foner, p. 448.

228 (States): Hillquit, pp. 209-210. Foner, pp. 448-452.

228 (again): Burbank, p. 32. Hillquit, pp. 213-214.

229 (Capital): *Workingman's Advocate*, 5/19/77. *Labor Standard*, 7/28/77. *Irish World*, 7/28/77.

229 (inventions): *Labor Standard*, 8/4/77, 8/11/77.

229 (interest): "Protokoll Buch" of the Hoboken section of the Workingmen's Party, 7/3/77, 7/17/77 and April-July 1877, *passim*, in Joseph A. Labadie Collection. "Philadelphia Tageblatt, Protokoll Buch der Verhandlunger des Verwaltungs Rathes," 1877, *passim*, Tamiment Institute Library, New York.

229 (shoestring): Entry for 8/5/77 in the blank book of H. Stein, Treas-

urer of the W.P.U.S., Labor Collection (U.S. MSS. 2A), Wisconsin Historical Society.

CHAPTER 12

230 (Cincinnati): McCabe, pp. 370-371.

231 (dynamite): Lafcadio Hearn's description is quoted in Burbank, p. 5. Vivian, pp. 190-191.

231 (violence): *Cincinnati Enquirer*, 7/23/77, 7/24/77. *Cincinnati Commercial*, 7/23/77, 7/24/77.

231 (good): *Idem.*

232 (sixteen): *Boston Globe*, 7/25/77.

232 (matter): All quotations are from the issues of 7/23/77. The "prominent official" is quoted in the *Philadelphia Times*, 7/24/77.

233 (find): *Ibid.*, 7/24/77, 7/25/77, 7/26/77. *Labor Standard*, 8/4/77.

233 (present): *Philadelphia Times*, 7/27/77, 7/30/77. *Philadelphia Telegraph*, 7/27/77. McClure, II, 458-459.

234 (closets, luckier, notified, Chicago): Bessie Louise Pierce, *A History of Chicago* (4 vols., New York, 1937-1957), III, 11-12, 20, 22-23, 33, 52-53, 55, 59, 234, 237-240, 243n, 516.

235 (English): David M. Behen, "The Chicago Labor Movement, 1873-1896: Its Philosophical Bases" (unpublished Ph.D. dissertation, University of Chicago, 1953), p. 70n. Photograph of Philip Van Patten in Labadie Collection. Howard H. Quint, *The Forging of American Socialism* (Columbia, S. C., 1953), p. 19.

235 (occasions): Lucy E. Parsons, *Life of Albert R. Parsons* (Chicago, 1889), pp. xv-xvi, 6-11.

236 (strikers): *Chicago Daily News*, 7/20/77, 7/22/77. Charles H. Dennis, *Victor Lawson* (Chicago, 1935), pp. 41-43.

236 (district): *Chicago Post*, 7/23/77. Pierce, III, 245-246.

237 (here): *Chicago Post*, 7/21/77. *Railroad Gazette*, IX (5/18/77), 225. In Burlington Archives: W. B. Strong to C. E. Perkins, 2:42 P.M., 7/22/77, CBQ 3.1; Perkins' return from Nebraska is noted in an office memorandum book, CBQ, 32.6:1877.

237 (city): Pierce, III, 247. AGO, Ltrs. Rec'd., 1877, #4212. *Annual Report of the Division of the Missouri for 1877*, printed copy in Sherman MSS., p. 2.

238 (night): *Chicago Post*, 7/23/77.

238 (police): Pierce, III, 246-247. *Chicago Post*, 7/24/77.

239 (receding): W. Strong to C. Perkins, 12:47 A.M., 7/24/77, CBQ 33 1870 2.1, in Burlington Archives.

239, 240 (Burlington, older, easily): *Chicago Times*, 7/25/77.

240 (day): *Idem. Chicago Post, 7/24/77.*

240 (idleness): *Idem.*

241 (boys): *Chicago Times, 7/25/77.*

241 (captains): *Chicago Post, 7/24/77. Chicago Times, 7/25/77.*

241 (him): AGO, Ltrs. Rec'd., 1877, #4299, 4306, 4312.

242 (duty): *Chicago Times, 7/25/77.* J. Seymour Curry, *Chicago: Its History and Builders* (4 vols., Chicago, 1912), II, 298.

242 (forefront): Parsons, pp. 11-13.

243 (crowd): *Chicago Daily News, 7/24/77. Chicago Times, 7/25/77.*

243 (committee, silver, completely): *Idem.*

244 (temper): *Chicago Post, 7/25/77. Chicago Times, 7/26/77.* Pierce, III, 249.

244 (strength): *Chicago Times, 7/26/77.* In Burlington Archives: W. Strong to C. Perkins, 10:46 A.M., 12:12 P.M., 4:58 P.M., CBQ 33 1870 3.1; R. Harris to J. Griswold, 7/25/77, CBQ B1.5 Box 31. C. Perkins to J. Forbes, 8/2/77, Letterbook 3, pp. 391-393, in Cunningham-Overton Collection.

245 (custody): *Chicago Times, 7/26/77.*

245 (evening): Pierce, III, 250. *Chicago Times, 7/26/77.* AGO, Ltrs. Rec'd., 1877, #4690.

246(dead): *Chicago Times, 7/26/77. Chicago Daily News, 7/26/77.*

247 (rioters): *Chicago Times, 7/26/77.*

247 (rioters): *Idem.* AGO, Ltrs. Rec'd., 1877, #4341, 4352, 4509 (enclosures 28, 44, 45).

248 (Vicksburg): *Chicago Times, 7/27/77. Chicago Post, 7/26/77.* W. Ackerman to W. Osborn, 7/26/77, in Ill. Cent. Archives.

248 (again): *Chicago Daily News, 7/26/77. Chicago Post, 7/27/77. Chicago Times, 7/27/77.*

249 (afternoon): *Chicago Post, 7/26/77. Chicago Times, 7/27/77.*

249 (erupted): *Chicago Post, 7/26/77. Chicago Daily News, 7/26/77. Chicago Times, 7/27/77.*

250 (children): *Idem. Chicago Post, 7/26/77. Chicago Inter Ocean, 4/25/79, 4/26/79, 5/6/79.* Pierce, III, 253n.

250 (moved, wounded): *Chicago Post, 7/27/77. Chicago Times, 7/27/77.*

251 (stock): *Chicago Daily News, 7/26/77. Chicago Post, 7/26/77. Chicago Times, 7/27/77.* F. Matthews to C. McCormick, 7/27/77, in Cyrus McCormick MSS., Wisconsin Historical Society.

251 (torch): *Chicago Post, 7/26/77. Chicago Times, 7/27/77.* John Moses and Joseph Kirkland, eds., *The History of Chicago* (2 vols., Chicago, 1895), I, 766. W. Strong to C. Perkins, 3:40 P.M., 7/26/77, in Burlington Archives.

356 1877: YEAR OF VIOLENCE

252 (quarters): *Chicago Times,* 7/27/77. AGO, Ltrs. Rec'd., 1877, #4412, 4509 (enclosure 40).
252 (broken): *Chicago Times,* 7/27/77. W. Ackerman to W. Osborn, 7/26/77, in Ill. Cent. Archives.
252 (reported): *Chicago Times,* 7/27/77. Pierce, III, 251.
253 (invertebrate): *Chicago Post,* 7/26/77. *Chicago Times,* 7/27/77.
253 (population): Burbank, pp. 1-2, 8.
253 (kept): *Ibid.,* pp. 2, 8, 45. *St. Louis Times,* 7/22/77.
254 (mid-July, embryo, starvation): Burbank, pp. 1, 3-4, 7, 33-34, 40-41, 54.
255 (business): James Harrison Wilson, *Under the Old Flag* (2 vols., New York, 1912), II, 381-383, 389-400, 542. In James Harrison Wilson MSS.: J. Wilson to J. Schiff, 7/19/77; J. Wilson to J. Boyle, 9/6/77.
255 (be): J. Wilson to C. Schurz, 7/22/77, in Schurz MSS.
256 (allies): *St. Louis Times,* 7/23/77. Burbank, p. 46.
256 (Cheers): *St. Louis Times,* 7/23/77. Burbank, pp. 47, 50.
256 (often): *Ibid.,* pp. 51, 176, 217.
257 (necessary): *St. Louis Times,* 7/23/77. Burbank, p. 53. J. Wilson to C. Schurz, 7/22/77, in Schurz MSS. AGO, Ltrs. Rec'd., 1877, #4250.
257, 258 (thereafter, all): *St. Louis Times,* 7/24/77. Burbank, pp. 61-66.
258 (hours): J. Schiff to J. Wilson, 7/24/77, in Wilson MSS. *St. Louis Times,* 7/24/77. AGO, Ltrs. Rec'd., 1877, #4264, 8135 (enclosure 84).
258 (punishment): Burbank, p. 61.
259 (for): *St. Louis Times,* 7/24/77. Burbank, pp. 68-69.
259, 260 (strikers, trains): *St. Louis Times,* 7/25/77. Burbank, pp. 78, 81.
260 (themselves): J. Wilson to C. Schurz, 7/24/77, in Schurz MSS. AGO, Ltrs. Rec'd., 1877, #4300.
260 (stage): *St. Louis Times,* 7/25/77. Burbank, p. 77.
260 (any): *Ibid.,* p. 83. Hillquit, p. 202.
260 (age): *St. Louis Times,* 7/25/77.

CHAPTER 13

261 (England): Boston & Maine Railroad, *Annual Report for 1877,* p. 8.
262 (this): *Arkansas Gazette,* 7/27/77. *Raleigh Observer,* 7/24/77.
262 (days): *Arkansas Gazette,* 7/24/77, 7/26/77, 7/27/77, 7/31/77.
262 (direction): Burbank, p. 101. *New Orleans Times,* 7/19/77, 7/28/77, 7/30/77.

262 (work): *Savannah News,* 7/26/77, 7/27/77, 7/28/77. *Charleston News and Courier,* 7/28/77.

263 (rioters): *New Orleans Times,* 7/25/77, 7/30/77. *Charleston News and Courier,* 7/24/77, 7/25/77.

263 (rule): *Galveston News,* 7/17/77, 7/24/77 to 8/5/77 *passim.*

264 (town): *Louisville Courier-Journal,* 7/25/77. *Louisville Commercial,* 7/24/77, 7/25/77.

265 (First): *Louisville Courier-Journal,* 7/25/77. *Louisville Commercial,* 7/25/77. Alpheus T. Mason, *Brandeis: A Free Man's Life* (New York, 1946), pp. 47-48.

265 (week): *Louisville Commercial,* 7/26/77, 7/27/77, 7/28/77. Mason, *Brandeis,* p. 48.

266 (order): Northern Pacific Railroad, *Annual Report for 1877,* p. 3. *Wyandott Herald,* 7/26/77. Missouri, Kansas & Texas Railroad, *Annual Report for 1877,* pp. 19, 46.

266 (property): *Omaha Republican,* 7/19/77 to 7/26/77 *passim.* AGO, Ltrs. Rec'd., 1877, #8131.

266 (cracker): *Rocky Mountain News,* 7/27/77.

267 (monopoly): John S. Hittell, *A History of the City of San Francisco* (San Francisco, 1878), pp. 422-424. Hubert H. Bancroft, *History of the Pacific States of North America* (39 vols., San Francisco, 1882-1891), XIX, 351-352. Oscar Lewis, *The Big Four* (New York, 1938), p. 365.

267 (pay): Nevins, *Emergence,* pp. 150-152, 375.

267 (onslaught): *San Francisco Call,* 7/23/77.

267 (authorities): *Ibid.,* 7/23/77, 7/24/77. H. Linderman to J. Sherman, 8/4/77, in Sherman MSS. Ira B. Cross, *A History of the Labor Movement in California* (Berkeley, 1935), p. 88.

268 (quietly): *San Francisco Bulletin,* 7/24/77. *San Francisco Call,* 7/24/77.

268 (order): *Ibid.,* 7/24/77, 7/25/77.

269 (ruins): *San Francisco Bulletin,* 7/25/77. *San Francisco Call,* 7/25/77, 7/26/77.

269, 270 (soon, generally): *San Francisco Bulletin,* 7/26/77. *San Francisco Call,* 7/26/77.

270 (fire): *Ibid.,* 7/26/77. *San Francisco Bulletin,* 7/26/77.

270 (normal): *San Francisco Call,* 7/27/77.

271 (elsewhere): *Detroit News,* 7/23/77, 7/24/77, 7/25/77, 7/26/77. AGO, Ltrs. Rec'd., 1877, #4298. Harlow, p. 238.

271 (case): *Detroit News,* 7/26/77. Michigan Central Railroad, *Annual Report for 1877,* p. 6. The Lehigh Valley Railroad Superintendent's 1877 report furnishes another example of the contradiction.

271 (running): Regional mileage figures for 1877 are in *Poor's Manual of Railroads for 1878-1879*, pp. iii-iv.

272 (securities): *New York Tribune*, 8/2/77. *New York World*, 7/23/77. *Boston Globe*, 7/23/77. J. Schiff to J. Wilson, 7/27/77, in Wilson MSS. J. Sherman to C. Conant, 7/23/77, in Sherman MSS.

272 (rose): *The Nation*, 8/2/77. E. Febber to J. Garrett, 7/25/77, in Garrett MSS. AGO, Ltrs. Rec'd., 1877, #5409 (enclosure 15).

272 (Thomas): *New York Clipper*, 8/4/77. *Chicago Post*, 7/28/77. Charles Edward Russell, *The American Orchestra and Theodore Thomas* (Garden City, 1927), pp. 110, 194-196.

273 (on): *Buffalo Commercial Advertiser*, 7/26/77. *New York Clipper*, 8/4/77. *Altoona Evening Mirror*, 7/23/77. *Fort Wayne* (Ind.) *Gazette*, 7/26/77. *Chicago Times*, 7/27/77. P. T. Barnum Route Book, entries for 7/24/77 to 7/27/77, in the John P. Grace Circus Route Book Collection in possession of Mr. Richard E. Conover, Xenia, O.

273 (terms): *Philadelphia Evening Bulletin*, 7/28/77. George S. Merriam, *The Life and Times of Samuel Bowles* (2 vols., New York, 1885), II, 426-427. W. Smith to M. Halstead, 7/31/77, in William Henry Smith MSS. *San Francisco Call*, 7/25/77. J. Wilson to W. Gresham, in Walter Q. Gresham MSS. *Detroit News*, 7/21/77. *Galveston News*, 8/3/77.

274 (latitude): *St. Louis Times*, 7/26/77. Burbank, pp. 96-97.

274 (organization): Sgt. F. Hinn to Chief Signal Officer, 7/24/77, Telegram #13, in Hayes MSS.

274 (Market): *St. Louis Times*, 7/26/77. Burbank, pp. 98-99.

275 (crowd): *St. Louis Times*, 7/26/77. Burbank, pp. 102-103. *Missouri Republican*, 7/26/77.

275 (success): *St. Louis Times*, 7/26/77. *Missouri Republican*, 7/26/77. Burbank, p. 100.

275 (procession): *Ibid.*, pp. 110-111.

276 (States): *Ibid.*, 111. *St. Louis Times*, 7/26/77.

276 (opportuneness): *Labor Standard*, 8/19/77. A. Bebel and E. Bernstein, eds., *Der Briefwechsel zwischen Friedrich Engels und Karl Marx, 1844 bis 1883* (Stuttgart, Germany, 1913), K. Marx to F. Engels, 7/25/77, quoted in Burbank, p. 93.

276 (city): *New York Evening Mail*, 7/23/77.

277 (demagogue): *New York Sun*, 7/24/77. *New York Times*, 7/24/77.

277 (elsewhere): *New York Sun*, 7/26/77. *Army and Navy Journal*, 8/4/77. AGO, Ltrs. Rec'd., 1877, #8135 (enclosure 21).

278 (Texas): *Ibid.*, #4309, 4312, 4341, 4359, 4414, 8135 (enclosure 20). Notes on cabinet meeting of 7/25/77, in Hayes MSS.

278 (communication, witticism): AGO, Ltrs. Rec'd., 1877, #4304, 4317.

278 (officers): *New York Herald*, 7/22/77. C. Perkins to R. Harris, 7/23/77, "Strike Telegrams," in Burlington Archives. H. Slocum to R. Hayes, 7/23/77, in Hayes MSS.

279 (morning): Milwaukee Chamber of Commerce, Philadelphia Corn Exchange, Baltimore Merchant's Exchange, etc., to R. Hayes, 7/25/77, in Hayes MSS. *Philadelphia North American*, 7/23/77. J. Holt to C. Schurz, 7/26/77, in Schurz MSS. Hayes's notes on cabinet meeting, 7/25/77, in Hayes MSS. AGO, Ltrs. Rec'd., 1877, #5409 (enclosure 15), 8128 (enclosures 1, 2), 8135 (enclosure 66).

279 (so): *Philadelphia Times*, 7/23/77, 7/24/77. S. Randall to J. Black, 8/14/77, in Jeremiah S. Black MSS.

280 (hands): C. Bond to J. Sherman, 7/23/77, in Hayes MSS. W. Smith to M. Halstead, 7/31/77, Letterbook 22, in Smith MSS. C. Nordhoff to C. Schurz, 7/25/77, in Schurz MSS.

280, 281 (stations, land, morning): *New York World*, 7/26/77. *New York Tribune*, 7/26/77.

281 (prevailed): *Louisville Commercial*, 7/27/77. *Cincinnati Star*, 7/25/77. AGO, Ltrs. Rec'd., 1877, #4509 (enclosures 34, 75).

282 (people): *St. Louis Times*, 7/27/77. Burbank, pp. 120, 121, 131, 135.

282 (restored): *St. Louis Times*, 7/27/77. Burbank, pp. 122, 123, 125, 128. AGO, Ltrs. Rec'd., 1877, #4358. J. Wilson to C. Schurz, 7/26/77, in Schurz MSS.

282 (committee): AGO, Ltrs. Rec'd., 1877, #4477. *St. Louis Times*, 7/28/77. *Missouri Republican*, 7/28/77. Burbank, pp. 150-153.

283 (lines): *Irish World*, 8/4/77, gives a partial list of management concessions.

283 (pay): In Burlington Archives: Telegrams from W. Strong to C. Perkins, 7/23/77 *passim;* G. Tyson to C. Perkins, 7/23/77; J. Griswold to R. Harris, 7/24/77.

283 (companies): W. Ackerman to W. Osborn, 7/24/77, in Ill. Cent. Archives.

284 (up): In Burlington Archives, "Strike Telegrams": C. Perkins to R. Harris, 7/23/77, 7/24/77, 7/25/77; C. Perkins to W. Strong, 7/23/77.

284 (all): *Scranton Republican*, 7/25/77. In Schurz MSS.: M. Church to C. Schurz, 7/26/77. C. Nordhoff to C. Schurz, 7/25/77. E. Smith to C. Perkins and to J. Joy, 7/25/77, "General Material, 1875-1878," pp. 164-167, in Cunningham-Overton Collection. In Burlington Archives: P. Geddes to R. Harris, 8/7/77; R. Harris to J. Forbes, 7/24/77; W. Strong to C. Perkins, 7/24/77.

284 (leadership): R. Carr to H. Villard, 8/2/77, Box 7, in Villard MSS. G. Tyson to C. Perkins, 7/25/77, "Strike Telegrams," in Burlington Archives.

285 (Erie): *Rochester Express*, 7/26/77. *Syracuse Journal*, 7/26/77.

285 (running): *New York World*, 7/24/77 to 7/26/77. Mott, p. 440. *Corning* (N.Y.) *Democrat*, 8/2/77.

286 (followed): *Report of Riots Committee*, p. 597. Otis, pp. 303-304. AGO, Ltrs. Rec'd., 1844, #4413, 4905 (enclosure 56).

286 (day): McCabe, pp. 159-161. AGO, Ltrs. Rec'd., 1877, #4715.

287 (full): *Pittsburgh Commercial Gazette*, 7/30/77, 7/31/77.

287 (government): Matilda Gresham, *Life of Walter Quintin Gresham* (2 vols., Chicago, 1919), I, 374-375, 383.

287 (these): Edwin W. Sigmund, "Railroad Strikers in Court," in *Journal* of the Illinois State Historical Society (Summer 1956), pp. 191-193. Gresham, I, 384.

288 (city): *Fort Wayne Gazette*, 7/23/77, 7/24/77, 7/26/77, 7/27/77. *Fort Wayne Sentinel*, 7/25/77. *Indianapolis News*, 7/24/77.

288 (Arsenal): *Ibid.*, July 26, 1902, and March 9, 1905. Frederick D. Kershner, Jr., "A Social and Cultural History of Indianapolis, 1860-1914" (unpublished Ph.D. dissertation, University of Wisconsin, 1950), pp. 74, 182-184.

288 (action): Adlai E. Stevenson, *Something of Men I Have Known* (Chicago, 1909), pp. 33-34. Gresham, pp. 385-393. In Gresham MSS.: C. Devens to W. Gresham, 7/24/77. J. Claybrook to W. Gresham, 7/24/77. *Indianapolis News*, 7/25/77. *Indianapolis Sun*, 7/28/77.

289 (troops): Notes on cabinet meeting of 7/26/77, in Hayes MSS. AGO, Ltrs. Rec'd., 1877, #4509 (enclosure 59). Captain Arnold to General Hancock, 7/26/77, in Hayes MSS.

289 (courts): Notes on cabinet meeting of 7/26/77, in Hayes MSS. AGO, Ltrs. Rec'd., 1877, #4340, 4509 (enclosure 50).

289 (face): W. Evarts to T. Weed, 7/27/77, in Weed MSS.

290 (trains): Gresham, pp. 397-400.

290 (Schiff): Sigmund, p. 203. AGO, Ltrs. Rec'd., 1877, #4479. J. Wilson to W. Gresham, 7/28/77, in Gresham MSS. J. Schiff to J. Wilson, 8/8/77, in Wilson MSS.

290 (August 3): *Detroit News*, 7/27/77. Burbank, p. 169. AGO, Ltrs. Rec'd., 1877, #4637. *Cleveland Herald*, 8/4/77.

291 (unconditionally): *Cumberland Civilian*, 7/29/77. *Wheeling Register*, 7/30/77 to 8/1/77. *Wheeling Intelligencer*, 8/1/77 to 8/4/77. In Barry MSS.: W. Hancock to W. Barry, 7/29/77; R. Stewart to W. Barry, 8/2/77.

291 (chance): *New York Sun,* 7/27/77.
291 (trip): AGO, Ltrs. Rec'd., 1877, #4408, 4642, 4722, 5050.
291 (*Ubique*): In Hayes MSS.: T. Scott to R. Hayes, 7/31/77. A. Meyer to R. Hayes, 8/5/77.

CHAPTER 14

292 (desperately): *Pittsburgh Commercial Gazette,* 7/30/77, 8/1/77, 9/19/77. *Cumberland Civilian,* 8/12/77. *New York Times,* 8/10/77.
293 (blacklisted): Illinois Assembly, *Report of Special Committee on Labor* (Springfield, 1879), pp. 58-62.
293 (miners): *Labor Standard,* 6/30/77. *Workingman's Advocate,* 5/5/77. George J. Stevenson, "The Brotherhood of Locomotive Engineers and Its Leaders, 1863-1920" (Ph.D. dissertation, Vanderbilt University, 1954), pp. 29-31.
293 (years): *Labor Standard,* 5/12/77, 6/30/77. *New York Times,* 4/7/77. In Joy MSS.: J. Walker to J. Joy, 4/27/77; circular to stockholders of the Chicago, Wilmington & Vermillion Coal Company, 7/1/77. In Cyrus Woodman MSS., Wisconsin Historical Society: A. Sweet to C. Woodman, 6/21/77, 6/25/77; C. Woodman to A. Sweet, 6/28/77.
294 (Promise): A. Sweet to C. Woodman, 7/2/77, in *ibid.*
294 (terms): *Chicago Times,* 7/28/77 to 7/30/77. *Chicago Post,* 7/30/77. AGO, Ltrs. Rec'd., 1877, #4522. *New York Times,* 11/9/77.
294 (prices): *New York Sun,* 8/4/77.
295 (supply): *Iron Molders' Journal,* XIII (6/10/77), 355. *Cumberland Daily News,* 7/25/77. *Pottsville Evening Chronicle,* 7/19/77.
295 (union): Delaware & Hudson Canal Company, *Annual Report for 1877,* p. 3. "Minutes of the Board of Managers," V, 140-141, in Delaware, Lackawanna & Western Railroad Archives.
295 (Easton): *New York Times,* 6/12/77. *Scranton Republican,* 7/17/77, 7/20/77, 7/21/77, 7/25/77. *Easton Express,* 7/25/77, 7/27/77.
296 (region): *Ibid.,* 7/25/77. "Minutes of the Board of Managers," V, 156, 169, in D L & W Archives.
296 (settlement): AGO, Ltrs. Rec'd., 1877, #5516. *Report of Riots Committee,* pp. 597, 703-705, 712-713, 778. "Minutes of the Board of Managers," V, 169-170, D L & W Archives.
297 (shops): *Report of Riots Committee,* pp. 718-719, 743-744, 746. Terence V. Powderly, *Thirty Years of Labor* (Columbus, 1889), p. 214.

297 (here, head): *Report of Riots Committee,* pp. 707-708, 725, 759, 777.

298 (Denmark): *Ibid.,* pp. 733-734, 756-757, 769-770. McCabe, pp. 208-209. Jacob A. Riis, *The Making of an American* (New York, 1901), p. 190.

298 (success): *Report of Riots Committee,* pp. 383, 596, 716. AGO, Ltrs. Rec'd., 1877, #4738. *New York Herald,* 8/3/77.

298 (whortleberries): AGO, Ltrs. Rec'd., 1877, #4608, 4689, 4710, 4711, 4725, 4864, 4888. Otis, pp. 311-314.

299 (did): *Ibid.,* pp. 321-322. *New York Times,* 8/19/77, 8/21/77, 8/27/77, 9/9/77, 9/15/77, 9/26/77, 10/17/77. AGO, Ltrs. Rec'd., 1877, #6297, 6671. A. Pinkerton to F. Gowen, 10/18/77, in "Molly Maguire MSS.," Philadelphia & Reading Railroad Archives. C. Pike to H. Wright, 10/29/77, in Wright MSS.

299 (guessed): "Minutes of the Board of Managers," V, 170, in D L & W Archives. J. Hickey to H. Wright, 11/3/77, in Wright MSS.

300 (decade): *New York Journal of Commerce,* quoted in *Engineers' Monthly Journal,* XI (September 1877), 416. *Railroad Gazette,* X (1/4/78), 4. Bureau of Census, pp. 200-201.

300 (1877): W. Painter to W. Chandler, 8/2/77, in William E. Chandler MSS., Library of Congress. *Railway World,* VI: (1/31/80), 111; (10/2/80), 941-942. Kuritz, p. 83. *Pittsburgh Press,* July 26, 1908. Schotter, p. 178.

300 (staff): *Iron Molders' Journal,* XIII (8/10/77), 421, 443. C. Nordhoff to S. Randall, 7/25/77, in Randall MSS. S. Randall to J. Black, 8/14/77, in Black MSS.

301 (all): Nevins, *Study in Power,* pp. 243-248.

301 (1877): Burgess and Kennedy, p. 383.

301 (head): Paul Winchester, *The Baltimore and Ohio Railroad* (Baltimore, 1927), pp. 41, 43. Croffut, p. 240. Schlegel, p. 287.

301 (same): Records of discharges, July 1877, CBQ 33 1870 3.4, in Burlington Archives.

301 (them): *New York Times,* 7/27/77. *New Orleans Times,* 8/1/77.

302 (depression): *Commercial and Financial Chronicle,* XXV (7/28/77), 73. *Iron Age,* quoted in *Iron Molders' Journal,* XIII (9/10/77), 454.

302 (Pennsylvania): Samuel Yellen, *American Labor Struggles* (New York, 1936), p. 25. *New York Times,* 8/18/77. Croffut, pp. 211, 218. Hungerford, *Men of Iron,* p. 287. G. J. Stevenson, p. 161.

303 (considerable): In Garrett MSS.: M. Jessup to R. Morse, 10/18/77; R. Morse to J. Garrett, 11/30/77. *Martinsburg Independent,* 8/25/77. *New York Times,* 8/28/77, 8/31/77. W. Ackerman to E.

Jeffery, 8/8/77, Ackerman Out-Letters, I, 360 in Ill. Cent. Archives.
Minute Book VIII, p. 18, in Pennsylvania Railroad Archives.

303 (men): Cochran, pp. 175-176. *Railroad Gazette*, X (1/4/78), 4.

303 (this): In Burlington Archives: R. Harris to J. Forbes, 7/31/77; R.
Harris to J. Griswold, 8/1/77, 8/2/77; J. Griswold to R. Harris,
8/5/77.

303 (endlessly): In *ibid.*: J. Forbes to R. Harris, 7/25/77; R. Harris to J.
Forbes, 8/29/77, 9/6/77.

304 (eighties): Bogen, p. 126. A. Towne to R. Harris, 12/7/77, in Burlington Archives. Cochran, p. 178.

304 (time): C. Perkins to J. Forbes, 8/9/77. Letterbook III, pp. 404-405,
in Cunningham-Overton Collection. In Burlington Archives: C. Perkins to R. Harris, 12/7/77, 12/15/77; R. Harris to J. Forbes,
11/9/77.

305 (disturbances): Kuritz, pp. 310-311. "Executive Minutes" (July-
September 1877) *passim*, Pennsylvania Division of Public Records
(Harrisburg). *Miners' Journal*, 8/10/77, 8/11/77. *New York Times*,
8/28/77. Minute Book XVIII, p. 125, in Penn. Archives.

305 (care): *Engineers' Monthly Journal*, XII (January 1878), 31. *Report
of Riots Committee*, p. 672.

305 (them): *Ibid.*, pp. 508-509, 600, 679, 949-950. *Pittsburgh Commercial Gazette*, 7/25/77.

305 (movement): *Ibid.*, 7/31/77. *Pittsburgh Telegraph*, 1/17/78. *Pittsburgh Post*, 7/22/87. Mr. Roscoe A. Ammon to author, January 12,
1958.

306 (change): *Richmond County* (N.Y.) *Advance*, May 21, 1915. Roscoe
A. Ammon to author, January 12, 1958. George I. Reed, ed., *The
Century Cyclopedia of History and Biography of Pennsylvania* (Chicago, 1904), II. *Boston Herald*, November 14, 1908. *New York
Times*: August 8 and 28, 1903; August 4, 1904; May 16, 1915. *Pittsburgh Dispatch*, September 10, 1919.

306 (them): In Burlington Archives: C. Perkins to W. Strong, 7/26/77;
W. Strong to C. Perkins, 7/27/77; G. Tyson to J. Griswold, 7/29/77.
New York Times, 8/9/77, 8/10/77, 8/15/77, 10/2/77, 10/3/77,
10/11/77. AGO, Ltrs. Rec'd., 1877, #4888. W. Herron to R. Hayes,
8/8/77, in Hayes MSS.

307 (strikes): *New York Times*, 9/3/77, 12/28/77. *Engineers' Monthly
Journal*, XI (September 1877), 411; XII (March 1878), 127; XIII
(December 1878), 553. G. J. Stevenson, pp. 161-165. I. L. Sharfman,
The American Railroad Problem (New York, 1921), pp. 319-320.

307 (severe): *New York Times*, 11/9/77, 11/29/77. *Baltimore American*, 8/1/77.

307 (penitentiary): *New York Times*, 10/25/77, 12/2/77, 12/8/77. *Pittsburgh Post*, 7/22/87.
308 (melodrama): *New York Times*, 10/3/77, 10/8/77, 10/10/77, 10/23/77. Morton L. Montgomery, *History of Berks County in Pennsylvania* (Philadelphia, 1886), p. 692.
308 (free): *New York Times*, 8/11/77, 8/15/77, 11/27/77, 12/18/77, 12/28/77. *Louisville Commercial*, 7/27/77 to 7/29/77. Moses and Kirkland, I, 293. Burbank, pp. 180, 184.
308 (statute): Mott, p. 440. Commons and associates, II, 191.
309 (court): T. Drummond to C. Devens, 8/7/77, Chronological Files, Northern District of Illinois, National Archives Record Group 60 "General Records of the Department of Justice." *Easton Weekly Argus*, 9/7/77.
309 (cases): Sigmund, p. 208. *Columbia Law Review*, XXXIII (May 1933), 885-886.
309 (time): Vivian, p. 71. AGO, Ltrs. Rec'd., 1877, #4982. J. Schiff to J. Wilson, 7/23/77, in Wilson MSS. T. Hillhouse to J. Sherman, 7/27/77, Assistant Treasurer's Correspondence, National Archives Record Group 56. "Jarvis" to J. Garfield, 7/27/77, in Garfield MSS.
310 (suppressed): *Congressional Record*, 45th Congress, 1st Session, VI, 296-298, 301, 312, 326. William T. Sherman, *Home Letters of General Sherman* (New York, 1909), p. 387.
310 (petroleum): *New York World*, 7/23/77.
310 (Streeter): *Idem. Rochester Express*, 7/23/77. B. Butler to J. Gould, 7/21/77, 7/23/77, in Benjamin F. Butler MSS., Library of Congress. *Cincinnati Enquirer*, 7/23/77. A. Holmes to H. Villard, 8/4/77, in Villard MSS.
311 (inflation): "Hal" to "Dallas," 7/30/77, in Daniel A. Tompkins MSS., Duke University Library. Jesse G. Cramer, ed., *Letters of Ulysses S. Grant* (New York, 1912), p. 133. *The Nation*, 8/22/78.
311 (faded): *Rocky Mountain News*, 7/27/77. *Railway World*, III, (11/17/77), 1090. *National Republican*, 7/23/77. *New York Graphic*, 7/25/77. *Cumberland News*, 7/24/77. *Boston Advertiser*, 7/28/77. *Commercial and Financial Chronicle*, 7/28/77.
311 (later): Reichley, p. 128. *Pittsburgh Press*, July 26, 1908. *Pittsburgh Telegraph*, 1/12/78. Whipple, pp. 92-94. *Rocky Mountain News*, 4/7/78. WPA, *Mathews Papers*, p. 94. Richard E. Fast and Hu Maxwell, *The History and Government of West Virginia* (Morgantown, 1901), p. 188.
312 (summer): *San Francisco Call*, 7/26/77. *Reading Eagle*, 8/1/77. *Pittsburgh Commercial Gazette*, 7/30/77. *New York Times*, 12/24/77, 12/30/77.

312 (*Poverty*): Charles A. Barker, *Henry George* (New York, 1955), p. 243. Henry George, Jr., *The Life of Henry George* (2 vols., New York, 1904), I, 291-292.

312 (come): Smith, p. 541.

313 (applauded): Paxton Hibben, *Henry Ward Beecher; An American Portrait* (New York, 1927), p. 288. H. Beecher to D. Wells, 7/24/77, in David A. Wells MSS., Library of Congress. *New York Times*, 7/23/77.

313 (mattered): Henry F. May, *Protestant Churches and Industrial America* (New York, 1949), pp. 92-94. *Presbyterian Quarterly and Princeton Review*, VI (October 1877), 729-730. *The Independent*, 8/2/77.

313 (Beecher): *Iron Molders' Journal*, XIII (8/10/77), 421. *Cincinnati Enquirer*, 7/25/77. Notes under "Labor–History–Detroit," in Labadie Collection.

314 (Hell): *New York World*, 7/24/77. *Commercial and Financial Chronicle*, 7/28/77. *New York Times*, 7/30/77. Hibben, *Beecher*, p. 289.

314 (Sam): *New York Times*, 8/8/77. *New York Graphic*, 7/25/77. *Harpers Monthly*, LV, 935. *Minneapolis Tribune*, 7/31/77.

314 (used): *St. Louis Journal*, 7/31/77. *New York Times*, 7/31/77, 8/20/77. *Cincinnati Daily Gazette*, 7/28/77. *Cleveland Leader*, 8/3/77. Hazard, *et al.*, eds., Fourth Series, IX, 602. *New York Evening Mail*, 8/2/77. Commons and associates, II, 325-326. *Atlantic Monthly*, LXXIV (October 1894), 534.

315 (unemployed): Fred Harvey Harrington, *Fighting Politician: Major General N. P. Banks* (Philadelphia, 1948), pp. 1, 205-207. In Nathaniel P. Banks MSS., Essex Institute (Salem, Massachusetts): W. Goodwin to N. Banks, 8/3/77; G. Roberts to N. Banks, 8/4/77; G. Craig to N. Banks, 8/11/77; M. Kirsch to N. Banks, 8/20/77. *Frank Leslie's Illustrated Newspaper*, 8/11/77. *Detroit Tribune*, 8/21/77. *Atlantic Monthly*, XL (November 1877), 621.

315 (might): AGO, Ltrs. Rec'd., 1877, #8131. R. Harris to T. Clark, *et al*, 7/29/77, in Burlington Archives. S. Hurlbut to J. Garfield, 7/28/77, in Garfield MSS. Scott, pp. 355-361. *New York Journal of Commerce*, 9/1/77. *New York Times*, 8/9/77, 9/11/77. *National Republican*, 8/3/77, 9/5/77. *Philadelphia Inquirer*, 8/6/77.

315 (power): Notes on cabinet meeting of 7/31/77, in Hayes MSS.

316 (horizon): Williams, ed., III, 441. *New York Times*, 8/17/77, 8/20/77 to 8/25/77 *passim*. *Buffalo Commercial Advertiser*, 8/24/77.

316 (August 6): *Chicago Inter Ocean*, 8/12/77. J. Barr to S. Randall, 8/6/77, in Randall MSS.

316 (common): J. Dalzell to J. Sherman, 8/8/77, in Sherman MSS. Edward McPherson, ed., *A Handbook of Politics* (Washington, D. C., 1878), p. 157. Mary L. Hinsdale, ed., *Garfield-Hinsdale Letters* (Ann Arbor, 1949), p. 375. *New York Tribune,* 8/14/77.

317 (out): *Workingman's Advocate,* 4/14/77, 5/5/77. *Philadelphia Record,* 7/16/77. *National Labor Tribune,* 5/5/77. Garfield diary, entries for 7/22/77, 8/5/77, in Garfield MSS. In Wilson MSS.: E. Upton to J. Wilson, 7/25/77; J. Schiff to J. Wilson, 12/13/77. W. Gresham to "Dear Tom" (not Thomas Drummond), 8/6/77, in Gresham MSS. *The National Socialist,* 6/15/78. *Raleigh Observer,* 7/29/77. *The Independent,* 8/30/77.

317 (Party): *Altoona Evening Mirror,* 7/30/77, 8/1/77. *Louisville Courier-Journal,* 8/7/77, 8/10/77. *Boston Post,* 8/13/77. *Albany Evening Journal,* 8/14/77. *Martinsburg Independent,* 8/18/77. Edward T. James, "American Labor and Political Action, 1865-1896" (Ph.D. dissertation, Harvard University, 1954), pp. 128-130, 137, 140-143. Nathan Fine, *Labor and Farmer Parties in the United States, 1828-1928* (New York, 1928), pp. 64-67.

318 (generations): Cross, pp. 96-97. Quint, p. 23. Burbank, p. 226. Commons and associates, II, 394.

319 (succor): Samuel Gompers, *Seventy Years of Life and Labor* (2 vols., New York, 1925), I, 140-143. Hermann Schluter, *The Brewing Industry and the Brewery Workers' Movement in America* (Cincinnati, 1910), p. 100. *Labor Standard,* 8/4/77. *Proceedings of Iron and Steel Workers,* p. 73.

319 (militia): *The New Englander,* XXXVII (July 1878), 532. *New York Times,* 5/21/78, 6/5/78, 12/15/78. *International Review,* V (July 1878), 515. A. Roberts to E. Sayres, 7/19/78, in "Personal Recollections of the National Guard," I, 85, in Sayres MSS.

319 (best-seller): Parsons, pp. 120, 127. Burbank, p. 229. George B. Mayberry, "Industrialism and the Industrial Worker in the American Novel, 1814-1890" (Ph.D. dissertation, Harvard University, 1943), pp. 97, 107, 148-153. Dennett, pp. 101, 103-118.

319 (1892): Democratic leaflet of August 1888, in Benjamin Harrison MSS., Library of Congress. Reichley, p. 130.

320 (mark): Almont Lindsey, *The Pullman Strike* (Chicago, 1942), p. 239. Ginger, pp. 71-72, 135. Gresham, pp. 418-419.

320 (prison): Williams, ed., IV, 278, 374, 383.

321 (instantly): Conversations with Mr. T. Raymond Zepp of Washington, D. C., December 13 and 15, 1957. *Chicago Inter Ocean,* July 7, 1894.

321 (on): *Chicago Times,* July 7, 1894. Lindsey, *Pullman Strike,* pp. 207-209.

Bibliography

Newspapers are omitted, as are other sources when their first and last citations are not more than five paragraphs apart.

I. PRIMARY MANUSCRIPT SOURCES

A. National Archives

Adjutant General's Office ("AGO"):
Letters Received. (Most of the items cited have been consolidated under "Letters Received, 1877, File #4042." Because of the size of the consolidated file, the original file numbers are cited in this book.)
Office of the Secretary of War ("Off. Sec. War"):
Record Group 107.

B. Library of Congress Collections.

Jeremiah Black	Public Record Office
James A. Garfield	Carl Schurz
John W. Garrett	Philip Sheridan
Walter Q. Gresham	John Sherman
Pinkerton	James Harrison Wilson

C. Other Manuscript Collections.

William F. Barry MSS., Maryland Historical Society
John Bigelow MSS., New York Public Library.
Cunningham-Overton Collection, in the custody of Mr. Richard C. Overton, Manchester Depot, Vermont.
Thomas C. Donaldson Memoirs, Rutherford B. Hayes Library, Fremont, Ohio.
Rutherford B. Hayes MSS., Rutherford B. Hayes Library, Fremont, Ohio.
Cornelius B. Hite MSS., Duke University Library.
James F. Joy MSS., Detroit Public Library.
Joseph A. Labadie Collection, University of Michigan Library.
Samuel J. Randall MSS., University of Pennsylvania Library.

Edward S. Sayres MSS., Pennsylvania Historical Society.
William Henry Smith MSS., Ohio Historical Society.
Henry Villard MSS., Houghton Library, Harvard University.
Thurlow Weed MSS., University of Rochester Library.
Hendrick B. Wright MSS., Wyoming Historical and Geographical
Society, Wilkes-Barre, Pa.

D. Railroad Company Archives.

Baltimore & Ohio Railroad Archives ("B & O"), Office of the Sec-
retary, Baltimore & Ohio Railroad Company, Baltimore, Md.
Boston & Maine Railroad Archives.
Chicago, Burlington & Quincy Railroad Archives ("Burlington"),
Newberry Library, Chicago, Ill.
Delaware, Lackawanna & Western Railroad Archives ("D L & W"),
Office of the Secretary, Delaware, Lackawanna & Western Rail-
road Company, New York City.
Illinois Central Railroad Archives.
Northern Pacific Railroad Archives, Northern Pacific Railroad Com-
pany, St. Paul, Minn.
Pennsylvania Railroad Archives ("Pennsy"), Office of the Secre-
tary, Pennsylvania Railroad Company, Philadelphia, Pa.

II. SOURCES FREQUENTLY CITED

Adams, Charles Francis, Jr. Notes on Railroad Accidents (New York,
1879).
————. Railroads: Their Origin and Problems (New York, 1878).
Aler, F. Vernon. Aler's History of Martinsburg and Berkeley County, West
Virginia (Hagerstown, Md., 1888).
Barnard, Harry. Rutherford B. Hayes and His America (Indianapolis,
1954).
Bogen, Jules I. The Anthracite Railroads (New York, 1927).
Burbank, David T. City of Little Bread: The St. Louis General Strike of
1877 (St. Louis, 1957).
Bureau of the Census. Historical Statistics of the United States, 1789-
1945 (Washington, D.C., 1949).
Burgess, George H., and Kenedy, Miles C. Centennial History of the
Pennsylvania Railroad Company, 1846-1946 (Philadelphia, 1949).
Casey, Robert J., and Douglas, W. A. S. The Lackawanna Story (New
York, 1951).

Cochran, Thomas C. *Railroad Leaders, 1845-1880* (Cambridge, Mass., 1953).

Commons, John R., and associates. *History of Labour in the United States* (4 vols., New York, 1921).

Croffut, William A. *The Vanderbilts and the Story of Their Fortune* (Chicago, 1886).

Cross, Ira B. *A History of the Labor Movement in California* (Berkeley, Calif., 1935).

Davis, George L. "Greater Pittsburgh's Commercial and Industrial Development, 1850-1900" (unpublished Ph.D. dissertation, University of Pittsburgh, 1952).

Dennett, Tyler. *John Hay* (New York, 1933).

Feder, Leah H. *Unemployment Relief in Periods of Depression* (New York, 1936).

Foner, Philip S. *History of the Labor Movement in the United States* (New York, 1947).

Ginger, Ray. *The Bending Cross* (New Brunswick, 1949).

Gordon, Sanford D. "Public Opinion as a Factor in the Emergence of a National Anti-Trust Program, 1873-1890" (unpublished Ph.D. dissertation, New York University, 1954).

Gowen, Franklin B. *To the Public* (Philadelphia ?, 1877).

Gresham, Matilda. *Life of Walter Quinten Gresham* (2 vols., Chicago, 1919).

Guillot, Ellen Elizabeth. *Social Factors in Crime as Explained by American Writers of the Civil War and Post Civil War Period* (Philadelphia, 1943).

Harlow, Alvin E. *The Road of the Century: The Story of the New York Central* (New York, 1947).

Hayes, Rutherford B. See Charles R. Williams, ed.

Hazard, Samuel, *et al.,* ed. *Pennsylvania Archives* (9 series, 138 vols., Philadelphia, 1852-1949).

Hillquit, Morris. *History of Socialism in the United States* (New York, 1903).

Holbrook, Stewart. *The Story of American Railroads* (New York, 1947).

Hungerford, Edward. *Men and Iron: The History of the New York Central* (New York, 1938).

―――.*The Story of the Baltimore & Ohio Railroad, 1827-1927* (2 vols., New York, 1928).

Illinois Railroad and Warehouse Commission. *Seventh Annual Report* (1878).

―――. *Eighth Annual Report* (1879).

Kahn, E. J., Jr. *The Merry Partners* (New York, 1955).

Kuritz, Human. "The Pennsylvania State Government and Labor Controls from 1856 to 1922" (unpublished Ph.D. dissertation, Columbia University, 1953).

Leng, John. *America in 1876* (Dundee, Scotland, 1877).

Marshall, W. G. *Through America; or, Nine Months in the United States* (London, 1881).

Martin, Edward W. See James D. McCabe.

Massachusetts Bureau of Statistics of Labor, *Tenth Annual Report* (Boston, 1879).

McCabe, James D. (Edward W. Martin, pseud.). *The History of the Great Riots* (Philadelphia, 1877).

McClure, Alexander K. *Old Time Notes of Pennsylvania* (2 vols., Philadelphia, 1905).

Moses, John, and Kirkland, Joseph, eds. *The History of Chicago* (2 vols., Chicago, 1895).

Mott, Edward H. *Between the Ocean and the Lakes: The Story of Erie* (New York, 1901).

Nevins, Allan. *The Emergence of Modern America, 1865-1876* (New York, 1927).

————. *Study in Power: John D. Rockefeller, Industrialist and Philanthropist* (2 vols., New York, 1953).

————, and Thomas, Milton, eds. *The Diary of George Templeton Strong* (4 vols., New York, 1952).

Otis, Elwell S. "The Army in Connection with the Labor Riots of 1877," *Journal of the Military Service Institute of the United States* (V, 1884).

Overseers of the Poor of the City of Boston. *Eleventh Annual Report* (Boston, 1875).

————. *Thirteenth Annual Report* (Boston, 1877).

Parsons, Lucy E. *Life of Albert Parsons.* (Chicago, 1889).

Pierce, Bessie L. *A History of Chicago* (4 vols., New York, 1937-1957).

Pinkerton, Allan. *Strikers, Communists, Tramps and Detectives* (New York, 1882).

Proceedings of the National Forge of the United Sons of Vulcan (Pittsburgh, 1875).

Proceedings of the Second Annual Convention of the National Amalgamated Association of Iron and Steel Workers of the United States (Pittsburgh, 1887).

Quint, Howard H. *The Forging of American Socialism* (Columbia, S. C., 1953).

Reichley, Marlin S. "Federal Military Intervention in Civil Disturbances" (unpublished Ph.D. dissertation, Georgetown University, 1939).

Report of the Committee Appointed to Investigate the Railroad Riots in July, 1877 (Harrisburg, Pa., 1878).

Rich, Bennett M. *The Presidents and Civil Disorder* (Washington, D.C., 1941).

Riis, Jacob A. *How the Other Half Lives* (New York, 1890).

Schlegel, Marvin W. *Ruler of the Reading: The Life of Franklin B. Gowen* (Harrisburg, Pa., 1947).

Schneider, David M., and Deutsch, Albert. *The History of Public Welfare in New York State, 1867-1940* (Chicago, 1941).

Schotter, H. W. *The Growth and Development of the Pennsylvania Railroad Company, 1846-1926* (Philadelphia, 1927).

Scott, Thomas A. "The Recent Strikes," *North American Review* (September 1877).

Sigmund, Elwin W. "Railroad Strikers in Court," *Journal of the Illinois State Historical Society* (Summer 1956).

Sipes, William B. *The Pennsylvania Railroad, Its Origins, Construction and Connections* (Philadelphia, 1875).

Smith, Goldwin. "The Labour War in the United States," *The Contemporary Review* (September 1877).

Stevenson, George J. "The Brotherhood of Locomotive Engineers and Its Leaders, 1863-1920" (unpublished Ph.D. dissertation, Vanderbilt University, 1954).

Strong, George T. See Allan Nevins and Milton Thomas, eds.

Sumner, William Graham. "What Our Boys Are Reading," *Scribner's Monthly* (March 1878).

United States Bureau of Labor Statistics. *History of Wages in the United States from Colonial Times to 1928*, Bulletin No. 604 (Washington, D.C., 1934).

United States Commissioner of Labor. *Sixteenth Annual Report* (Washington, D.C., 1901).

Vivian, Henry H. *Notes of a Tour in America* (London, 1878).

Wells, O. V. "The Depression of 1873-79," *Agricultural History* (XI, 1937).

Whipple, James B. "Cleveland in Conflict: A Study in Urban Adolescence, 1876-1900" (unpublished Ph.D. dissertation, Western Reserve University, 1951).

Williams, Charles R., ed. *Diary and Letters of Rutherford Birchard Hayes* (5 vols., Columbus, Ohio, 1922-1926).

Woodward, C. Vann. *Reunion and Reaction* (Boston, 1951).

Works Progress Administration, comp. *Annals of Cleveland, a Digest and Index of the Newspaper Record of Events and Opinions* (59 vols., Cleveland, 1937-1938).

————. *Calendar of the Henry Mason Mathews Letters and Papers* (Charleston, W. Va., 1941).

Wright, Carroll D. *The Battles of Labor* (Philadelphia, 1906).

Yearley, Clifton K. "The Baltimore and Ohio Railroad Strike of 1877," *Maryland Historical Magazine* (September 1956).

Acknowledgments

MY RESEARCH for this book took me to more than a hundred libraries in thirty-nine cities and towns. In all, I found not only efficient helpfulness but also the friendliness that turns a journey into a joy. To them, and to the many others with whom I have corresponded, I say again: thank you. In particular, I wish to thank Mr. Watt Marchman and the Rutherford B. Hayes Library at Fremont, Ohio, for generously furnishing extensive microfilms of the Hayes papers and scrapbooks; and Mr. David T. Burbank of St. Louis for permission to read and use his excellent, trail-breaking study of the Great Strike in St. Louis.

A grant from the John Simon Guggenheim Memorial Foundation enabled me to devote a year to uninterrupted research and writing, thus hastening the completion of this book by three or four years. Boston University has been generous in grants for clerical work and for the able assistance of Mr. Philip N. Backstrom and Mr. James C. Desmond in bibliography and checking.

I owe more than I can say to my sister, Mrs. Wendell J. Greene, and to my mother, Mrs. Robert G. Bruce.

Index